# LITERATURE
## *for Life and Work*
### BOOK 1

**Christine Bideganeta LaRocco**
Integrated and Applied Curriculum Consultant
English Instructor
Arlington, Virginia

**Elaine Bowe Johnson, Ph.D.**
Associate Dean
Language and Literature Division
Mt. Hood Community College
Gresham, Oregon

## National Textbook Company
*a division of* NTC/CONTEMPORARY PUBLISHING GROUP
Lincolnwood, Illinois USA

| | |
|---|---|
| Cover Design: | Photonics Graphics |
| Series Design: | Learning Design Associates, Inc., Columbus, Ohio |

**Cover Photography Credits:** Holland windmill—Photograph by Jack K. Blonk, Laval, Quebec, Canada; all other photos royalty free.

## ACKNOWLEDGEMENT

"A Mother in Mannville" by Marjorie Kinnan Rawlings. Reprinted with permission of Sribner, a
    Division Simon & Schuster from *When the Whippoorwill* by Marjorie Kinnan Rawlings.
    Copyright © 1936, 1940 by Marjorie Kinnan Rawlings; Copyright © 1964 by Norton Baskin.
"The Elk Tooth Dress" by Dorothy M. Johnson. Copyright © 1957by Triangle Publications, Inc. Copyright
    renewed © 1985 by Dorothy M. Johnson. Reprinted by permission of McIntosh and Otis, Inc.
"Amanda and the Wounded Birds" by Colby Rodowsky, copyright © 1987 by Colby Rodowsky, from
    *Visions* by Donald R. Gallo, Editor. Used by permission of Dell Books, a division of Bantam
    Doubleday Dell Publishing Group, Inc.

*Continued on page 400*

ISBN: 0-538-66713-3

Published by National Textbook Company,
a division of NTC/Contemporary Publishing Group, Inc.
4255 West Touhy Avenue,
Lincolnwood, Illinois 60712-1975 U.S.A.
© 1998 NTC/Contemporary Publishing Group, Inc.

7 8 9 10 11 12 13 14 15 16 17 18 19  071  10 09 08 07 06 05 04 03 02

*For Larry, and for the most important students I ever taught,*
*Anna and Matthew*

*Christine B. LaRocco*

**The authors and editors of *Literature for Life and Work* gratefully acknowledge the following educators for their insightful reviews of literature selections, sample lessons, and manuscript:**

Nancy Barker
Norwood High School
Cincinnati, OH

Ken Brown
Lakeland, FL

Susan Clark
Michel Junior High School
Biloxi, MS

Audie Cline
California High School
Jefferson City, MO

Jerry Collins
Wilson High School
Tacoma, WA

Dr. Willard Daggett
International Center for
    Leadership in Education, Inc.

Stephanie Dew
Santa Monica High School
Santa Monica, CA

Randy Gingrich
Hughes High School
Cincinnati, OH

Donna Helo
Rayne High School
Crowley, LA

Nicole Hochholzer
Kaukauna High School
Kaukauna, WI

Dorothy Hoover
Huntingdon Area High School
Huntingdon, PA

Judy Kayse
Huntsville High School
Huntsville, TX

Marcia Lubell
Yorktown High School
Yorktown Heights, NY

Carter Nicely
Old Mill High School
Arnold, MD

Jan Smith
Upsala Area Schools
Little Falls, MN

Theresa Spangler
Brunswick High School
Brunswick, GA

Alice Jane Stephens
Triton Central High School
Fairland, IN

Ruth Townsend
Yorktown High School
Yorktown Heights, NY

## Special Contributors

Vicky Coelho
Boise High School
Boise State University
Boise, ID

James Coughlin
Capital High School
Boise, ID

Ilene Berman
Sidwell Friends School
Washington, DC

# TABLE OF CONTENTS

# UNIT 5 TURNING POINTS ................. 212

## To the Student:

When you first looked at this book, you probably thought, "Oh, sure, I've seen this kind of textbook before. It's just another collection of readings with predictable questions for me to answer."

But this textbook differs from any you have used before because everything in it connects with your own experiences, interests, and ambitions. All the poetry, fiction, and nonfiction, both classical and modern, were chosen because they deal with life experiences shared by people of all times and places.

This book takes you seriously. It asks you to develop the art of thinking. It encourages you to apply what you read in a way that affects your daily life. That's what makes it unique. We hope you enjoy it and discover the excitement of connecting literature to life and work.

The literature is arranged in units under a common theme. Our goal was to allow you to read about experiences and ideas that matter in your lives. Once the literature was chosen, we then set out to challenge you with real world assignments that connect the course with your experience.

The assignments in the "Exploring," "Understanding," and "Connecting" sections invite you to express your own views, to share them with others, to work on teams, and to make a significant difference in your community. You learn best when you connect learning to your own experiences and knowledge. The assignments invite you to learn not only by studying, but also by becoming involved in activities in the real world. You learn to write, read, and think critically by doing work that joins academic material with everyday life.

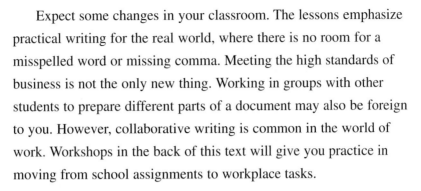

Expect some changes in your classroom. The lessons emphasize practical writing for the real world, where there is no room for a misspelled word or missing comma. Meeting the high standards of business is not the only new thing. Working in groups with other students to prepare different parts of a document may also be foreign to you. However, collaborative writing is common in the world of work. Workshops in the back of this text will give you practice in moving from school assignments to workplace tasks.

Our approach to writing assignments trains you in skills you'll actually use in your lifetime as an individual, a family member, worker, customer, and consumer. You will practice the reading, writing, listening, and speaking skills expected of you by employers, clients, colleagues, neighbors, businesses, and the person on the other end of the phone. Whether you go on to college, vocational school, the military, special training, or the world of work, the exercises in this book will prepare you for success.

This book will help you discover how much you already know. We challenge you to become involved in your English class this year in a new way and because of one simple fact: you'll be using these communication skills every day of your life.

Christine B. LaRocco

Elaine B. Johnson

P.S. Be sure to visit the *Literature for Life and Work Home Page* at **www.litlinks.com** for exciting Internet activities related to the units in this text!

# UNIT
## ①
# FAMILY AND FRIENDS

*Family and friends are important support systems in our lives. Our families teach us what is right and wrong, through words and actions. They encourage us to become independent and counsel us when we have doubts. Often, the most important lesson we can learn is that we are loved.*

*Like our families, close friends support us in good times and bad. They help us distinguish what is important from all we are exposed to each day. They listen and care. Family and friends help us discover who we are and what we truly value.*

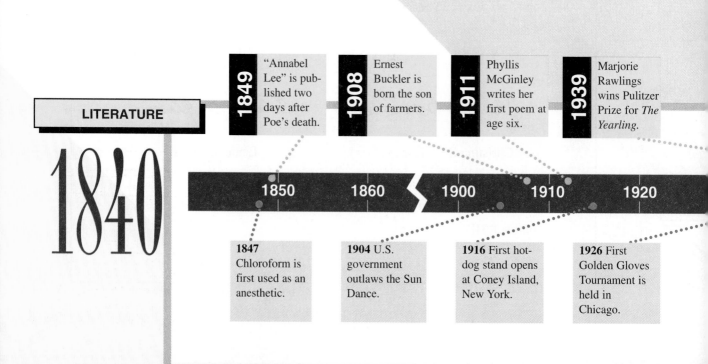

**LITERATURE**

**1849** "Annabel Lee" is published two days after Poe's death.

**1908** Ernest Buckler is born the son of farmers.

**1911** Phyllis McGinley writes her first poem at age six.

**1939** Marjorie Rawlings wins Pulitzer Prize for *The Yearling*.

1840

1850  1860  1900  1910  1920

**1847** Chloroform is first used as an anesthetic.

**1904** U.S. government outlaws the Sun Dance.

**1916** First hot-dog stand opens at Coney Island, New York.

**1926** First Golden Gloves Tournament is held in Chicago.

# A Mother in Mannville
—Marjorie Kinnan Rawlings

# The Elk Tooth Dress
—Dorothy M. Johnson

# Annabel Lee
—Edgar Allan Poe

# Amanda and the Wounded Birds
—Colby Rodowsky

# A Man
—Ernest Buckler

# First Lesson
—Phyllis McGinley

# Amigo Brothers
—Piri Thomas

# Good Hot Dogs/
# Buenos Hot Dogs
—Sandra Cisneros

## 2000

1930    1940    1950    1960    1970

**1929** Great Depression begins in the United States.

**1944** Streptomycin is first drug to control tuberculosis.

**1950** Adolescence is first described as a stage of life.

**1980s** Satellites allow easy syndication of talk shows.

**LIFE and WORK**

# A Mother in Mannville

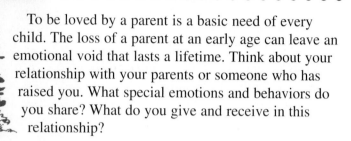

## EXPLORING

To be loved by a parent is a basic need of every child. The loss of a parent at an early age can leave an emotional void that lasts a lifetime. Think about your relationship with your parents or someone who has raised you. What special emotions and behaviors do you share? What do you give and receive in this relationship?

## THEME CONNECTION...
## A MOTHER'S LOVE

The boy in this story is an orphan who "adopts" a kind woman. Hungry for a mother's love, he offers to do her chores so he can be near her. While an orphanage provides for the child's physical needs, such as food and shelter, his need for love cannot be fulfilled by an institution.

## TIME & PLACE

During the Great Depression of the 1930s, the standard pay rate for chopping wood was ten cents an hour, and gloves cost a dollar. Jerry, the young boy in the story, lives in an orphanage in the Carolina mountains and would have been considered lucky to have earned a dollar for taking care of the narrator's dog for a weekend. Though the orphanage provides the children with meals and clothing, it cannot afford small comforts like gloves during the winter.

## THE WRITER'S CRAFT
### POINT OF VIEW

In any piece of literature, the point of view is the perspective from which the story is told. In this story, the main character speaks from the first person point of view, using *I* and *me.* Readers experience events along with her and know only the limited amount of information that she knows. All details about the boy's past are hidden from readers because the main character does not possess that information. The author chose this technique so readers can experience the main character's surprise at the story's end.

# A Mother in Mannville

Marjorie Kinnan Rawlings

he orphanage is high in the Carolina mountains. Sometimes in winter the snow drifts are so deep that the institution is cut off from the village below, from all the world. Fog hides the mountain peaks, the snow swirls down the valleys, and a wind blows so bitterly that the orphanage boys who take the milk twice daily to the baby cottage reach the door with fingers stiff in an agony of numbness.

"Or when we carry trays from the cookhouse for the ones that are sick," Jerry said, "we get our faces frostbit, because we can't put our hands over them. I have gloves," he added. "Some of the boys don't have any."

He liked the late spring, he said. The rhododendron was in bloom, a carpet of color, across the mountainsides, soft as the May winds that stirred the hemlocks. He called it laurel.

"It's pretty when the laurel blooms," he said. "Some of it's pink and some of it's white."

I was there in the autumn. I wanted quiet, isolation, to do some troublesome writing. I wanted mountain air to blow out the malaria from too long a time in the sub-tropics. I was homesick, too, for the flaming of maples in October, and for corn shocks and pumpkins and black-walnut trees and the lift of hills. I found them all, living in a cabin that belonged to the orphanage, half a mile beyond the orphanage farm. When I took the cabin, I asked for a boy or man to come and chop wood for the fireplace. The first few days were warm, I found what wood I needed about the cabin, no one came, and I forgot the order.

I looked up from my typewriter one late afternoon, a little startled. A boy stood at the door, and my pointer dog, my companion, was at his side and had not barked to warn me. The boy was probably twelve years old, but undersized. He wore overalls and a torn shirt, and was barefooted.

He said, "I can chop some wood today."

I said, "But I have a boy coming from the orphanage."

"I'm the boy."

"You? But you're small."

"Size don't matter, chopping wood," he said. "Some of the big boys don't chop good. I've been chopping wood at the orphanage a long time."

I visualized mangled and inadequate branches for my fires. I was well into my work and not inclined to conversation. I was a little blunt.

"Very well. There's the ax. Go ahead and see what you can do."

I went back to work, closing the door. At first the sound of the boy dragging brush annoyed me. Then he began to chop. The blows were rhythmic and steady, and shortly I had forgotten him, the sound no more of an interruption

## About the Author

Marjorie Kinnan Rawlings (1896–1953) attended the University of Wisconsin and began her working career as a journalist in New York. In 1928 she focused on writing stories and novels at her farm in Cross Creek, Florida. Her writing often deals with the relationships between people trying to make a living in difficult, rural surroundings. Rawlings won the Pulitzer Prize in 1939 for her novel *The Yearling,* a story about a boy growing up in rural Florida in the 1870s.

## FOCUS ON...
## ECONOMICS

In the 1930s, the time setting for this story, the United States endured the longest and worst business slump in its history. Unemployment was at an all-time high, and thousands of banks, factories, and stores went out of business. Interview an adult you know who lived during this time. Find out what life was like for young people then. How did the economic conditions affect their lives? With the person's permission, record the interview to share with classmates.

◆ ◆ ◆ ◆ ◆ ◆ ◆ ◆ ◆ ◆ ◆ ◆

suffused—
spread over

shocks and his eyes, very direct, were like the mountain sky when rain is pending—gray, with a shadowing of that miraculous blue. As I spoke, a light came over him, as though the setting sun had touched him with the same **suffused** glory with which it touched the mountains. I gave him a quarter.

"You may come tomorrow," I said, "and thank you very much."

than a consistent rain. I suppose an hour and a half passed, for when I stopped and stretched, and heard the boy's steps on the cabin stoop, the sun was dropping behind the farthest mountain, and the valleys were purple with something deeper than the asters.

The boy said, "I have to go to supper now. I can come again tomorrow evening."

I said, "I'll pay you now for what you've done," thinking I should probably have to insist on an older boy. "Ten cents an hour?"

"Anything is all right."

We went together back of the cabin. An astonishing amount of solid wood had been cut. There were cherry logs and heavy roots of rhododendron, and blocks from the waste pine and oak left from the building of the cabin.

"But you've done as much as a man," I said. "This is a splendid pile."

I looked at him, actually, for the first time. His hair was the color of the corn

He looked at me, and at the coin, and seemed to want to speak, but could not, and turned away.

"I'll split kindling tomorrow," he said over his thin ragged shoulder. "You'll need kindling and medium wood and logs and backlogs."

At daylight I was half wakened by the sound of chopping. Again it was so even in texture that I went back to sleep. When I left my bed in the cool morning, the boy had come and gone, and a stack of kindling was neat against the cabin wall. He came again after school in the afternoon and worked until time to return to the orphanage. His name was Jerry; he was twelve years old, and he had been at the orphanage since he was four. I could picture him at four, with the same grave gray-blue eyes and the same—independence? No, the word that comes to me is "integrity."

The word means something very special to me, and the quality for which I use it is a rare one. My father had it— there is another of whom I am almost sure—but almost no man of my acquaintance possesses it with the clarity, the purity, the simplicity of a mountain stream. But the boy Jerry had it. It is bedded on courage, but it is more than brave. It is honest, but it is more than honesty. The ax handle broke one day. Jerry said the woodshop at the orphanage would repair it. I brought money to pay for the job and he refused it.

"I'll pay for it," he said. "I broke it. I brought the ax down careless."

"But no one hits accurately every time," I told him. "The fault was in the wood of the handle. I'll see the man from whom I bought it."

It was only then that he would take the money. He was standing back of his own carelessness. He was a free-will agent and he chose to do careful work, and if he failed, he took the responsibility without **subterfuge.**

And he did for me the unnecessary thing, the gracious thing, that we find done only by the great of heart. Things no training can teach, for they are done on the instant, with no **predicated** experience. He found a cubbyhole beside the fireplace that I had not noticed. There, of his own accord, he put kindling and "medium" wood, so that I might always have dry fire material ready in case of sudden wet weather. A stone was loose in the rough walk to the cabin. He dug a deeper hole and steadied it, although he came, himself, by a short cut over the bank. I found that when I tried to return

his thoughtfulness with such things as candy and apples, he was wordless. "Thank you" was, perhaps, an expression for which he had had no use, for his courtesy was instinctive. He only looked at the gift and at me, and a curtain lifted, so that I saw deep into the clear well of his eyes, and gratitude was there, and affection, soft over the firm granite of his character.

He made simple excuses to come and sit with me. I could no more have turned him away than if he had been physically hungry. I suggested once that the best time for us to visit was just before supper, when I left off my writing. After that, he waited always until my typewriter had been some time quiet. One day I worked until nearly dark. I went outside the cabin, having forgotten him. I saw him going up over the hill in the twilight toward the orphanage. When I sat down on my stoop, a place was warm from his body where he had been sitting.

He became intimate, of course, with my pointer, Pat. There is a strange communion between a boy and a dog. Perhaps they possess the same singleness of spirit, the same kind of wisdom. It is difficult to explain, but it exists. When I went across the state for a weekend, I left the dog in Jerry's charge. I gave him the dog whistle and the key to the cabin, and left sufficient food. He was to come two or three times a day and let out the dog, and feed and exercise him. I should return Sunday night, and Jerry would take out the dog for the last time Sunday afternoon and then

● ● ● ● ● ● ●
"It is honest, but it is more than honesty."
● ● ● ● ● ● ●

subterfuge—a purposely deceptive action

predicated—previous, or practiced

leave the key under an agreed hiding place.

My return was belated and fog filled the mountain passes so treacherously that I dared not drive at night. The fog held the next morning, and it was Monday noon before I reached the cabin. The dog had been fed and cared for that morning. Jerry came early in the afternoon, anxious.

"The superintendent said nobody would drive in the fog," he said. "I came just before bedtime last night and you hadn't come. So I brought Pat some of my breakfast this morning. I wouldn't have let anything happen to him."

"I was sure of that. I didn't worry."

"When I heard about the fog, I thought you'd know."

He was needed for work at the orphanage and he had to return at once. I gave him a dollar in payment, and he looked at it and went away. But that night he came in the darkness and knocked at the door.

"Come in, Jerry," I said, "if you're allowed to be away this late."

"I told maybe a story," he said. "I told them I thought you would want to see me."

"That's true," I assured him, and I saw his relief. "I want to hear about how you managed with the dog."

He sat by the fire with me, with no other light, and told me of their two days together. The dog lay close to him, and found a comfort there that I did not have for him. And it seemed to me that being with my dog, and caring for him, had brought the boy and me, too, together, so that he felt that he belonged to me as well as to the animal.

"He stayed right with me," he told me, "except when he ran in the laurel. He likes the laurel. I took him up over the hill and we both ran fast. There was a place where the grass was high and I lay down in it and hid. I could hear Pat hunting for me. He found my trail and he barked. When he found me, he acted crazy, and he ran around and around me, in circles."

We watched the flames.

"That's an apple log." he said. "It burns the prettiest of any wood."

We were very close.

He was suddenly **impelled** to speak of things he had not spoken of before, nor had I cared to ask him.

"You look a little bit like my mother," he said. "Especially in the dark, by the fire."

"But you were only four, Jerry, when you came here. You have remembered how she looked, all these years?"

"My mother lives in Mannville," he said.

For a moment, finding that he had a mother shocked me as greatly as anything in my life has ever done, and I did not know why it disturbed me. Then I understood my distress. I was filled with a passionate resentment that any woman should go away and leave her son. A fresh anger added itself. A son like this one— The orphanage was a wholesome place, the executives were kind, good people, the food was more than adequate, the boys were healthy, a ragged shirt was no hardship, nor the doing of clean labor. Granted, perhaps, that the boy felt no lack, what blood fed the bowels of a woman who did not yearn over this child's lean body that had come in **parturition** out of her own? At four he would have looked the same as

## SPOTLIGHT ON... INTERVIEWING

Effective interviewing skills are useful in many lines of work. They are particularly helpful to journalists and writers. Gathering valuable information in an interview requires asking thoughtful questions that result in informative answers. When you interview someone, keep the following tips in mind:

1. Identify a specific topic about which your subject—the interviewee—is extremely knowledgeable.
2. Request an interview at your subject's convenience. Ask permission to record the interview.
3. Write a list of specific questions.
4. Conduct the interview. Listen attentively.
5. Take careful and thorough notes. Write down quotations accurately. Don't be afraid to repeat something to verify its accuracy.
6. Be sure to thank your subject in person and in writing after the interview.

now. Nothing, I thought, nothing in life could change those eyes. His quality must be apparent to an idiot, a fool. I burned with questions I could not ask. In any, I was afraid, there would be pain.

"Have you seen her, Jerry—lately?"

"I see her every summer. She sends for me."

I wanted to cry out, "Why are you not with her? How can she let you go away again?"

He said, "She comes up here from Mannville whenever she can. She doesn't have a job now."

His face shone in the firelight.

"She wanted to give me a puppy, but they can't let any one boy keep a puppy. You remember the suit I had on last Sunday?" He was plainly proud. "She sent me that for Christmas. The Christmas before that"—he drew a long breath, savoring the memory—"she sent me a pair of skates."

"Roller skates?"

My mind was busy, making pictures of her, trying to understand her. She had not, then, entirely deserted or forgotten him. But why, then—I thought, "I must not condemn her without knowing."

"Roller skates. I let the other boys use them. They're always borrowing them. But they're careful of them."

What circumstance other than poverty—"I'm going to take the dollar you gave me for taking care of Pat," he said, "and buy her a pair of gloves."

I could only say, "That will be nice. Do you know her size?"

"I think it's 8½," he said.

He looked at my hands.

"Do you wear 8½?" he asked.

abstracted—
absentminded

anomalous—dif-
ferent from the
usual arrange-
ment, irregular

vermilion—bright
reddish orange

"No. I wear a smaller size, a 6."

"Oh! Then I guess her hands are bigger than yours."

I hated her. Poverty or no, there was other food than bread, and the soul could starve as quickly as the body. He was taking his dollar to buy gloves for her big stupid hands, and she lived away from him, in Mannville, and contented herself with sending him skates.

"She likes white gloves," he said. "Do you think I can get them for a dollar?"

"I think so," I said.

I decided that I should not leave the mountains without seeing her and knowing for myself why she had done this thing.

The human mind scatters its interests as though made of thistledown, and every wind stirs and moves it. I finished my work. It did not please me, and I gave my thoughts to another field. I should need some Mexican material.

I made arrangements to close my Florida place. Mexico immediately, and doing the writing there, if conditions were favorable. Then, Alaska with my brother. After that, heaven knew what or where.

I did not take time to go to Mannville to see Jerry's mother, nor even to talk with the orphanage officials about her. I was a trifle **abstracted** about the boy, because of my work and plans. And after my first fury at her—we did not speak of her again—his having a mother, any sort at all, not far away, in Mannville, relieved me of the ache I had had about him. He did not question the **anomalous**

relation. He was not lonely. It was none of my concern.

He came every day and cut my wood and did small helpful favors and stayed to talk. The days had become cold, and often I let him come inside the cabin. He would lie on the floor in front of the fire, with one arm across the pointer, and they would both doze and wait quietly for me. Other days they ran with a common ecstasy through the laurel, and since the asters were now gone, he brought me back **vermilion** maple leaves, and chestnut boughs dripping with imperial yellow. I was ready to go.

● ● ● ● ● ● ●

"I wanted to talk with you about his mother…"

● ● ● ● ● ● ●

I said to him. "You have been my good friend, Jerry, I shall often think of you and miss you. Pat will miss you too. I am leaving tomorrow."

He did not answer. When he went away, I remember that a new moon hung over the mountains, and I watched him go in silence up the hill. I expected him the next day, but he did not come. The details of packing my personal belongings, loading my car, arranging the bed over the seat, where the dog would ride, occupied me until late in the day. I closed the cabin and started the car, noticing that the sun was in the west and I should do well to be out of the mountains by nightfall. I stopped by the orphanage and left the cabin key and money for my light bill with Miss Clark.

"And will you call Jerry for me to say good-by to him?"

"I don't know where he is," she said. "I'm afraid he's not well. He didn't eat his dinner this noon. One of the other boys saw him going over the hill into the laurel. He was supposed to fire the boiler this afternoon. It's not like him; he's unusually reliable."

I was almost relieved, for I knew I should never see him again, and it would be easier not to say good-by to him.

I said, "I wanted to talk with you about his mother—why he's here—but I'm in more of a hurry than I expected to be. It's out of the question for me to see her now too. But here's some money I'd like to leave with you to buy things for him at Christmas and on his birthday. It will be better than for me to try to send him things, I could so easily duplicate— skates, for instance."

She blinked her honest spinster's eyes.

"There's not much use for skates here," she said.

Her stupidity annoyed me.

"What I mean," I said, "is that I don't want to duplicate things his mother sends him. I might have chosen skates if I didn't know she had already given them to him."

She stared at me.

"I don't understand," she said. "He has no mother. He has no skates." ❖

# ON THE JOB

## FREELANCE WRITER

The tools of freelance writers range from pencils and notebooks to laptop computers and modems. Whatever their methods, most writers agree that peace and quiet are essential to productivity. Because most writers work alone, self-motivation and the ability to manage time are valuable personal qualities. An ability to organize and express ideas clearly is also a vital skill. Freelance writers create stories, poems, or articles for books and magazines. They may also contribute to newspapers, company newsletters, radio and television broadcasts, and advertisements. To prepare for this highly competitive profession, course work in communications, journalism, or English is essential. In addition, gaining expertise in a specific field, such as tourism or environmental science, could help a writer focus his or her skills and market them to particular publications.

# UNDERSTANDING

1. The writer in the story seeks solitude, whereas the boy wants to be *connected* to something. Which of his actions suggest this? Make a list of the needs he exhibits and write how he tries to fill each need. Now compare yourself to Jerry. What needs do you have in common? How do you fill those needs?

2. The writer describes Jerry's special quality as "integrity." Write your own definition of "integrity." Then find examples of Jerry's integrity throughout the story. Next find examples that seem to disprove Jerry's integrity. Explain why you think Jerry wants the narrator to believe he has a mother.

Write a private journal entry about a time when you deceived someone and why you chose to do so. Was lying your only option, or did you have choices? What were the results of your actions?

3. Jerry has a strong work ethic—he works hard and feels responsible to do a good job. Find examples that show he is a conscientious worker both at the orphanage and for the narrator.

   Think about yourself as a worker. Would you describe yourself as diligent? In two columns, list your positive work habits and an example of each. Then write a letter of recommendation for yourself that describes your characteristics as a worker. Use examples of your past actions to support your points.
   *Workshop 17*

## A LAST WORD

If you had been the narrator, what would you have done regarding Jerry once you learned the truth about his mother? For what reasons should we become involved in the lives of others?

## CONNECTING

1. Research the statistics on orphaned children in this country and in at least two other nations. Where and with whom do the children live, what is the quality of their lives, and what agencies and individuals are working to help them? Write a letter to one of these agencies requesting information on the services they provide. Share the information with the class in an oral presentation.
   *Workshops 17 and 25*

2. The writer paid Jerry ten cents an hour, a fair price for household chores at the time the story takes place. What would be a fair hourly wage for household chores today? What was the value of a dollar during the 1940s, 1950s, and 1960s compared to today's dollar? You might talk to older relatives or neighbors to find out what they remember about wages and prices during those decades. Write a short report on rising prices and the changes in wages over the past fifty years. Use charts or graphs as visual representations of the information you found.
   *Workshop 22*

## ACCENT ON...
### SOCIAL SERVICES

A well-run orphanage can meet the day-to-day physical needs of children, as the narrator in the story discovers. However, young people have other needs, whether or not they are orphans. Suppose you are a social worker providing services for needy young people. Develop a two-week plan of activities or opportunities for a group of children. Choose whatever age group interests you. Your plan should consider the particular needs of the age group you choose.

# The Elk Tooth Dress

## EXPLORING

• • • • • • • • • • • • • • • • • • • •

In most cultures, bonds of family loyalty form the foundation of personal growth. In what ways are you loyal to your family? What traits and traditions have you learned from your family? Describe a time when your family members stood together. How did that make you feel?

## THEME CONNECTION...
## FAMILY RELATIONSHIPS

Natalie has been raised by her grandparents to respect her Native American heritage. Although she is interested in modern customs and current styles, she chooses to remain faithful to the teachings of her people. While many teenagers might resent the tight hold of the family, Natalie learns that having patience and trust can bring her what she wants.

## TIME & PLACE

This story focuses on the conflict between two cultures, one traditional and one modern. Natalie Root Digger lives with her grandparents, who teach her Salish, the native language of the Flathead Indians. As a teenager in the 1950s, however, she learns French and algebra at school and wants to follow current fashions. Her tribe lives in Montana, home of many Native American tribes. Often the tribes hold day- or weekend-long meetings to discuss important issues, display their native crafts, and perform dances handed down from their ancestors.

## THE WRITER'S CRAFT

### PLOT

The sequence of actions or events in a story is called the plot. Most short stories have the same general five-step plan. First comes the introduction or the exposition where the story opens. Readers are introduced to the characters and the story's setting. As the plot continues, the action rises as the main character enters a conflict. In the climax, readers see the character making an important discovery or decision. The events after the climax are called the falling action. They lead to the resolution, the part where all the conflicts are settled.

• • • • • • • • • • • • • • • • • • • • • • • • • • • • • • • • • •

# The Elk Tooth Dress

Dorothy M. Johnson

## About the Author

Dorothy M. Johnson (1905–1984) always wanted to write. During her career she was a magazine editor in New York, then a news editor in Montana, and finally an assistant professor of journalism at the University of Montana. She wrote a number of short stories about the West, and several of them were made into feature films, such as *The Man Who Shot Liberty Valance.* She died in Missoula, Montana, her home for more than thirty years.

Missoula—a town in western Montana

Salish—(SAY-lish) a family of North American Indian languages of the northwest U.S. and southwest Canada

Joe Red Crane came over to talk about our going to the Indian Institute in **Missoula.** It is a big gathering at the University, with meetings for several days, to talk about the problems of Indians; and have we got problems! Grandpa said that this year he would let the professors talk about the problems, and he would just as soon be in the big show in the University Field House after they got the problems all talked about.

Sometime, maybe, I will learn how to get around Grandma; but Grandpa still can't do it, and he has been married to her for thirty-five years. I am only sixteen years old.

They are both old-fashioned, but Grandpa is not so stubborn.

Grandpa wanted to wear his own grandfather's feather war bonnet in the big show, but Joe Red Crane talked him out of it. That shows the difference between Grandpa and Grandma. Nobody ever talked her out of anything.

"That is absolutely right," said Grandpa.

"So you will dance at the Indian Institute in Missoula, maybe?"

"Now you put it that way, maybe I will," said Grandpa. "But I won't wear tail feathers or no mail-order war bonnet. I will just wear my beaded vest."

"You will also wear pants," Grandma said to him over her shoulder.

Grandpa said, "All the time I meant to wear pants. Women should stay out of serious conversations."

"There would be serious conversations if you went to Missoula with no pants," Grandma answered.

Then Mr. Red Crane got around to noticing me. I was doing my homework, and you can bet it is hard to memorize irregular French verbs when you are listening to a conversation that switches from English to **Salish** and back.

"We got to have a nice display of art work for the exhibit," he said. "You going to bring something pretty, Natalie? I bet you are. Some nice beadwork."

"I don't like beadwork," I said. "It's old-fashioned. I don't think I will go anyway. Not unless I can get my hair cut short and have a permanent."

Grandma said to the wall, "Natalie will go, and she will not have a permanent. She will wear her hair in braids like she was meant to. She has not got her exhibit finished yet, but she will. It is a bag all covered with beads." Grandma switched to Salish and muttered, "She is lazy. Bad girl."

I am only kind of lazy and not very bad, but I did not argue, because getting a permanent is something we have not agreed about for two years or more.

Joe Red Crane saved his talk with Grandma till last, because it was going to be the toughest.

"And you will wear your fringed **buckskin** dress with the elk teeth all over it," he said to her with a big smile, "and you will be in the Grass Dance."

"I will not do any such thing," said Grandma. "I am going to wear my go-to-town clothes and sit in the audience and watch everybody and see whether my old man is wearing his pants. Natalie can wear my dress with the elk teeth if she wants to. I guess she won't want to, though, because she has all these modern ideas."

I almost jumped out of my chair. She had never let me wear that dress before. It is very old and valuable. If I asked her for it, she would have said, "No, you are care-less; you would lose some of the elk teeth."

"That's all settled then," Mr. Red Crane said, getting up off the floor.

After he left, I went to work on Grandma, figuring that if I said no, she would say yes.

"I don't want to get my braids cut off and have a permanent," I said. "I have decided to wear my hair long even if you do have to work so hard brushing it."

"Good thing," she said, "because that is how it is going to be."

At school all the kids were talking about going to Missoula, and when I found out some more about the plans, I got pouty.

"I am not going to go," I told Grandma. "Mary MacTavish is going to be introduced as a princess because her great-grandfather was a chief and signed some old treaty. She would have flunked algebra if I had not helped with her homework. So now she is a princess. Mary MacTavish—some Indian!"

Grandma got a firm look on her face and said, "Just be proud you're a full-blood and never mind that princess stuff. But you will go."

Now I am glad I went, because it was a lovely time. It was the most wonderful time I can remember.

That was a big affair, that Indian Institute at the University Field House in Missoula. Grandpa even washed the station wagon. He spent so much time on it that Grandma got nervous and said she would rather ride in a car with mud on it than get there after everybody else had left. But we got there early.

We had the biggest bunch of people from our reservation because we only had to go a few miles. There were people from tribes all over Montana, strangers, handsome people in beautiful costumes. Second to us, the Blackfeet had the biggest bunch, and Grandma said, "Huh! The women wear rouge."

There were more languages being spoken than I had ever heard before—Indian languages all different. Absolutely nobody said one word in French. Sometimes I wonder why I go to all the trouble with those irregular verbs. One good thing about Salish, nobody fusses about grammar. You just talk it.

It was a wonderful time, the gathering of all those dark, dignified people—my people, even if they were from other tribes with other languages. The whites came too, of course, lots of them, but they were just there to see us.

In the big crowd we lost track of Grandpa.

"Now where is that Indian exhibit?" Grandma muttered, and I said, "I don't want to go see that."

"I should think you wouldn't," she answered, "but we are going to see it anyway."

buckskin—soft leather made from a deer's hide

It was embarrassing because I never did finish my beadwork exhibit, and Grandma had to. She fussed because she had to do it kind of sloppy so nobody would know it wasn't all mine. But after all, when a girl is a junior in high school and studying French, and she's in a lot of activities, how much time has she got for beadwork?

We found the exhibit. Grandma asked an Indian where it was. She wouldn't ask a white person because she wouldn't admit they might know something she didn't.

Mary MacTavish was hanging around the exhibit, because her entry for art work was a drawing of **Marilyn Monroe** that she copied out of a movie magazine. Mary MacTavish, that princess, stood around in her mail-order buckskin dress, batting her eyelashes; and I must admit that she had two fellows from our football team and two others hanging around with her.

"Oh, hello, Natalie," she said very sweetly, for fear I wouldn't notice all those fellows; and I said, "Hi ya, princess, old kid."

Grandma said in a carrying voice, "We will not look at any drawings copied out of magazines. We will look at the real Indian art. Well, that bag you beaded looks pretty good, Natalie. They displayed it nice."

I kind of nudged my arm against her arm to tell her I was grateful that she didn't give away my guilty secret about not finishing it myself, and she nudged back. When Grandma is for you, she is

for you all the way, especially if somebody else is against you.

"Where did that old man of mine go?" she grumbled.

"He just came in," I said, "with a white woman," and Grandma said, "What!"

Grandpa was being very Noble Red Man. He is not very tall, but he can look awful noble. He was just looking past this white woman in a baggy **tweed** suit and not answering her, and she was getting more and more earnest, pointing at her camera and talking her idea of Indian English: "Me take picture, okay? You stand still, me take nice picture?"

I was so grateful to Grandma for being on my side that I walked over and rescued him from her, because she wouldn't lower herself by chasing after him.

I said to him in Salish, "Come on with me if you want to get away."

The white woman said, "Little girl, maybe you talk English—just tell him I want to take his picture."

So if she wanted to, why didn't she go ahead?

I murmured, *"Je ne parle pas l'anglais. Mon grandpère ne parle pas l'anglais."*

She shook her head and said, "Oh, dear. They all talk Indian," and walked away.

Then we three went to the Field House and got settled in the front row of the audience.

We looked around, and I saw the most beautiful thing I ever laid eyes on. He was tall and lean, in tight jeans and cowboy boots, and he had long hair. Long, thick, glossy braids, even if he

> • • • • • • • •
> **"I was so grateful to Grandma for being on my side."**
> • • • • • • • •

was young like me—long hair like the old men, but ah, how pretty it looks on a young fellow!

He was as handsome as a calendar, with a sharp profile and his head held high. He wore a cowboy hat, sort of tipped back so it wouldn't hide the soft way his hair came down over his ears, because he was proud of his hair, and that was right.

Alongside him, all the boys I know look just plain stupid. My heart hurt. I kind of wanted to cry.

I said in a whisper, "Grandma, look."

"Look at what?" she asked. "All those strange Indians?"

Then I saw he was not by himself but in a group of five or six men, all older; but do you know, I hadn't noticed them before. They were Indians, but wearing business suits, and a couple of them had braids.

Grandma saw the young man then and said, "Ah." She said something to Grandpa and he looked and said, "Ah."

Then he got up and ambled over to these men halfway across the arena, and they all got acquainted and shook hands. The young long-hair didn't talk. He just stood there listening, the way a young

## FOCUS ON... MUSIC AND DANCE

Tribal dances are an important aspect of nearly all Native American ceremonies. Are you familiar with an authentic dance from any culture? What is the dance's significance within that culture? Find out about a dance and its music performed by an Indian nation or by some cultural group. Use print or video resources, or contact a source on the Internet. Videotape a performance of the dance and its music. Show the video to your class and give an oral report on the meaning of the dance to members of the cultural group.

◆ ◆ ◆ ◆ ◆ ◆ ◆ ◆ ◆ ◆ ◆ ◆ ◆ ◆ ◆

man should in the presence of his betters; only generally they don't.

Grandma said, "They are Cheyennes," and I asked, "How can you tell from here?"

"Your grandpa just told me in sign talk," she answered. "If you'd keep your eyes open, you might learn something. The young fellow is going to be in the show." She squinted and added, "His name is something like water."

It just goes to show you how much good French does a girl when something really important comes up. I don't pay much attention to sign talk; it's old-fashioned. We used to use it in grade school when we wanted to make remarks about a new teacher.

"Oh, look at that mail-order princess," I said, shocked. "She is going right over to interrupt the men. She is going to get that Cheyenne boy for herself."

conservative—
tending to
preserve estab-
lished traditions

Minnehaha—
"Indian girl"; a
reference to the
heroine of
Longfellow's
poem "The
Song of
Hiawatha"

"I don't think she is," said Grandma. "Keep still and trust your grandpa. Sometimes he is a no-good, but in a pinch you can depend on him."

Mary was heading for the men, with two other girls, all giggling and wiggling. But Grandpa fixed her wagon. It was cute how he did it. He never saw them, but every time Mary moved a little to one side, he moved too, so his back was always toward her while he talked to the other men.

There was quite a crowd of Indians around there, making a quiet fuss over the long-hair boy. The old people approved because he was **conservative,** old-fashioned; and the boys hung around because he was twirling a rope, sort of playing with it; and the girls edged up because he was so cute. And I had to stay by Grandma because we are conservative.

Grandma said, "Never mind that phony **Minnehaha,** making eyes. You make eyes at the ground. . . . Listen, I saw some other women from other reservations with elk teeth on their dresses, but not so many as on the dress you're wearing. Don't you worry."

She dug in the big bag she carried and brought out something. It was her little old short cape embroidered with porcupine quills, dyed in soft colors long ago. She hung it over my shoulders, and I felt warm and cared for because I know she thought a lot of me and was on my side.

Even when I was a child, not many women were embroidering with porcupine quills; they used all beads because it was easier. This cape was very old, made by my grandmother. The buckskin

● ● ● ● ● ● ●
"He will think
you are bold."
● ● ● ● ● ● ●

was soft and gray, not dirty but not glaring white. Wearing it, I felt like a queen and was not very jealous of Princess MacTavish.

The men and boys from our reservation were buckling on the bells they wear on their legs for dancing, and you couldn't hear yourself think. They are big, round bells with something noisy inside. And Grandpa had gone over to the middle and started beating a drum. The only thing he doesn't like about a show is that he can't beat a drum and dance at the same time.

Then a man said, "Woof, woof, testing," into the public-address system, and asked everybody to take his seat because the show was going to begin. The young long-hair walked past us with his friends, but he did not look our way at all.

Grandma said, "Natalie, stop looking at him all the time."

"What does he wear long hair for if he doesn't want to be looked at?" I answered.

"I don't know what he wants," said Grandma, "but I want you to stop looking. He will think you are bold."

"He doesn't know I'm alive," I moaned, and she said with a satisfied chuckle, "Oh, yes, he does. What do you think your grandpa went over there for? To talk about the hay crop, maybe?"

I was so happy I even stopped staring.

Grandma said, "Doesn't Mary MacTavish look silly with her short hair in that Indian dress from mail order? But you look just right."

"I am a bad girl and lazy," I said. "You had to finish my beadwork."

"Oh, not so bad," she answered, always arguing.

Somebody on the public-address system made a long speech about the significance of all this and named all the tribes that were represented, and then he said the Flatheads would please take their places. So I left Grandma and went drifting out to the arena with the rest of our people and stood with the other girls in the back.

## SPOTLIGHT ON... USING NON-VERBAL CUES

The characters in Johnson's story often communicate without speaking. Using nonverbal cues can be an effective communication tool. Look for the following nonverbal cues as others communicate with you:
• body movements
• hand gestures
• facial expressions
• silences
• physical actions

The men sat down in chairs in a long row. The chairs were turned backward, because if a man wears tail feathers he has to straddle when he sits down. But Grandpa turned his chair around and leaned back and was comfortable, because he wouldn't be caught dead in those mail-order tail feathers. He had a big silver ornament on each braid, but he wasn't dressed up except for a beaded vest. He wore his pants all right, blue jeans. He wore his silver-rimmed glasses, too, and Grandma didn't like that; she says it is too modern. But he says, "I am nearsighted, and I wear glasses. You want me to fall over something and break my neck, maybe?"

Mary MacTavish said to me, "Hi, kid. It's too bad they won't let me present you to the audience. Alice and Elizabeth are my maids-in-waiting, you know. I am going to present them to the audience. But I can't do a thing for you, because their ancestors signed the same treaty mine did, but your ancestors wouldn't sign."

"My ancestors never gave the country away," I said. "They wanted to hang onto it."

"What are you looking at the ground for?" she asked. "Lost something?"

"Indian girls are supposed to be modest," I said. "Didn't anybody ever tell you? I am a full-blood, so I am going to be modest while I've got this elk tooth dress on and this old and valuable embroidered cape all covered with dyed porcupine quills."

"I guess you're just jealous because I'm not going to present you too," Mary MacTavish said.

"I guess you better be kind of polite," I said, "if you don't want to flunk French."

Then we had to quit talking, because Mr. Red Crane started to talk on the public-address system, introducing our people.

There were a couple of dances for the men, good and noisy, with all the drumming and all those bells on their legs clanging with every step, and I was in the Grass Dance with Mary and the rest of them.

Mr. Red Crane introduced Princess Mary MacTavish, and she walked forward with her beaded moccasins on her feet and her permanent on her head, looking so modest it would kill you, making eyes at the ground.

"Princess Mary will now present her maids-in-waiting," Mr. Red Crane said, and everybody waited, but she didn't. She was being so modest, she just stood there. So Alice had to walk out by herself, and so did Elizabeth.

Then *they* just stood there, the modest Indian maidens, until the announcer told them twice they could go sit down now.

Then he said, "One of the girls from the Flathead Reservation is wearing a very rare costume, very old, that I am sure you will want to see. Natalie Root Digger, will you please walk forward so the audience can see you?"

Well, I just about died. I went forward about three steps and stood there with my eyes down, feeling those thousands of people staring. He told about the old dress with the elk teeth on it and the precious cape embroidered with porcupine quills, and the people clapped. I went back without anybody telling me.

I never took my eyes off the ground, but I saw that long-hair Cheyenne in the front row sitting by Grandma. She looked good. She wore her black dress with red figures in it, and her best purple silk handkerchief draped around her head in folds, with her long, dark braids looped to hang down under it.

Our people did more dances, and Grandpa would sneak out in front of the rest and kind of clown with his dancing. Everytime he did that, the audience would laugh and clap. Then we went out of the arena and finally I got over to where Grandma was. She said in Salish, "Sit down. Lots of room," and the long-hair started to get up out of the way. But Grandma said in English, "Stay there. She's little; she won't crowd you."

He said, "She sure won't," and we sat close because we had to, both looking at the ground but seeing each other just the same. He had the most wonderful voice, deep and soft and bashful. The announcer said now the Blackfeet would come and perform, and Grandma said, "Huh!"

All the other Indians, when they had gone into the arena, had just sort of drifted in. But those Blackfeet came marching to a drum, very showy, and their leader gave them signals with an eagle wing fan. Real fancy.

The long-hair boy said, "Tourist stuff," and Grandma looked at him with approval.

They did some dances, and they were so popular with the silly crowd of white people that they kept right on doing dances. The Cheyenne boy made a thoughtful sound and got up and walked across the arena toward Grandpa and the rest of our Flathead men. In a minute, Grandpa and the others from our reservation started walking from one end of the arena toward the other.

You should have heard it. They didn't do anything but just walk and mind their own business, but when two dozen Indians walk from one place to another with strings of big bells on their legs, not keeping step—well. The racket was so loud, with the clanging of the bells drowning out the Blackfeet drums, that the audience forgot about the Blackfeet dancing so smart and sassy. People got kind of fidgety and started looking at their programs, and when they clapped for the Blackfeet, Grandma and I clapped for the Flatheads.

Grandma said, "Well, I guess we won that battle."

When the young long-hair came back, drifting, Grandma moved over so he would sit between us.

"What's your name, Cheyenne?" she asked.

"George Standing in the Water," he answered.

"You're a smart boy," Grandma said, "and I would like to meet your folks sometime."

He didn't say anything, but he blushed. A blush under a bronze skin is pretty.

"Your folks are old-fashioned?" Grandma asked him, and he knew it was a compliment, and nodded.

"My brother fasted in the Sun Dance last year," he said. "Maybe I will someday."

We don't do the Sun Dance—we have our own customs—but I knew a little about that, and I shivered. They starve and don't drink any water for four days, the few men who dare to dance the Sun Dance; then they dance until they faint sometimes.

"Maybe we'll come to your reservation sometime," Grandma purred.

"I wouldn't want to see the Sun Dance if anybody I knew was in it," I said, feeling terrible.

"My brother's girl, she was kind of proud of him," George said.

So then I thought I could watch him if the time came, and I would be proud too.

The announcer said on the public-address system, "A young Cheyenne from the Tongue River Reservation will demonstrate his skill in roping. I present George Standing in the Water, of the Northern Cheyenne."

George went out in the arena, not very far, not looking up at the audience, but as if he were there all by himself with nobody around. It was all quiet, no drumming. He twirled his rope in little circles and big circles. He danced into the spinning rope circle and danced out of it again. The rope was like a live thing that did just what he wanted it to do, and his hands hardly moved, but the rope spun its circle and rippled and flashed like water.

People were taking pictures—flash, flash went the cameras, taking pictures of the fine long-hair. Grandpa's white-woman friend was jumping around in her baggy tweed suit, putting new flash bulbs in her camera, and taking pictures and talking to herself.

It was as if George were there all alone, in the big Field House, dreaming with the spinning rope. When he stopped, there was nothing dramatic about the stopping. He didn't bow to the audience like some performers do. Why should he bow? He didn't owe them anything. He just gathered up his rope when he was through, while the audience clapped and hollered, and he walked over to sit by us again.

bitterroot—a plant found in western North America having an edible root and a pink or white flower

lithe—flexible, graceful

I thought, I wish I had a camera. I wish I could have a picture of George Standing in the Water to keep forever.

Somebody made another long speech about the significance of all this, and some other tribes danced, and then the whole show was over. Grandpa drifted over to us, and that white woman in the tweed suit made a dive at him.

"Well, I'll take care of this," said Grandma, and marched toward them like an army with banners.

"You going home tonight?" George asked, looking at the ground.

I said, "Yes. To Arlee." And maybe I will never see you again, I thought. That will be worse than if I never had known you were alive. "Where you going?"

"Staying at a motel with my friends. Long drive to Tongue River. We'll start early in the morning. Listen, where would a fellow write you a letter if he wanted to, maybe? Just Arlee?"

"That's right. Natalie Root Digger, Arlee, Montana." Then I got really bold. "You know, we dig **bitterroot** around Missoula in the spring, pretty soon. We're old-fashioned. We don't mind if our friends come dig bitterroot with us. Or maybe you have to go to school."

"This year I have to go to school. I am on the track team. Maybe next year. If your folks come to our rodeo. I ride bucking horses."

"Maybe Grandma and Grandpa would like to go to your rodeo," I answered. "I guess they would probably take me along."

We never looked at each other all that time, but I saw his black, soft, shining braids; and he saw my braids, and the buckskin dress trimmed with elk teeth and the little cape with the faded-color porcupine quill embroidery.

"Well, so long," he said.

I said, "Okay. See you around."

He walked away, so **lithe** and slim, and my heart wanted to cry.

My folks came back, their faces straight, but I could tell they were laughing inside about something. I didn't feel like laughing.

"Well, that white woman got your grandpa's picture," Grandma said. "It's hard talking this Injun English she likes, but I got the idea across that she could take his picture if she would send me a print; also, she has to send me some other pictures that are on the same roll of film."

"That's nice," I said with my heart jumping. Because she had taken pictures of George while he was spinning the rope.

"Where'd that Cheyenne go?" Grandma asked.

"He had to catch up with his friends. Grandma, he asked us to their rodeo, and I asked him to help us dig bitterroot, and is it all right? If you say it's wrong and I'm not a nice, modest girl, I'll just die!"

"It is all right and you are a good girl," she answered. "I think we will maybe go to the Cheyennes' rodeo when the time comes."

When my letter comes from the Tongue River Reservation, it will have his return address on it, I guess. But I wouldn't ask him for it, because it is a good thing to be old-fashioned, even for a girl who is a junior in high school and learning French. ❖

## UNDERSTANDING

1. Find lines in the text that reveal how Natalie and her grandmother feel about one another. Summarize your findings in a one-sentence statement.

   Interview classmates or friends who have close relationships with a grandparent. Ask questions whose answers will provide information that shows how the two feel about one another. Pool the information and categorize the different elements of the relationships. Produce a list of benefits of having a close relationship with a grandparent. *Workshop 26*

2.  Humor is used in this story in both subtle and obvious ways. With a partner, find ways the author has used humor. Choose one humorous situation and create a cartoon from it. Use lines from the text as a caption for the cartoon.

3. Write the five elements of plot on a sheet of paper, leaving space between them. Under each, write the events from the story that fall into that element. What do we learn in the introduction? What is the sequence of events as the action rises? What do you consider the climax of the story? What occurs during the falling action? How is the conflict finally resolved? *Workshop 1*

## CONNECTING

1. Research the ethnic groups that settled in your region. Choose one of these groups and explore the culture of the people, including their language, customs, traditional dress, country of origin, foods, and so on. Deliver an oral presentation of your findings to the class. If possible, invite a speaker from this ethnic group to discuss the culture with the class. *Workshop 21*

2. Suppose you are organizing a one-day cultural event. Your event may focus on your own culture or one in which you are interested. Prepare a brochure describing the events that would take place during the day. Assume you are advertising the event for tourists, townspeople, and relatives of the performers. *Workshop 20*

### A LAST WORD

What conflicts do you perceive in your own culture? What parts of your culture do you embrace? What aspects might you question? Why?

# Annabel Lee

## EXPLORING
● ● ● ● ● ● ● ● ● ● ● ● ● ● ● ● ● ● ● ● ●

Today's music addresses love, happiness, distress, and many other emotions. Some songs tell stories in addition to express emotions. What stories do you know through songs? Write about or share one such story with a group or with the class. Describe the author's point and how he or she uses melody, rhythm, and rhyme to capture emotion.

## THEME CONNECTION...
## LOVE RELATIONSHIPS

Edgar Allan Poe is known not only for his frightening and fantastic tales but also for his rhythmic poetry. He writes in this poem about his lovely bride who died at a young age. Through his grief we see a deep, abiding love and devotion to her. Much of their life together was spent in a struggle against poverty and illness. Poe's depression on losing the beautiful woman he loved moved him to write with great feeling. Only three years later, Poe died penniless and in despair.

## TIME & PLACE

The story of Annabel Lee takes place in the mid-1800s, probably on the east coast of the United States. Poe and his wife, who was also his young cousin, Virginia Clemm, moved around looking for opportunities where he could work as a writer. Besides writing stories about frightening events and deadly diseases, Poe worked in journalism. He became world famous after his death for his themes of loss and isolation and as a master of mystery and suspense.

## THE WRITER'S CRAFT
### NARRATIVE POETRY

Simply stated, narrative poetry tells a story. It looks like, sounds like, and has the rhythm of poetry, but its story has a setting, characters, a plot, and a theme. Narrative poetry is an ancient form of storytelling introduced as far back as the Greek and Roman empires. Sometimes poetry describing the adventures of brave soldiers was sung to entertain the ruler and the court.

● ● ● ● ● ● ● ● ● ● ● ● ● ● ● ● ● ● ● ● ● ● ● ● ● ● ● ● ●

# Annabel Lee

Edgar Allan Poe

It was many and many a year ago,
    In a kingdom by the sea,
That a maiden there lived whom you may know
    By the name of Annabel Lee;—
And this maiden she lived with no other thought
    Than to love and be loved by me.

*I* was a child and *she* was a child,
    In this kingdom by the sea,
But we loved with a love that was more than love—
    I and my Annabel Lee—
With a love that the wingèd **seraphs** in Heaven
    **Coveted** her and me.

And this was the reason that, long ago,
    In this kingdom by the sea,
A wind blew out of a cloud, chilling
    My beautiful Annabel Lee;
So that her high-born kinsmen came
    And bore her away from me,
To shut her up in a **sepulchre**
    In this kingdom by the sea.

The angels, not half so happy in Heaven,
    Went envying her and me:—
Yes!—that was the reason (as all men know,
    In this kingdom by the sea)
That the wind came out of the cloud, by night,
    Chilling and killing my Annabel Lee.

But our love it was stronger by far than the love
    Of those who were older than we—
    Of many far wiser than we—
And neither the angels in Heaven above,
    Nor the demons down under the sea,
Can ever **dissever** my soul from the soul
    Of the beautiful Annabel Lee:—

## About the Author

Born in Boston, Edgar Allan Poe (1809–1849) led a troubled life. His mother died when he was three, and his father left the family. Taken in by a wealthy family, Poe received a good education. He wrote his first book of poetry at age 18 and soon started writing short stories. He married Virginia Clemm in 1836 and worked as a magazine editor. When his wife died in 1847, Poe's life seemed to dissolve. Though he had a short life, Poe's writing made him one of the most influential American writers.

seraphs—angels

coveted—desired what belonged to someone else

sepulchre—a place of burial, a tomb

dissever—to separate

For the moon never beams without bringing me dreams
    Of the beautiful Annabel Lee;
And the stars never rise but I feel the bright eyes
    Of the beautiful Annabel Lee;
And so, all the night-tide, I lie down by the side
Of my darling,—my darling,—my life and my bride,
    In her sepulchre there by the sea—
    In her tomb by the sounding sea. ❖

## UNDERSTANDING

1. Find words and phrases the narrator uses to describe his feelings for his bride. What feelings does the narrator's description create in you? What images come to mind as you read the poem? How do you picture Annabel Lee? How old is she? What are her hair and eye colors, skin tone, and other physical features? Imagine her voice and her actions. Write a paragraph describing Annabel Lee. *Workshops 7, 8, and 10*

2. Setting is an important element in this poem. Find phrases that describe the setting. Discuss in a group how the setting contributes to the sound and feel of the poem. Write a one-page paper exploring other possible settings for this poem. How would different settings alter the sound and feel of the poem?

3.  Find lines in the poem that indicate how Annabel Lee died. In groups discuss what the lines mean. Decide as a group on a possible cause of death. Share your decision with the class, using evidence from the poem. Write a short news article telling the story of her death. *Workshop 19*

4. Write the last word of each line in a list. These words represent the poem's rhyme scheme. Examine the pattern of each stanza. Note where the author chose to abandon the pattern. What is the effect of the rhyme scheme as you read the poem aloud? *Workshop 2*

### A LAST WORD

Some literary critics maintain that an artist must suffer deeply to produce work of beauty and insight. Do you agree? Can a writer produce excellent literature without enduring tragedy or severe disappointment?

## CONNECTING

1. Make a list of our society's traditions concerning death. The first might be the taking of food to the grieving family. What others do you know? To expand your list, ask relatives or neighbors to explain their traditions. As a class, prepare a list of all these customs.

   One common custom is to write a sympathy letter to the deceased person's family. Pretend someone you know has lost a family member or close friend. Write a sympathy letter to that person. Express your feelings and offer your support. *Workshop 16*

2. Grief may last for months and even years. The narrator in the poem still mourns Annabel Lee every night. Check your library for information on the process of grieving. Other good resources are a school counselor, school nurse, minister, or social worker. Invite one of these people to your class to speak on death and grieving. Using information from your research and from the guest speaker, work in groups to create a short pamphlet that advises young people on how to deal with grief and provides sources for further help or advice. *Workshop 20*

## ACCENT ON...
### HEALTH CARE TECHNOLOGY

The narrator in the poem laments the death of his love from a chill wind; likewise, Poe lamented the death of his young wife from tuberculosis. How is tuberculosis diagnosed today? What are its treatments? Find out what kind of preventive health care is available and what technology is used in the prevention and treatment of respiratory diseases such as tuberculosis. Write a two-page report explaining how tuberculosis is detected and treated today.

# Amanda and the Wounded Birds

## EXPLORING

Stress affects both young and old in today's fast-paced world. Emotions and relationships can become strained. What causes stress in your life? What physical symptoms of stress do you experience? Describe a time when stress weakened your family relationships. How did you resolve the situation?

## THEME CONNECTION... FAMILY RELATIONSHIPS

The family is the basic unit of society around the world. Whether a family consists of two, three, four, or more people, its strength depends on the love and respect its members have for one another. Family relationships are nurtured, in part, through spending time together and communicating. In this story, the everyday responsibilities of work and school interfere with the time a mother and her daughter would like to spend together. The teenage daughter has begun to feel like a "wounded bird" who needs the warmth and attention only her mother can provide.

## TIME & PLACE

Radio talk shows have become extremely popular in cities across America. The subjects of these programs vary. Some talk show hosts interview local and national celebrities. Some give opinions on current events, politics, and religion, urging callers to discuss these often controversial subjects over the airwaves. Others offer advice to their callers, like Dr. Hart in the story.

## THE WRITER'S CRAFT

### SHORT STORY

A short story presents a specific event in a compact time frame. It generally focuses on one major conflict and how it is resolved. The story can usually be read in a short amount of time. Elements of a short story are setting, characters, plot, and theme. Writers must carefully craft short stories because they must complete the telling of an event in only a few words.

Short stories as we know them today first appeared in America in the 1800s. Edgar Allan Poe, O. Henry, and Nathaniel Hawthorne were among those who developed clever and appealing stories.

# Amanda and the Wounded Birds

Colby Rodowsky

It's not that my mother doesn't understand, because she does. In fact, she understands so well, and so much, and so single-mindedly that half the time she goes around with a glazed look in her eyes and forgets to get her hair cut, and go to the dentist and that we're almost out of toilet paper or tuna fish.

She makes her living understanding, which may make more sense when I tell you that my mother is Dr. Emma Hart. Now, if that doesn't help, then probably, like me until my **consciousness** was raised, you've always thought of radio as the place to hear the Top 40 or sometimes the weather report when you're heading for the shore on a summer Friday afternoon. But just try twiddling the dial and you'll find her, way over to the left on the band, next to the country and western station.

Maybe what I should do is go back a little and explain. You see, my mother is a psychotherapist, which means that she counsels people and tries to help them find ways of dealing with their problems. She's also a widow. My father died when I was a baby and sometimes I try to imagine what it must have been like for her, taking care of a baby alone and trying to establish a practice all at the same time. One thing I'm sure of is that knowing Mom, she handled it gracefully, and **stoically,** and with that funny habit she has of biting her lower lip so that for all her hanging-in-there attitude she still looks like a ten-year-old kid—the kind you want to do something for because she's not always whining or sniffling. I guess you'd have to say that as much as possible my mother is in charge of her own life, which is the way she tries to get the people who call in to her on the radio to be.

The way the radio program got started was that several years ago the producer was looking for something to put on in the late afternoon when people were mostly fixing dinner or driving car pool or just sitting with their feet up. It wasn't exactly prime time. Then he remembered how he'd heard Mom speak at a dinner once and had thought at the time that putting someone like her on radio would be a real public service. Besides, the ratings couldn't be any lower than they had been for the Handy Home Fixit show he'd had on before. Anyway, he tracked her down, arranged for a test, and then Mom was on the air.

I never will forget that first show. I mean, there was my mother's voice coming out of our kitchen radio, sounding slightly frantic and giving those first callers more than they bargained for: I guess she was afraid if she let them off the line there wouldn't *be* any more. That day even the producer called with a question. And the boy in the studio who went for coffee. But Mom hung in there,

## About the Author

As a young girl, Colby Rodowsky wanted to become a writer, and her mother encouraged her. Born in Baltimore in 1932, Rodowsky earned an English degree from the College of Notre Dame of Maryland. She taught school for three years, then focused on raising her six children with her husband. Rodowsky did not start her writing career until after she was forty. She won the American Library Association's Best Books for Young Adults citation for her novel *Julie's Daughter.*

consciousness—awareness

stoically—not showing any feelings

downtrodden—
burdened with
difficulties

and calls continued to come in, and then they started backing up, and it wasn't long before people opened by saying, "I didn't think I'd *ever* get through to you." After only a month on the air the Emma Hart show went from one hour to two; and the way I figured it, a lot of people were eating dinner later than they ever had before. Including us.

Mom really cared about the people who telephoned her, and almost right from the beginning she was calling them her "wounded birds." Not on the air, of course, and *never* to anyone but me. I got used to her looking up in the middle of dinner or from watching the late news on TV and saying, "I hope my wounded bird with the abusive husband will get herself into counseling," or "The wounded bird with those children who walk all over her had better learn to assert herself before it's too late." And I *sure* learned not to joke around: once I referred to one of her callers as a fractured canary and almost started World War III.

Not long after this, things really started to happen. First, Mom's show was moved to a better time slot. Then it was syndicated, so that she wasn't just on the air here but in a bunch of other cities, too. The way "Doonesbury" and "Dick Tracy" are in a bunch of newspapers. Now, I have to say that for the most part my mother's pretty cool about things, but the day she found out that the Emma Hart show was being syndicated she just about flipped. She called from the studio and told me to meet her at the Terrace

Garden for dinner, to be sure and get spiffed up because we were going all out.

During dinner Mom spent a lot of time staring into the candlelight and smiling to herself. Finally she said, "Just think of all those people who'll be listening now." And let me tell you, I *was* thinking about them, and it worried me a lot. I mean the way I saw it, there were going to be even more problems: more victims who were **downtrodden** or mis-understood. More stories about people who had been abused or who had kids on drugs or dropping out, or ne'er-do-well relatives moving in. But when I tried to say that, Mom was suddenly all atten-tion. "Don't be silly, Amanda. It's the same amount of time and the same number of calls—you'll hardly notice any difference. Only now I'll have wounded birds in Phoenix and Pittsburgh and Philadelphia."

● ● ● ● ● ● ●
"Just think of all those people who'll be listening now."
● ● ● ● ● ● ●

In one way she was right: the show sounded pretty much the same. (Except that *I* found out that when your husband/lover/friend walks out on you it hurts as much in Peoria as it does in Perth Amboy.)

In another way she was wrong: she was busier than she had ever been before, what with travelling and lectur-ing and doing guest shows from other cities. For a while there, it was as if I was spending as much time at my best friend Terri's as I was at my own house. Then eventually Mom decided I could stay at our place when she had to be out of town, as long as Terri stayed there with me, which wasn't as good or as bad as it sounds, because Terri lives right across the street and her mother has X-ray eyes. I mean we can hardly manage to reach for our favorite breakfast of Twinkies and Oreo ice cream with an orange juice chaser before her mother is on the telephone telling us to eat cornflakes instead—and to wash the dishes.

Sometimes I felt that life was nothing but a revolving door: Mom going out while I was coming in. I know there are some kids who would've thought I was lucky, but the thing about my mother is that she's okay. And I wanted to see more of her. Besides that, I needed to talk to her. I don't know why, but all of a sudden it seemed that things were piling up around me. No major crises, you understand. Nothing that would exactly stop traffic.

I'll give you an example.

Take my friend Terri. I have a terrible feeling that she has a secret crush on my boyfriend Josh. If she does, it would be a disaster, because how could we really be friends anymore? But then again how could Terri and I *not* be friends? I'm not sure *why* I think this, unless it's because she gets quiet and acts bored when I talk about him a lot—the way you do when you don't want to let on about liking someone. I mean she couldn't *really* be bored. Could she?

Then there's Miss Spellman, my English teacher, who has this really **atrocious** breath and is forever leaning into people as she reads poetry in class. Imagine somebody breathing garbage fumes on you as she recites Emily Dickinson. If something doesn't happen soon I may never like poetry again.

Now, maybe these aren't world problems, any more than the incident with the guidance counselor was, but it bugged me all the same. Our school has an obsession about students getting into *good* colleges **a.s.a.p.** and knowing what they want to do with the rest of their lives (Terri and I call it the life-packaging syndrome). Anyway, this particular day I was coming out of gym on my way to study hall when Mr. Burnside, the guidance counselor, stopped me and started asking me all this stuff, like what my career goals were and had I decided what I wanted to major in in college.

What I said (only politer than it sounds here) was that how did I know what I

atrocious—
exceptionally
bad

a.s.a.p.—
abbreviation for
"as soon as
possible"

wanted to major in when I didn't even know where I wanted to *go* to college. Mr. Burnside got a wild look in his eyes and started opening and closing his mouth so that all I could see was a shiny strand of spit running between his top and his bottom teeth while he lectured me on how I was going about this whole college thing the wrong way. He said I should come into the guidance office someday and let him feed me into the computer—well, not me exactly, but stuff like my grades, extra curricular activities, and whether or not I needed financial aid.

"And what does your mother say?" he asked as he rooted in his pocket for a late pass to get me into study hall. "You'll certainly have it easier than anybody else in your class, or the school either for that matter—living with Dr. Emma Hart." He laughed that horselaugh of his and slapped me on the back. "She'll get right to the *Hart* of it." Another laugh. "Anybody else would have to call her on the telephone." His laughter seemed to follow me all the way to study hall. I even heard it bouncing around in my head as I settled down to do my Spanish.

"Anybody else would have to call her on the telephone," he had said.

Why not? I thought as I was walking home from school.

Why not? I asked myself when Josh and I were eating popcorn and playing Scrabble on the living room floor that night.

And pretty soon *why not?* changed to *when?* The answer to that one was easy enough though, because spring vacation was only a week and a half away and that would give me the perfect opportunity.

The funny thing was that once I'd decided to do it, I never worried about getting through. Maybe that was because I'd heard Mom say plenty of times that they always liked it when kids called into the show, and I guess I figured that unless everybody on spring vacation decided to call the Dr. Emma Hart Show, I wouldn't have any trouble. Besides I practiced in the shower making my voice huskier than usual and just a little breathless, hoping that it would sound sincere and make an impression on Jordan, the guy who screens the calls and tries for just the right balance of men, women, and kids, with not too much emphasis on busted romances as opposed to anxiety attacks.

The next funny thing was that once I'd made up my mind to call Dr. Emma Hart, I began to feel like a wounded bird myself, and I was suddenly awfully glad that she cared about them the way she did. I had a little trouble deciding what I wanted to ask her on the show, and even before I could make up my mind I began to think of other things that bothered me too. Not problems, but stuff I'd like to talk over with Mom. Like Vietnam, for example. I'd watched **Apocalypse Now** on TV and there were a lot of things I didn't understand. And what about the sixties?—was Mom ever involved in sit-ins or walkouts or any of that? I somehow doubted it, but it would be important to know for sure. Finally it came to me: what I wanted to ask Dr. Hart about was not being able to talk to

## SPOTLIGHT ON...
## ACTIVE LISTENING

Amanda's mother needed to be an active listener in her work as a psychologist, and Amanda needed her mother to be a more active listener at home. In school, at home, and on the job, you too will need to develop good listening skills. Here are some suggestions to help you become a more active listener.
- Pay close attention to the speaker. Don't become distracted.
- Take detailed notes or draw diagrams.
- If you don't understand something, jot down questions to ask.
- Think about what is being said. Do you agree? Does it make sense? What is your reaction to what you have heard? Write down your thoughts and reactions.
- Re-read your notes to help you remember what you heard.

Mom because there she was all wrapped up with her wounded birds. Only the whole thing got confusing, one being the other and all.

Anyway, I did it. I put the call in just before eleven on the Monday morning of spring vacation and almost chickened out when Jordan answered. I had met him a couple of times down at the studio, and I could almost see him now, looking like some kind of an intense juggler who is trying to keep everything going at once. I heard my voice, as if it were coming from somewhere far away, giving my name as Claire (it's my middle name) and outlining my problem. When I got finished, Jordan said that he was putting me on hold and not to go away, that Dr. Hart would be with me shortly.

And all of a sudden she was. I mean, there I was talking to my own mother and telling her how I couldn't talk to my mother, and how the things I wanted to talk to her about weren't actually big deals anyway, but still—

Dr. Hart let me go on for a while and then she broke in and said that it was important for me to know that my concerns were as real as anybody else's and it sounded as if my mother and I had a pretty good relationship that had just gotten a little off the track and what I had to do was be really up-front with her and let her know how I felt. Then she suggested that I make a date with my mother for lunch so that I could tell her (Mom) exactly what I'd told her (Dr. Emma Hart), and that I should be sure to call back and let her know how it worked out.

After that I said, "OK" and "Thank you." Then I hung up.

The only trouble was that as soon as Mom got home that day I knew it wasn't going to work.

She was sort of coming unglued. It had been a bad day, she told me. One of her private patients was in the midst of a crisis; the producer of the show was having a fight with his wife and wanted to tell Mom all about it. She had a dinner speech to give Saturday night and didn't have a thought about what to say, and my uncle Alex had called from Scranton to ask Mom to try to talk some sense into his teenage son, who was driving them all crazy.

Then she looked at me and said, "Thank heavens you've got it all together."

Talk about guilt. Right away I knew I was going to break rule number one: I wasn't going to be able to be up-front.

The thing was, I knew I couldn't take what was already one rotten week for Mom and dump all my problems (which seemed to be getting bigger by the minute) on her. Even though I felt like I was going to explode.

By Friday I knew I needed another talk with Dr. Hart. After all, she'd said to call back, hadn't she?

Getting through Jordan was even easier the second time. All I had to say was that I'd spoken to Dr. Hart earlier in the week and that she'd said to let her know what happened.

"Oh, good, a success story," Jordan said right away, jumping to conclusions. I guess he knew what kind of a week it had been too. "Hold on; Dr. Hart will be with you soon," he said.

And there was Dr. Emma Hart again. And suddenly there I was, unloading about how what she had suggested wasn't going to work.

"Why not?" she wanted to know. "Did you try?"

"Yes—no," I said. Then I was going on again, all about Bad-Breath Spellman, the guidance counselor, and how maybe my best friend had a thing for my boyfriend. She kept steering me back to the subject of my mother and why I hadn't arranged to have lunch with her.

I said that my mother had a bad week. That she was swamped, preoccupied, distracted, and running behind. And then it happened. I mean, I heard the words sliding off my lips and couldn't stop them. I said, "The thing about my mother is that she has all these wounded birds who have really important problems and they take all the time she has."

A silence ballooned up between us and was so loud I couldn't hear anything else—and if you know anything about radio, you know that the worst thing that can happen is silence. It lasted forever, and while it was going on I gave serious thought to running away from home, or at least hanging up.

When Mom finally spoke, her voice sounded choked, as if she had swallowed a gumball.

"We've been talking to Claire this morning, who is really Amanda," she said. "And one of the things we talk a lot about on this show is saying what you have to say—even if that's not always easy. Are you still there, Amanda?"

"Yes," I squeaked.

"If I know Amanda," my mother went on, "she would rather have run away, or hung up, but instead she did something harder. She hung on."

I gulped.

# ACCENT ON...
## BROADCAST TECHNOLOGY

Once the Dr. Emma Hart Show was syndicated, its audience increased tremendously. How is a radio program broadcast nationally? What are the steps in the process of syndicating a program? How is a program transmitted live? What is done about the differences in time zones? Time delays? Exactly what technology is used? Does syndication guarantee success?

Interview a program director at a local radio station or search for information on the Internet. Present your findings in an oral report.

# ON THE JOB
## RADIO ANNOUNCER

Because radio announcers, in general, read commercials and messages to listeners, their most valuable asset is a good speaking voice and style. High school courses and after-school activities in writing, communications, and public speaking can provide basic training. Additional training in acting, broadcasting, or videotape production may also be helpful. A good place to gain experience is at a small radio station, where announcers may perform a variety of tasks, including selling commercial time, writing commercials and news scripts, and running broadcasting equipment. To get a job as a radio announcer, it is essential for an applicant to provide a taped audition demonstrating his or her speaking skills and style.

"Amanda is my daughter, and it seems we have some things to talk about, so what I'm going to do is to ask my assistant to make a reservation for lunch at the Terrace Garden." Then it sounded as though Mom had moved closer to the microphone and was speaking just to me. "If you hurry, Amanda, I'll meet you at 1:30. So we can talk."

And we did: about Bad-Breath Spellman, and Terri, and how it's okay not to know what I want to do with the rest of my life.

We talked about saving the whales, and our two weeks at the shore this summer, and how some day we're going to Ireland. About books and movies and the time in fourth grade when I got the chicken pox and Mom caught them from me.

And we talked about how we had missed talking to each other and what we could do about it.

We ate lunch slowly, and took ages deciding on dessert, and ages more eating it.

We sat there all afternoon, until the light streaking in the windows changed from yellow to a deep, burning gold and the busboys started setting the tables for dinner. ❖

## UNDERSTANDING

1. Find statements in the text that indicate how Amanda admires her mother. What can you conclude about Amanda? Write a one-paragraph character sketch of Amanda. Next, make a list of qualities you admire in a relative. Write a character sketch that states how he or she shows these qualities. Try to imitate the tone of Amanda's introduction of her mother. *Workshop 8*

2. Find lines in the text that indicate Dr. Hart has raised Amanda to be independent and responsible. How important are these characteristics? Consider a specific activity you are involved in, such as participating on a team. Write a paragraph that describes why being responsible and independent contributes to success in your activity. *Workshop 8*

3. Make a chart that outlines how Amanda solved her problem. Next to each point, note the pros and cons involved in taking that course of action. Next, think about a problem you have recently solved. Make a chart for the steps you took to solve the problem. List the pros and cons of each step. Write a paragraph that explains the advantages or disadvantages of your approach. Explain how else you might have solved the problem.

### A LAST WORD

What role does communication play in your relationship with your family? What happens when communication is interrupted? How can the lines of communication among family members remain open and strong?

## CONNECTING

1.  In a group, research the availability of counseling and therapy in your town or region. Include both private counselors and the services provided through government agencies. Locate information on fees as well as funding that helps people with low incomes. Design a flier, on computer, if possible, that presents the information in an easy-to-read format. *Workshop 20*

2. List times you have been annoyed when someone like a clerk, a waiter, or even a doctor did not listen carefully to you. Then work in a group to brainstorm all the occupations in which listening is important. Choose an occupation that interests you and arrange to interview someone who works in that field. Prepare interview questions about the necessity of listening, the benefits of listening, and how *not* listening hinders effectiveness. Following the interview, write several paragraphs on the importance of strong listening skills in this occupation. Be sure to write a letter of thanks to the individual you interviewed. *Workshops 6 and 26*

# Fathers

· *A Man*

· *First Lesson*

## EXPLORING

Sometimes an accident or a narrow escape brings people closer together. Such an incident might make you realize how deeply the loss of the person involved would affect you. Consider a time when you experienced this situation. How did you feel about the person before, during, and after the incident? What actions did you take? How did you let the person know your feelings?

## THEME CONNECTION...
## A FATHER'S LOVE

Protecting their children is a responsibility most fathers take seriously. The father in "A Man" is practical. When he sends his son out to bring home the cows, it never occurs to him that danger awaits. Later, concerned for his injured son, the father expresses affection toward him for the first time.

"First Lesson" shows us a protective father through a daughter's eyes. She senses his feelings of loss as outside forces pull her away from him.

## TIME & PLACE

The story takes place during the early 1900s in a remote rural area. In medical emergencies, farm families depended on the good will of neighbors, and doctors made house calls. Oranges, grown in tropical climates, would have been a rare treat for a farm boy like Mark, because fruits and vegetables were not transported easily at that time.

The young woman of the poem encounters a situation that is common in any time or place. Most fathers worry about their daughters and are reluctant to see them grow up.

## THE WRITER'S CRAFT

### SETTING

Setting includes the time and place of the story. Successful writers know that when and where a story takes place affects the tone and mood—the general feeling—of the entire piece. Setting, therefore, is a critical element in a short story. A writer must carefully craft the setting to bring about the desired response in the reader. Sometimes writers do not give an exact time and place, but readers usually can gather hints from the behaviors of the characters or the background of the plot.

province—
sphere, area of
specialty

forlorn—sad and
lonely

Plantagenet—
the ruling family
of England from
1154 to 1399

# A Man
### Ernest Buckler

all the man Joseph. Call his son Mark. Two scars had bracketed Mark's left eye since he was twelve. But they were periods, not brackets, in the punctuation of his life. The reason had to do with his father.

Joseph had none of the stiffness that goes with rock strength. He was one of those men who cast the broadest shadow, without there being any darkness in them at all. Yet there was always a curious awkwardness between him and his son. In a neighbor's house of a Sunday afternoon Mark might stand nearer to him than anyone else; but he never got onto his lap like the other kids got onto their fathers' laps. Joseph never teased him. He never made him any of those small-scale replicas of farm gear that the other men made their sons: tiny ox carts or trail sleds.

In any case, that kind of fussy workmanship was not his **province.** His instrument was the plow.

One day he came across Mark poking seeds between the potato plants.

"What's them?" he said.

Mark could dodge anyone else's questions; he could never answer his father with less than the whole truth.

"They're orange seeds," he said.

He'd saved them from the Christmas before. Oranges were such a seldom thing then that it was as if he was planting a mystery.

"They won't grow here," Joseph said.

Mark felt suddenly ridiculous, as he so often did when his father came upon anything fanciful he was doing: as if he had to shift himself to the sober footing of common sense. He dug the seeds out and planted them, secretly, behind the barn.

The night of the accident was one of those cold, drizzly nights in early summer when animals in the pasture huddle like **forlorn** statues. The sort of night when the cows never come.

School had ended that very day. This was the third year Mark had graded twice and he was very excited. All the time his mother washed the supper dishes he kept prattling on about the kings and queens of England he'd have in his studies next term. He felt so much taller than the "kid" he'd been yesterday.

His father took no part in the conversation, but he was not for that reason outside it—and everything Mark said was for his benefit too.

Joseph was waiting to milk. "Ain't it about time you got after the cows?" he said at last. He never ordered Mark. It would have caused the strangest sort of embarrassment if he ever had.

Cows! Mark winced. Right when he could almost see the boy **Plantagenet**

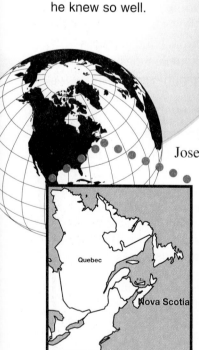

Joseph does not often express his thoughts or feelings. Mark and his family can usually figure out, or infer, what Joseph feels or thinks by drawing conclusions based on his actions. As you read, you should look for stated facts, but you must also try to infer meaning from what may not be stated directly. When you make accurate inferences, you can draw more meaningful conclusions. Here are some suggestions to help you make inferences and conclusions:

- Read carefully what the writer has stated directly.
- Think about your own knowledge of an experience with the facts the writer includes.
- Think about the implications of the facts. What information can you infer?
- Draw conclusions based on the facts as well as on the inferences you have made from your own knowledge and experience.

robed in **ermine** and wearing the jewelled crown!

"They'll come, won't they?" he said. (He knew better.) "They come last night."

He never used good speech when his father was around. He'd have felt like a girl. (Though Joseph was a far wiser, far better educated man in the true sense than Mark would ever be.)

"They won't come a night like this," Joseph said. "They're likely holed up in a spruce thicket somewheres, outa the rain."

"I'll see if I can hear the bell," Mark said.

He went out on the porch steps and listened. There wasn't a sound.

"It's no use to wait for the bell," Joseph called. "They won't budge a hair tonight."

"Well, if they ain't got sense enough to come themselves a night like this," Mark said, as near as he'd ever come to sputtering at his father, "why can't they just stay out?"

"I'd never get em back to their milk for a week," Joseph said.

Mark went then, but, as Joseph couldn't help seeing, grudgingly.

He sat on the bars of the pasture gate and called. "*Co*-boss, *co*-boss . . ." But there wasn't the tinkle of a bell.

He loved to be out in a good honest rain, but this was different. He picked his steps down the pasture lane to avoid the clammy drops that showered from every bush or fern he touched.

He came to the first clearing, where Joseph had planted the burntland potatoes last year. The cows were nowhere to be

ermine—a weasel whose brown or white fur is often used to line capes or hoods seen. But Pedro, the horse, was there—hunched up and gloomy-looking in the drizzle. Mark couldn't bear to see him so downcast and not try to soothe him.

He went close and patted his rump. Pedro moved just far enough ahead to shake off his touch. It was the kind of night when the touch of anything sent a shivery feeling all through you.

He should have known that the horse wanted to be left alone. But he kept at it. He'd touch him, the horse would move ahead, he'd follow behind and touch him again. The horse laid back his ears.

And then, in a flash, Mark saw the big black haunch rear up and the hoof, like a sudden devouring jaw, right in front of his left eye. The horse wasn't shod or Mark would have been killed.

He was stunned. But in a minute he got to his feet again. He put his hand to his face. It came away all blood. He began to scream and run for home.

Joseph could hear him crying before he came in sight. He started to meet him. When Mark came through the alder thicket below the barn and Joseph saw he was holding his hand up to his face, he broke into a run. Before he got to the bars he could see the blood.

He didn't stop to let down a single bar. He leapt them. Mark had never seen him move like that in his life before. He grabbed Mark up and raced back to the house.

Within minutes the house was a hubbub of neighbors. Mark gloried in the breathless attention that everyone bent

● ● ● ● ● ● ●

## "He didn't stop to let down a single bar. He leapt them."

● ● ● ● ● ● ●

on him. He asked Joseph to hold him up to the mirror over the sink. "No, no, Joseph, don't . . ." his mother pleaded, but Joseph obeyed him. His face was a mass of cuts and bruises. He felt like a Plantagenet borne off the field with royal wounds.

Afterward, he remembered all the head-shakings: "That biggest cut there don't look too good to me. Pretty deep . . ."

And the offers of help: "I got some **b'racit acit** for washin out cuts, down home. I could git in a minute . . ."

And the warnings: "No, *don't* let him lay down. Anyone's had a blow on the head, always keep em moving around . . ."

And he remembered his mother beseeching him over and over: "Can you see all right? Are you sure you can see all right?"

He didn't remember his father doing or saying anything flustered, unusual. But Joseph would be the one who'd quietly put the extra leaves in the dining-room table so they could lay him on it when the doctor came at last, to have the stitches taken. And when the doctor put him to sleep (though he confessed that this was risky, with Mark's weak heart) it would be Joseph's hand that held the **chloroform** cone without a tremor. The doctor said that Mark must stay in bed for two whole weeks. Joseph came in to see him once each day and again just before bedtime. Mark's eye was now swollen shut and the color of thunder sunsets. Maybe he'd have the mirror in his hand, admiring his eye,

when he heard his father coming. He'd thrust the mirror in under the bedclothes. They exchanged the same awkward sentences each time. Joseph was the sort of man who looks helplessly out of place in a bedroom. He never sat down.

The first morning Mark was allowed outdoors again he had planned to walk; but Joseph picked him up without a word and carried him.

He didn't protest. But this time there was no **tumult** of excitement as before to leave him mindless of his father's arms about him; now the unaccustomed feel of them seemed to make him aware of every gram of his own weight. And yet, though it was merely an ordinary fine summer's morning, it struck him as the freshest, greenest, sunniest he had ever seen.

The moment they left the house it was plain to him that this wasn't just an aimless jaunt. His father was taking him somewhere.

Joseph carried him straight across the house field and down the slope beyond—to where he'd stuck the orange seeds in the ground.

Mark saw what they were headed for before they got there. But he couldn't speak. If he had tried to, he'd have cried.

Joseph set him down beside a miniature garden.

Miniature, but with the rows as perfectly in line as washboard ribs. This had

## FOCUS ON... SCIENCE

Joseph explains to his son that orange trees simply will not flourish where they live. Instead he plants melons, red peppers, and citron in the miniature garden. Where *are* oranges grown? Find out what conditions oranges require and why. Then determine which parts of the United States offer the sort of conditions in which oranges thrive. Create a map to show your findings.

◆ ◆ ◆ ◆ ◆ ◆ ◆ ◆ ◆ ◆ ◆ ◆ ◆ ◆ ◆

been no rough job for the plow. It had been the painstaking work of fork and spade and then the careful molding of his hands. He must have started it right after the accident, because the seeds were already through the ground. And he hadn't mentioned it to a soul.

"This can be yours," he said to Mark.

"Oh, Father," Mark began, "it's . . ." But how could he tell him what it was? He bent down to examine the sprouts. "What's them?" he said, touching the strange plants in the outside row.

"Melons," Joseph said, pointing, "and red peppers and **citron.**"

He must have got them from the wealthy man who had the big glass hothouse in town. Things almost as fanciful as orange seeds.

"You never know," he said. "They might grow here."

Mark could not speak. But his face must have shown the bright amazement that raced behind it, or else what Joseph said next would never have broken out.

tumult—noisy confusion

citron—a small, hard-fleshed watermelon

"You don't think I'da made you go for them cows if I'd a knowed you was gonna get hurt, do you?" he said. Almost savagely. "I wouldn'ta cared if they'd a never given another drop o' milk as long as they lived!"

Mark gave him a crazy answer, but it didn't seem crazy to either of them then, because a sudden something seemed to bridge all the gaps of speech.

"You jumped right over the bars when you saw I was hurt, didn't you!" he said. "You never even took the top one down. You just jumped right clear over em!"

His father turned his face away, and it looked as if his shoulders were taking a long deep breath.

Joseph let him walk back to the house.

When they went to the kitchen, Mark's sister said, "Where did you go?"

For no reason he could explain Mark felt another sudden **compact** with his father, that this should be some sort of secret.

"Just out," he said.

"Just out around," Joseph echoed.

And Mark knew that never again would he have to . . . shift . . . himself at the sound of his father's footsteps. Not ever. ❖

# ON THE JOB
## AGRICULTURAL TECHNICIAN

Agricultural technicians work in all phases of agribusiness—the business of farming. Technicians who work on farms are called "technical farm workers." They are usually in charge of sowing and harvesting crops and protecting them from hazards such as diseases and pest infestations. Their other responsibilities often include supervising other workers, deciding when and how to plant and harvest, and experimenting with crop improvement. Communication and decision-making skills are essential for a technical farm worker, as is a thorough knowledge of agribusiness.

# ACCENT ON...
## AGRICULTURAL TECHNOLOGY

The types of produce a farmer can grow successfully depend on the climate and geography of a region. However, through advanced agricultural research and technology, farmers can now grow some crops in areas where they would not naturally grow. Find out which crops in your area fall into this category. What techniques do farmers use to grow these crops despite unfavorable climatic conditions? Could hydroponics (growing plants in nutrient-enriched water instead of soil) improve the volume or quality of any produce grown in your area? Why or why not?

# First Lesson

Phyllis McGinley

The thing to remember about fathers is, they're men.
A girl has to keep it in mind.
They are dragon-seekers, bent on improbable rescues.
Scratch any father, you find
Someone **chock-full** of **qualms** and romantic terrors,
Believing change is a threat—
Like your first shoes with heels on, like your first bicycle
It took such months to get.

Walk in strange woods, they warn you about the snakes there.
Climb, and they fear you'll fall.
Books, **angular** boys, or swimming in deep water—
Fathers mistrust them all.
Men are the worriers. It is difficult for them
To learn what they must learn:
How you have a journey to take and very likely,
For a while, will not return. ❖

chock-full—full to the brim

qualms— uneasiness

angular—bony and lean, gaunt

# UNDERSTANDING

1. Find passages in "A Man" that describe Joseph. Explain how Joseph's actions provide insight into his overall character. Next, list the qualities of a good neighbor. Write a journal entry describing the kind of neighbor Joseph would be.

2. Why doesn't Mark use "good speech" in his father's presence? Find examples in the text of "non-standard" English. Listen to the speech of those around you in school and in your neighborhood. Keep notes on the phrases that you believe are non-standard English. Next to each, write the way the phrase would be spoken in standard English.

In groups, discuss situations in which using non-standard English hinders a speaker's effectiveness. Also note some situations when it might be acceptable to use non-standard English. Write a short dramatic scene in which someone using non-standard English communicates effectively; he or she might be returning an item to a store or applying for a job. Present the scene to the class. ***Workshop 4***

3. Consider the title "A Man." Why did the author choose this simple title? What are your thoughts when you read the title? To whom does the title refer?

4. Note the subtle use of rhyme in "First Lesson." Compare it with the use of rhyme in other poems throughout the text. Which do you prefer, rhymed or unrhymed lines? When would you use rhyme in a poem? What is the effect of rhyme? Write a poem similar to "First Lesson," but about Joseph from the viewpoint of his son, Mark. Or write a poem about a similar or special relationship in your own life. ***Workshop 2***

**A LAST WORD**

To what extent is what we *don't* say to loved ones and friends just as important, or more so, than what we *do* say? What are the risks of saying too much? Too little?

## CONNECTING

1. Actions speak louder than words. In "A Man," Mark learns through his father's actions how intensely Joseph loves him. The young woman in "First Lesson" also learns about her father's feelings through his actions. Find articles in weekly news magazines or newspapers in which someone's character shows through his or her actions. For example, perhaps a young person has performed a daring rescue. What do the person's actions tell us? What can we infer or assume about his or her character? Present your article and discuss it with the class. ***Workshop 25***

2. Research the kinds of fruits and vegetables that grow well in your region. In groups, plan a garden for your families. Decide on the appropriate size for the garden and draw a diagram of it. Determine the cost of planting the garden, including seeds, special soil, fertilizer, water, and other necessary elements. Last, write an action plan for your garden that includes your proposal to plant the garden, the layout, the time needed for preparation and maintenance, a cost estimate, and the expected yield. Divide the research and writing tasks, assigning each person in the group responsibility for a specific part of the action plan. Be sure everyone has an opportunity to revise and edit the different parts of the plan. ***Workshops 11 and 27***

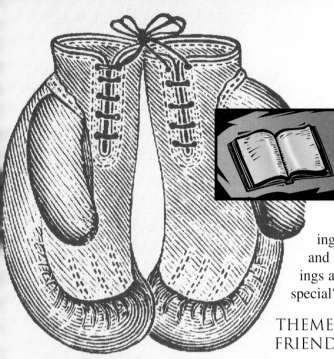

# Friends

- *Amigo Brothers*
- *Good Hot Dogs*
- *Buenos Hot Dogs*

## EXPLORING

Strong friendships are valuable and worth preserving. A good friend rejoices with you in your triumphs and supports you in your struggles. Consider your feelings about a close friend. What makes your relationship special? What qualities do you expect in a close friend?

## THEME CONNECTION...
## FRIENDSHIPS

In the story, two best friends have the same dream, to become lightweight boxing champion of the world. The day has come for them to meet each other in the ring. How will their competition affect the bond between them?

The narrator of the poem fondly recalls eating hot dogs for lunch with a childhood friend. Life's simplest pleasures are richer when shared.

## TIME & PLACE

The lower east side of Manhattan runs east of Fifth Avenue and south of 14th Street in New York City. Many multicultural communities are located there. Felix and Antonio's lives center around their apartment building and the nearby Boys' Club and pro's gym. The community rallies behind their heroes, so the prize fight must be held in a local park in order to accommodate the many spectators.

Cisneros often writes about another geographic area that has been greatly influenced by immigration, the southwestern United States. In her poem, two friends devour hot dogs at a nearby store during their school lunch break.

## THE WRITER'S CRAFT

### THEME

Short stories intend to make a point about human nature in an interesting way. The author's main idea or central insight is the theme. To determine the theme, look for the point or idea that the author seems to emphasize most throughout the story. This idea is the theme. Consider how the story's events and the characters' actions help to define the theme.

# Amigo Brothers

Piri Thomas

tenement—low-rent, often run-down apartment building

## About the Author

Piri Thomas (b. 1928), the son of Puerto Rican parents, grew up in what he calls "the mean streets" of Spanish Harlem in New York City. As a youth, Thomas participated in street violence, gangs, and drugs, and he ended up in prison for armed robbery. After serving his sentence, Thomas began a new life, working in rehabilitation centers in New York and Puerto Rico. He then became a staff member at the Center for Urban Education in New York. A writer and film producer, Thomas has also been an active advocate for prison reform.

lightweight—one of the weight classifications in boxing, from 126 to 135 pounds

street negatives—undesirable or unlawful behavior

Antonio Cruz and Felix Vargas were both seventeen years old. They were so together in friendship that they felt themselves to be brothers. They had known each other since childhood, growing up on the lower east side of Manhattan in the same **tenement** building on Fifth Street between Avenue A and Avenue B.

Antonio was fair, lean, and lanky, while Felix was dark, short, and husky. Antonio's hair was always falling over his eyes, while Felix wore his black hair in a natural Afro style.

Each youngster had a dream of someday becoming **lightweight** champion of the world. Every chance they had the boys worked out, sometimes at the Boys' Club on 10th Street and Avenue A and sometimes at the pro's gym on 14th Street. Early morning sunrises would find them running along the East River Drive, wrapped in sweat shirts, short towels around their necks, and handkerchiefs Apache style around their foreheads.

While some youngsters were into **street negatives,** Antonio and Felix slept, ate, rapped, and dreamt positive. Between them, they had a collection of *Fight* magazines second to none, plus a scrapbook filled with torn tickets to every boxing match they had ever attended, and some clippings of their own. If asked a question about any given fighter, they would immediately zip out from their memory banks divisions, weights, records of fights, knockouts, **technical knockouts,** and **draws** or losses.

Each had fought many **bouts** representing their community and had won two gold-plated medals plus a silver and bronze medallion. The difference was in their style. Antonio's lean form and long reach made him the better boxer, while Felix's short and muscular frame made him the better slugger. Whenever they had met in the ring for sparring sessions, it had always been hot and heavy.

Now, after a series of elimination bouts, they had been informed that they were to meet each other in the division finals that were scheduled for the seventh of August, two weeks away—the winner to represent the Boys' Club in the **Golden Gloves** Championship Tournament.

The two boys continued to run together along the East River Drive. But even when joking with each other, they both sensed a wall rising between them.

One morning less than a week before their bout, they met as usual for their daily work-out. They fooled around with a few jabs at the air, slapped skin, and then took off, running lightly along the dirty East River's edge.

Antonio glanced at Felix, who kept his eyes purposely straight ahead, pausing from time to time to do some fancy leg work while throwing one-twos followed by upper cuts to an imaginary jaw. Antonio then beat the air with a **barrage** of body blows and short devastating lefts with an overhand jaw-breaking right.

After a mile or so, Felix puffed and said, "Let's stop a while, bro. I think we both got something to say to each other."

Antonio nodded. It was not natural to be acting as though nothing unusual was happening . . . .

They rested their elbows on the railing separating them from the river. Antonio wiped his face with his short towel. The sunrise was now creating day.

Felix leaned heavily on the river's railing and stared across to the shores of Brooklyn. Finally, he broke the silence.

". . . I don't know how to come out with it."

Antonio helped. "It's about our fight, right?"

"Yeah, right." Felix's eyes squinted at the rising orange sun.

"I've been thinking about it too, **panín.** In fact, since we found out it was going to be me and you, I've been awake at night, pulling punches on you, trying not to hurt you."

"Same here. It ain't natural not to think about the fight. I mean, we both are **cheverote** fighters and we both want to win. But only one of us can win. There ain't no draws in the eliminations."

Felix tapped Antonio gently on the shoulder. "I don't mean to sound like I'm bragging, bro. But I wanna win, fair and square."

Antonio nodded quietly. "Yeah. We both know that in the ring the better man wins. Friend or no friend, brother or no . . ."

Felix finished it for him. "Brother. Tony, let's promise something right here. Okay?"

"If it's fair, **hermano,** I'm for it." Antonio admired the courage of a tug boat pulling a barge five times its **welterweight** size.

"It's fair, Tony. When we get into the ring, it's gotta be like we never met. We gotta be like two heavy strangers that want the same thing and only one can have it. You understand, don'tcha?"

"**Sí,** I know." Tony smiled. "No pulling punches. We go all the way."

"Yeah, that's right. Listen, Tony. Don't you think it's a good idea if we don't see each other until the day of the fight? I'm going to stay with my Aunt Lucy in the Bronx. I can use Gleason's Gym for working out. My manager says he got some sparring partners with more or less your style."

Tony scratched his nose **pensively.** "Yeah, it would be better for our heads." He held out his hand, palm upward. "Deal?"

"Deal." Felix lightly slapped open skin.

"Ready for some more running?" Tony asked lamely.

"Naw, bro. Let's cut it here. You go on. I kinda like to get things together in my head."

"You ain't worried, are you?" Tony asked.

> ● ● ● ● ● ● ●
> "The amigo brothers were not ashamed to hug each other tightly."
> ● ● ● ● ● ● ●

**technical knockout**—when a referee declares a winner because one of the boxers is too hurt or dazed to continue, even though there has been no knockout

**draw**—a tie

**bout**—an athletic match; a fight

**Golden Gloves**—a series of amateur boxing tournaments held throughout the U.S.

**barrage**—a rapid, heavy series of blows

**panín**—Puerto Rican slang for "buddy"

**cheverote**—Puerto Rican for "great," "super"

**hermano**—Spanish for "brother," meaning friend in this case

**welterweight**—the middle weight classification in boxing; Antonio sees the tug boat as medium-sized

**sí**—Spanish for "yes"

**pensively**—thoughtfully

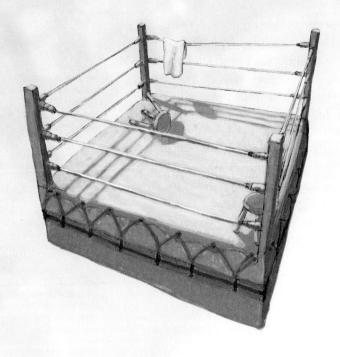

In the quiet early dark, he peered over the ledge. Six stories below the lights of the city blinked and the sounds of cars mingled with the curses and the laughter of children in the street. He tried not to think of Felix, feeling he had succeeded in psyching his mind. But only in the ring would he really know. To spare Felix hurt, he would have to knock him out, early and quick.

Up in the South Bronx, Felix decided to take in a movie in an effort to keep Antonio's face away from his fists. The flick was *The Champion* with Kirk Douglas, the third time Felix was seeing it. . . .

Felix became the champ and Tony the challenger.

The movie audience was going out of its head, roaring in blood lust at the butchery going on. The champ hunched his shoulders grunting and sniffing red blood back into his broken nose. The challenger, confident that he had the championship in the bag, threw a left. The champ countered with a dynamite right that exploded into the challenger's brains.

Felix's right arm felt the shock. Antonio's face, **superimposed** on the screen, was shattered and split apart by the awesome force of the killer blow. Felix saw himself in the ring, blasting Antonio against the ropes. The champ had to be forcibly restrained. The challenger was allowed to crumble slowly to the canvas, a broken bloody mess.

When Felix finally left the theater, he had figured out how to psyche himself for tomorrow's fight. It was Felix the Champion vs. Antonio the Challenger.

*suavecito*—
Spanish for "take it easy"

*sabe*—
Spanish for "understand?"

superimposed—
placed over or above

"No way, man." Felix laughed out loud. "I got too much smarts for that. I just think it's cooler if we split right here. After the fight, we can get it together again like nothing ever happened."

The amigo brothers were not ashamed to hug each other tightly.

"Guess you're right. Watch yourself Felix. I hear there's some pretty heavy dudes up in the Bronx. *Suavecito,* okay?"

"Okay. You watch yourself too, *sabe*?"

Tony jogged away. Felix watched his friend disappear from view, throwing rights and lefts. Both fighters had a lot of psyching up to do before the big fight.

The days in training passed much too slowly. Although they kept out of each other's way, they were aware of each other's progress via the ghetto grapevine.

The evening before the big fight, Tony made his way to the roof of his tenement.

He walked up some dark streets, deserted except for small pockets of wary-looking kids wearing gang colors. Despite the fact that he was Puerto Rican like them, they eyed him as a stranger to their turf. Felix did a fast shuffle, bobbing and weaving, while letting loose a torrent of blows that would demolish whatever got in its way. It seemed to impress the brothers, who went about their own business.

Finding no takers, Felix decided to split to his aunt's. Walking the streets had not relaxed him, neither had the fight flick. All it had done was to stir him up. He let himself quietly into his Aunt Lucy's apartment and went straight to bed, falling into a fitful sleep with sounds of the gong for Round One.

Antonio was passing some heavy time on his rooftop. How would the fight tomorrow affect his relationship with Felix? After all, fighting was like any other profession. Friendship had nothing to do with it. A gnawing doubt crept in. He cut negative thinking real quick by doing some speedy fancy dance steps, bobbing and weaving like mercury. The night air was blurred with perpetual motions of left hooks and right crosses. Felix, his *amigo* brother, was not going to be Felix at all in the ring. Just an opponent with another face. Antonio went to sleep, hearing the opening bell for the first round. Like his friend in the South Bronx, he prayed for victory, via a quick clean knockout in the first round.

Large posters plastered all over the walls of local shops announced the fight between Antonio Cruz and Felix Vargas as the main bout.

The fight had created great interest in the neighborhood. Antonio and Felix were well liked and respected. Each had his own loyal following. Betting fever was high and ranged from a bottle of coke to cold hard cash on the line.

Antonio's fans bet with **unbridled** faith in his boxing skills. On the other side, Felix's admirers bet on his dynamite-packed fists.

Felix had returned to his apartment early in the morning of August 7th and stayed there, hoping to avoid seeing Antonio. He turned the radio on to **salsa** music sounds and then tried to read while waiting for word from his manager.

The fight was scheduled to take place in Tompkins Square Park. It had been decided that the gymnasium of the Boys' Club was not large enough to hold all the people who were sure to attend. In Tompkins Square Park, everyone who wanted could view the fight, whether from ringside or window fire escapes or tenement rooftops.

The morning of the fight Tompkins Square was a beehive of activity with numerous workers setting up the ring, the seats, and the guest speakers' stand. The scheduled bouts began shortly after noon and the park had begun filling up even earlier.

The local junior high school across from Tompkins Square Park served as the dressing room for all the fighters. Each was given a separate classroom with desk tops, covered with mats, serving as resting tables. Antonio thought he caught a glimpse of Felix waving to him from a room at the far end of the corridor. He waved back just in case it had been him.

unbridled—set loose, unrestrained

salsa—lively Caribbean dance music

The fighters changed from their street clothes into fighting gear. Antonio wore white trunks, black socks, and black shoes. Felix wore sky blue trunks, red socks, and white boxing shoes. Each had dressing gowns to match their fighting trunks with their names neatly stitched on the back.

The loudspeakers blared into the open windows of the school. There were speeches by **dignitaries,** community leaders, and great boxers of yesteryear. Some were well prepared, some improvised on the spot. They all carried the same message of great pleasure and honor at being part of such a historic event. This great day was in the tradition of champions emerging from the streets of the lower east side.

Interwoven with the speeches were the sounds of the other boxing events. After the sixth bout, Felix was much relieved when his trainer Charlie said, "Time change. Quick knockout. This is it. We're on."

Waiting time was over. Felix was escorted from the classroom by a dozen fans in white T-shirts with the word FELIX across their fronts.

Antonio was escorted down a different stairwell and guided through a roped-off path.

As the two climbed into the ring, the crowd exploded with a roar. Antonio and Felix both bowed gracefully and then raised their arms in acknowledgment.

Antonio tried to be cool, but even as the roar was in its first birth, he turned slowly to meet Felix's eyes looking directly into his. Felix nodded his head and Antonio responded. And both as one, just as quickly, turned away to face his own corner.

Bong—bong—bong. The roar turned to stillness.

"Ladies and Gentlemen, *Señores y Señoras.*"

The announcer spoke slowly, pleased at his bilingual efforts.

"Now the moment we have all been waiting for—the main event between two fine young Puerto Rican fighters, products of our lower east side."

**"Loisaida,"** called out a member of the audience.

"In this corner, weighing 134 pounds, Felix Vargas. And in this corner, weighing 133 pounds, Antonio Cruz. The winner will represent the Boys' Club in the tournament of champions, the Golden Gloves. There will be no draw. May the best man win."

The cheering of the crowd shook the window panes of the old buildings surrounding Tompkins Square Park. At the center of the ring, the referee was giving instructions to the youngsters.

"Keep your punches up. No low blows. No punching on the back of the head. Keep your heads up. Understand. Let's have a clean fight. Now shake hands and come out fighting."

Both youngsters touched gloves and nodded. They turned and danced quickly to their corners. Their head towels and dressing gowns were lifted neatly from their shoulders by their trainers' nimble fingers. Antonio crossed himself. Felix did the same.

"May the best man win."

BONG! BONG! ROUND ONE. Felix and Antonio turned and faced each other squarely in a fighting pose. Felix wasted no time. He came in fast, head low, half hunched toward his right shoulder, and lashed out with a straight left. He missed a right cross as Antonio slipped the punch and countered with one-two-three lefts that snapped

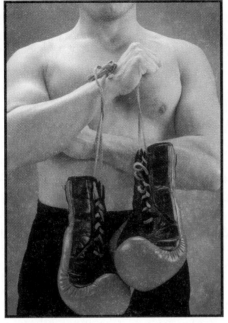

### FOCUS ON... SPANISH

In the childhood homes of both Piri Thomas and Sandra Cisneros, Spanish was the primary language spoken, though both writers learned English as well. The influence of the Spanish language on American English is extensive. The words *salsa, taco, tortilla, canyon, plaza, patio, fiesta, pronto, tornado,* and *bonanza* all have Spanish origins. Investigate the many Spanish words and phrases that have become part of the American vocabulary. Create a data bank of such words and their meanings.

Felix's head back, sending a mild shock coursing through him. If Felix had any small doubt about their friendship affecting their fight, it was being neatly **dispelled.**

Antonio danced, a joy to behold. His left hand was like a piston pumping jabs one right after another with seeming ease. Felix bobbed and weaved and never stopped boring in. He knew that at long range he was at a disadvantage. Antonio had too much reach on him. Only by coming in close could Felix hope to achieve the dreamed-of knockout.

Antonio knew the dynamite that was stored in his *amigo* brother's fist. He ducked a short right and missed a left hook. Felix trapped him against the ropes just long enough to pour some punishing rights and lefts to Antonio's hard midsection. Antonio slipped away from Felix, crashing two lefts to his head, which set Felix's right ear to ringing.

Bong! Both *amigos* froze a punch well on its way, sending up a roar of approval for good sportsmanship.

Felix walked briskly back to his corner. His right ear had not stopped ringing. Antonio gracefully danced his way toward his stool none the worse, except for glowing glove burns, showing angry red against the whiteness of his midribs.

"Watch that right, Tony." His trainer talked into his ear. "Remember Felix always goes to the body. He'll want you to drop your hands for his overhand left or right. Got it?"

Antonio nodded, spraying water out between his teeth. He felt better as his sore midsection was being firmly rubbed.

Felix's corner was also busy.

"You gotta get in there, fella." Felix's trainer poured water over his curly Afro locks. "Get in there or he's gonna chop you up from way back."

dispelled—
driven away

feinted—faked

bedlam—a
scene of
confusion

haymaker—a
powerful blow

*Bong! Bong!* Round two. Felix was off his stool and rushed Antonio like a bull, sending a hard right to his head. Beads of water exploded from Antonio's long hair.

Antonio, hurt, sent back a blurring barrage of lefts and rights that only meant pain to Felix, who returned with a short left to the head followed by a looping right to the body. Antonio countered with his own flurry, forcing Felix to give ground. But not for long. Felix bobbed and weaved, bobbed and weaved, occasionally punching his two gloves together.

Antonio waited for the rush that was sure to come. Felix closed in and **feinted** with his left shoulder and threw his right instead. Lights suddenly exploded inside Felix's head as Antonio slipped the blow and hit him with a pistonlike left, catching him flush on the point of his chin.

**Bedlam** broke loose as Felix's legs momentarily buckled. He fought off a series of rights and lefts and came back with a strong right that taught Antonio respect.

Antonio danced in carefully. He knew Felix had the habit of playing possum when hurt, to sucker an opponent within reach of the powerful bombs he carried in each fist.

A right to the head slowed Antonio's pretty dancing. He answered with his own left at Felix's right eye that began puffing up within three seconds.

Antonio, a bit too eager, moved in too close and Felix had him entangled into a rip-roaring, punching toe-to-toe slugfest that brought the whole Tompkins Square Park screaming to its feet.

Rights to the body. Lefts to the head. Neither fighter was giving an inch.

Suddenly a short right caught Antonio squarely on the chin. His long legs turned to jelly and his arms flailed out desperately. Felix, grunting like a bull, threw wild punches from every direction. Antonio, groggy, bobbed and weaved, evading most of the blows. Suddenly his head cleared. His left flashed out hard and straight catching Felix on the bridge of his nose.

Felix lashed back with a **haymaker,** right off the ghetto streets. At the same instant, his eye caught another left hook from Antonio. Felix swung out trying to clear the pain. Only the frenzied screaming of those along ringside let him know that he had dropped Antonio. Fighting off the growing haze, Antonio struggled to his feet, got up, ducked, and threw a smashing right that dropped Felix flat on his back.

Felix got up as fast as he could in his own corner, groggy but still game. He didn't even hear the count. In a fog, he heard the roaring of the crowd, who seemed to have gone insane. His head cleared to hear the bell sound at the end of the round. He was . . . glad. His trainer sat him down on the stool.

In his corner, Antonio was doing what all fighters do when they are hurt. They sit and smile at everyone.

The referee signaled the ring doctor to check the fighters out. He did so and then gave his okay. The cold water sponges brought clarity to both *amigo* brothers. They were rubbed until their circulation ran free.

*Bong!* Round three—the final round. Up to now it had been tic-tac-toe, pretty much even. But everyone knew there could be no draw and that this round would decide the winner.

This time, to Felix's surprise, it was Antonio who came out fast, charging across the ring. Felix braced himself but couldn't ward off the barrage of punches. Antonio drove Felix hard against the ropes.

The crowd ate it up. Thus far the two had fought with **mucho corazón.** Felix tapped his gloves and commenced his attack anew. Antonio, throwing boxer's caution to the winds, jumped in to meet him.

Both pounded away. Neither gave an inch and neither fell to the canvas. Felix's left eye was tightly closed. Claret red blood poured from Antonio's nose. They fought toe-to-toe.

The sounds of their blows were loud in contrast to the silence of a crowd gone completely mute. The referee was stunned by their savagery.

*Bong! Bong! Bong!* The bell sounded over and over again. Felix and Antonio were past hearing. Their blows continued to pound on each other like hailstones.

Finally the referee and the two trainers pried Felix and Antonio apart. Cold water was poured over them to bring them back to their senses.

They looked around and then rushed toward each other. A cry of alarm surged through Tompkins Square Park. Was this a fight to the death instead of a boxing match?

The fear soon gave way to wave upon wave of cheering as the two *amigos* embraced.

No matter what the decision, they knew they would always be champions to each other.

*BONG! BONG! BONG!* "Ladies and Gentlemen. *Señores* and *Señoras.* The winner and representative to the Golden Gloves Tournament of Champions is . . ."

The announcer turned to point to the winner and found himself alone. Arm in arm the champions had already left the ring. ❖

*mucho corazón—* Spanish for "much courage"

# ON THE JOB
## ATHLETIC TRAINER

Working in the field of sports medicine, athletic trainers examine and give first aid to athletes who have been hurt. They also show athletes how to build their strength and avoid injuries. Often, athletic trainers work with team doctors to provide physical therapy for athletes recovering from injuries. Interested students can gain experience by helping high school athletic trainers and coaches. Usually, athletic trainers must be certified by the National Athletic Trainers Association (NATA). To become certified, prospective athletic trainers should complete an approved four-year college program in athletic training. Two years of experience working under the supervision of NATA-approved trainers is also required for certification.

# Good Hot Dogs

Sandra Cisneros

## About the Author

Sandra Cisneros (b. 1954) is the daughter of a Mexican-American mother and a Mexican father. She grew up in Chicago, where she experienced insecurity and loneliness as well as the simple joys of growing up. After attending college, Cisneros taught high school English, then made writing her obsession. She has written several books and received many awards and honors. When she is not writing, she shares her love of writing by lecturing and teaching.

for Kiki

Fifty cents apiece
To eat our lunch
We'd run
Straight from school
Instead of home
Two blocks
Then the store
That smelled like steam
You ordered
Because you had the money
Two hot dogs and two pops for here
Everything on the hot dogs
Except pickle lily
Dash those hot dogs
Into buns and splash on
All that good stuff
Yellow mustard and onions
And french fries piled on top all
Rolled up in a piece of wax
Paper for us to hold hot
In our hands
Quarters on the counter
Sit down
Good hot dogs
We'd eat
Fast till there was nothing left
But salt and poppy seeds even
The little burnt tips
Of french fries
We'd eat
You humming
And me swinging my legs ❖

Unit 1: Family and Friends

# Buenos Hot Dogs
Translated from the English by the poet


para Kiki

Cincuenta centavos cada uno
Para comer nuestro lonche
Corríamos
Derecho desde la escuela
En vez de a casa
Dos cuadras
Después la tienda
Que olía a vapor
Tú pedías
Porque tenías el dinero
Dos hot dogs y dos refrescos para comer aquí
Los hot dogs con todo
Menos pepinos
Hecha esos hot dogs
En sus panes y salpícalos
Con todos esas cosas buenas
Mostaza amarilla y cebollas
Y papas fritas amontonadas encima
Envueltos en papel de cera
Para llevarlos calientitos
En las manos
Monedas encima del mostrador
Siéntate
Buenos hot dogs
Comíamos
Rápido hasta que no quedaba nada
Menos sal y semillas de amapola hasta
Las puntitas quemadas
De las papas fritas
Comíamos
Tu canturreando
Y yo columpiando mis piernas ❖

## UNDERSTANDING

1. List the times when Antonio and Felix *demonstrate* their friendship. In a paragraph, describe and explain the closeness of their relationship. ***Workshop 8***

2. Find examples of specific boxing terms in "Amigo Brothers" and explain how they are used. How does this special vocabulary, or jargon, add to the authenticity of the story?

   Choose an activity with which you are very familiar. What jargon do you use in connection with that activity? Write an explanation of what the special terms mean. Then explain how important it is for a participant in the activity to understand the jargon.

3.  Review the information about theme in The Writer's Craft on page 45. Working with a partner, decide what Piri Thomas's theme is in "Amigo Brothers." Based on the story, what are Thomas's beliefs about friendships, loyalty, and human nature? Share your findings with the class.

   Now relate Thomas's theme to your own life. Have you ever had to compete with a friend? How did the situation turn out? What did you learn from the experience? Write a journal entry describing the event and your emotional reaction to it. Remember to keep the author's theme in mind as you make connections to your own experiences.

4. Sandra Cisneros uses no rhyme in her poem "Good Hot Dogs." Instead she uses simple language to recreate a simple scene. What is the relationship between the two young people? What is the theme of the poem?

   Think of something you do often with a best friend. Describe the activity in a poem, paragraph, or diary entry. On your own or with the help of another student, teacher, or resource person, translate your text into another language as Cisneros has. ***Workshops 2, 8, and 10***

## ACCENT ON...
### INTERNATIONAL COMMUNICATIONS

Notice that in Cisneros's translation of her poem from English to Spanish, there is no Spanish word for "hot dog"; the term is the same in both languages. Certain words are universally understood, but most require careful and precise translation in order to be understood by speakers of another language. Explore careers in international communications. What opportunities are available? What knowledge and skills are required? Translating is one job in the field of international communications. Would a translator work with written materials or be required to translate *as* people speak—a much more difficult task? Write a one-page career outline for future reference. You may also want to provide a copy to your school guidance office.

# CONNECTING

1. Problem solving is a skill we use every day. What problem in your school or community needs solving? Perhaps your community needs to clean up its parks, or your school has a problem with graffiti. Using a problem-solving method, decide upon an appropriate plan of action to solve the problem. Write the solution in the form of an action plan. **Workshop 11**

2. In a group of eight students, design and write an inspirational book on friendship. Agree on a design that reflects each person's beliefs about being a good friend. Each page could hold an inspirational saying or quotation to serve as a reminder for all good friends. You may want to start each page with, "When you have a best friend, you . . ." or "To be a best friend means . . . ." Each group member should be responsible for completing a specific task. Lay out and illustrate the booklet (on computer if possible), design a cover, and bind the book. Display your booklets at a community gathering or school open house. **Workshops 20 and 27**

## UNIT 1

# WRAP IT UP

1. In "A Mother in Mannville," "The Elk Tooth Dress," and "Amanda and the Wounded Birds," the main characters seek approval and/or support from a parental figure. What exactly does each young character want? Why is this important to them? Use details from the stories to support your ideas.

   Think about a time when you sought approval or support from a family member. What if you had not been successful? Where could you have turned for help? Create a brochure of teen outreach programs or social services. Describe in the brochure the support each agency provides.

2. Loyalty and friendship are extremely important to the characters in "Amigo Brothers." In "A Man," Mark discovers a strong bond with his father. How do these stories treat the theme of loyalty and love differently? How do the characters show affection differently?

   Examine the ways you convey your feelings of friendship and affection to the people close to you. Are there times when you could communicate those feelings more clearly? Do you *give* the same support that you expect to receive from others? Explain how families and friends might improve the ways they show support for one another.

# UNIT
## ②
# A HEROIC SPIRIT

*Who are the heroes in our lives? The selections in this unit offer a wide range of answers, from legendary characters to the courageous men and women who face challenges every day. The heroic spirit survives not only in ancient tales but also appears in our everyday lives.*

*Sometimes heroism means facing mythic monsters. Other times, it involves putting your life on the line for the sake of others. Sometimes heroism is the courage to face great odds against you. It can also mean staying true to your principles, in spite of ridicule and resistance.*

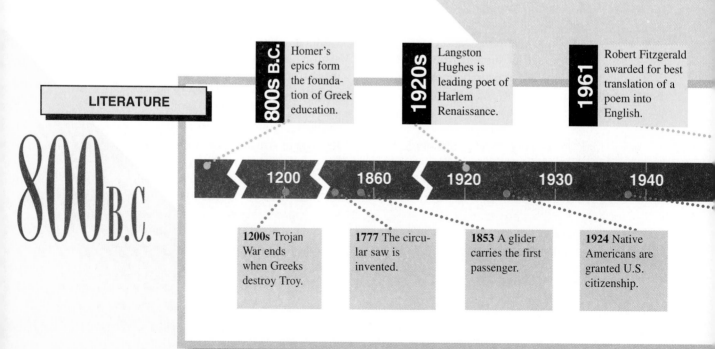

**LITERATURE**

**800 B.C.**

**800s B.C.** Homer's epics form the foundation of Greek education.

**1920s** Langston Hughes is leading poet of Harlem Renaissance.

**1961** Robert Fitzgerald awarded for best translation of a poem into English.

1200   1860   1920   1930   1940

**1200s** Trojan War ends when Greeks destroy Troy.

**1777** The circular saw is invented.

**1853** A glider carries the first passenger.

**1924** Native Americans are granted U.S. citizenship.

**1963** Martin Luther King, Jr., writes and delivers his historic "I Have a Dream" speech.

**1984** Bernard Evslin publishes *Hercules,* which wins the Washington Irving Children's Book Award.

**1986** *Challenger: The Inspiring Life Stories of Seven Brave Astronauts of Shuttle Mission 51-L* is published.

1950  1960  1970  1980  1990

2000

**1939** The first smokejumpers battle forest fires.

**1968** Martin Luther King, Jr., is assassinated.

**1986** The shuttle *Challenger* explodes.

LIFE and WORK

# Why Gartersnake Wears a Green Blanket

## EXPLORING

Sometimes society allows wrongdoing because no one recognizes the wrong or speaks out against it. One generation may teach the next to tolerate injustice. Today, globally televised news reports broadcast countless cases of wrongdoing. Until someone leads the fight to stop an evil practice, it will continue. What wrongs should we speak out against today?

## THEME CONNECTION...
## LEGENDARY HEROES

A legend is a popular story that comes from past generations. The hero of a legend performs amazing deeds and has unbelievable strength or skills. Often animals are heroes of legends and have human abilities like speaking and thinking. Famous American legendary heroes are Davy Crockett, Johnny Appleseed, and Paul Bunyan.

## TIME & PLACE

Many stories passed down through generations explain the customs and beliefs of a people. These stories were often told to children to teach them lessons and to pass along traditions and practices. This example comes from the American Northwest. The author is a member of the Okanogan and Colville tribes in Washington and Oregon.

## THE WRITER'S CRAFT
### LEGEND

Most legends contain no historical information that can be proven, though people like to think they are at least *based* on facts. Legends play a major role in the cultures of many ethnic groups. Many legends offer explanations of how things came to be. For example, how the stars appeared in the sky and how the elephant got its trunk are the subjects of legends. This Native American legend explains the origins of thunder, lightning, and the garter snake's colorful skin.

## Why Gartersnake Wears a Green Blanket

### Mourning Dove (Humishuma)

hunder-bird—used to fly from the Warm-land (South) once every **snow** to devour the most beautiful of the maidens. He always wanted a maiden as soon as he appeared—at his first rolling among the clouds. He would not stand for any delay. He came at the blooming of the woods-flowers, and then there was wailing in the villages— sorrow for the girl who must give herself to the monster. This maiden, chosen by the tribes because of her great beauty, would have to walk out and meet the monster, and be eaten. Then *Thing-that-hits* would not harm the other people. That was the custom. No one ever thought of trying to change it, of defying the terrible Thunder-bird.

It happened one spring that the girl who was loved by little *Sku-qua-wel'-hau*—Gartersnake—was chosen to be the sacrifice to Thunder-bird. That made Gartersnake very sad. He had no wish to live without her, so he decided to go with her when she went to meet the monster.

Thunder-bird could be seen high in the clouds when the maiden started toward the sacrifice-place. Putting on his best war-shirt, Gartersnake followed her. She looked around and saw him. She begged him to go back, to leave her. She did not want him to be killed, too. But Gartersnake hurried his steps and caught up with her.

"Oh, go back! Go back to our people," she said. "You cannot stand before the awful Thunder-bird. Let me die alone."

"No! If you must die, I will die with you," answered Gartersnake, and he kept by her side.

Soon they heard the noise of the monster's wings. The maiden cried, and Gartersnake felt weak, but he tried not to show his fear. Thunder-bird roared over them. His great wings shook the air and made the sky dark. He swooped low and from his mouth came a stream of fire. Gartersnake spat back.

"This person must be powerful," said Thunder-bird to himself. "He spits fire as I do." Then, thinking to discover his small enemy's weakness, Thunder-bird asked: "What do you fear? Of what are you afraid?"

"Nothing! There is nothing I fear," replied Gartersnake. "And you cannot hurt me. Nothing can hurt me. If you feel like fighting me, I will show you how to spit real fire. My fire-spit is worse than yours."

Thunder-bird believed those words, for none of the people ever had dared to talk to him like that. Only the frightened, wailing maidens ever had come to meet him. But he hoped to scare the other, and he spat a fearful streak of fire. Gartersnake then spat a stream of sizzling fire that flashed right in the monster's face. Thunder-bird couldn't stand that. He

### About the Author

Christine Quintasket (1885–1936) devoted the final years of her life to writing *Coyote Stories,* the folklore collection in which this legend appears. Under the name Mourning Dove, Quintasket carefully wrote Salish legends she had heard from relatives and visiting elders. She was an enrolled member of the Colville Reservation in Washington, where she actively worked for Native American rights and became the first woman elected to the Colville Tribal Council.

snow—winter

turned and fled, heading for the Warm-land. Spitting his hardest, Gartersnake ran after him, and not until he was sure that the monster really was beaten did Gartersnake stop chasing him. Then he shouted:

"A New People are coming to the world. From this day you will not come down out of the sky to eat people. You may roam the sky, but you shall make only rumblings and crashings in the storm."

Thunder-bird never returned to eat any more maidens or to destroy the tribes. But sometimes he clashes his wings and spits his fire through the clouds.

For his bravery the people gave Garter-snake a pretty green blanket with stripes on it. *Sku-qua-wel'-hau*, the Ground Twister, still wears that blanket. ❖

## FOCUS ON... SCIENCE

"Why Gartersnake Wears a Green Blanket" explains the origin of the garter snake's striped skin. One of the most common snakes, the garter inhabits vacant lots and gardens from Canada to Central America. Find out about the garter snake's various forms, as well as its habits, habitats, diet, and physical features. Write your findings in the form of a brief report, and include illustrations, if possible.

◆◆◆◆◆◆◆◆◆◆◆◆◆◆

## UNDERSTANDING

1. Find evidence in the text that Thunder-bird represents thunder and lightning. How is he a threat to this community? In modern communities of people who live and work alongside each other, what basic guidelines should all parties follow for harmony and peaceful coexistence? Develop a "Good Neighbors" newsletter that includes articles on how neighbors can improve the ways they relate to each other. *Workshop 19*

2. Gartersnake stands up to Thunder-bird, spitting fire back at him. What does each of their "fires" represent?

   Speaking out on an issue or defending yourself in daily matters must be handled carefully. Consider a time when you fought back in a way that only made a situation worse. What other actions could you have taken? Write a letter to another person involved in the conflict to explain why your behavior was counterproductive and to identify what you had wished or intended to accomplish. *Workshop 16*

3. What famous Americans have spoken out and made positive changes for society? Choose one, conduct research, and take notes on the person's actions and the results of his or her efforts. Write a speech that the person might have delivered. In the speech, outline the person's beliefs and the changes for which he or she fought.

## CONNECTING

A LAST WORD

What heroic stories are told repeatedly in your family? How do these stories enrich your life?

1. Choose a natural phenomenon such as a volcanic eruption or a tornado. Research the scientific reason it occurs. Then write a legend that Native Americans might have told to explain the occurrence.

2. Speak out on a topic that matters to you and affects your life. Your topic might be school dress codes or neighbors who don't shovel their snowy sidewalks. Gather information on this topic. Write a letter to the editor of your school or community newspaper that explains why change is needed and what action you recommend.

# Heroes of Old

- *Daedalus*
  - *Be Daedalus*
  - *I, Icarus*
  - *Theseus and the Minotaur*

## EXPLORING

Sometimes the world spins so quickly we feel tangled up in problems, which seem dark and threatening. During such times, we may feel we are moving through a labyrinth, a complex maze that leads nowhere. Of course, there is *one* path out, but it is difficult to detect. Describe a time when you searched for an answer but felt surrounded by darkness. What did you discover as you searched for the passage out of your labyrinth?

## THEME CONNECTION...
## HEROES AND GODS

Mythology tells us of individuals who are half-god, half-human. Their godlike side gives them great strength; their human side gives them a weakness. Some are good; some are evil. In myths, the gods interfere in the lives of humans in direct ways. Heroism may come *from* the gods, or it may occur *in spite of* the gods.

## TIME & PLACE

Many ancient Greek and Roman myths have been preserved for us by Ovid, a Roman poet born in 43 B.C. Writing in Latin, he produced a number of collections of poems. Evidence of Ovid's popularity is that so many of his works have survived the centuries for us to enjoy. Poets and writers all over the world have crafted their own versions of these myths, usually based at least loosely on Ovid's poems.

## THE WRITER'S CRAFT
### CHRONOLOGICAL ORDER AND FLASHBACK

When presenting the events of a story, writers often choose to use chronological order, or the actual order in which events occur in time. Most stories and myths are told in this way, moving from the beginning straight through to the end of the action. This method allows readers to make discoveries right along with the characters. When writers use flashback, they describe events that took place at a time before present events in the story.

# Daedalus

Retold by Bernard Evslin

## About the Author

A prolific author of books that retell myths and legends, Bernard Evslin was also a film producer, playwright, and novelist. Born in Philadelphia in 1922, Evslin traveled widely in the United States, Europe, and Asia. He wrote about Greek myths in such books as *The Greek Gods, Heroes and Monsters of Greek Myth,* and *Hercules,* which won the Washington Irving Children's Book Choice Award. Evslin died in 1993.

he gods, being all-powerful, needed a more subtle praise than obedience. They preferred their intention to become man's **aspiration**, their **caprice**, his law. **Athene**, in particular, liked to be served this way. The gray-eyed goddess of wisdom, whose sign was the owl, taught men the arts they needed to know, not through **gross decree**, but through firing the brightest spirits to a white heat wherein they perceived the secret laws of nature and made discoveries and inventions.

Now, in those times, her favorite among all **mortals** was an Athenian named Daedalus. In the white city of the goddess, Daedalus was honored among all the men, and treasure after treasure flowed from his workshop—the wheel, the plough, the loom. Finally, as happens to many men, his pride raced away with his wits; and he fell into a black envy of his nephew, Talos, a most gifted lad, whom he had taken into his workshop, and who, everyone said, was bound to follow in his footsteps.

"Aye, but he's following too fast," grumbled Daedalus to himself. "He's treading on my heels."

Daedalus, at that time, was working on a special project, a blade to cut wood more quickly than knife or ax. He had puzzled, tested, and tried many things, but nothing seemed to work. Then, one day, coming early to his workshop, he heard a curious sound. It was his nephew, Talos, who had come even earlier. He was leaning over, holding a board pinned to a low table under his knee, and swiftly cutting into it with what looked like the backbone of a fish.

The boy turned to him, smiling. "Look, Uncle," he cried. "See, how splendid! Yesterday I saw a large fish stranded on the beach, half-eaten by gulls, and a notion came to me that his spine with its many sharp teeth might be just the thing we're looking for. So I took it from the fish who had no more need of it and tried it right there. I cut through a great piece of driftwood. Isn't that wonderful? Don't you think the goddess, Athene, herself, washed the fish on shore for me to see? Why are you looking at me that way, Uncle? Are you not pleased?"

"Very pleased, my boy. I have long been considering your case and have been weighing how to reward you according to your merit. Well, now I think I know. But first we must go to Athene's temple to give thanks for this timely inspiration."

He took the boy by the hand and led him up the sunny road to the top of the hill, to the **Acropolis** where the temple of Athene stood—and still stands. Daedalus led him to the roof of the marble building; and there, as the lad stretched his arms toward heaven, Daedalus stepped softly behind him,

aspiration— strong desire

caprice—whim

Athene— goddess of the hunt and the moon; patron goddess of Athens

gross decree— outright command

placed his hands on his shoulders, and pushed. The boy went tumbling off the temple, off the hill, to the rocks below. But Athene, who had heard the first words of the boy's prayer, caught him in mid-air, and turned him into a partridge, which flew away, drumming. She then withdrew her favor from Daedalus.

Word of the boy's death flashed through the city. Nothing could be proved against Daedalus, but he was the target of the darkest suspicions, which, curiously enough, he took as an **affront**, for nothing could be proved, and so he felt unjustly accused.

"Ungrateful wretches!" he cried. "I will leave this city. I will go elsewhere and find more appreciative neighbors."

He had not told them about his invention of the saw, but he took the model Talos had made and set out for **Crete**. Arriving there, he went directly to the palace of King Minos, who, at that time, was the most powerful king in all the world, and made him a gift of the marvelous tool that could cut wood more swiftly than knife or ax. Minos, delighted, immediately appointed Daedalus Court **Artificer**, Smith Extraordinary, and **fitted out** a workshop for him with the likeliest lads for apprentices. Minos also gave the old fellow a beautiful young slave girl for his own.

Now, the Cretan women were the loveliest in the world, and Crete's court the most glittering. The capital city of Knossos made Athens seem like a little village. Women and girls alike wore . . . dresses, gems in their hair and a most beguiling scent made by their slaves who had been blinded so that their noses would be more keen. Daedalus was an honored figure at this court—and a **novelty** besides. The Cretans were mad for novelties, so the old man was much flattered and content.

He was a special favorite with the young princesses, **Ariadne** and **Phaedra**, who loved to visit him at his workshop and watch him make things. He became very fond of the girls and made them marvelous jointed wooden dolls with springs cunningly set and coiled so that they curtsied and danced and winked their eyes. Queen **Pasiphae** also came to see him often. He made her a perfume flask that played music when it was uncorked, and a looking glass that allowed her to see the back of her head. She spent hours with him gossiping, for she was very bored.

The queen kept coaxing Daedalus to tell her why he had really left Athens, for she sensed a secret; but all he would ever say was that the goddess, Athene, had withdrawn her favor, so he had been forced to leave her city.

"Goddess Athene!" she cried. "Goddess this and god that . . . What nonsense! These are old wives' tales, **nursery vapors**, nothing for intelligent men and women to trouble themselves about."

"Oh, my lady," cried Daedalus. "In heaven's name, take care what you say. The gods will hear and you will be punished."

"And I took you for a sophisticated man," said the queen. "A man of the

> ● ● ● ● ● ● ●
> "The goddess, Athene, had withdrawn her favor."
> ● ● ● ● ● ● ●

## FOCUS ON... SOCIAL STUDIES

Daedalus refers to the Acropolis in Athens as the place where Athene's temple stood. In ancient Greek cities, an acropolis was usually a central point, located for defense on the highest part of a hill. For the ancient Greeks, the founding of a city was a religious act—a basic factor in Greek city planning was the establishment of a local home for the gods. Research the Athenian Acropolis. Then write a two-page report about its structures and their functions in the daily life of Athens. Present your report to the class orally, using visuals of the district's plan and buildings, if possible.

◆ ◆ ◆ ◆ ◆ ◆ ◆ ◆ ◆ ◆ ◆ ◆ ◆

Hephaestus—
god of fire and
of the forge;
lame because
he was once
thrown off of Mt.
Olympus, the
home of the
Greek gods

Aphrodite—
goddess of love
and beauty

prate—chatter

discounted—
ignored

vengeance—
punishment in
return for an
insult

derisively—
laughingly,
cruelly

world, a traveler, a scientist. I am disappointed in you. Gods, indeed! And are you not, my Smith, more clever by far than that lame **Hephaestus**? And am I not more beautiful than **Aphrodite**?"

She stood up tall and full-bodied, and indeed very beautiful. The old man trembled.

"Come here. Come closer. Look at me. Confess that I am more beautiful than the Cytherean . . . Aphrodite. Of all the gods, she is the one I disbelieve in most. Love . . . my serving maids **prate** of it, my daughters frisk with the idea. All through the island men meet women by rock and tree, their shadows mingle; and I, I have Minos, the crown on a stick who loves nothing but his own decrees."

"Softly, madame, softly," said Daedalus. "You are not yourself. It is midsummer, a confusing time for women; what they say then must be **discounted**. Your wild words will be forgiven, but please do not repeat them. Now, see what I have made for you, even as you were saying those foolish things: a parasol, lighter than a butterfly's wing, and yet so constructed that it opens by itself like a flower when it feels the sun."

But Aphrodite had heard, and she planned a terrible **vengeance** . . . .

After a while, the queen gave birth to a child, who attracted a great deal of notice as he was half bull. People **derisively** called him the Minotaur, or Minos' bull.

Even in his most cruel fury, Minos was a careful planner. He decided to hide his shame, knowing that the world forgets what it does not see. He had Daedalus construct a tangled maze on the palace grounds, a place of thorny hedges and sudden rooms, called the Labyrinth. There were paths running this way and that, becoming corridors, plunging underground, crossing each other, crossing themselves, each one leading back to the middle, so there was no way out.

Here King Minos imprisoned Pasiphae and the Minotaur—and Daedalus too. Minos wanted to make very sure that the old craftsman would never **divulge** the secret of the Labyrinth, so here Daedalus dwelt. His workshop was in the Labyrinth, but he did not work well. At his bench he could hear Pasiphae howling, and the hideous, broken bellowing of the bull-man, who grew more loathsome and ferocious each day.

His only comfort was his son, Icarus, who, of his own free will, chose to live with him because he so loved and admired his father. It was Icarus who said to him one day, "Father, I grow weary of this maze. Let us leave this place and go to places I have not seen."

"Alas, dear boy," said Daedalus, "we cannot. It is forbidden to leave the Labyrinth."

"You know the way out, do you not? You built the thing, after all."

"Yes, certainly, I know the way out. But I dare not take it. Minos would have us put to death immediately. All I can do is petition the king to allow you to go, but I must remain."

"No. We go together."

"But I have explained to you that we cannot."

"Minos is a great king," said Icarus. "But he does not rule the whole earth. Let us leave the island. Let us leave Crete and cross the sea."

"You are mad, dear boy. How can we do this? The sea is locked against us. Every boatman on every craft, large and small, is under strict **interdict** against allowing me voyage. We cannot leave the island."

"Oh, yes, we can," said Icarus. "I'll tell you how. Just make us wings."

"Wings?"

"To fly with. Like the birds—you know—wings."

"Is it possible? Can I do this?"

"Birds have them; therefore, they have been made. And anything, dear father, that has been made you can duplicate. You have made things never seen before, never known before, never dreamed before."

"I will start immediately," cried Daedalus.

He had Icarus set out baits of fish and capture a gull. Then, very carefully, he copied its wings—not only the shape of them, but the hollow bone **struts**, and the feathers with their wind-catching overlaps and hollow stems, and he improved a bit on the model. Finally, one day, he completed two magnificent sets of wings with real feathers plucked from the feather cloaks the Cretan dancers used. They were huge, larger than eagles' wings.

He fitted a pair to Icarus, sealing the **pinions** to the boy's powerful shoulders with wax. Then he donned his own.

"Goodbye to Crete!" cried Icarus joyfully.

"Hear me, boy," said Daedalus. "Follow me closely and do not go off the way. Do not fly too low or the spray will wet your wings, not too high or the sun will melt them. Not too high and not too

divulge—make known

interdict—command

struts—the stiff, supporting part of a wing

pinions—wings

low, but close by me, through the middle air."

"Oh, come, come," cried Icarus, and he leaped into the air, spreading his wings and soaring off above the hedges of the Labyrinth as if he had been born with wings. Daedalus flew after him.

They flew together over the palace grounds, over the beaches, and headed out to sea. A shepherd looked up and saw them; and a fisherman looked up and saw them; and they both thought they saw gods flying. The shepherd prayed to **Hermes**, and the fisherman prayed to **Poseidon**, with glad hearts. Now, they knew, their prayers would be answered.

Icarus had never been so happy. In one leap his life had changed. Instead of **groveling** in the dank tunnels of the Labyrinth, he was flying, flying free under the wide, bright sky in a great drench of sunlight, the first boy in the history of the world to fly. He looked up and saw a gull, and tried to hold his

wings steady and float on the air as the gull was doing, as easily as a duck floats on water. He felt himself slipping, and he slipped all the way in a slanting dive to the dancing surface of the water before he could regain his balance. The water splashing against his chest felt deliciously cool.

"No . . . no . . . ," he heard his father call from far above. "Not too low and not too high. Keep to the middle air . . ."

Icarus yelled back a wordless shout of joy, beat his wings, and soared up, up toward the floating gull.

"Ha . . . ," he thought to himself. "Those things have been flying all their lives. Wait till I get a little practice. I'll outfly them all."

Crete was a brown dot behind them now; there was no land before them, just the diamond-glittering water. Old Daedalus was beating his way through the air, steadily and cautiously, trying this wing-position and that, this body angle and that, observing how the gulls thrust and soared. He kept an eye on Icarus, making mental notes about how to improve the wings once they had landed. He felt a bit tired. The sun was heavy on his shoulders. The figures spun in his head.

"I must not go to sleep," he said to himself. "I must watch the boy. He may do something **rash**."

But Icarus was flying easily alongside so Daedalus hunched his shoulders, let his chin fall on his chest, and half-coasted on a column of air. He shut his eyes for a moment . . . just for a moment . . .

In that moment Icarus saw a great white swan climb past him, wings spread, shooting like a great white arrow straight for the sun and uttering a long honking call. Icarus looked after him; he had already dwindled and was a splinter of light, moving toward the sun.

"How splendid he is, flying so swiftly, so proudly, so high. How I should like to get a closer look at the sun. Once and for all I should like to see for myself what it really is. Is it a great, burning eye looking through an enormous spyhole, as some Libyans say; or is it **Apollo** driving a golden coach drawn by golden horses, as the Athenians believe; or perhaps it is a great flaming squid swimming the waters of the sky, as the barbarians say; or, maybe, as my father holds, it is a monster ball of burning gas that Apollo moves by its own motion? I think I shall go a bit closer, anyway. The old man seems to be napping. I can be up and back before he opens his eyes. How splendid if I could get a really good look at the sun and be able to tell my father something he doesn't know. How that would delight him. What a joke we will have together. Yes . . . I must follow that swan."

So Icarus, full of strength and joy, blood flaming in his veins, stretched his home-made wings and climbed after the swan. Up, up, up, he flew. The air seemed thinner, his body heavier; the sun was swollen now, filling the whole sky, blazing down at him. He couldn't see any more than he had before; he was dazed with light.

"Closer . . ." he thought. "Higher . . . closer . . . up and up. . ."

He felt the back of his shoulders growing wet.

"Yes," he thought. "This is hot work."

But the wetness was not what he supposed; it was wax—melting wax. The wax bonds of his wings were melting in the heat of the sun. He felt the wings sliding away from him. As they fell away and drifted slowly down, he gazed at them, stupefied. It was as if a great golden hand had taken him in its grasp and hurled him toward the sea. The sky tilted. His breath was torn from his chest. The diamond-hard sea was rushing toward him.

"No," he cried. "No . . . no . . ."

Daedalus, dozing and floating on his column of air, felt the cry ripping through his body like an arrow. He opened his eyes to see the white body of his son hurtling down. It fell into the sea and disappeared. ❖

Apollo—god of the sun and of music

# Be Daedalus

Nanina Alba

parching—hotly
drying

tax—cost

Be Daedalus: make wings,
Make feathered wings;
Bind them with wax
    Avoid the **parching** sun that brings
    Death as its **tax**.
    Suns can be brutal things.

Be Daedalus; make wings,
If Icarus be unwise
And swing up toward the flame,
    Forget his prejudice and prize,
    The price, the name.

Be Daedalus; make wings,
Make even feathered wings . . . ❖

## ON THE JOB
### ENTREPRENEUR

Entrepreneurs organize, operate, and assume the risks for business ventures. For such a multi-faceted job, organizational talent, exceptional communication skills, and the ability to solve problems and make decisions are essential. Although no specific training is required to become an entrepreneur, some college or business school is helpful. Advances in computer technology have enabled many people to become entrepreneurs and establish home-based businesses.

## ACCENT ON...
### ENTREPRENEURIAL ENTERPRISES

Daedalus offered his unique services to the king and queen. Providing personal services can be a lucrative enterprise. Many people are interested in purchasing items created by individuals with unique talents such as cabinet-makers, jewelry makers, and potters. Also, many people need assistance with household tasks such as yard work or pet care. The first step for any entrepreneur is to make a business plan—a statement of what the business will be, how it will operate, and how it is being financed. Plan your own personal-service firm. Decide on a service that you will provide and create a brief business plan.

# I, Icarus

Alden Nowlan

propelled—
moved

There was a time when I could fly. I swear it.
Perhaps, if I think hard for a moment, I can even tell you the year.
My room was on the ground floor at the rear of the house.
My bed faced a window.
Night after night I lay on my bed and willed myself to fly.
It was hard work, I can tell you.
Sometimes I lay perfectly still for an hour before I felt
 my body rising from the bed.
I rose slowly, slowly until I floated three or four feet
 above the floor.
Then, with a kind of swimming motion, I **propelled** myself
 toward the window.
Outside, I rose higher and higher, above the pasture fence,
 above the clothesline, above the dark, haunted trees
 beyond the pasture.
And, all the time, I heard the music of flutes.
It seemed the wind made this music.
And sometimes there were voices singing. ❖

# Theseus and the Minotaur

Gavin O. Rahilly

wharves—piers along the shore

upswept—lined; the cypresses' branches "curl" upward

rank—row

omen—sign

manling—young man

*King Minos of Crete demands a tribute from Athens. Each year, seven young men and seven young women sail to Crete to be fed to the Minotaur. Theseus is determined to bring an end to the sacrifices— and to the Minotaur. As he boards his black-sailed ship, Theseus promises his father that if he is successful, he will return in a ship with white sails.*

lowly, the bright-eyed ship pulled out onto the rolling sea, the sailors straining at their oars until a steady breeze came up, and the sunlit headlands fell behind.

Standing at the ship's prow, Theseus offered up a prayer to his divine father. "Oh great Poseidon, lord of the dark sea and the dark places under the earth where the bright sun never looks, if you are indeed my father give me victory in the darkness of the Labyrinth." So he prayed to great Poseidon, and the god sent up dolphins from the depths to play around the ship as darkness fell.

On they sailed to Crete, to the harbor city where King Minos ruled. Terrace after terrace of white-walled houses rose up the hills, to heights roofed over with bright gold. On the broad-planked **wharves** the armored soldiers of the king were waiting, to lead the hero and his companions through the streets. With cries and weeping, the Cretans crowding round threw flowers at the young people doomed to die.

Theseus and his followers were led along a pathway **upswept** with cypresses, until past the pillars of the palace gates a **rank** of women greeted them. One above all stood out, a girl in her first womanhood, full of grace and swiftness, clad in simple white. As she looked upon the captives, Theseus met her eyes, until she blushed and looked away. Some god made him call out "Hail, princess!" and drop upon one knee, before the guards led them into the place where grim Minos sat. The arms of his gold throne were shaped like dolphins, and Theseus smiled at the **omen**.

"Why is it that you smile, you whom the gods have already given up to death?" asked Minos.

"Because, oh king, I know the deathless gods give victory to those they wish to honor," Theseus replied.

Minos gave the slight suggestion of a nod. "As great Zeus is my father, why will the gods honor you, **manling**?"

"Because Poseidon the Earthshaker is my father, and he has sent me here to sacrifice this dark thing you keep underground." As Theseus said this, there was a stir about the throne, and the priestess he had hailed slipped through the guards to take her place beside Minos.

"Sister's daughter Ariadne," said the king, "whom do you name first to go to meet the Dweller in the Labyrinth?"

"This one, lord," the princess said, pointing to Theseus. And again she turned her face away.

"So be it," said the king. "Let the others stay under guard, and send this one into the Labyrinth."

They took Theseus to the temple, to wash him and paint him with strange

## SPOTLIGHT ON... EXHIBITING SELF-CONTROL

Icarus's inability to control his curiosity about the sun proved fatal. Theseus, however, maintained his self-control in the Labyrinth by shaking off fearful thoughts and stilling his mind. You, too, will face situations in which you may be tempted to lose your self-control. Here are some ways to maintain self-control:

1. Identify your goal.
2. Understand your options.
3. Listen to other points of view.
4. Communicate your thoughts calmly. Never shout or scream.
5. Try to put yourself in someone else's shoes.
6. Back off or revisit the question later if you start to lose control.

designs. They gave him rich foods and wines, which he refused to eat, fearing they were drugged; and in the night the priestess Ariadne, sister's daughter of the king, came to him.

"Stranger, who are you?" she whispered when she stood before him.

"My mother named me Theseus. My father is **Aegeus**, King of Athens, but by my mother's oath I truly am the son of great Poseidon."

Ariadne bowed her head. "Then by the Goddess I serve, you are the one foretold. The **oracles** said this dark one of the earth could never die, until one of the gods sent one to kill him." She took his hand a moment.

Then she opened out the bundle hid beneath her **mantle** and gave Theseus a sword, wrought with patterns and designs on blade and hilt. He held the cold blade a moment close against his forehead.

"This you'll need more," she said, and she gave him a wound ball of woolen twine. "Tie the end upon the door when you go in and let this roll out in front of you. It will lead you to the maze's heart and leave a track for you to follow out, a track you'd never find unaided. For those who enter in the Labyrinth have never yet come out." Theseus took the slight ball in his hand.

"Come," she said, and by the altar fire she lit a torch. Black-hooded priestesses waited at the Labyrinth's bronze-plated door, and silently they swung it back, revealing darkness. On the threshold Ariadne handed him the torch, and behind him swung shut the heavy gate.

Aegeus—pronounced ee-JEE-us

oracles—persons through whom the gods make their wishes known

mantle—cloak

guttering—flick-
ering

straitly—nar-
rowly

Dionysus—god
of wine

In **guttering** red torchglow Theseus could scarcely see the magic ball of twine as it unwound before him down the steep incline into the earth. Holding the torch low to light the ground before his feet, he started down and ever down into the darkness, gripping his sword.

A few steps into the maze, he could not tell which way led down, or—save for the thread—which way he'd come. Around him pressed the darkness, oppressing him with dread and emptiness, so that he was afraid to go on.

Theseus shook off these thoughts, stilling his mind to listen for the monster's presence. The Minotaur was at home in the darkness—it might be waiting on the path ahead of him, might be listening to his footfalls now, might burst upon him from any of the passages that ran ghostly off to either side of the track marked by the dim unrolling thread.

Never level, never straight, the path twisted on. Once bones almost stopped his feet at where the passage narrowed so **straitly** that he had to wind and stretch his way through sideways; yet in that place the dark cold rock was smoothed, as if by constant passage of some enormous body.

Once past, another long stretch wound down and round, until the wall fell away from his outstretched hand. This unseen cavern must be the earth's womb, at the center of the Labyrinth. He saw the ball of twine had stopped at last.

All was darkness, and silence, while Theseus listened with all his powers. Was there a sound of something breathing in the dark? At the edge of the dim torchlight a shadowed shape suggested itself, humped like a bull, but stretched out like a man. The monster was asleep, betrayed to him by the god, lying on the naked rock beside a bed of bones.

With a cry to great Poseidon, Theseus leapt across the monster's back. He grasped a horn, twisting the grotesque head to one side to expose the throat to his keen blade. The dark shape roared as it tried to rise up under him. Then it sank back, and black blood poured over his hand holding the sword. Giving thanks to the immortal gods, Theseus wiped clean his blade, before he caught up the end of Ariadne's thread and started up again from that place to daylight.

Ariadne was waiting at the door. She washed off from him the monster's blood, and then led him down to where the other young Athenians waited by the black-sailed ship. So they left Crete before King Minos could pursue.

The victorious hero sailed back to Athens, with his companions and Cretan bride. But Theseus left Ariadne on the island of Naxos, where some say the god **Dionysus** claimed her as his bride. Theseus continued to Athens, but whether distracted by mourning Ariadne or by rejoicing for his homecoming, he forgot to hoist the white sail that would give his father hope of his return. Aegeus saw the black sail from the cliff on which he watched, and despairing that his son was dead, he leapt into the sea. Ever since it has been called the Aegean Sea.

Theseus returned to Athens and ruled as king. ❖

# UNDERSTANDING

1. The Minotaur lives in the Labyrinth with Pasiphae, Daedalus, and Icarus. Identify the human weaknesses of the characters who dwell in the Labyrinth. Draw a line, and along it list in chronological order the events that occur as a result of human weakness.

2.  Theseus travels to Crete to rid the island of the Minotaur. Find evidence in the text of how well Theseus's plan worked.

   Suppose that you and a group of classmates have experienced a "sighting" of a modern-day "monster" such as Bigfoot. Choose a group member to be a reporter, and plan and write out an interview between the reporter and the group members. The reporter's questions should focus on details of the setting, why you were there, what you saw, and what the beast was doing. Videotape or role-play your interview. *Workshop 27*

3. Based on what you know about Daedalus and Icarus from the myth, what is the reason for the advice given in the poem "Be Daedalus?" Assume the poet is counseling parents on how to raise children. Create a list of rules to follow when disciplining and protecting children, promoting their creativity, and other issues. Use the message of the poem as a guide.

4. Remembering a time when he wished to fly, the author of "I, Icarus" envies Icarus's adventure. Did you ever wish you could perform superhuman acts? Write a journal entry on this topic and turn it into a poem that begins with a line such as, "There was a time when I could . . . "

## A LAST WORD

Are some people simply destined for greatness? What qualities do successful people possess?

# CONNECTING

1.  A myth is a story about a superhuman being or an unlikely event. The characters in myths include gods, heroes, and ordinary people. Work with several classmates to write another short episode in the Labyrinth myth. Use the same characters with the same traits. Design an illustrated children's book of your story and present it to a local elementary school. *Workshop 7*

2. Myths exist today as they did in ancient times. Consider people, places, and beliefs that have an element of mythology. Was there really a lost continent of Atlantis? In groups, choose a mysterious and almost mythical subject that remains unexplained today. Read about it and present a debate for the class, arguing both for and against the possibility that it exists.

# from *The Odyssey*

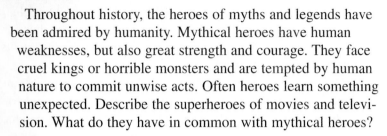

## EXPLORING

Throughout history, the heroes of myths and legends have been admired by humanity. Mythical heroes have human weaknesses, but also great strength and courage. They face cruel kings or horrible monsters and are tempted by human nature to commit unwise acts. Often heroes learn something unexpected. Describe the superheroes of movies and television. What do they have in common with mythical heroes?

## THEME CONNECTION... THE HEROIC VOYAGE

*The Odyssey* is the adventure of a clever Greek hero and king on his way home from war. Because the gods are angry, he must travel for 10 long years. He encounters many dangers, and narrowly escapes from each one. The voyage emphasizes the courage, cunning, and wit of the hero. In these tales, Odysseus and his men must escape the strong Cicones army and the vicious, one-eyed monster Polyphemus.

## TIME & PLACE

In ancient Greece, storytellers memorized and retold the stories that make up *The Odyssey*. Around 850 B.C., the Greek poet Homer, who is said to have been blind, recorded the stories. His version is the one preserved for us through the centuries.

The Greeks defeated the Trojans in the legendary war, and Odysseus is returning to Greece. On the way, however, he encounters many obstacles. His journey lasts for 10 years.

## THE WRITER'S CRAFT

### EPIC

An epic is a long poem that tells a story of great adventure, usually relating somehow to the development of a nation or race of people. Epic heroes have superhuman qualities that enable them to perform extraordinary acts, often through the help of supernatural forces—in the form of gods and goddesses. The storyteller does not make judgments on the hero's actions, so readers see both strengths and weaknesses.

## from *The Odyssey*

Homer (translated by Robert Fitzgerald)

**Sailing from Troy**

"I am **Laertes'** son, Odysseus.
Men hold me
**formidable** for **guile** in peace and war:
this fame has gone abroad to the sky's
   rim.
My home is on the peaked sea-mark of
   **Ithaca**
under Mount Neion's wind-blown robe
   of leaves,
in sight of other islands—Dulichium,
**Same**, wooded Zacynthus—Ithaca
being most lofty in that coastal sea,
and northwest, while the rest lie east
   and south.
A rocky isle, but good for a boy's
   training:
I shall not see on earth a place more
   dear,
though I have been **detained** long by
   **Calypso**,
loveliest among goddesses, who held me
in her smooth caves, to be her heart's
   delight,
as **Circe of Aeaea**, the enchantress,
desired me, and detained me in her hall.
But in my heart I never gave consent.
Where shall a man find sweetness to
   surpass
his own home and his parents? In far
   lands
he shall not, though he find a house of
   gold.

What of my sailing, then, from Troy?

What of those
   years
of rough adven-
   ture, weath-
   ered under
   Zeus?
The wind that
   carried west
   from **Ilium**
brought me to
Ismarus, on the
   far shore,
a strongpoint on the
   coast of **Cicones**.
I stormed that place and
   killed the men who fought.
Plunder we took, and we enslaved
   the women,
to make division, equal shares to
   all—
but on the spot I told them: 'Back,
   and quickly!
Out to sea again!' My men were
   mutinous,
fools, on stores of wine. Sheep
   after sheep
they butchered by the surf, and
   **shambling** cattle,
feasting,—while fugitives went
   inland, running
to call to arms the main force of
   Cicones.
This was an army, trained to fight on
   horseback
or, where the ground required, on foot.
   They came
with dawn over that terrain like the
   leaves
and blades of spring. So doom
   appeared to us,
dark word of Zeus for us, our evil days.

### About the Author

Little is known about the poet Homer who is traditionally credited with writing *The Iliad* and *The Odyssey*. Homer is thought to have lived sometime between 900 and 700 B.C. in ancient Greece, although some scholars today question whether he ever existed. One theory suggests that the two epics were actually composed from pieces written by a number of poets. Although *The Odyssey* is written in verse, it has been called the first novel because of its exciting action and effective flashbacks.

Laertes—
pronounced
lay-AR-teez

formidable—
causing fear
or awe

guile—
cleverness

My men stood up and made a fight
  of it—
backed on the ships, with **lances** kept
  in play,
from bright morning through the blaze
  of noon
holding our beach, although so far
  outnumbered;
but when the sun passed toward
  **unyoking** time,
then the **Achaeans**, one by one, gave
  way.
Six benches were left empty in every
  ship

that evening when we pulled away
  from death.
And this new grief we bore with us
  to sea:
our precious lives we had, but not our
  friends.
No ship made sail next day until some
  shipmate
had raised a cry, three times, for each
  poor ghost
unfleshed by the Cicones on that
  field. ❖

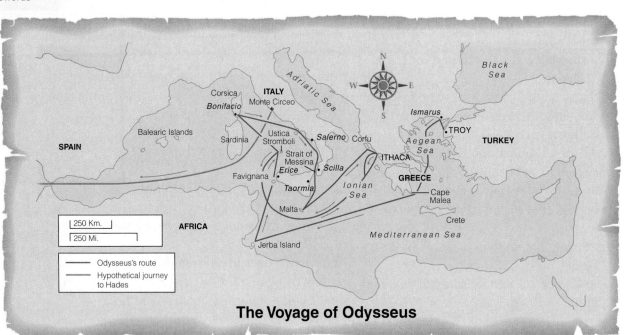

**The Voyage of Odysseus**

# from The Odyssey

Homer (retold by Barbara Leonie Picard)

## Polyphemus the Cyclops

he next land that they reached was the country of the **Cyclopes**, a simple, savage folk, of more than human size, who never tilled their land, or built ships or houses, or traded with other nations. Instead they lived in caves in the rocks and spent their time pasturing their flocks on their rich green fields.

Just off the mainland lay a wooded island, the home of many wild goats, and to this island the twelve ships came on a misty night. The men disembarked and slept; and in the morning, when the mist had cleared, they saw opposite them the land of the Cyclopes and were surprised, for in the fog they had not imagined the mainland to be so close.

All that day they rested from their labors on the sea and feasted on the flesh of the island goats. Keeping a careful watch upon the land, Odysseus was just able to make out the huge flocks of sheep and the cattle of the Cyclopes browsing in the fields, and the smoke from the fires of the herdsmen. "Tomorrow," he said, "I shall go with one ship to the mainland to see who lives in that rich country. It may well be a friendly folk who will give us welcome hospitality after our days at sea."

Accordingly, in the morning Odysseus sailed to the mainland and beached his ship on the shore below a rocky cliff which towered above their heads, with shrubs growing among rocks and little yellow wallflowers springing from every cleft.

Close by, halfway up the cliff and approached by a zigzag pathway, was the opening of a wide cave, half hidden by laurel bushes and surrounded by a wall of huge stones. It was plain to see that the cave was someone's home, and picking out twelve of his best men, Odysseus set off up the cliff carrying a skin of the finest wine he had on board, as a gift for whoever might live there.

Beyond the wall they found a court-yard with pens for sheep and goats; though the pens were empty when they saw them, for the flocks were out at pasture with their owner.

"There is no one here," said Odysseus. "Let us wait in the cave for the shepherd to return." And they passed beneath the glossy **foliage** of the overhanging laurels and went inside.

Within, the light was dim, but when their eyes grew used to it, they saw that the huge cave held many pens of lambs and **kids**, all separated according to their ages. There were, too, great pails of milk, and cheeses stacked in baskets hanging from the roof. But, for all this abundance of good food, the cave did not seem a friendly place, and Odysseus' men urged him to let them take as many cheeses and lambs as they could carry and return at once to the ship. But he would not hear of this. "We could not rob a stranger in his absence," he said. "Besides, when he returns it may please him to give us far more gifts than thirteen men can carry off, and it would be folly to miss the chance of filling our

Cyclopes—pronounced sigh-KLOH-peez, plural of *Cyclops*

foliage—leaves

kids—young goats

savory—
delicious

faggots—a
bundle of sticks
used for kindling

ship with **savory** cheeses and tender kids which we might share with our comrades waiting on the island."

So they remained in the cave, and towards evening the herdsman returned with his flocks. He was as tall as three men and broad, with but one eye in the middle of his forehead; and as soon as Odysseus and his men caught sight of him, they knew that they had been unwise to wait.

He came to the entrance of the cave and flung inside a huge bundle of logs, large branches lopped from tall pines and oaks, as **faggots** for his fire; and in terror the Greeks fled to the darkest corner of the cave and hid themselves. The monster penned his rams and goats in the courtyard and drove the ewes and she-goats into the cave for milking, blocking the entrance with a great stone. And even his sheep and goats were larger than any Odysseus had ever seen before.

When the milking was over, the monster penned the ewes with their lambs and the goats with their kids, and set himself to make a fire from the wood he had brought home. As soon as he had a blaze, he was able to see, by the light of the leaping flames, Odysseus and his men, crouching in the very farthest corner. "Who are you, strangers?" he asked in a voice like thunder.

For all his terror Odysseus stepped forward and answered boldly enough. "We are Greeks, sailing home to Ithaca from the war with Troy. The winds have carried us somewhat from our course,

● ● ● ● ● ● ●

"We have come to you in hope that you may be our host."

● ● ● ● ● ● ●

and we have come to you in hope that you may be our host until we can set sail once more."

The giant roared, "I am Polyphemus the Cyclops, and I entertain no guests unless it pleases me. But tell me this, where have you beached your ship? Is she close by?"

Odysseus suspected the question and guessed the Cyclops meant harm to his ship and the men guarding her, and he answered cunningly, "Our ship was wrecked upon your shore, and only I and these twelve men escaped alive from the sea."

But Polyphemus gave no word of sympathy in reply. Instead, he seized a man in each hand, and dashing out their brains against the rocky floor, he tore them in pieces and ate them for his supper before the eyes of their horrified comrades. Then after drinking several large pailfuls of milk, he lay down by the fire to sleep.

Odysseus would have drawn his sword and crept upon him while he slept and killed him, but that he knew it would be impossible for him and his men to move away by themselves the great stone that blocked the opening of the cave. So, terrified, they waited all night, whispering together and trying to devise some means of outwitting the cruel monster.

At dawn Polyphemus rekindled the fire and milked his ewes and goats again. That done, he snatched up two more of Odysseus' men and ate them as a wild beast might have done. Then he rolled aside the great stone from the mouth of the cave and drove out his flocks; and replacing the stone once more, he went towards the mountain pastures, whistling cheerfully at the thought of the good supper which awaited his return.

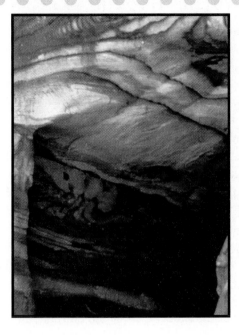

Odysseus and the eight men left to him sat down beside the fire to think how they might escape the fate which would surely be theirs unless they could find a way to leave the cave; and at last a plan came to Odysseus. In the cave there lay a long pole of green olive-wood, drying so that it might serve the Cyclops for a staff. From this pole Odysseus hacked off with his sword a piece the length of a tall man, and set his companions to sharpen one end into a point and harden it in the fire.

"Tonight," he said, "when the monster sleeps, we will heat the wood red-hot and with it put out his single eye."

When the point of the stake was hard and sharp, they hid it and then chose by lot the four men who should help Odysseus use it in the night.

When evening came the Cyclops returned with his flocks, and this time he drove all the sheep into the cave, rams and ewes alike, and penned them safely. When he had milked the ewes and goats, he thought of his own supper and seized two more men. While he sat by the fire eating them, Odysseus poured out a huge

SPOTLIGHT ON...
PROBLEM
SOLVING

While trying to make his way back home, Odysseus encounters and solves a number of problems. Like other skills, problem solving can be improved through experience and practice. To solve a problem, follow these steps:
1. Identify the problem.
2. Consider your options.
3. Decide on the best course of action.
4. Carry out your decision.
5. Evaluate the results.

◆ ◆ ◆ ◆ ◆ ◆ ◆ ◆ ◆ ◆ ◆ ◆ ◆ ◆ ◆

bowlful of the wine he had brought with him, and coming forward, he offered it to Polyphemus. "Such wine as this our ship held before it was wrecked upon your shores," he said. "Come, taste of it and tell me if you think it is not good."

The Cyclops took the wooden bowl and drained it at one **draught**. He held it out to Odysseus. "Give me more," he said.

Odysseus filled it a second time, and again the monster drank. "Give me yet more of your wine, stranger," he demanded, "and tell me your name, that I may give you a gift in return."

A third time Odysseus filled the bowl and the Cyclops drank. "My name is No-one," said Odysseus. "Tell me now what gift you will give to No-one in exchange for his good wine."

"I will eat you last of all your comrades. A few more hours of life, that shall be my gift to you." And with a mighty laugh that echoed through the

draught—pronounced draft; drink, inhaling

cave Polyphemus lay down beside the fire; and made drowsy by the wine, he fell deeply asleep at once.

Odysseus thrust the stake into the embers and held it there until it was red-hot; then taking it, he and the four men on whom the lot had fallen drove it deep into the Cyclops' eye.

With screams and with shouts of rage, Polyphemus awoke and pulled the stake from the socket of his eye, and wildly flinging his arms about and stumbling around the cave, he tried to catch Odysseus and his friends, who crouched trembling against the wall.

The neighboring Cyclopes who dwelt in caverns nearby heard his cries, and coming to his cave, stood outside the great stone and called to him. "What ails you, Polyphemus? Why do you wake us with your cries? Does someone steal your sheep or kill you?"

"Good neighbors," said Polyphemus, "it is the cunning wiles of No-one that are killing me."

"If no one is killing you," answered the neighbors, "you must be sick, and illness comes from the gods, and we can be of no help to you. You have woken us in vain. May your sickness have left you by the morning." And they returned to their own homes.

But the Cyclops groped his way to the entrance of the cave and pushed away the great stone, and sitting down in the doorway, waited to catch any of the men who might try to pass him; so that they saw that there was no escape for them that way.

At the far end of the cave Odysseus and his companions made whispered plans; and taking **reeds** from Polyphemus' bed, Odysseus bound together eighteen of the finest rams in threes, with one of his six men tied beneath each middle ram. Then he himself laid hold of the largest ram of all, a great creature with a splendid fleece, and lay underneath it, clinging on and hidden by the shaggy wool that hung down from its broad sides.

By that time it was dawn, and the rams were eager to be grazing in the rich pastures. Bleating, they moved together to the entrance of the cave, where Polyphemus felt across the back of each one as it came to him, before passing it through the courtyard. But he never thought to feel beneath the animals, so the six men went safely out. Last of all to come was the leader of the flock, walking slowly under the weight of Odysseus, clinging to its fleece.

As Polyphemus felt its back he spoke to it. "My good ram, you are ever the foremost of the flock, leading the others to their grazing ground. Why are you last today? Are you grieved for your master, blinded by wicked No-one, and would stay to comfort him? I would that you could speak and tell me where he hides, that wretch who took away my sight. But go, dear ram, join your companions in the fields." And Polyphemus moved his hand aside and the ram stepped through the opening into the sunlight, bearing Odysseus.

Once outside the courtyard, Odysseus freed himself from his hiding-place and went to release his companions. Then hastily they drove the sheep down to the ship and their comrades waiting on the shore. With no delay they stowed the flock on board and set out to row back to the island where the fleet was moored.

A little way from the shore Odysseus stood up in the ship and shouted with all his might, "Now indeed, wicked Cyclops, do you know what **ills** your cruelty to helpless strangers has brought to you."

Polyphemus heard him and came out from his cave in fury, and breaking off a huge piece of rock, he flung it into the sea in the direction of Odysseus' voice. It fell in the water by the bows, and the great waves made by its fall washed the ship back towards the shore; but Odysseus seized a long pole and pushed off again, and his men fell to rowing hard once more.

Again Odysseus stood up to shout his taunts to the Cyclops, and though his men tried to restrain him, for they feared another rock might be cast at them, he called out, "Polyphemus, if anyone should ever ask you how you lost your sight, you may tell him that Odysseus, king of Ithaca, put out your eye."

And Polyphemus cried out with a loud voice, "Alas, it was foretold that great grief would come to me through Odysseus, king of Ithaca, but I had thought he would be a fine big man, a worthy enemy for me, not a tiny weakling like yourself. But evil will come to you as well from this, for Poseidon, god of the sea **whereon** you sail, is my father, and he will avenge my eye." And then he held out his hands over the water and prayed to his father for vengeance. "Great Poseidon, lord of all the seas,

grant your son this one request. May Odysseus and his men never reach their home in Ithaca. But if, in spite of all his misdeeds, it is the will of the gods that Odysseus should gain the shores of his own land, let it be alone and friendless, and may he find sorrow awaiting him in his house."

And again Polyphemus tore off and hurled into the sea a rock. But this time it fell to the stern of the ship and sent her rushing forward to the island.

Once safely with the men from his other ships, Odysseus divided the sheep among them, a fair share to each. But his companions allotted him the fine ram by the help of which he had escaped, as an extra gift, because he was their leader and because he had saved six of his men from the Cyclops. ❖

ills—troubles

whereon—on which

# ON THE JOB

## TRAVEL AGENT

Travel agents make arrangements for transportation and hotel accommodations, as well as plan tour, business, and vacation packages. Because they need to consult a variety of computer-based sources for information, travel agents must have strong computer abilities. Excellent communication skills are also needed for working with clients and presenting travel promotions. Specialized training in travel and tourism is highly recommended. Helpful high school courses include geography, computer science, foreign languages, and history.

## UNDERSTANDING

1. In the opening lines of *The Odyssey*, the hero introduces himself. What information does he use to identify himself? What is the point he will emphasize in the story that follows?

   Write an introduction of yourself as if you were a storyteller. What information will you include? If you were to state your core or central belief, what would it be? Introduce yourself to the class and explain your core belief.

2. The Cyclopes are a fearsome people. Find examples in the text that describe the personalities and behaviors of the Cyclopes, and of Polyphemus in particular. Write several entries in a ship's log describing the people Odysseus's men encounter in this land.

3. While trapped in Polyphemus's cave, Odysseus devises a plan to escape. Describe this clever scheme in detail.

   Plan an event or activity—such as a family reunion, a camping trip, or a class outing—down to the last detail. Write an action plan describing the participants, the equipment needed, the location, the transportation, and other details. Write the plan to inform the participants of the details. ***Workshops 11 and 18***

## CONNECTING

1. Read or view a modern or ancient adventure story. Afterward, consider the qualities and accomplishments its hero has in common with Odysseus. Create a two-column chart on a sheet of paper. List each hero's personal traits, qualities, and goals. Deliver an oral presentation with a short overview of the story, but focus mainly on the comparison with Odysseus. ***Workshops 15 and 25***

2. Think of yourself as the hero in your own life story. What "giants" do you have to overcome? How do you approach them? A "giant" might be finishing school, getting along with family members, or finding a first job. Where can you go for help when a situation becomes overwhelming?

   Many schools have peer counseling programs—does yours? If so, find out the qualifications for becoming a peer counselor. Write an article for the school newspaper to let other students know about the program and how they can get involved. If your school does *not* have a program, plan one. Determine who would train the peer counselors and how much time it would take. In a proposal to the principal, explain the benefits of such a program and recommend that the school support the program. ***Workshop 19 or 13***

> ### A LAST WORD
> As we go on our life journeys, we encounter many challenges. Why is it important that we know how to think for ourselves, especially when facing a challenge? Why might those situations call for us to think and act on behalf of others as well?

# Heroes in the Forest

- *Natural and Right*
- *Wildfires in the West*

## EXPLORING

Some heroes may save not only human lives but also forests and wildlife. Whether set by humans or sparked by lightning, a wildfire destroys natural resources. Every summer, newscasts relate stories of raging forest fires and brushfires all across the nation. Armies of firefighters jump from planes to preserve waterways, forests, and wildlife, as well as people's homes. Discuss the importance of protecting these natural resources. How do you and others benefit from these resources?

## THEME CONNECTION... WORKING HEROES

The author of this essay has spent thousands of hours risking his life to control fires in America's most remote forests. Learn about the dangerous occupation of fighting wildfires as you drop in on a day in the life of a smokejumper.

## TIME & PLACE

Drought strikes often in the western United States. When it does, smokejumpers know they are going to have a busy summer. The National Forest Service employs hundreds of firefighters and calls on many volunteers to help battle wildfires. These people prepare food, transport food and supplies, and relay information, but smokejumpers have the riskiest job.

## THE WRITER'S CRAFT

### PERSONAL ESSAY

In a personal essay, a writer shares experiences, thoughts, and opinions on a topic familiar to him or her. Some essays describe people, places, or things. Others are narrative, telling a true story. The expository essay gives readers information or explains a process. Writers also use essays to persuade readers to adopt a point of view or take a specific action.

# Natural and Right

Clay Morgan

## About the Author

Clay Morgan has fought hundreds of fires and made over 150 parachute jumps for the U.S. Forest Service. He has also worked as a lookout, a trail builder, a teacher, and a pizza cook. His novel, *Santiago and the Drinking Party* is a "philosophical adventure story" set in the Amazon river valley of South America.

We are smokejumpers, Tim Farrell, Catfish Bates, Bob Shoemaker and I. We each wear 75 pounds of gear and protection: two parachutes, a heavily padded jumpsuit, a Bell helmet, pilot's gloves, logger's boots, a mountain climber's **rappelling line**, and a one-man emergency fire shelter.

It is 1987. Idaho. We are riding in a Forest Service DC-3. Below us, the 7,000-foot-deep Salmon River canyon falls away, and all around us glacier-gouged peaks rise over granite basins crowded with alpine lakes. In the cliffs above one lake, Partridge Lake, a wildfire is blazing.

We put on our helmets and lower the steel grids of our facemasks. We see the fire burning in a patch of firs near **treeline**. As we watch, whole trees explode. Fire rolls off their pointed tops and spins into the air. The fire flashes bright hot orange, a dazzling contrast to the cool granite grays and the dark greens of forest and meadow.

It is a wondrous sight, and in many ways this fire is natural and right. It was started by lightning, unseen and unaided by man. Now, its smoke gently wreathes the mountainside and drapes a meadow turned white with hail. There is nothing above the fire to burn, only snowbanks and rocks, and nothing around it but cliffs. We could argue to let this fire go, to let the fire run its natural course. But things are different below the fire. The mountainside descends into a heavy forest of tall fir, spruce, and ponderosa pine. If the fire rolls down the cliffs and into the forest, the whole canyon could erupt into flames. It has happened here before. In 1985, Catfish Bates jumped another small fire only ten miles northeast of here. A month later, the famed French Creek fire had consumed more than 14,000 acres.

We circle the fire. It attracts our eyes as if it were a flag waving in the wind, but we have to look past it now, to the cliffs and trees, all the obstacles that wait at the end of our jump. "Bad stuff down there," somebody says, and we all nod. But it is all beautiful to our eyes and it charges our hearts.

Our spotter, Barry Koncinsky, has dropped a set of crepe-paper streamers and we watch them drift. They show us the secret intentions of the invisible wind, how far our chutes might carry us. For a landing zone, we choose a long and narrow meadow separating two opposing cliffs. The cliff on the east side stands 800 feet tall. A jumble of **talus** lies at its base. The meadow itself is

● ● ● ● ● ● ● ●

"In many ways this fire is natural and right."

● ● ● ● ● ● ● ●

rappelling line—rope used by mountain climbers

treeline—elevation above which trees do not grow on mountainsides

talus—rock debris at the base of a cliff

## FOCUS ON... SCIENCE

An ecosystem is an ecological community together with its physical environment. An ecosystem is not confined or defined by size. It may be a square meter of a mountainside, a square mile of forest, a pond, an aquarium, an empty lot, or a farm. Research a small ecosystem by observing it. Find out what substances and organisms make up its main components. Create illustrations of the ecosystem and its components.

strewn with boulders and logs. A creek winds through them, then it leaps off a ledge and falls toward Partridge Lake. From this angle, Partridge Lake is a perfect mirror reflecting the stormy sky.

We decide we'll jump out above the mountain where two cliffs meet. Then we'll drift back with the wind and land in the long meadow.

We bank around and begin our first jump run. Tim and Catfish are the first out. They make sounds of small explosions as they charge into the wind. Their **static lines snake** after them and pull open their chutes. Their two canopies spin away. Barry pulls in the empty lines.

I hook my own static line to the cable by the door and place my left foot in the doorway, with my toes out in the wind. Barry crouches beside me. "Big things down there, Clay," he tells me, "and that's no lie. Have fun!" He puts his hand over my toe and puts his head into the blast. I feel Bob Shoemaker getting into position behind me. I grab both

sides of the doorway. The pilots steady the plane until it feels like a rock and I flex my knees, thinking, here comes, here comes. I search the horizon for a landmark peak and I lock my eyes on it.

Barry slaps my calf and I launch through the door, pushing for the peak. The **slipstream** grabs me, I pitch to my left and my parachute pops open above me, full and bright and beautiful. I take a breath. Wind and rain hit my face. I grab my guideline **toggles** and pull shut some guideslots to turn me back toward the meadow.

The taller cliff rises past me on my right, with patches of last winter's snow. I want to stay directly between the two cliffs, but the wind is funnelling here, and it causes my canopy to **oscillate**. I begin to swing like a watch on a chain, so I turn back toward the cliff and hold. I'm steady by the time I'm halfway down it. Tim and Catfish land near the end of the meadow. Bob is almost down. Now I see the rocks and logs again, everywhere. I do some last corrections

static lines— cords attached to a parachute pack and to an airplane to open the parachute after the jumper clears the plane

snake—wind or curl

slipstream—the stream of air driven backward by a propeller

toggles— handles used to control slots in a parachute to aid in steering

oscillate—swing back and forth

# SPOTLIGHT ON...
# WORKING
# COOPERATIVELY

Smokejumpers Morgan, Farrell, Bates, and Shoemaker work as a team. In such hazardous work as theirs, working cooperatively is essential to the team's survival. In any working relationship, people must work as a team. As you establish such working relationships, keep the following guidelines in mind:

- Discuss with your team members the nature of your goals and tasks.
- Divide the tasks up evenly among the members of the team.
- Discuss and resolve problems as they occur.
- Encourage each other and let your partners know you appreciate their efforts.

bivouac—
temporary camp

limbo—a
neutral,
temporary
waiting place

and get ready to hit. The ground rush is always hypnotic.

I land between two braids of the creek, in the middle of the meadow. I'm laughing. I hear the others hollering. The DC-3 makes a low pass over the fire and drops our food and fire gear. Through the trees, I can see the flames, about 100 yards above us. We are here, out of the sky, to fight that fire. For all of the natural and rational considerations, there is another reason we are here. We are humans. And to humans, fire is downright irresistible.

Fires are like human beings. They express themselves dramatically. And in the Western highlands, fires still call the shots. They dictate the progression of natural communities, of species succession, of life. Fly over the West on any summer day, over Alaska and British Columbia, over Washington, Oregon, Idaho, on down to New Mexico— usually a wildfire is in sight. Here in the

West, fire is common. In fact, most natural fires are as right as rain.

Right as rain. But the big ones can cause more destruction than the worst spring floods. . . .

For more than 50 years, the rule of the Forest Service was to stop every fire. That slowed the destruction, but without natural fire the forests filled up with fuel. Now, many fires are allowed to burn. They are monitored and studied, with the hope that their effects on nature will approximate nature itself. . . .

During a big fire, a fire camp springs up to sustain the hundreds of firefighters. This camp looks like a cross between a hobo convention and an army **bivouac**, just before retreat is sounded. The camp sprawls around for about two weeks, but while it lasts, it's a community.

It's a community like **limbo**. A fire camp is never as nice as where you came from, but it's more comfortable than where you're going. That's the inferno, the fireline, maybe a nightshift spent digging up rocks and dodging rolling boulders.

Fire camp consists of dozens of tents, arranged by the whims of geography. The tents range from the big Army wall tents to those bright little $300 jobs you can get from Eddie Bauer. The firebosses have the tents. The firefighters sleep in the open or under pieces of plastic. It's all the same, until it rains. Then the bosses can expect company.

If the fire camp is near a road, it has a kitchen trucked into it. In fireman's talk, the fire is "catered." You set up folding tables under awnings and eat your ham and mashed potatoes. If the fire camp is farther out, the food may be army C-rations. "Rats" is the firefighter's word for it: canned meat, canned fruit, and John Wayne crackers. You take your fruit can after you're done and you boil up your coffee. . . .

It's morning, before dawn, and I've got my nose in my coffee can. The coffee is hot and as hard as gasoline. It's been boiling in an oil tin that was run over by a jeep. The coffee curls my tongue and grits my teeth with ash and acid. I try to strain out the caffeine. The fire has bled the sky all night and the dawn seems to die in grays the smoke drags down and flattens around our feet. . . .

I keep my eyes above my coffee rim and look at my buddies. We start to grin. What are we, here, idiots? We love this life. We start to laugh. We can hear the helicopters spin awake across a meadow lost in smoke. We pick up our tools. The day shift will be hot.

Fighting forest fires is the best job I've ever had. Every summer, I gave up all my time. In return, I got to keep my bad habits and forget about routine. It was a life of guaranteed surprise. We'd fly in the jump plane over the wilderness, never knowing what was next. Maybe we'd parachute into a mountain glade, or into a solid canopy of tall Douglas fir. Or, maybe, we'd be in the doorway ready to jump—with our faces in the wind, our hearts in our throats, our muscles tense and shaking—and we'd be called back to base and sent somewhere else, to the Cascades near Canada, to the Gila near Old Mexico, or to the tundra north of Nome.

Our lives were sudden and changing and sometimes beyond our control. Out of control, we felt free. We felt like the fires. ❖

# ON THE JOB
## FIREFIGHTER

Firefighters help protect the public from the danger of fire. A high school education is generally sufficient background, but completion of community college courses in fire science may improve an applicant's chances for appointment. Firefighting is one of the most hazardous occupations. Because of its complex and dangerous nature, firefighting requires organization and teamwork. Applicants undergo a number of tests, including tests of strength and physical stamina, coordination, and agility. Many fire departments offer accredited apprenticeship programs.

# Wildfires in the West
Gary Visgaitis

NEWS WRITING

## August 15, 1994

With the wildfire season just half over, this year is shaping up to be one of the worst in recent history. A state-by-state look at fires and a comparison to previous years:

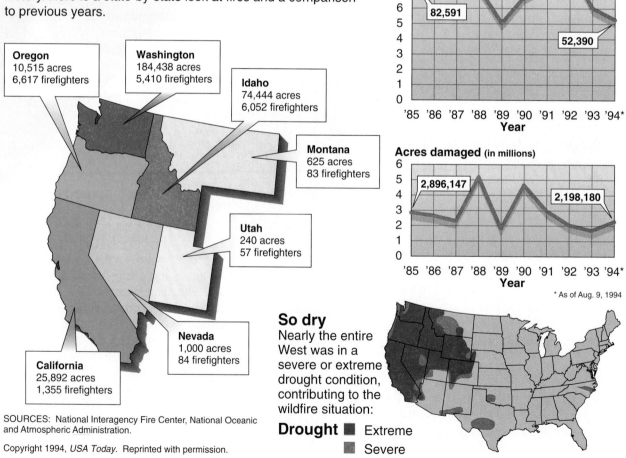

# Wildfires in the West

In 1994, the wildfire season was one of the worst in recent history. Here is a state-by-state look at fires and a comparison to previous years.

**Oregon**
10,515 acres
6,617 firefighters

**Washington**
184,438 acres
5,410 firefighters

**Idaho**
74,444 acres
6,052 firefighters

**Montana**
625 acres
83 firefighters

**Utah**
240 acres
57 firefighters

**Nevada**
1,000 acres
84 firefighters

**California**
25,892 acres
1,355 firefighters

**Number of fires** (in thousands)

82,591

52,390

'85 '86 '87 '88 '89 '90 '91 '92 '93 '94*
**Year**

**Acres damaged** (in millions)

2,896,147

2,198,180

'85 '86 '87 '88 '89 '90 '91 '92 '93 '94*
**Year**

* As of Aug. 9, 1994

## So dry
Nearly the entire West was in a severe or extreme drought condition, contributing to the wildfire situation:

**Drought** ■ Extreme
■ Severe

SOURCES: National Interagency Fire Center, National Oceanic and Atmospheric Administration.

Copyright 1994, *USA Today*. Reprinted with permission.

## UNDERSTANDING

1. The author describes in detail what the smokejumpers wear and do. Using phrases from the text, make a list of the smokejumpers' gear and activities. Circle the action verbs in these phrases. Using the action verbs as evidence, what can you conclude about the occupation of smokejumping? Write a topic sentence that states your conclusion. *Workshop 8*

2. In a simile, a writer compares one thing to another. The purpose of using a simile is to create a strong image in the reader's mind. Find examples of similes or comparisons Morgan uses in his essay. Next to each, draw a picture of the comparison as you see it in your mind.

3.  With a partner, find evidence in the text that suggests teamwork is a significant element of firefighting. Write a paragraph on teamwork and its role in firefighting. Start with a strong topic, or main idea, sentence and use examples from the article to prove your point. *Workshop 8*

4. Study the map and graphs on page 92. From the information given, write a news story on the fire situation. Present specific data clearly to help the reader understand the seriousness of the fires. In your lead, or opening sentence, "grab" the reader's attention. Then continue your article with answers to the questions *who, what, when, where,* and *why. Workshop 19*

## CONNECTING

1. Assume you are the fire dispatcher for the western United States. After reviewing the large map on page 92, you realize some firefighters must be shifted to handle the various sizes of fires. As dispatcher, you decide that the ratio of firefighters to acres burning should be 1 to 15. Based on that ratio, determine how many firefighters each state *should* have. Then decide which states should gain and which should lose firefighters. Now write a memo to all western state fire management supervisors to explain your plan for balancing the number of firefighters in the region. *Workshop 18*

2.  In groups, choose an occupation that involves extreme risks, such as search and rescue work, construction, or law enforcement. Research the occupation to discover the duties, skills, uniforms and gear, and other aspects of the job. Write a job description of someone in this occupation. *Workshop 10*

A LAST WORD

Smokejumpers such as Clay Morgan struggle against the natural elements of fire, wind, and rain as they battle forest fires. Why might firefighters be considered modern-day heroes? What hero qualities do firefighters display?

# Heroes at Risk

- *The Mission Continues*
- *Last Ride*

## EXPLORING

Heroes take risks to reach goals. Sometimes they know the risks are so great that their own safety is endangered, but many daring individuals ignore the danger. Name some adventurers who have acquired fame or whom we consider heroes because of the greatness of their achievements. Explain why they are heroes.

## THEME CONNECTION...
## LOST HEROES

Some heroes have risked and lost their lives, yet their fame lasts throughout the years. Martin Luther King, Jr., was murdered in the midst of his struggle for civil rights. The astronauts of the space shuttle *Challenger* planned to change history by taking the first civilian, a teacher, into space on January 28, 1986. Instead, they gave their lives. The memory of their courage continues to inspire their families, the nation, and the world.

## TIME & PLACE

In 1986, the space shuttle *Challenger* was launched into space in Cape Canaveral, Florida, with teacher Christa McAuliffe, the winner of NASA's space travel contest, on board. Millions of Americans, including schoolchildren, were watching the spectacle on television—and witnessed the burst of smoke as the mission failed.

## THE WRITER'S CRAFT
### BIAS IN WRITING

Many writers express their opinions on specific subjects in both fiction and nonfiction works. However, journalists must be careful to keep their writing free of personal commentary unless they are writing editorials. As readers, we should determine the author's purpose and keep it in mind as we evaluate and make judgments about what we read.

# The Mission Continues
Claudia Glenn Dowling

hree, two, one . . . "Roger. Go with throttle up," shuttle commander Dick Scobee radioed on a freezing January morning 10 years ago. His daughter Kathie, 25, huddled with her mother, brother and infant son on a roof at Cape Canaveral, along with the assembled families of the six other *Challenger* astronauts about to blast into space. She felt the rumble of liftoff and hugged her baby closer in the cold. "Wow, look how pretty," she said 74 seconds later. "Is that normal?" someone else in the crowd asked. "They're gone," said Jane, wife of pilot Michael Smith. "What do you mean, Mom?" asked her son. "They're lost," she replied. All over the country, the millions watching that awful bloom spread across their television screen realized that something had gone wrong before they heard the voice of Mission Control: "Obviously . . . a major malfunction." Blam.

The bolt out of the blue shattered the U.S. space program. The 25th shuttle flight was scheduled to kick off the busiest year ever for the National Aeronautics and Space Administration, a year in which Halley's comet would be observed, the Hubble telescope lofted and no fewer than 15 shuttle missions flown. Moreover, space travel for everyman was to be popularized by Christa McAuliffe, a gung-ho schoolteacher from Concord, N.H., selected from 11,000 applicants to be the first average American in space. Her motto was "reach for the stars." During four months of training at Johnson Space Center in Houston, Christa kidded that her greatest fear of flying was a waste compartment malfunction. Calling himself a "space husband," lawyer Steve McAuliffe cared for their two children, who seemed to take space exploration for granted. Christa, more aware of the risks, told LIFE's David Friend, "If anything happened, my husband would have to deal with that as the time came."

On January 28, 1986, as schoolchildren everywhere gazed skyward, what Christa had promised would be "the ultimate field trip" ended in disaster. The families were hustled off the roof, down elevators, into buses. Still bewildered, Kathie clung to baby Justin and eyed the NASA staff. "The looks on their faces told me something was really, absolutely, terribly wrong," she recalls. The families waited for the news in the crew's quarters. Steve McAuliffe, with Scott, nine, and Caroline, six, sat in Christa's dorm room, her sneakers still on the floor. "This is not how it's supposed to be," he said.

Mission Control turned rapidly to spin control. Rather than delivering the State of the Union address that evening as scheduled, President Ronald Reagan made a brief speech. "We'll continue our

## About the Author
The managing editor of *Life* magazine refers to Claudia Dowling as a writer "who can do anything." Dowling has been a writer for *Life* for more than 13 years. In that time, she has done remarkable things to get a story, such as paddling the Amazon with a Cofan Indian chief, making an emergency landing in Kyrgyzstan, and climbing 21,500 feet up Mount Everest.

quest in space," he promised traumatized Americans, for whom the word *shuttle* had once sounded so routine. "There will be more shuttle flights and more shuttle crews and, yes, more volunteers, more civilians, more teachers in space." But there would be no shuttle flights for almost three years. There would be no teacher in space. And for those left on the ground, for the families of the seven adventurers who died, there would be years of bitterness, of grief and pain and anger before, finally, lives could heal. On the tenth anniversary of the explosion, this January 28, the *Challenger* commander's son, Rich Scobee, now an Air Force pilot, will fly his F-16 over the Super Bowl in Tempe, Ariz., leading a formation of jets in a memorial tribute.

Ten years ago, NASA planes flew the McAuliffes home to New Hampshire, the Scobees and three other families who lived near Johnson Space Center back to Houston. Each family was assigned an astronaut to help out— to run interference with the reporters camped on their lawns, respond to roomfuls of mail, arrange insurance payments. In the midst of their own mourning, the parents' first concern was for the children. Cheryl, the wife of astronaut Ronald McNair and a technical writer for NASA explained to her toddlers that "we won't be able to see Daddy anymore, physically, but that we would be able to feel him, spiritually." In addition to their grief, the children had practical worries. Hawaiian-born astronaut Ellison Onizuka's daughters asked:

● ● ● ● ● ● ●
## "Twenty-four other shuttle flights went off O.K."
● ● ● ● ● ● ●

"Are we going to have enough money to eat? Am I like a child from a divorced family? Will we still live in this house?" Recalls mother Lorna, "There were so many things to be done, so many wounds to **salve**."

In those early months, the Houston women often gathered in the Scobees' living room. "As the commander's wife I felt such responsibility," recalls June. "I needed help myself, and I was trying to carry the weight of the world." With new information, the wounds reopened. At the outset of a search for shuttle debris that would take seven months, 31 ships, 52 aircraft and 6,000 workers, Christa McAuliffe's lesson plans for space were found floating in the Atlantic Ocean. The crew compartment was found 40 days later. When the bodies were brought up, it became clear that some of the astronauts had been alive during the three-to-four-minute fall to the sea.

Shortly after the last funerals were held, a commission chaired by former Secretary of State William Rogers revealed the conclusions of its investigation: The explosion of the $1.2 billion spacecraft was due to a faulty O-ring seal on the solid rocket fuel booster, a $900 synthetic rubber band that engineers had warned was vulnerable at temperatures below 51°. The *Challenger* launch, canceled three times, had finally taken place in 36° weather. The Rogers Commission found both the company that made the O-rings, Morton Thiokol, and NASA itself guilty of allowing an avoidable accident to occur.

## SPOTLIGHT ON...
## INTERPERSONAL SKILLS

For the families of the *Challenger* astronauts, "the mission continues." Whether founding a center to promote space science for kids, working for a foundation for teenage mothers, or continuing their work for NASA, these people work together to lead and teach others. You can develop and strengthen your interpersonal skills by practicing these tasks:

- Work on teams.
- Teach and share information with others.
- Negotiate resolutions to problems.
- Work with people from culturally diverse backgrounds.

The survivors' first response was anger. "It shouldn't have happened," says Christa's mother, Grace Corrigan. "They were told not to launch, and they decided, 'Twenty-four other shuttle flights went off O.K.' They were **complacent**."

The government scrambled to settle with the survivors. In December 1986, the families of Christa McAuliffe, Ellison Onizuka, Bruce Jarvis and Dick Scobee accepted some $7.7 million from the U.S. and Morton Thiokol. The unrevealed sums designated for each family were based on age and number of dependents of the deceased. The families of Ronald McNair and unmarried astronaut Judith Resnick sued Morton Thiokol and settled independently more than a year later, reportedly for multiple millions. The last suit to be resolved was that of Jane Smith, who, on the second anniversary of the *Challenger* accident, filed a $1.5 billion suit against Morton Thiokol. "No one in big business should be allowed to make a faulty product and profit from it," she said. Her suit was settled for an undisclosed sum in 1988, just before the shuttle resumed flying. Like several of the other widows— Cheryl McNair works for a foundation for teenage mothers, and Marcia Jarvis clears hiking trails near her Mammoth Mountain, Calif., home—Jane has a favorite charity, the Virginia Beach Society for the Prevention of Cruelty to Animals. Her dogs, she says, helped her through mourning. Despite her marriage five years ago to a Naval Academy pal of her first husband's and a move to Virginia, she still misses Mike Smith every day: "I waited, and he never came back."

At the time of the accident, television host Larry King asked June Scobee, "Do you think you will ever remarry?" She responded, "Dick Scobee loved me enough to last a lifetime." But two and a half years afterward, she felt "alone." Her son, Rich, was in the Air Force, as his father would have wished. Her

complacent— unconcerned, unwilling to act

daughter, Katie, had her own problems with an unraveling marriage. And suddenly, June found, "I couldn't function." She checked into a hospital, then saw a psychologist. "I knew that I had to let Dick Scobee go," she says. In 1989 she married Lt. Gen. Don Rodgers, whose wife had died, and they moved to Tennessee. For her part, after agonizing about a decision contrary to her Christian upbringing, daughter Katie got a divorce: "Daddy was so young when he died—I just thought, life is too short."

There were delayed reactions in other families, too. Lorna Onizuka, who hasn't remarried, noticed the changed dynamics without a man in the house: "He was an **equilibrium** for us. With no El to come in and say, 'Ladies,' it was like a den of she-lions." When she overheard her younger girl "talking" to her father on the telephone, she built a house without so many memories. In her attic is a cedar closet storing her husband's fishing

tackle and flight bag. On the household's Buddhist altar, she makes offerings of flowers [and] favorite foods . . . . The older daughter, now out of college, works for NASA like her mother, who deals with the Japanese space agency. "Ten years down the road, there are still moments that my daughters break down and cry," Lorna says. "Moments, usually, of accomplishment. When one wins a soccer tournament, when she's invited to be a debutante and doesn't have her father to escort her, when she graduates and we're missing one person." But the anger has long passed. "I could spend the rest of my life being angry at something I couldn't change," says Lorna. "My husband believed that this mission was worth his life."

The families wanted a living memorial. "We didn't want to dwell on how the crew died, but what they had lived for," says Chuck Resnick, brother of astronaut Judy. June Scobee quit her job

## FOCUS ON...
## SCIENCE

At the Challenger Center, teams of students study space science. With a small group, research the process of launching a space probe. Then write a report that describes the process of a space probe launch. Your team may also wish to prepare a three-dimensional model of a space probe that helps illustrate the launch process.

◆ ◆ ◆ ◆ ◆ ◆ ◆ ◆ ◆ ◆ ◆ ◆ ◆ ◆ ◆ ◆ ◆ ◆ ◆ ◆ ◆

## ACCENT ON...
## SAFETY
## TECHNOLOGY
● ● ● ● ● ● ● ● ● ● ● ● ● ● ● ● ● ● ● ● ●

A faulty product caused the tragic explosion of the space shuttle *Challenger*. The astronauts' families strongly felt that businesses should not be allowed to profit from the production and sale of faulty products. Discuss with local manufacturers ways in which modern technology is currently used to create safe, accurate products.

as an education professor at the University of Houston to found the Challenger Center, an organization promoting space science for kids. Members of each of the seven astronauts' families sit on the board. Among the initial supporters: Morton Thiokol and Rockwell International, which built the orbiter.

"O.K., astronauts, let's go." A team of fifth-graders at a Challenger Center in Framingham, Mass., one of 30 around the U.S., receives its orders: Launch a probe to Halley's comet. "We don't dwell on the sad part," says teacher Mary Liscombe. "We say, 'The mission continues.'" Grace Corrigan, who lives nearby, often visits the center, which she supports with proceeds of her 1993 book, *A Journal for Christa*. "That's Christa's mom," the kids whisper. Christa's own kids, kept out of the public eye, are big now. Scott is in college, downloading musical riffs from the Internet. Caroline is 16 and a horsewoman. Their father, now a federal judge, took up flying and, three years ago, married a reading teacher. He too supports the centers. The faculty nationwide includes some of the 114 Teacher in Space finalists—not least, Christa's backup, Idaho teacher **Barbara Morgan.** NASA chief Daniel Goldin has appointed a committee to decide whether to end the Teacher in Space program. But for now, Barbara, 44, still has a flight physical

every year. "What happened was horrible, and you can't ever erase that," she says. "But our job as teachers is to help kids reach their potential. *Challenger* reminds us that we should never quit reaching for the stars."

One frequent visitor to the Challenger Center in Houston is Dick Scobee's grandson, the infant in Katie's arms when she watched that fatal flowering in the sky. "I like the shuttle simulator best," says Justin. "It would be fun in space. You can float because it's **zero g**. I would like to become an astronaut." ❖

zero g—zero gravity; the absence of gravity's pull in space allows the astronauts to float inside the orbiter

Note of interest: Barbara Morgan is the wife of Clay Morgan—smokejumper and author of "Natural and Right."

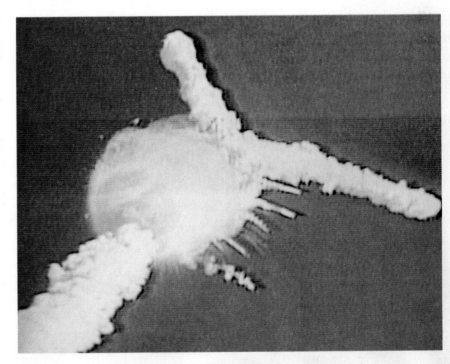

# *Last Ride*

Andrea Holtslander

We watch in horror as
the booster rockets twist
crazily through the sky
like balloons
whipped free
From a child's grasp.

The horror is the reality on the screen.

"On this day of tragedy . . . we watch in horror
as . . ."
    And for the benefit of those who
missed the live show
                we will run the
                fireworks once again.

    The spotlight moves to the grief-stricken
families and we can have our
                heart-strings pulled
    with 20 million others
as we watch their
tears fall,
        LIVE.

    Having wrung all the tears from his
audience the ringmaster can now turn to sports
          as seven families try to put
    together their lives
                scattered over the Atlantic
                Ocean. ❖

# UNDERSTANDING

1.  Make a list of all the people Dowling interviewed for her article "The Mission Continues." Write a journal entry describing the effort and amount of work it would take to compile this information. With a group, assemble a list of personal qualities, skills, and attitudes needed to research and write nonfiction articles.

2. In "Last Ride" the poet comments on more than just the *Challenger* disaster. Write a thesis statement—one sentence that tells what the poet's purpose is. Discuss the issue of news coverage of major events and its impact on the audience.

3. Compare Dowling's purpose in the article with Holtslander's purpose in the poem. Write a paragraph describing, comparing, and contrasting the author's and poet's purposes. ***Workshops 8 and 15***

## A LAST WORD

Christa McAuliffe's motto was "reach for the stars." How can you adopt that motto as your own and reach for the stars?

# CONNECTING

1. Research other disasters that have had worldwide news coverage. For instance, you might investigate the Apollo 13 near-disaster, or the eruption of Mt. Pinatubo. Design a poster with drawings that show details of the situation and its causes and consequences. Display your poster and explain your findings in an oral presentation. ***Workshop 25***

2. Watch a 30-minute local news program on television. As you watch, take notes on the stories presented and the reporting style. Determine whether the news is reported in a straightforward manner or presented out of proportion to its actual importance or content. Assume you are the editor in a newsroom. Write a memo to the reporters, film crews, and programming department outlining the network's policy on objective and balanced news reporting. ***Workshop 18***

# The Courage to Dream

- *Dreams*
- *I Have a Dream*

## EXPLORING

Heroism is greatness, and heroes are those who win the admiration of many through the courage and strength of their actions and beliefs. Today's heroes are honest, generous, and intelligent, have deep convictions, and work toward positive change. The timeless quality of their fame sets them apart from celebrities, whose fame passes quickly. List three people you believe have these heroic qualities because they fight for positive change. How does each qualify as a hero?

## THEME CONNECTION... HERO FOR A CAUSE

In a world full of dreamers and doers, heroes are those who hold onto their visions of how the world should be and take action to realize those visions.

## TIME & PLACE

On August 28, 1963, Martin Luther King, Jr., stood on the steps of the Lincoln Memorial and shared with America his dream of racial equality. King had called for a "March on Washington" to wage civil protest for equal rights. This peaceful demonstration was a turning point in King's life. The "I Have a Dream" speech drew national attention to causes King had been promoting for many years throughout the South.

## THE WRITER'S CRAFT

### METAPHOR

In both prose and poetry, authors use metaphors to create vivid images in readers' minds. A metaphor makes a comparison between two ideas or things by stating that one *is* the other, rather than saying that one is *like* the other (as in a simile). Metaphors are stronger than similes—they actually identify one thing as another. Consider the difference between "Mornings at my house *are like* a fire drill," and "Mornings at my house *are* a fire drill." In the second example, the metaphor makes the image more vivid for the reader.

## Dreams

Langston Hughes

Hold fast to dreams
For if dreams die
Life is a broken-winged bird
That cannot fly.

Hold fast to dreams
For when dreams go
Life is a barren field
Frozen with snow. ❖

### About the Author

Langston Hughes (1902–1967) grew up in Lawrence, Kansas, and in Cleveland, Ohio. After a year at Columbia University, he withdrew to write. He supported himself by serving as messman on ships in Africa and Europe and washing dishes in a Paris night club. By 1929, Hughes had published two books of poetry including *The Weary Blues.* These works confirmed his status as the best poet of the 1920s Harlem Renaissance, a period when Harlem, New York, blossomed as a cultural center.

# I Have a Dream

Martin Luther King, Jr.

*Washington D.C.,*
*August 28, 1963*

am happy to join with you today in what will go down in history as the greatest demonstration for freedom in the history of our nation.

**Fivescore** years ago, a great American, in whose symbolic shadow we stand today, signed the Emancipation Proclamation. This momentous decree came as a great beacon light of hope to millions of Negro slaves who had been seared in the flames of withering injustice. It came as a joyous daybreak to end the long night of their captivity.

But one hundred years later, the Negro still is not free; one hundred years later, the life of the Negro is still sadly crippled by the **manacles** of segregation and the chains of discrimination; one hundred years later, the Negro lives on a lonely island of poverty in the midst of a vast ocean of material prosperity; one hundred years later, the Negro is still languished in the corners of American society and finds himself in exile in his own land.

So we've come here today to dramatize a shameful condition. In a sense we've come to our nation's capital to cash a check. When the architects of our republic wrote the magnificent words of the Constitution and the Declaration of Independence, they were signing a **promissory note** to which every American was to fall heir. This note was the promise that all men, yes, black men as well as white men, would be guaranteed the unalienable rights of life, liberty, and the pursuit of happiness.

It is obvious today that America has **defaulted** on this promissory note in so far as her citizens of color are concerned. Instead of honoring this sacred obligation, America has given the Negro people a bad check; a check which has come back marked "insufficient funds." We refuse to believe that there are insufficient funds in the great vaults of opportunity of this nation. And so we've come to cash this check, a check that will give us upon demand the riches of freedom and the security of justice.

We have also come to this **hallowed** spot to remind America of the fierce urgency of now. This is no time to engage in the luxury of cooling off or to take the **tranquilizing** drug of

> "Now is the time to lift our nation from the quicksands of racial injustice to the solid rock of brotherhood."

**fivescore**—100 years, since a score is 20 years

**manacles**—a type of handcuff once used on African slaves

**promissory note**—a written promise to pay a sum of money in the future

In his speech, Martin Luther King, Jr., pleads for justice and freedom. When trying to bring about change, whether to improve your community or your own skills, you should plan carefully. You can use the following steps as a starting point.

1. Identify the change you want to make.
2. Lay out your plan in a logical manner.
3. List specific ways in which change can be successfully achieved.
4. Itemize the resources needed, including time, money, and human effort.
5. Plan ways to acquire those resources.
6. Review your plan periodically and update it if necessary.

**gradualism.** Now is the time to make real the promises of democracy; now is the time to rise from the dark and desolate valley of segregation to the sunlit path of racial justice; now is the time to lift our nation from the quicksands of racial injustice to the solid rock of brotherhood; now is the time to make justice a reality for all God's children. It would be fatal for the nation to overlook the urgency of the moment. This **sweltering** summer of the Negro's **legitimate** discontent will not pass until there is an invigorating autumn of freedom and equality.

Nineteen sixty-three is not an end, but a beginning. And those who hope that the Negro needed to blow off steam and will now be content, will have a rude awakening if the nation returns to business as usual.

There will be neither rest nor tranquility in America until the Negro is granted his citizenship rights. The whirlwinds of revolt will continue to shake the foundations of our nation until the bright day of justice emerges.

But there is something that I must say to my people who stand on the warm threshold which leads into the palace of justice. In the process of gaining our rightful place we must not be guilty of wrongful deeds.

Let us not seek to satisfy our thirst for freedom by drinking from the cup of bitterness and hatred. We must forever conduct our struggle on the high plane of dignity and discipline. We must not allow our creative protest to **degenerate** into physical violence. Again and again we must rise to the majestic heights of meeting physical force with soul force.

defaulted—
failed to meet an
obligation

hallowed—
sacred

tranquilizing—
excessively
calming

gradualism—
taking action
over an
extended period
of time

sweltering—
extremely hot

legitimate—
rightful

degenerate—
sink

The marvelous new militancy which has engulfed the Negro community must not lead us to a distrust of all white people, for many of our white brothers, as evidenced by their presence here today, have come to realize that their destiny is tied up with our destiny and they have come to realize that their freedom is **inextricably** bound to our freedom. This offense we share mounted to storm the battlements of injustice must be carried forth by a biracial army. We cannot walk alone.

And as we walk, we must make the pledge that we shall always march ahead. We cannot turn back. There are those who are asking the **devotees** of civil rights, "When will you be satis- fied?" We can never be satisfied as long as the Negro is the victim of the unspeakable horrors of police brutality.

We can never be satisfied as long as our bodies, heavy with fatigue of travel, cannot gain lodging in the motels of the highways and the hotels of the cities. We cannot be satisfied as long as the Negro's basic mobility is from a smaller ghetto to a larger one.

We can never be satisfied as long as our children are stripped of their self- hood and robbed of their dignity by signs stating "for whites only." We cannot be satisfied as long as a Negro in Mississippi cannot vote and a Negro in New York believes he has nothing for which to vote. No, we are not satisfied, and we will not be satisfied until justice rolls down like waters and righteousness like a mighty stream.

I am not unmindful that some of you come here out of excessive trials and **tribulation.** Some of you have come fresh from narrow jail cells. Some of you have come from areas where your quest for freedom left you battered by the storms of persecution and staggered by the winds of police brutality. You have been the veterans of creative suffering. Continue to work with the faith that unearned suffering is **redemptive.**

Go back to Mississippi; go back to Alabama; go back to South Carolina; go back to Georgia; go back to Louisiana; go back to the slums and ghettos of the northern cities, knowing that somehow this situation can, and will be changed. Let us not **wallow** in the valley of despair.

So I say to you, my friends, that even though we must face the difficulties of today and tomorrow, I still have a dream. It is a dream deeply rooted in the American dream that one day this nation will rise up and live out the true meaning of its creed—we hold these truths to be self-evident, that all men are created equal.

I have a dream that one day on the red hills of Georgia, sons of former slaves and sons of former slave-owners will be able to sit down together at the table of brotherhood . . . .

I have a dream my four little children will one day live in a nation where they will not be judged by the color of their skin but by the content of their character. I have a dream today! . . .

I have a dream that one day **every valley** shall be exalted, every hill and mountain shall be made low, the rough places shall be made plain, and the crooked places shall be made straight and the glory of the Lord will be revealed and all flesh shall see it together.

This is our hope. This is the faith that I go back to the South with.

With this faith we will be able to hew out of the mountain of despair a stone of hope. With this faith we will be able to transform the jangling **discords** of our nation into a beautiful symphony of brotherhood.

With this faith we will be able to work together, to pray together, to struggle together, to go to jail together, to stand up for freedom together, knowing that we will be free one day. This will be the day when all of God's children will be able to sing with new meaning—"my country 'tis of thee; sweet land of liberty; of thee I sing; land where my fathers died, land of the pilgrim's pride; from every mountain side, let freedom ring"—and if America is to be a great nation, this must become true.

So let freedom ring from the **prodigious** hilltops of New Hampshire.

Let freedom ring from the mighty mountains of New York.

Let freedom ring from the heightening Alleghenies of Pennsylvania.

Let freedom ring from the snow-capped Rockies of Colorado.

Let freedom ring from the **curvaceous** slopes of California.

But not only that.

Let freedom ring from Stone Mountain of Georgia.

Let freedom ring from Lookout Mountain of Tennessee.

Let freedom ring from every hill and molehill of Mississippi, from every mountainside, let freedom ring.

And when we allow freedom to ring, when we let it ring from every village and hamlet, from every state and city, we will be able to speed up that day when all of God's children—black men and white men, Jews and Gentiles, Catholics and Protestants—will be able to join hands and to sing in the words of the old Negro spiritual, "Free at last, free at last; thank God Almighty, we are free at last." ❖

discords—con-
tradictions; in
music, tones
that are out of
harmony

prodigious—
numerous and
lofty

curvaceous—
rolling, hilly

## ACCENT ON...
### LAW

In his speech, Martin Luther King, Jr., talks about justice and equality for all. Working with social studies or history students, discuss existing laws that protect against discrimination based on race, religion, and gender. What other laws are pending? Write to a congressional representative or local politician in support of any current rights legislation.

## FOCUS ON...
### HISTORY

Martin Luther King, Jr., delivered the memorable "I Have a Dream" speech at the March on Washington on August 28, 1963. This event was the climax of the civil rights movement. Find out about the March on Washington and the Freedom Marchers who demonstrated in support of the civil rights legislation that was pending in Congress. What legislation was enacted because of this massive, nonviolent demonstration?

# UNDERSTANDING

1. In "Dreams," Langston Hughes uses two distinct metaphors to describe the loss of one's dreams. Write a paragraph to explain each metaphor and how you envision its connection to a lost dream. Then create a sketch, painting, or photo of the image Hughes creates. *Workshop 8*

2. Make a list of direct quotations from King's speech that are metaphors. In a second column, describe each image King creates.

3.  King spoke for a specific audience and purpose. With a partner, agree on King's purpose. Then find lines in the speech that directly state this purpose.

4. The "I Have a Dream" speech is written as a persuasive essay. Outline the major points or arguments King makes. What is his "call to action" at the end?
    Write an essay to persuade someone to change his or her behavior. Start with a statement of what the problem is and what change must occur. Then list in logical order the reasons for change and the goals the change will meet. Conclude with an emphasis on the importance of the new behavior and how it will affect future outcomes. Present your essay to the class as a persuasive speech. *Workshops 13 and 25*

5. Poet Gwendolyn Brooks wrote a tribute poem to Martin Luther King, Jr., in which she said, "He was a prose poem. He was a tragic grace. He was a warm music." What images do these metaphors create in your mind?
    Write a poem as a tribute to someone you respect, such as a parent, teacher or mentor, coach, or friend. Begin by brainstorming a list of that person's qualities and why those are important. Focus on a few major characteristics of the person. Use metaphor in your poem to let readers "see" this person as you do.

## A LAST WORD

More than 30 years have passed since Martin Luther King, Jr., gave his "I Have a Dream" speech. What can we do to keep his dream for America alive?

# CONNECTING

1. Martin Luther King, Jr., had a cause for which he fought and to which he dedicated his life. Discover service programs or clubs in your town or community that improve the health, safety, or lifestyles of residents. The Lions Club, Jaycees, Hospice, and Red Cross are just a few common community organizations. In groups, choose a service club to contact. Develop a list of questions for a phone interview with a leader of the organization. Ask for information on the projects the organization undertakes, the services it provides, who may

become a member, and how many members exist. Design a flier promoting the group's programs and encouraging membership. If possible, volunteer to participate in an activity. ***Workshops 20 and 26***

2. Working with several classmates, choose an aspect of King's life to research: his childhood, education, beliefs and teachings, or role in the politics of the 1960s, or the effects of the civil rights movement and the changes it brought. Write a dialogue between King and another person. Through King's words, allow listeners to learn some specific information about his life, his teachings, his beliefs, or the civil rights movement. Present your dialogue for the class or tape it as a radio program. ***Workshop 21***

# WRAP IT UP

1. Langston Hughes urges, "Hold fast to dreams." Think about the real-life heroes in "Natural and Right," "The Mission Continues," and "I Have a Dream." How do these people react to the difficult situations or tragedies they encounter? How do they hold fast to their dreams? What similarities exist between holding fast to dreams and having a heroic spirit?

2. In "Why Gartersnake Wears a Green Blanket" "Daedalus," and the excerpt from *The Odyssey,* mythic characters perform courageous, wise, and heroic deeds. Describe the meaning of the word *hero* and explain the significance of the heroes in these particular stories.

   Each family and culture keeps its spirit and identity alive through stories, myths, and legends. What stories are repeated in your family? At what special occasions are they told? Do certain characters or people appear in the stories? Explain the significance of these stories to your family.

3. What are the similarities and differences between celebrities and heroes? Make a list of characteristics that define true heroes.

# UNIT ③

# ACTION AND REACTION

*In physics we learn that every action causes a reaction. This is also true in our daily lives. We must constantly act or react to someone or something. What we do or say can solve problems or cause bigger ones. Our actions can overcome obstacles or create new ones.*

*Some people think that their lives depend on other people's decisions or on luck. The fact is, most people have more control over their lives than they realize. Things don't just happen to them. Their happiness or unhappiness is often a result of their own actions and reactions.*

**LITERATURE**

**350 B.C.**

**1880** de Maupassant publishes a short story titled "Ball of Fat."

**1941** Jeanne W. Houston and her family enter an internment camp.

**1948** Fredric Brown wins Edgar Allan Poe Award for *The Fabulous Clipjoint.*

**1972** Wallace Stegner wins Pulitzer Prize for *Angle of Repose.*

200 B.C.    1830    1840    1920    1930

**350 B.C.** Chinese begin to use round bronze coins as money.

**200 B.C.** An ancient Asian king is the first to study poisoning.

**1838** Henry Brougham designs a one-horse carriage.

**1869** The first Japanese settle in the United States.

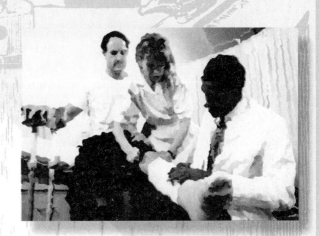

**LIFE and WORK**

# The Necklace

## EXPLORING

Throughout the world, advertisers tempt people to try new products, buy better cars, or move to finer homes. The push to have bigger and better things can make us dissatisfied with what we *do* have and envious of those who have what we do not. Sometimes we think that if we have more possessions we will be happier. Consider the things you *need* and the things you *want*. How do they differ? If you possessed everything you *needed,* would you be happy? If you possessed everything you *wanted,* would you be happier?

## THEME CONNECTION...
## THE EFFECTS OF PRIDE

Pride and ambition can be the ruin of a person who allows these traits to overpower good sense. The main character of this classic French short story suffers such a disaster, followed by a tragic twist of fate, all brought on by her own actions. Because she wants more than she has, this character's pride changes her life entirely.

## TIME & PLACE

"The Necklace" is set in Paris during the late 1800s. Madame Loisel and her husband are on the fringes of the French aristocracy, or ruling class. As an employee of the Ministry of Education, Madame Loisel's husband is a lower-ranking government official. They are close enough to the French aristocracy to be aware of fancy parties and social customs, but they do not have the money to keep up with the material requirements of the upper classes.

## THE WRITER'S CRAFT
### CHARACTERIZATION

Writers characterize, or show the qualities of characters, in a number of ways. First, readers learn about characters from their words and actions. Then, a writer's physical description helps readers "see" characters. Finally, readers learn about characters through the words, thoughts, and actions of *other* characters.

# The Necklace
## Guy de Maupassant

She was one of those pretty, charming young women who are born, as if by an error of Fate, into a petty official's family. She had no **dowry,** no hopes, not the slightest chance of being appreciated, understood, loved, and married by a rich and distinguished man; so she slipped into marriage with a minor civil servant at the Ministry of Education.

Unable to afford jewelry, she dressed simply; but she was as wretched as a *déclassée,* for women have neither caste nor breeding—-in them beauty, grace, and charm replace pride of birth. **Innate** refinement, instinctive elegance, and suppleness of wit give them their place on the only scale that counts, and these qualities make humble girls the peers of the grandest ladies.

She suffered constantly, feeling that all the attributes of a gracious life, every luxury, should rightly have been hers. The poverty of her rooms—-the shabby walls, the worn furniture, the ugly uphol-stery-—caused her pain. All these things that another woman of her class would not even have noticed, tormented her and made her angry. The very sight of the little **Breton** girl who cleaned for her awoke **rueful** thoughts and the wildest dreams in her mind. She dreamt of thick-carpeted reception rooms with Oriental hangings, lighted by tall, bronze torches, and with two huge footmen in knee breeches, made drowsy by the heat from the stove, asleep in the wide armchairs. She dreamt of great drawing rooms upholstered in old silks, with fragile little tables holding priceless knickknacks, and of enchanting little sitting rooms **redolent** of perfume, designed for tea-time chats with intimate friends—- famous, sought-after men whose attentions all women longed for.

When she sat down to dinner at her round table with its three-day-old cloth, and watched her husband opposite her lift the lid of the soup **tureen** and exclaim, delighted: "Ah, a good homemade beef stew! There's nothing better . . ." she would visualize elegant dinners with gleaming silver amid tapestried walls peopled by knights and ladies and exotic birds in a fairy forest; she would think of exquisite dishes served on gorgeous china, and of **gallantries** whispered and received with **sphinx-like** smiles while eating the pink flesh of trout or wings of grouse.

She had no proper wardrobe, no jewels, nothing. And those were the only things that she loved—-she felt she was made for them. She would have so loved to charm, to be envied, to be admired and sought after.

She had a rich friend, a schoolmate from the convent she had attended, but

dowry—the property that a woman brings to her husband at marriage

*déclassée*—a woman who has fallen in social position

innate—inborn; possessed at birth

Breton—a person from the French province of Brittany

rueful—regretful

redolent—full of fragrance

tureen—large serving bowl

gallantries—polite gestures or remarks

sphinx-like—mysterious

Georges Ramponneau—pronounced ZHORZH rahm puh NO

M. and Mme. Loisel—Monsieur and Madame, the French equivalent of *Mr. and Mrs;* pronounced Iwa ZEL

Mathilde—pronounced mah TELD

she didn't like to visit her because it always made her so miserable when she got home again. She would weep for whole days at a time from sorrow, regret, despair, and distress.

Then one evening her husband arrived home looking triumphant and having a large envelope.

"There," he said, "there's something for you."

She tore it open eagerly and took out a printed card which said:

"The Minister of Education and Madame **Georges Ramponneau** request the pleasure of the company of **M. and Mme. Loisel** at an evening reception at the Ministry on Monday, January 18th."

Instead of being delighted, as her husband had hoped, she tossed the invitation on the table and muttered, annoyed:

"What do you expect me to do with that?"

"Why, I thought you'd be pleased, dear. You never go out and this would be an occasion for you, a great one! I had a lot of trouble getting it. Everyone wants an invitation; they're in great demand and there are only a few reserved for the employees. All the officials will be there."

She looked at him, irritated, and said impatiently:

"I haven't a thing to wear. How could I go?"

It had never even occurred to him. He stammered:

"But what about the dress you wear to the theater? I think it's lovely . . ."

He fell silent, amazed and bewildered to see that his wife was crying. Two big tears escaped from the corners of her eyes and rolled slowly toward the corners of her mouth. He mumbled:

"What is it? What is it?"

But, with great effort, she had overcome her misery; and now she answered him calmly, wiping her tear-damp cheeks:

"It's nothing. It's just that I have no evening dress and so I can't go to the party. Give the invitation to one of your colleagues whose wife will be better dressed than I would be."

He was overcome. He said:

"Listen, **Mathilde,** how much would an evening dress cost—-a suitable one that you could wear again on other occasions, something very simple?"

She thought for several seconds, making her calculations and at the same time estimating how much she could ask for without **eliciting** an immediate refusal and an exclamation of horror from this economical government clerk.

At last, not too sure of herself, she said:

"It's hard to say exactly but I think I could manage with four hundred francs."

He went a little pale, for that was exactly the amount he had put aside to buy a rifle so that he could go hunting the following summer near Nanterre, with a few friends who went shooting larks around there on Sundays.

However, he said:

"Well, all right, then. I'll give you four hundred francs. But try to get something really nice."

As the day of the ball drew closer, Madame Loisel seemed depressed, disturbed, worried—despite the fact that her dress was ready. One evening her husband said:

"What's the matter? You've really been very strange these last few days."

And she answered:

"I hate not having a single jewel, not one stone, to wear. I shall look so **dowdy.** I'd almost rather not go to the party."

He suggested:

"You can wear some fresh flowers. It's considered very **chic** at this time of year. For ten francs you can get two or three beautiful roses."

That didn't satisfy her at all.

"No . . . there's nothing more humiliating than to look poverty-stricken among a lot of rich women."

Then her husband exclaimed:

"Wait—you silly thing! Why don't you go and see Madame Forestier and ask her to lend you some jewelry. You certainly know her well enough for that, don't you think?"

She let out a joyful cry.

"You're right. It never occurred to me."

The next day she went to see her friend and related her tale of woe.

Madame Forestier went to her mirrored wardrobe, took out a big jewel case, brought it to Madame Loisel, opened it, and said:

"Take your pick, my dear."

Her eyes wandered from some bracelets to a pearl necklace, then to a gold Venetian cross set with stones, of very fine workmanship. She tried on the jewelry before the mirror, hesitating, unable to bring herself to take them off, to give them back. And she kept asking:

"Do you have anything else, by chance?"

"Why yes. Here, look for yourself. I don't know which ones you'll like."

All at once, in a box lined with black satin, she came upon a superb diamond necklace, and her heart started beating with overwhelming desire. Her hands trembled as she picked it up. She fastened it around her neck over her high-necked dress and stood there gazing at herself **ecstatically.**

Hesitantly, filled with terrible anguish, she asked:

"Could you lend me this one—just this and nothing else?"

"Yes, of course."

She threw her arms around her friend's neck, kissed her ardently, and fled with her treasure.

eliciting—bringing out

dowdy—shabby

chic—fashionable

ecstatically—excitedly and extremely happily

# SPOTLIGHT ON...
# MAKING INFERENCES

In the short story "The Necklace," the narrator does not tell the reader exactly what Madame or Monsieur Loisel believes or feels. Rather, he lets the reader infer, or conclude, what each character is like based on evidence, or context clues, in the story. The author may give you the following context clues:

- Comparison of the character to others
- Examples of behaviors that are clues to the character's personality
- Supplying details about the character's surroundings, possessions, or relationships.

◆ ◆ ◆ ◆ ◆ ◆ ◆ ◆ ◆ ◆ ◆ ◆ ◆ ◆ ◆ ◆ ◆ ◆ ◆ ◆ ◆ ◆ ◆ ◆ ◆

**enraptured—**
filled with delight

**homage—**publicly expressed honor or respect

**Seine—**pronounced SEN; a river flowing through Paris

**broughams—**pronounced BROHMZ; horse-drawn carriages

The day of the party arrived. Madame Loisel was a great success. She was the prettiest woman there—resplendent, graceful, beaming, and deliriously happy. All the men looked at her, asked who she was, tried to get themselves introduced to her. All the minister's aides wanted to waltz with her. The minister himself noticed her.

She danced **enraptured**—carried away, intoxicated with pleasure, forgetting everything in this triumph of her beauty and the glory of her success, floating in a cloud of happiness formed by all this **homage,** all this admiration, all the desires she had stirred up—by this victory so complete and so sweet to the heart of a woman.

When she left the party, it was almost four in the morning. Her husband had been sleeping since midnight in a small, deserted sitting room, with three other gentlemen whose wives were having a wonderful time.

He brought her wraps so that they could leave and put them around her shoulders—the plain wraps from her everyday life whose shabbiness jarred with the elegance of her evening dress. She felt this and wanted to escape quickly so that the other women, who were enveloping themselves in their rich furs, wouldn't see her.

Loisel held her back.

"Wait a minute. You'll catch cold out there. I'm going to call a cab."

But she wouldn't listen to him and went hastily downstairs. Outside in the street, there was no cab to be found; they set out to look for one, calling to the drivers they saw passing in the distance.

They walked toward the **Seine,** shivering and miserable. Finally, on the embankment, they found one of those ancient nocturnal **broughams** which are only to be seen in Paris at night, as if they were ashamed to show their shabbiness in daylight.

It took them to their door in the Rue des Martyrs, and they went sadly upstairs to their apartment. For her, it was all over. And he was thinking that he had to be at the Ministry by ten.

She took off her wraps before the mirror so that she could see herself in all her glory once more. Then she cried out. The necklace was gone; there was nothing around her neck.

Her husband, already half undressed, asked:

"What's the matter?"

She turned toward him in a frenzy:

"The . . . the . . . necklace—-it's gone."

He got up, thunderstruck.

"What did you say? . . . What! . . . Impossible!"

And they searched the folds of her dress, the folds of her wrap, the pockets, everywhere. They didn't find it.

He asked:

"Are you sure you still had it when we left the ball?"

"Yes. I remember touching it in the hallway of the Ministry."

"But if you had lost it in the street, we would have heard it fall. It must be in the cab."

"Yes, most likely. Do you remember the number?"

"No. What about you—-did you notice it?"

"No."

They looked at each other in utter dejection. Finally Loisel got dressed again.

"I'm going to retrace the whole distance we covered on foot," he said, "and see if I can't find it."

And he left the house. She remained in her evening dress, too weak to go to bed, sitting crushed on a chair, lifeless and blank. Her husband returned at about seven o'clock. He had found nothing.

He went to the police station, to the newspapers to offer a reward, to the offices of the cab companies—-in a word, wherever there seemed to be the slightest hope of tracing it.

She spent the whole day waiting, in a state of utter hopelessness before such an appalling catastrophe.

Loisel returned in the evening, his face lined and pale; he had learned nothing.

"You must write to your friend," he said, "and tell her that you've broken the clasp of the necklace and that you're getting it mended. That'll give us time to decide what to do."

She wrote the letter at his dictation.

By the end of the week, they had lost all hope.

Loisel, who had aged five years, declared: "We'll have to replace the necklace."

The next day they took the case in which it had been kept and went to the jeweler whose name appeared inside it. He looked through his ledgers:

"I didn't sell this necklace, Madame. I only supplied the case."

Then they went from one jeweler to the next, trying to find a necklace like the other, racking their memories, both of them sick with worry and distress.

In a fashionable shop near the Palais Royal, they found a diamond necklace which they decided was exactly like the other. It was worth 40,000 francs. They could have it for 36,000 francs.

They asked the jeweler to hold it for them for three days, and they stipulated

> "We'll have to replace the necklace."

that he should take it back for 34,000 francs if the other necklace was found before the end of February.

Loisel possessed 18,000 francs left him by his father. He would borrow the rest.

He borrowed, asking a thousand francs from one man, five hundred from another, a hundred here, fifty there. He signed promissory notes, borrowed at **exorbitant** rates, dealt with **usurers** and the entire race of moneylenders. He compromised his whole career, gave his signature even when he wasn't sure he would be able to honor it, and horrified by the anxieties with which his future would be filled, by the black misery about to descend upon him, by the prospect of physical privation and moral suffering, went to get the new necklace, placing on the jeweler's counter 36,000 francs.

When Madame Loisel went to return the necklace, Madame Forestier said in a faintly waspish tone:

"You could have brought it back a little sooner! I might have needed it."

She didn't open the case as her friend had feared she might. If she had noticed the substitution, what would she have thought? What would she have said? Mightn't she have taken Madame Loisel for a thief?

Madame Loisel came to know the awful life of the poverty-stricken. However, she resigned herself to it with unexpected **fortitude.** The crushing debt had to be paid. She would pay it. They dismissed the maid: they moved into an attic under the roof.

She came to know all the heavy household chores. The loathsome work of the kitchen. She washed the dishes, wearing down her pink nails on greasy casseroles and the bottoms of saucepans. She did the laundry, washing shirts and dishcloths which she hung on a line to dry; she took the garbage down to the street every morning, and carried water upstairs, stopping at every floor to get her breath. Dressed like a working-class woman, she went to the fruit store, the grocer, and the butcher with her basket on her arm, bargaining, out-raged, contesting each *sou* of her pitiful funds.

Every month some notes had to be honored and more time requested on others.

Her husband worked in the evenings, putting a shopkeeper's ledgers in order, and often at night as well, doing copying at twenty-five centimes a page.

And it went on like that for ten years.

After ten years, they had made good on everything, including the usurious rates and the compound interest.

Madame Loisel looked old now. She had become the sort of strong woman, hard and coarse, that one finds in poor families. **Disheveled,** her skirts askew, with reddened hands, she spoke in a loud voice, slopping water over the floors as she washed them. But sometimes, when her husband was at the office, she would sit down by the window and muse over that party long ago when she had been so beautiful, the belle of the ball.

How would things have turned out if she hadn't lost that necklace? Who could tell? How strange and fickle life is! How little it takes to make or break you!

Then one Sunday when she was strolling along the **Champs Elysees** to forget the week's chores for a while, she suddenly caught sight of a woman taking a child for a walk. It was Madame Forestier, still young, still beautiful, still charming.

Madame Loisel started to tremble. Should she speak to her? Yes, certainly she should. And now that she had paid everything back, why shouldn't she tell her the whole story?

She went up to her.

"Hello, Jeanne."

The other didn't recognize her and was surprised that this plainly dressed woman should speak to her so familiarly. She murmured:

"But . . . Madame! . . . I'm sure . . . You must be mistaken."

"No, I'm not. I am Mathilde Loisel."

Her friend gave a little cry.

"Oh! Oh, my poor Mathilde, how you've changed!"

"Yes, I've been through some pretty hard times since I last saw you and I've had plenty of trouble—-and all because of you!"

"Because of me? What do you mean?"

"You remember the diamond necklace you lent me to wear to the party at the Ministry?"

"Yes. What about it?"

"Well, I lost it."

"What are you talking about? You returned it to me."

"What I gave back to you was another one just like it. And it took us ten years to pay for it. You can imagine it wasn't easy for us, since we were quite poor . . . . Anyway, I'm glad it's over and done with."

Madame Forestier stopped short.

"You say you bought a diamond necklace to replace that other one?"

"Yes. You didn't even notice then? They really were exactly alike."

And she smiled, full of a proud, simple joy.

Madame Forestier, profoundly moved, took Mathilde's hands in her own.

"Oh, my poor, poor Mathilde! Mine was false. It was worth five hundred francs at the most!" ❖

## ACCENT ON...
### INSURANCE

In "The Necklace," Madame and Monsieur Loisel borrow thousands of francs to repay the debts they owe to replace Madame Forestier's necklace. Today, most people who own fine jewelry carry insurance policies that protect the value of the jewelry against loss or theft. An insurance agent can help individuals select the right policy for their needs. Find out from talking to an insurance broker what kinds of policies are offered in the category of property liability.

# UNDERSTANDING

1. Madame Loisel comes alive for readers through her appearance, her thoughts and desires, and her actions. In three columns labeled "Appearance," "Thoughts," and "Actions," list appropriate quotations from the text.

   Choose someone you know very well. Brainstorm about this person's personality in the same three categories. Then write a character sketch of this person. ***Workshop 10***

2. Though Madame Loisel is dissatisfied, her life is not all bad from an outsider's point of view. Consider her caring and hard-working husband. What else does she have that others would envy?

   Review your own qualities, possessions, and lifestyle. Remember the everyday things we take for granted, such as food to eat and books to read. Now write yourself a letter, reminding yourself of the good in your life and advising yourself to make what you have work for you. ***Workshop 16***

3. Readers and characters alike are surprised by the ironic ending of "The Necklace." Irony is the contrast between what is expected and what actually occurs. Describe the irony in the plot.

   Describe a situation from your life, a novel, or a movie in which the outcome of an effort surprised everyone involved. Write about the situation in a narrative essay that explains the expected outcome and the surprising twist. ***Workshop 9***

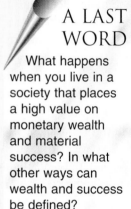

## A LAST WORD

What happens when you live in a society that places a high value on monetary wealth and material success? In what other ways can wealth and success be defined?

# CONNECTING

1.  Working with several classmates, brainstorm the different professions in which people study, mine, craft, or sell minerals and precious gems. Choose one profession that interests you. As a group, determine how, where, and at what cost a person could become trained in one of these professions. Compile your data in a neat, concise, word-processed report.

2.  Working in groups, gather data on the cost of supporting a family of four for one month in your community. Your group should choose one of these specific categories to research: housing, groceries, child care, transportation, utilities, or insurance. One group should also research average earnings of men and women. Then pool your information as a class to design and produce a brochure entitled, "Can You Afford It?" ***Workshop 20***

# The Colt

## EXPLORING

Sometimes we want something to happen so badly that we give up all other activities to strive for that one thing. Recall a time when you wanted something this much. What did you do to try to make it happen? Were the results rewarding or disappointing?

## THEME CONNECTION...
## CHAIN REACTION

A neglected chore rarely has serious consequences. In most cases, a person can simply do the job later. Sometimes, however, innocent actions, such as putting off or neglecting a chore, can have terrible consequences. In this story, the main character is a young man who learns a hard lesson about life when he forgets to complete his chores.

## TIME & PLACE

"The Colt" was published in 1943. Although the story takes place near that time, motor vehicles were not yet in common use in the somewhat remote farming country of Wyoming and Montana. Horse-drawn wagons were the primary form of transportation. This makes the fate of a newborn colt all the more critical; horses were necessary to the success of a farm.

## THE WRITER'S CRAFT
### CAUSE AND EFFECT

Everything that happens has at least one cause, and *nearly* everything that happens has at least one effect. Identifying cause-and-effect relationships in anything we read helps us understand the material better.

Plots in short stories move along through cause and effect. One person's actions cause a specific effect, negative or positive, on others. In this story, an unfinished chore sets off a chain reaction of effects. The result is inevitable.

# The Colt
## Wallace Stegner

It was the swift coming of spring that let things happen. It was spring, and the opening of the roads, that took his father out of town. It was spring that clogged the river with floodwater and ice pans, sent the dogs racing in wild aimless packs, ripped the railroad bridge out and scattered it down the river for **exuberant** townspeople to fish out piecemeal. It was spring that drove the whole town to the river-bank with pike-poles and coffeepots and boxes of sand-wiches for an impromptu picnic, lifting their sober respon-sibilities out of them and making them whoop bless-ings on the Canadian Pacific Railroad for a winter's firewood. Nothing might have gone wrong except for the coming of spring. Some of the neighbors might have noticed and let them know; Bruce might not have forgotten; his mother might have remem-bered and sent him out again after dark.

But the spring came, and the ice went out, and that night Bruce went to bed **drunk** and exhausted with excitement. In the restless sleep just before waking he dreamed of wolves and wild hunts, but when he awoke finally he realized that he had not been dreaming the noise. The window, wide open for the first time in months, let in a shivery draught of fresh, damp air, and he heard the faint yelping far down in the bend of the river.

He dressed and went downstairs, crowding his bottom into the warm oven, not because he was cold but because it had been a ritual for so long that not even the sight of the sun outside could convince him it wasn't necessary. The dogs were still yapping; he heard them through the open door.

"What's the matter with all the pooches?" he said. "Where's Spot?"

"He's out with them," his mother said. "They've probably got a porcupine treed. Dogs go crazy in the spring."

"It's dog days they go crazy."

"They go crazy in the spring, too." She hummed a little as she set the table. "You'd better go feed the horses. Breakfast won't be for ten minutes. And see if Daisy is all right."

Bruce stood perfectly still in the middle of the kitchen. "Oh my gosh!" he said. "I left Daisy **picketed** out all night!"

His mother's head jerked around. "Where?"

"Down in the bend."

"Where those dogs are?"

"Yes," he said, sick and afraid. "Maybe she's had her colt."

"She shouldn't for two or three days," his mother said. But just looking at her he knew that it might be bad, that there was something to be afraid of. In another moment they were both out the door, both running.

But it couldn't be Daisy they were barking at, he thought as he raced around

### About the Author

Born in Iowa and educated in Utah, Wallace Stegner (1909–1993) has taught at several universities, including Stanford. Many of his richly written novels and short stories explore American rural life. Also characteristic of his work are a strong sense of place, accurate detail, and characters who are extremely honest and ethical.

His novel *Angle of Repose* won a Pulitzer Prize in 1972. In 1977, *The Spectator Bird* won the National Book Award. Stegner's *Collected Stories* appeared in 1990.

exuberant—joyously enthusiastic

drunk—dominated by a feeling

picketed—tied to a stake in the ground

Chance's barn. He'd picketed her higher up, not clear down in the U where the dogs were. His eyes swept the brown, wet, close-cropped meadow, the edge of the brush where the river ran close under the north bench. The mare wasn't there! He opened his mouth and half turned, running, to shout at his mother coming behind him, and then sprinted for the deep curve of the bend.

As soon as he rounded the little clump of brush that fringed the cutbank behind Chance's he saw them. The mare stood planted, a bay spot against the gray brush, and in front of her, on the ground, was another smaller spot. Six or eight dogs were leaping around, barking, sitting. Even at that distance he recognized Spot and the Chapmans' Airedale.

He shouted and pumped on. At a gravelly patch he stooped and clawed and straightened, still running, with a handful of pebbles. In one pausing, straddling, aiming motion he left fly a rock at the distant pack. It fell far short, but they turned their heads, sat on their haunches and let out defiant short barks. Their tongues lolled as if they had run far.

Bruce yelled and threw again, one eye on the dogs and the other on the chestnut colt in front of the mare's feet. The mare's ears were back, and as he ran Bruce saw the colt's head bob up and down. It was all right then. The colt was alive. He slowed and came up quietly. Never move fast or speak loud around an animal, Pa said.

The colt struggled again, raised its head with white eyeballs rolling, spraddled its white-stockinged legs and tried to stand. "Easy, boy," Bruce said. "Take it easy, old fella." His mother arrived, getting her breath, her hair half down, and he turned to her gleefully. "It's all right, Ma. They didn't hurt anything. Isn't he a beauty, Ma?"

He stroked Daisy's nose. She was heaving, her ears pricking forward and back; her flanks were **lathered,** and she trembled. Patting her gently, he watched the colt, sitting now like a dog on its haunches, and his happiness that nothing had really been hurt bubbled out of him. "Lookit, Ma," he said. "He's got four white socks. Can I call him Socks, Ma? He sure is a nice colt, isn't he? Aren't you Socks, old boy?" He reached down to touch the chestnut's forelock, and the colt struggled, pulling away.

Then Bruce saw his mother's face. It was quiet, too quiet. She hadn't answered a word to all his jabber. Instead she knelt down, about ten feet from the squatting colt, and stared at it. The boy's eyes followed hers. There was something funny about . . .

"Ma!" he said. "What's the matter with its front feet?"

He left Daisy's head and came around, staring. The colt's **pasterns** looked bent—-*were* bent, so that they flattened clear to the ground under its weight. Frightened by Bruce's movement, the chestnut flopped and floundered to its feet, pressing close to its mother. And it walked, Bruce saw, flat on its **fetlocks,** its hooves sticking out in front like a movie comedian's too-large shoes.

Bruce's mother pressed her lips together, shaking her head. She moved

**"It was all right then. The colt was alive."**

lathered—sweaty

pastern—the area just above a horse's hoof

fetlock—a protruding joint on the back of a horse's leg just above the pastern

so gently that she got her hand on the colt's **poll,** and he bobbed against the pleasant scratching. "You poor broken-legged thing," she said with tears in her eyes. "You poor little friendly ruined thing!"

Still quietly, she turned toward the dogs, and for the first time in his life Bruce heard her curse. Quietly, almost in a whisper, she cursed them as they sat with hanging tongues just out of reach. "Damn you," she said. "Damn your wild hearts, chasing a mother and a poor little colt."

To Bruce, standing with trembling lip, she said, "Go get Jim Enich. Tell him to bring a wagon. And don't cry. It's not your fault."

His mouth tightened, a sob jerked in his chest. He bit his lip and drew his face down tight to keep from crying, but his eyes filled and ran over.

"It is too my fault!" he said, and turned and ran.

Later, as they came in the wagon up along the cutbank, the colt tied down in the wagon box with his head sometimes lifting, sometimes bumping on the boards, the mare trotting after with chuckling vibrations of **solicitude** in her throat, Bruce leaned far over and tried to touch the colt's haunch. "Gee!" he said. "Poor old Socks."

His mother's arm was around him, keeping him from leaning over too far. He didn't watch where they were until he heard his mother say in surprise and relief, "Why, there's Pa!"

Instantly he was terrified. He had forgotten and left Daisy staked out all night. It was his fault, the whole thing. He slid back into the seat and crouched between Enich and his mother, watching from that narrow space like a gopher from its hole. He saw the Ford against the barn and his father's big body leaning into it pulling out gunny sacks and straw. There was mud all over the car, mud on his father's pants. He crouched deeper into his crevice and watched his father's face while his mother was telling what had happened.

Then Pa and Jim Enich lifted and slid the colt down to the ground, and Pa stooped to feel its fetlocks. His face was still, red from windburn, and his big square hands were muddy. After a long examination he straightened up.

"Would've been a nice colt," he said. "Damn a pack of mangy mongrels, anyway." He brushed his pants and looked at Bruce's mother. "How come Daisy was out?"

"I told Bruce to take her out. The barn seems so cramped for her, and I thought it would do her good to stretch her legs. And then the ice went out, and the bridge with it, and there was a lot of excitement . . . ." She spoke very fast, and in her voice Bruce heard the echo of his own fear and guilt. She was trying to protect him, but in his mind he knew he was to blame.

"I didn't mean to leave her out, Pa," he said. His voice squeaked, and he swallowed. "I was going to bring her in before supper, only when the bridge . . ."

His father's somber eyes rested on him, and he stopped. But his father didn't fly into a rage. He just seemed tired. He looked at the colt and then at Enich. "Total loss?" he said.

Enich had a leathery, withered face, with two deep creases from beside his nose to the corner of his mouth. A brown

## SPOTLIGHT ON...
## PAYING ATTENTION TO
## DETAILS

In "The Colt," Wallace Stegner describes the colt and Bruce's care of him in careful detail. The details an author chooses to include alert you to what the author considers important. As you read, you can improve your attention to details and enjoy your reading more by doing the following:
1. Note characters' names and descriptions.
2. Note or highlight unfamiliar words or phrases.
3. Look for context clues to help you understand the plot and unfamiliar terms.

mole hid in the left one, and it emerged and disappeared as he chewed a dry grass stem. "Hide," he said.

Bruce closed his dry mouth, swallowed. "Pa!" he said. "It won't have to be shot, will it?"

"What else can you do with it?" his father said. "A crippled horse is no good. It's just plain mercy to shoot it."

"Give it to me, Pa. I'll keep it lying down and heal it up."

"Yeah," his father said, without sarcasm and without mirth. "You could keep it lying down about one hour."

Bruce's mother came up next to him, as if the two of them were standing against the others. "Jim," she said quickly, "isn't there some kind of brace you could put on it? I remember my dad had a horse once that broke a leg below the knee, and he saved it that way."

"Not much chance," Enich said. "Both legs, like that." He picked a weed and stripped the dry branches from the stalk. "You can't make a horse understand he has to keep still."

"But wouldn't it be worth trying?" she said. "Children's bones heal so fast, I should think a colt's would too."

"I don't know. There's an outside chance, maybe."

"Bo," she said to her husband, "why don't we try it? It seems such a shame, a lovely colt like that."

"I know it's a shame!" he said. "I don't like shooting colts any better than you do. But I never saw a broken-legged colt get well. It'd just be a lot of worry and trouble, and then you'd have to shoot it finally anyway."

"Please," she said. She nodded at him slightly, and then the eyes of both were on Bruce. He felt the tears coming up again, and turned to grope for the colt's ears. It tried to struggle to its feet, and Enich put his foot on its neck. The mare chuckled anxiously.

"How much this hobble brace kind of thing cost?" the father said finally. Bruce turned again, his mouth open with hope.

"Two-three dollars, is all," Enich said.

"You think it's got a chance?"

contrition—
sincere remorse;
regret for wrong-
doing

freshet—the
overflowing of a
stream due to
heavy rain or
melted snow

.22's—.22-
caliber rifles

revelation—
something that
is revealed

"One in a thousand, maybe."

"All right. Let's go see MacDonald."

"Oh, good!" Bruce's mother said, and put her arm around him tight.

"I don't know, whether it's good or not," the father said. "We might wish we never did it." To Bruce he said, "It's your responsibility. You got to take complete care of it."

"I will!" Bruce said. He took his hand out of his pocket and rubbed below his eye with his knuckles. "I'll take care of it every day."

Big with **contrition** and shame and gratitude and the sudden sense of immense responsibility, he watched his father and Enich start for the house to get a tape measure. When they were thirty feet away he said loudly, "Thanks, Pa. Thanks an awful lot."

His father half turned, said something to Enich. Bruce stooped to stroke the colt, looked at his mother, started to laugh and felt it turn horribly into a sob. When he turned away so that his mother wouldn't notice, he saw his dog Spot looking inquiringly around the corner of the barn. Spot took three or four tentative steps and paused, wagging his tail. Very slowly (never speak loud or move fast around an animal) the boy bent and found a good-sized stone. He straightened casually, brought his arm back, and threw with all his might. The rock caught Spot squarely in the ribs. He yiped, tucked his tail, and scuttled around the barn, and Bruce chased him, throwing clods and stones and gravel, yelling, "Get out! Go on, get out of here or I'll kick you apart. Get out! Go on!"

So all that spring, while the world dried in the sun and the willows emerged

from the floodwater and the mud left by the **freshet** hardened and caked among their roots, and the grass of the meadow greened and the river brush grew misty with tiny leaves and the dandelions spread yellow among the flats, Bruce tended his colt. While the other boys roamed the bench hills with **.22's** looking for gophers or rabbits or sage hens, he anxiously superintended the colt's nursing and watched it learn to nibble the grass. While his gang built a darkly secret hide-out in the deep brush beyond Hazard's, he was currying and brushing and trimming the chestnut mane. When packs of boys ran hare and hounds through the town and around the river's slow bends, he perched on the front porch with his slingshot and a can full of small round stones, waiting for stray dogs to appear. He waged a holy war on the dogs until they learned to detour widely around his house, and he never did completely forgive his own dog, Spot. His whole life was wrapped up in the hobbled, leg-ironed chestnut colt with the slow-motion lunging walk and the affectionate nibbling lips.

Every week or so Enich, who was now working out of town at the Half Diamond Bar, rode in and stopped. Always, with that expressionless quiet that was terrible to the boy, he stood and looked the colt over, bent to feel pastern and fetlock, stood back to watch the plunging walk when the boy held out a handful of grass. His expression said nothing; whatever he thought was hidden back of his leathery face as the dark mole was hidden in the crease beside his mouth. Bruce found himself watching that mole sometimes, as if **revelation** might lie there. But when he pressed Enich to tell him, when he said, "He's getting better, isn't he? He walks better, doesn't he, Mr. Enich? His ankles don't bend so much, do they?" the wrangler gave him little encouragement.

"Let him be a while. He's growin', sure enough. Maybe give him another month."

May passed. The river was slow and clear again, and some of the boys were already swimming. School was almost over. And still Bruce paid attention to nothing but Socks. He willed so strongly that the colt should get well that he grew furious even at Daisy when she some-times wouldn't let the colt suck as much as he wanted. He took a butcher knife and cut the long tender grass in the fence corners, where Socks could not reach, and fed it to his pet by the handful. He trained him to nuzzle for sugar-lumps in his pockets. And back in his mind was a fear: in the middle of June they would be going out to the homestead again, and if Socks weren't well by that time he might not be able to go.

"Pa," he said, a week before they planned to leave. "How much of a load are we going to have, going out to the homestead?"

"I don't know, wagonful, I suppose. Why?"

"I just wondered." He ran his fingers in a walking motion along the round edge of the dining table, and strayed into the other room. If they had a wagon load, then there was no way Socks could be loaded in and taken along. And he

●●●●●●
"His ankles
don't bend so
much, do they?"
●●●●●●

couldn't walk fifty miles. He'd get left behind before they got up on the bench, hobbling along like the little crippled boy in the Pied Piper, and they'd look back and see him trying to run, trying to keep up.

That picture was so painful that he cried over it in bed that night. But in the morning he dared to ask his father if they couldn't take Socks along to the farm. His father turned to him eyes as sober as Jim Enich's, and when he spoke it was with a kind of tired impatience. "How can he go? He couldn't walk it."

"But I want him to go, Pa!"

"Brucie," his mother said, "don't get your hopes up. You know we'd do it if we could, if it was possible."

"But Ma . . ."

His father said, "What you want us to do, haul a broken-legged colt fifty miles?"

"He'd be well by the end of the summer, and he could walk back."

"Look," his father said. "Why can't you make up your mind to it? He isn't getting well. He isn't going to get well."

"He is too getting well!" Bruce shouted. He half stood up at the table, and his father looked at his mother and shrugged.

"Please, Bo," she said.

"Well, he's got to make up his mind to it sometime," he said.

Jim Enich's wagon pulled up on Saturday morning, and Bruce was out the door before his father could rise from his chair. "Hi, Mr. Enich," he said.

"Hello, Bub. How's your pony?"

"He's fine," Bruce said. "I think he's got a lot better since you saw him last."

"Uh-huh." Enich wrapped the lines around the whipstock and climbed down. "Tell me you're leaving next week."

"Yes," Bruce said. "Socks is in the back."

When they got into the back yard Bruce's father was there with his hands behind his back, studying the colt as it hobbled around. He looked at Enich. "What do you think?" he said. "The kid here thinks his colt can walk out to the homestead."

unaccountable
—unexplainable

"Uh-huh," Enich said. "Well, I wouldn't say that." He inspected the chestnut, scratched between his ears. Socks bobbed, and snuffled at his pockets. "Kid's made quite a pet of him."

Bruce's father grunted. "That's just the trouble."

"I didn't think he could walk out," Bruce said. "I thought we could take him in the wagon, and then he'd be well enough to walk back in the fall."

"Uh," Enich said. "Let's take his braces off for a minute."

He unbuckled the triple straps on each leg, pulled the braces off, and stood back. The colt stood almost as flat on his fetlocks as he had the morning he was born. Even Bruce, watching with his whole mind tight and apprehensive, could see that. Enich shook his head.

"You see, Bruce?" his father said. "It's too bad, but he isn't getting better. You'll have to make up your mind . . ."

"He will get better though!" Bruce said. "It just takes a long time, is all." He looked at his father's face, at Enich's, and neither one had any hope in it. But when Bruce opened his mouth to say something else his father's eyebrows drew down in sudden, **unaccountable** anger, and his hand made an impatient sawing motion in the air.

"We shouldn't have tried this in the first place," he said. "It just tangles everything up." He patted his coat pockets, felt in his vest. "Run in and get me a couple cigars."

Bruce hesitated, his eyes on Enich. "Run!" his father said harshly.

Reluctantly he released the colt's halter rope and started for the house. At the door he looked back, and his father and Enich were talking together so low that their words didn't carry to where he stood. He saw his father shake his head, and Enich bend to pluck a grass stem. They were both against him, they both were sure Socks would never get well. Well, he would! There was some way.

He found the cigars, came out, watched them both light up. Disappointment was a sickness in him, and mixed with the disappointment was a question. When he could stand their silence no more he burst out with it. "But what are we going to *do*? He's got to have some place to stay."

"Look, kiddo," His father sat down on a sawhorse and took him by the arm. His face was serious and his voice gentle. "We can't take him out there. He isn't well enough to walk, and we can't haul him. So Jim here has offered to buy him. He'll give you three dollars for him, and when you come back, if you want, you might be able to buy him back. That is if he's well. It'll be better to leave him with Jim."

"Well . . ." Bruce studied the mole on Enich's cheek. "Can you get him better by fall, Mr. Enich?"

"I wouldn't expect it," Enich said. "He ain't got much of a show."

"If anybody can get him better, Jim can," his father said. "How's that deal sound to you?"

"Maybe when I come back he'll be all off his braces and running around like a house afire," Bruce said. "Maybe next time I see him I can ride him." The mole

disappeared as Enich tongued his cigar.

"Well, all right then," Bruce said, bothered by their stony-eyed silence. "But I sure hate to leave you behind, Socks, old boy."

"It's the best way all around," his father said. He talked fast, as if he were in a hurry. "Can you take him along now?"

"Oh, gee!" Bruce said. "Today?"

"Come on," his father said. "Let's get it over with."

Bruce stood by while they **trussed** the colt and hoisted him into the wagon box, and when Jim climbed in he cried out, "Hey, we forgot to put his hobbles back on." Jim and his father looked at each other. His father shrugged. "All right," he said, and started putting the braces back on the trussed front legs. "He might hurt himself if they weren't on," Bruce said. He leaned over the endgate stroking the white blazed face, and as the wagon pulled away he stood with tears in his eyes and the three dollars in his hand, watching the terrified straining of the colt's neck, the bony head raised above the endgate and one white eye rolling.

Five days later, in the sun-slanting, dew-wet spring morning, they stood for the last time that summer on the front porch, the loaded wagon against the front fence. The father tossed the key in his hand and kicked the door jamb. "Well, goodbye, Old Paint," he said. "See you in the fall."

As they went to the wagon Bruce sang loudly,

> "If he could have taken Socks along it would have been perfect."

The Colt

sloughlike—
swampy; pro-
nounced SLEW

"Goodbye Old Paint, I'm leavin'
Cheyenne,
I'm leavin' Cheyenne, I'm goin' to
Montana,
Goodbye, Old Paint, I'm leavin'
Cheyenne."

"Turn it off," his father said. "You
want to wake up the whole town?" He
boosted Bruce into the back end, where
he squirmed and wiggled his way neck-
deep into the luggage. His mother,
turning to see how he was settled,
laughed at him. "You look like a baby
owl in a nest," she said.

His father turned and winked at him.
"Open your mouth and I'll drop in a
mouse."

It was good to be leaving; the thought
of the homestead was exciting. If he
could have taken Socks along it would
have been perfect, but he had to admit,
looking around at the jammed wagon
box, that there sure wasn't any room for
him. He continued to sing softly as they
rocked out into the road and turned east
toward MacKenna's house, where they
were leaving the keys.

At the low, **sloughlike** spot that had
become the town's dumpground the road
split, leaving the dump like an island in
the middle. The boy sniffed at the old
familiar smells of rust and tarpaper and
ashes and refuse. He had collected a lot
of old iron and tea lead and bottles and
broken machinery and clocks, and once a
perfectly good amber-headed cane, in
that old dumpground. His father turned
up the right fork, and as they passed the
central part of the dump the wind,
coming in from the northeast, brought a
rotten, unbearable stench across them.

"Pee-you!" his mother said, and held
her nose. Bruce echoed her. "Pee-you!
Pee-you-willy!" He clamped his nose
shut and pretended to fall dead.

"Guess I better get to windward of
that coming back," said his father.

They woke MacKenna up and left the
key and started back. The things they
passed were very sharp and clear to the
boy. He was seeing them for the last
time all summer. He noticed things he
had never noticed so clearly before: how
the hills came down into the river from
the north like three folds in a blanket,
how the stovepipe on the shack east of
town had a little conical hat on it. He
chanted at the things he saw. "Goodbye,
old shack. Goodbye, old Frenchman

# ACCENT ON...
## ANIMAL HUSBANDRY
● ● ● ● ● ● ● ● ● ● ● ● ● ● ● ● ● ● ● ● ● ● ●

As Bruce learns when caring for
Socks, raising animals on a farm is hard
and sometimes heartbreaking work.
Animal husbandry, or the science of
raising livestock, has been practiced for
thousands of years. Livestock, or
domestic animals, include cattle, horses,
sheep, hogs, and goats that are raised
for home use or profit. Think about and
research raising animals on a farm of
your own. Write a one- to two-page proposal to raise your own livestock: What
types of animals would you raise? How
many of each? How much land would
you need? How would you house, feed,
breed, and care for the animals? For
what purpose would you raise the
animals—to provide food for your family,
or to sell for profit?

River. Goodbye old Dumpground, goodbye."

"Hold your noses," his father said. He eased the wagon into the other fork around the dump. "Somebody sure dumped something rotten."

He stared ahead, bending a little, and Bruce heard him swear. He slapped the reins on the team until they trotted. "What?" the mother said. Bruce, half rising to see what caused the speed, saw her lips go flat over her teeth, and a look on her face like the woman he had seen in the traveling dentist's chair, when the dentist dug a living nerve out of her tooth and then got down on his knees to hunt for it, and she sat there half raised in her seat, her face lifted.

"For gosh sakes," he said. And then he saw.

He screamed at them. "Ma, it's Socks! Stop! Pa! It's Socks!"

His father drove grimly ahead, not turning, not speaking, and his mother shook her head without looking around. He screamed again, but neither of them turned. And when he dug down into the load, burrowing in and shaking with long smothered sobs, they still said nothing.

So they left town, and as they wound up the dugway to the south bench there was not a word among them except his father's low, "I thought he was going to take it out of town." None of them looked back at the view they had always admired, the flat river bottom green with spring, its village snuggled in the loops of river. Bruce's eyes, pressed against the coats and blankets under him until his sight was a red haze, could still see through it the bloated, skinned body of the colt, the chestnut hair left a little way above the hooves, the iron braces still on the broken front legs. ❖

# UNDERSTANDING

1. The author opens the story with an event that sets off a chain reaction: Warm spring weather melts the river's ice. List the changes that this event causes.

   What changes do you notice in your community when a new season arrives? Pick a season and make a list of the changes that occur when that season arrives. Write a paragraph on the causes and effects of the changes and your reactions to them. *Workshop 14*

2. Find statements in the story that signal danger before the characters realize the colt is injured. How do Bruce's and his mother's actions forewarn us of the disaster?

   Sometimes in life we have warnings before an event occurs. We might ignore a warning, or a warning might set off a series of events. In our homes, many products come with troubleshooting charts. If a certain signal or warning occurs, the owner or repairperson knows to take a specific action. Develop a troubleshooting chart for an appliance or piece of equipment you use regularly, such as a washing machine. *Workshop 23*

3. His parents care for Bruce and do not want him to be hurt. Find evidence in the text that supports this statement.

   In your opinion, did Bruce's parents choose the best course? Did they have other options? What were they? Choose a different option and explain its possible consequences. Discuss the different effects this option would have had on Bruce, the colt, and Bruce's parents. *Workshop 14*

A LAST WORD

Unfortunately, our actions sometimes have serious or tragic consequences. How can we be more aware or careful of the actions we do take? How can we make ourselves more aware of the possible consequences of our actions?

# CONNECTING

1. In a group, choose a domestic pet and research the advantages and disadvantages of owning that pet. You might select dogs, cats, fish, birds, rabbits, guinea pigs, gerbils, mice, turtles, and so on. Then design a brochure for young children on the responsibilities of owning the pet you researched. Assign tasks to group members so that each person is responsible for some part of the research and/or brochure development. *Workshop 20*

2. Working with several classmates, find out what organizations promote the humane treatment of animals. What organizations work to save endangered species? As a group, agree on one organization to investigate and write a letter requesting information on its mission and activities. Report what you learn to the class. *Workshop 17*

# In Response to War

- *from Farewell to Manzanar*
- *In Response to Executive Order 9066*

## EXPLORING

● ● ● ● ● ● ● ● ● ● ● ● ● ● ● ● ● ● ● ● ●

Imagine that your own democratic government has decided to put you and your family members in a prison camp because of your ethnic background or skin color. What would you take with you to the camp? What and whom would you miss the most? As a result of this action by the government, what would you think of the "freedom" guaranteed to you under the Constitution?

## THEME CONNECTION...
## HASTY REACTIONS

Some events cause a hasty reaction that may seem right at the time but that actually may be done for all the wrong reasons. When the United States entered the war against Japan, was it reasonable to suspect that American-born Japanese would betray the United States? Was internment (imprisonment) the only option?

## TIME & PLACE

Between March 1942 and December 1944, the United States government relocated more than 120,000 people of Japanese descent. These people were moved from the West Coast to "relocation centers" in several interior states. The government feared that the Japanese Americans could communicate with Japan too easily from the West Coast. Two-thirds of those who were relocated were American citizens *who had been born in America.*

## THE WRITER'S CRAFT

### AUTOBIOGRAPHY

The word *autobiography* literally means "self life." An autobiography is a nonfiction work written by someone about his or her own life. The point of view is very personal—autobiography has an intimate dimension that cannot be found in other forms of writing. It is subjective, meaning it comes from the personal insight of the central character and may include that character's biases or prejudices. Readers should remember that writers of autobiography may not see facts or events as clearly as an outsider might.

● ● ● ● ● ● ● ● ● ● ● ● ● ● ● ● ● ● ● ● ● ● ● ● ● ● ● ● ● ●

# from *Farewell to Manzanar*

Jeanne Wakatsuki Houston and
James D. Houston

## About the Authors

Jeanne Wakatsuki Houston (b. 1934) was seven years old when her family was uprooted from its California home and sent to live for three-and-a-half years at Manzanar internment camp. Twenty-five years later, she was finally able to write about it. Wakatsuki Houston studied at San Jose State College, where she and her husband met.

James D. Houston (b. 1933), a writing instructor at the University of California at Santa Cruz, has published three novels, a collection of short stories, and two nonfiction works.

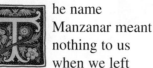

The name Manzanar meant nothing to us when we left Boyle Heights. We didn't know where it was or what it was. We went because the government ordered us to. And, in the case of my older brothers and sisters, we went with a certain amount of relief. They had all heard stories of Japanese homes being attacked, of beatings in the streets of California towns. They were as frightened of the Caucasians as Caucasians were of us. Moving, under what appeared to be government protection, to an area less directly threatened by the war seemed not such a bad idea at all. For some it actually sounded like a fine adventure.

Our pickup point was a Buddhist church in Los Angeles. It was very early, and misty, when we got there with our luggage. Mama had bought heavy coats for all of us. She grew up in eastern Washington and knew that anywhere inland in early April would be cold. I was proud of my new coat, and I remember sitting on a duffel bag trying to be friendly with the Greyhound driver. I smiled at him. He didn't smile back. He was befriending no one. Someone tied a numbered tag to my collar and to the duffel bag (each family was given a number, and that became our official designation until the camps were closed), someone else passed out box lunches for the trip, and we climbed aboard.

I had never been outside Los Angeles County, never traveled more than ten miles from the coast, had never even ridden on a bus. I was full of excitement, the way any kid would be, and wanted to look out the window. But for the first few hours the shades were drawn. Around me other people played cards, read magazines, dozed, waiting. I settled back, waiting too, and finally fell asleep. The bus felt very secure to me. Almost half its passengers were immediate relatives. Mama and my older brothers had succeeded in keeping most of us together, on the same bus, headed for the same camp. I didn't realize until much later what a job that was. The strategy had been, first, to have everyone living in the same district when the evacuation began, and, then, to get all of us included under the same family number, even though names had been changed by marriage. Many families weren't as lucky as ours and suffered months of anguish while trying to arrange transfers from one camp to another.

We rode all day. By the time we reached our destination, the shades were up. It was late afternoon. The first thing I saw was a yellow swirl across a blurred, reddish setting sun. The bus was being pelted by what sounded like splattering rain. It wasn't rain. This was my first look at something I would soon know very well, a billowing flurry of dust and sand churned up by the wind through Owens Valley.

We drove past a barbed-wire fence, through a gate, and into an open space where trunks and sacks and packages had been dumped from the baggage trucks that drove out ahead of us. I could see a few tents set up, the first rows of black barracks, and beyond them, blurred by sand, rows of barracks that seemed to spread for miles across this plain. People were sitting on cartons or milling around, with their backs to the wind, waiting to see which friends or relatives might be on this bus. As we approached, they turned or stood up, and some moved toward us expectantly. But inside the bus no one stirred. No one waved or spoke. They just stared out the windows, ominously silent. I didn't understand this. Hadn't we finally arrived, our whole family intact? I opened a window, leaned out, and yelled happily. "Hey! This whole bus is full of Wakatsukis!"

Outside, the greeters smiled. Inside there was an explosion of laughter, hysterical, tension-breaking laughter that left my brothers choking and whacking each other across the shoulders.

We had pulled up just in time for dinner. The **mess halls** weren't completed yet. An outdoor chow line snaked around a half-finished building that

● ● ● ● ● ● ● ● ●
### "Hey! This whole bus is full of Wakatsukis!"
● ● ● ● ● ● ● ● ●

broke a good part of the wind. They issued us army mess kits, the round metal kind that fold over, and plopped in scoops of canned Vienna sausage, canned string beans, steamed rice that had been cooked too long, and on top of the rice a serving of canned apricots. The Caucasian servers were thinking that the fruit poured over rice would make a good dessert. Among the Japanese, of course, rice is never eaten with sweet foods, only with salty or savory foods. Few of us could eat such a mixture. But at this point no one dared protest. It would have been impolite. I was horrified when I saw the apricot syrup seeping through my little mound of rice. I opened my mouth to complain. My mother jabbed me in the back to keep quiet. We moved on through the line and joined the others squatting in the lee of half-raised walls, dabbing courteously at what was, for almost everyone there, an inedible **concoction**.

After dinner we were taken to Block 16, a cluster of fifteen barracks that had just been finished a day or so earlier—although finished was hardly the word for it. The shacks were built of one thickness of pine planking covered with tarpaper. They sat on concrete footings, with about two feet of open space between the floorboards and the ground. Gaps showed between the planks, and as the weeks passed and the green wood dried out, the gaps widened. Knotholes gaped in the uncovered floor.

Each barracks was divided into six units, sixteen by twenty feet, about the

mess hall—a place where meals are served to a group of people

concoction— odd mixture

In Response to War

**135**

## SPOTLIGHT ON... WORKING WITH CULTURAL DIVERSITY

In the excerpt from *Farewell to Manzanar,* the food servers at the camp pour canned apricots over rice for dessert, not knowing that in Japanese culture rice is never eaten with sweet foods. You, too, may be unfamiliar with the practices and traditions of various ethnic groups. To work and communicate successfully with people from culturally diverse backgrounds, always strive for understanding.

- Recognize the value of the ethnic, social, and educational backgrounds of the people who work with you.
- Understand and respect different views and unfamiliar approaches to situations and problem solving.
- Learn about, respect, and understand the beliefs and values of others.

◆ ◆ ◆ ◆ ◆ ◆ ◆ ◆ ◆ ◆ ◆ ◆ ◆ ◆ ◆ ◆ ◆ ◆ ◆ ◆ ◆

**formulas**—a milk-like drink containing nutrients required by infants

**abate**—die down

size of a living room, with one bare bulb hanging from the ceiling and an oil stove for heat. We were assigned two of these for the twelve people in our family group; and our official family "number" was enlarged by three digits—16 plus the number of this barracks. We were issued steel army cots, two brown army blankets each, and some mattress covers, which my brothers stuffed with straw.

The first task was to divide up what space we had for sleeping. Bill and Woody contributed a blanket each and partitioned off the first room: one side for Bill and Tomi, one side for Woody and Chizu and their baby girl. Woody also got the stove, for heating **formulas**.

The people who had it hardest during the first few months were young couples like these, many of whom had married just before the evacuation began, in order

not to be separated and sent to different camps. Our two rooms were crowded, but at least it was all in the family. My oldest sister and her husband were shoved into one of those sixteen-by-twenty-foot compartments with six people they had never seen before—two other couples, one recently married like themselves, the other with two teenage boys. Partitioning off a room like that wasn't easy. It was bitter cold when we arrived, and the wind did not **abate**. All they had to use for room dividers were those army blankets, two of which were barely enough to keep one person warm. They argued over whose blanket should be sacrificed and later argued about noise at night—the parents wanted their boys asleep by 9:00 P.M.—and they continued arguing over matters like that for six months, until my sister and her husband left to harvest sugar beets in Idaho. It was grueling work up there, and wages were pitiful, but when the call came through camp for workers to alleviate the wartime labor shortage, it sounded better than their life at Manzanar. They knew they'd have, if nothing else, a room, perhaps a cabin of their own.

The first night in Block 16, the rest of us squeezed into the second room—Granny, Lillian, age fourteen, Ray, thirteen, May, eleven, Kiyo, ten, Mama, and me. I didn't mind this at all at the time. Being youngest meant I got to sleep with Mama. And before we went to bed I had a great time jumping up and down on the mattress. The boys had stuffed so much straw into hers, we had to flatten it some so we wouldn't slide off. I slept with her every night after that until Papa came back.

We woke early, shivering and coated with dust that had blown up through the knotholes and in through the slits around the doorway. During the night Mama had unpacked all our clothes and heaped them on our beds for warmth. Now our cubicle looked as if a great laundry bag had exploded and then been sprayed with fine dust. A skin of sand covered the floor. I looked over Mama's shoulder at Kiyo, on top of his fat mattress, buried under jeans and overcoats and sweaters. His eyebrows were gray, and he was starting to giggle. He was looking at me, at my gray eyebrows and coated hair, and pretty soon we were both giggling. I looked at Mama's face to see if she thought Kiyo was funny. She lay very still next to me on our mattress, her eyes scanning everything—bare rafters, walls, dusty kids—scanning

slowly, and I think the mask of her face would have cracked had not Woody's voice just then come at us through the wall. He was rapping on the planks as if testing to see if they were hollow.

"Hey!" he yelled. "You guys fall into the same flour barrel as us?"

"No," Kiyo yelled back. "Ours is full of Japs."

All of us laughed at this.

"Well, tell 'em it's time to get up," Woody said. "If we're gonna live in this place, we better get to work."

He gave us ten minutes to dress, then he came in carrying a broom, a hammer, and a sack full of tin can lids he had scrounged somewhere. Woody would be our leader for a while now, short, stocky, grinning behind his mustache. He had just turned twenty-four . . .

"Hey, brother Ray, Kiyo," he said. "You see these tin can lids?"

"Yeah, yeah," the boys said drowsily, as if going back to sleep. They were both young versions of Woody.

They looked around. You could see about a dozen.

Woody said, "You get those covered up before breakfast time. Any more sand comes in there through one of them knotholes, you have to eat it off the floor with ketchup."

"What about sand that comes in through the cracks?" Kiyo said.

Woody stood up very straight, which in itself was funny, since he was only about five-foot-six.

"Don't worry about the cracks," he said. "Different kind of sand comes in through the cracks."

He put his hands on his hips and gave Kiyo a sternly comic look, squinting at

## FOCUS ON... HISTORY

*Farewell to Manzanar* is the true story of one Japanese-American family's experiences during and after their camp internment in World War II. Find out more about this period in United States history and about the attitudes and feelings that motivated the creation of the internment camps. Write a two-page report with factual information about the events leading up to the decision to intern these people. Include in your report a summary of how Japanese Americans were treated and the effects of these experiences on them.

◆ ◆ ◆ ◆ ◆ ◆ ◆ ◆ ◆ ◆ ◆ ◆ ◆ ◆ ◆

buffeting—striking repeatedly

him through one eye the way Papa would when he was asserting his authority. Woody mimicked Papa's voice: "And I can tell the difference. So be careful."

The boys laughed and went to work nailing down lids. May started sweeping out the sand. I was helping Mama fold the clothes we'd used for cover, when Woody came over and put his arms around her shoulder. He was short; she was even shorter, under five feet.

He said softly, "You okay, Mama?"

She didn't look at him, she just kept folding clothes and said, "Can we get the cracks covered too, Woody?"

Outside the sky was clear, but icy gusts of wind were **buffeting** our barracks every few minutes, sending fresh dust puffs up through the floorboards. May's broom could barely keep up with it, and our oil heater could scarcely hold its own against the drafts.

"We'll get this whole place as tight as a barrel, Mama. I already met a guy who told me where they pile all the scrap lumber."

"Scrap?"

"That's all they got. I mean, they're still building the camp, you know. Sixteen blocks left to go. After that, they say maybe we'll get some stuff to fix the insides a little bit."

Her eyes blazed then, her voice quietly furious. "Woody, we can't live like this. Animals live like this."

It was hard to get Woody down. He'd keep smiling when everybody else was ready to explode. Grief flickered in his eyes. He blinked it away and hugged her tighter. "We'll make it better, Mama. You watch."

We could hear voices in other cubicles now. Beyond the wall Woody's baby girl started to cry.

"I have to go over to the kitchen," he said, "see if those guys got a pot for heating bottles. That oil stove takes too long—something wrong with the fuel line. I'll find out what they're giving us for breakfast."

"Probably hotcakes with soy sauce," Kiyo said, on his hands and knees between the bunks.

"No." Woody grinned, heading out the door. "Rice. With Log Cabin Syrup and melted butter."

As the months at Manzanar turned to years, it became a world unto itself, with its own logic and familiar ways. In time, staying there seemed far simpler than moving once again to another, unknown place. It was as if the war were forgotten, our reason for being there forgotten. The present, the little bit of busywork you had right in front of you, became the most urgent thing. In such a narrowed world, in order to survive, you learn to contain your rage and your despair, and you try to re-create, as well as you can, your normality, some sense of things continuing. The fact that America had accused us, or excluded us, or imprisoned us, or whatever it might be called, did not change the kind of world we wanted. Most of us were born in this country; we had no other models. Those parks and gardens lent it an oriental character, but in most ways it was a totally equipped American small town, complete with schools, churches, Boy Scouts, beauty parlors, neighborhood gossip, fire and police departments, glee clubs, softball leagues, Abbott and Costello movies, tennis courts, and traveling shows. (I still remember an Indian who turned up one Saturday billing himself as a Sioux chief, wearing bear claws and head feathers. In the firebreak he sang songs and danced his tribal dances while hundreds of us watched.)

In our family, while Papa puttered, Mama made her daily rounds to the mess halls, helping young mothers with their feeding, planning diets for the various ailments people suffered from. She wore a bright yellow, long-billed sun hat she had made herself and always kept stiffly starched. Afternoons I would see her coming from blocks away, heading home, her tiny figure warped by heat waves and that bonnet a yellow flower wavering in the glare.

● ● ● ● ● ● ●
## "It was called *Our World.*"
● ● ● ● ● ● ●

In their disagreement over serving the country, Woody and Papa had struck a kind of compromise. Papa talked him out of volunteering; Woody waited for the army to induct him. Meanwhile he clerked in the co-op general store. Kiyo, nearly thirteen by this time, looked forward to the heavy winds. They moved the sand around and uncovered obsidian arrowheads he could sell to old men in camp for fifty cents apiece. Ray, a few years older, played in the six-man touch football league, sometimes against Caucasian teams who would come in from Lone Pine or Independence. My sister Lillian was in high school and singing with a hillbilly band called The Sierra Stars—jeans, cowboy hats, two guitars, and a tub bass. And my oldest brother, Bill, led a dance band called The Jive Bombers—brass and rhythm, with cardboard fold-out music stands lettered J.B. Dances were held every weekend in one of the recreation halls. Bill played trumpet and took vocals on Glenn Miller arrangements of such tunes as *In the Mood, String of Pearls*, and *Don't Fence Me In*. He didn't sing *Don't Fence Me In* out of protest, as if trying quietly to mock the authorities. It just happened to be a hit song one year, and they all wanted to be an up-to-date American swing band. They would blast it out into recreation barracks full of bobby-soxed, jitter-bugging couples:

*Oh, give me land, lots of land*
*Under starry skies above,*
*Don't fence me in.*
*Let me ride through the wide*
*Open country that I love . . .*

Pictures of the band, in their bow ties and jackets, appeared in the high school yearbook for 1943–1944, along with pictures of just about everything else in camp that year. It was called *Our World*. ❖

# In Response to Executive Order 9066
## Americans of Japanese Descent Must Report to Relocation Centers

Dwight Okita

**About the Author**

Poet and playwright Dwight Okita (b. 1958) is a graduate of the University of Illinois at Chicago. His mother and father were relocated to an internment camp during World War II. Okita's poem is based on his parents' experiences during that period. Okita says that the poem is written in the voice of his mother, who "still survives and overcomes bad things by being stunningly innocent about everything that happens to her."

Dear Sirs:
Of course I'll come. I've packed my galoshes
and three packets of tomato seeds. Janet calls them
"love apples." My father says where we're going
they won't grow.

I am a fourteen-year-old girl with bad spelling
and a messy room. If it helps any, I will tell you
I have always felt funny using chopsticks
and my favorite food is hot dogs.
My best friend is a white girl named Denise—
we look at boys together. She sat in front of me
all through grade school because of our names:
O'Connor, Ozawa. I know the back of Denise's head very well.
I tell her she's going bald. She tells me I copy on tests.
We're best friends.

I saw Denise today in Geography class.
She was sitting on the other side of the room.
"You're trying to start a war," she said, "giving secrets away
to the Enemy. Why can't you keep your big mouth shut?"
I didn't know what to say.
I gave her a packet of tomato seeds
and asked her to plant them for me, told her
when the first tomato ripens
to miss me. ❖

# UNDERSTANDING

1. The story points out cultural differences between Americans and Japanese. Find examples in the text of some cultural differences and the reactions of the Japanese Americans to those differences.

   Cultural differences make American society rich and varied. In particular, we eat foods that have come to us from other cultures. Suppose a new restaurant called "House of International Cuisine" is opening. You attend the grand opening and write a feature article for the local newspaper. In your article, describe dishes from at least three different cultures. *Workshop 19*

2. Irony—the contrast between what is expected and what actually occurs—is a strong element in both the story and the poem. List several examples of irony from each selection. For example, in the first paragraph of the excerpt from *Farewell to Manzanar,* note the irony in "we went with a certain amount of relief." For each ironic statement you identify, briefly explain the irony.

3. "In Response to Executive Order 9066" is a letter written in the form of a poem. In what ways does the innocence of the fourteen-year-old girl come out in the poem? Would the message be different if it were written as a formal letter instead of as a poem?

   Choose a social issue that affects or concerns you, such as crime, drugs, indifference, racism, or pollution. Write a letter to a government official that explains your concerns. You may write a formal letter or a letter poem in the form of "In Response to Executive Order 9066." *Workshop 2 or 17*

> ## A LAST WORD
> Throughout history, people have suffered discrimination because they were part of a particular group. What causes humanity to behave this way? How can people learn to respect, rather than discriminate against, one another?

# CONNECTING

1. Many Japanese families came to live in California in the mid-1800s. Research Japanese immigration to the West Coast of the United States. Focus specifically on the contributions these new citizens made to America. Write a short report using maps and charts to illustrate the data. *Workshops 21 and 22*

2. As a class, brainstorm occasions in the past when specific groups were discriminated against because of race, nationality, or religious beliefs. An example is that of the Puritans, who fled England to make new homes in America. In small groups, research the causes of one of these occurrences and the extent of the discrimination. Determine the situation's effects on the nation or world. Present a panel presentation on the issue. *Workshop 25*

# Practice Makes Perfect

- *Ex-Basketball Player*
- *from Basketball for Women*

## EXPLORING
● ● ● ● ● ● ● ● ● ● ● ● ● ● ● ● ● ● ●

Sports stars are today's big heroes. They make unbelievably high salaries, live very public lives, and are worshipped by young and old alike. Do you think society admires these superstar athletes too much? Discuss whether athletes' salaries and fame are justified by how they perform for us. Is it fair that these athletic "entertainers" earn more than, for example, a nurse who works 12-hour shifts helping cancer patients deal with their illnesses?

## THEME CONNECTION...
## PREDICTING OUTCOMES

In the selections in this lesson, sometimes the actions are practiced and planned, and reactions are desirable and predictable. Sometimes the outcome is a matter of chance.

## TIME & PLACE

Basketball has been capturing the American imagination for more than 100 years. It is the object of dreams, poems, stories, and movies. Though professional basketball has become a multimillion-dollar business, many sportswriters still focus on the fundamentals of the game itself, rather than on the superstar players and high-tech arenas. In the poem and the technical manual in this lesson, readers can acquaint themselves with some of the details of the game— some of its essence.

In this lesson, the poem was written in the 1950s and the instructions are from a recent manual on women's basketball.

## THE WRITER'S CRAFT
### NONFICTION

Nonfiction is writing that informs the reader about real events and real people. It takes many forms, such as business proposals, manuals for operating or repairing machinery, instruction booklets, reports, and contracts. Newspapers and magazines contain mainly nonfiction writing, and essays, speeches, biographies, and autobiographies are also in this category. Because we are surrounded by nonfiction in our daily lives, more people read it than fiction.

● ● ● ● ● ● ● ● ● ● ● ● ● ● ● ● ● ● ● ● ● ● ● ● ● ● ● ● ● ● ● ● ● ●

# Ex-Basketball Player

John Updike

**About
the Author**

One of the most successful contemporary American authors, John Updike (b. 1932) has had his efforts honored by nearly every literary award, including the Pulitzer Prize. He grew up during the Great Depression in Shillington, Pennsylvania, where his parents encouraged his education and interest in art and writing. After a brief but highly successful career as a staff writer for *The New Yorker* magazine, Updike chose to pursue an independent writing career. He has produced more than 25 volumes of fiction, poetry, and criticism.

phosphates—
carbonated beverages

Pearl Avenue runs past the high-school lot,
Bends with the trolley tracks, and stops, cut off
Before it has a chance to go two blocks,
At Colonel McComsky Plaza. Berth's Garage
is on the corner facing west, and there,
Most days, you'll find Flick Webb, who helps Berth out.

Flick stands tall among the idiot pumps—
Five on a side, the old bubble-head style,
Their rubber elbows hanging loose and low.
One's nostrils are two S's, and his eyes
An E and O. And one is squat, without
A head at all—-more of a football type.

Once Flick played for the high-school team, the Wizards.
He was good: in fact, the best. In '46
He bucketed three hundred ninety points,
A county record still. The ball loved Flick.
I saw him rack up thirty-eight or forty
In one home game. His hands were like wild birds.

He never learned a trade, he just sells gas,
Checks oil, and changes flats. Once in a while,
As a gag, he dribbles an inner tube,
But most of us remember anyway.
His hands are fine and nervous on the lug wrench.
It makes no difference to the lug wrench, though.

Off work, he hangs around Mae's luncheonette.
Grease-gray and kind of coiled, he plays pinball,
Smokes those thin cigars, nurses lemon **phosphates**.
Flick seldom says a word to Mae, just nods
Beyond her face toward bright applauding tiers
Of Necco Wafers, Nibs, and Juju Beads. ❖

## from *Basketball for Women*

Nancy Lieberman Cline and
Robin Roberts

### Persistence

Persistence is your attitude. It's your frame of mind. It's not being satisfied. If you are persistent in basketball or in life, you can be successful. That quality will help you with skills and strategies. Eventually, you will figure out why you are successful on the court. Desire and hard work are a function of persistence. It's the only way to achieve success. Persistence has a domino effect. Everyone benefits except maybe your opponents. You've got the desire to play your best and if your opponents can't match that desire, watch out.

Building Persistence. You build persistence when you are willing to settle only for the best. There will be times in practice when hard work, repetition, and persistence pay off. Continue working when you think you can be better at a skill, drill, or learning the game. Don't be afraid to ask questions of coaches, mentors, and players. Get it right in your mind. That's how you can build persistence into your game. It's always doing, asking, and making sure it's correct. No matter how much or hard you work at something, apply those habits all the time. You'll be amazed at how being persistent can change a coach's or teammate's opinion of you. If you play hard for 2 hours in practice, your persistence should show your coaches you can give the same effort in a game. Take that focus and desire and use it every time you practice or play.

### Free Throws

How many games have been won or lost at the line? It happens at all levels—-the pros, college, high school, and rec league. Developing a consistent, reliable foul shot can change your success and your team's success. With all the bumping and grinding you deal with during a game while trying to shoot over a defender, the free throw is a blessing. When you are at the line, no one's in your face playing **D**. You have worked hard to get to the line. Now take a deep breath, relax, and concentrate. Here are some things to remember:

- Take deep breaths; relax your muscles. Take a moment to catch your breath. You rarely go to the line rested.

- Repetition is important. Take a few dribbles prior to shooting to find a rhythm. Do the same routine before each foul shot.

- Use a consistent technique; each shot must be the same motion. Foul shooting is rhythm, routine, and mechanics.

**About the Authors**

Nancy Lieberman Cline, or "Lady Magic," learned her aggressive style of playing basketball on New York playgrounds. She was the youngest member of the 1976 Olympic basketball team, which won the silver medal in Montreal.

ESPN Sportscaster Robin Roberts majored in communications and played basketball at Southeastern Louisiana University. After college, she worked at a number of small radio and television stations before joining ESPN.

D—defense

### "Persistence is your attitude."

Discuss how a person's self-confidence can affect performance on the job, at home, or at school. Identify specific skills at which you feel confident. What events or situations reinforce your sense of self-confidence?

◆ ◆ ◆ ◆ ◆ ◆ ◆ ◆ ◆ ◆ ◆ ◆ ◆ ◆ ◆

Stay balanced. Keep your elbow in; lean into your shot. Fix your eyes on the target and follow through.

- Line up properly. Most indoor courts have a nail placed in the middle of the foul line. Line up your foot with that nail. Line up with your right foot if you are right-handed; your left foot if you are left-handed.

- Think positively; you must believe in yourself and have confidence that you will make the shot. Confidence comes from success. Success comes from practicing your free throw shooting every day. ❖

# ON THE JOB

## DIESEL MECHANIC

If Flick Webb had learned a trade, he might have become a diesel mechanic. Diesel mechanics maintain, repair, and rebuild diesel engines that power buses, trucks, and trains. Because they often lift heavy parts, diesel mechanics should be in good physical condition. They usually work for diesel equipment dealers, manufacturers, or companies that use diesel equipment. Employers prefer applicants who have a high school education and mechanical ability. Helpful high school or vocational school courses include math, science, automobile repair, and machine shop work.

## UNDERSTANDING

1. In "Ex-Basketball Player," Flick had a dream that never materialized. Find evidence that the author believes that a person needs an education or training to make a living. What evidence is there that the author understands that relatively few athletes actually become superstars?

   Choose a sports star—past or present—whom you consider great. For instance, it might be Arthur Ashe, Florence Griffith Joyner, or Joe Montana. Research the athlete's life, including his or her childhood. Draw a diagram that illustrates the person's path to becoming a star. If possible, include quotations from the person. Share your diagram and describe it for the class. *Workshop 25*

2. Persistence is a quality needed for the success of any effort. Identify the main points the authors make about persistence in the excerpt from *Basketball for Women*. Then outline the essay.

   Choose another quality needed for success, whether of an athletic activity or another kind of challenge. Write an essay on why the quality is needed and how it contributes to the success of the effort or activity. *Workshop 3*

3. Re-read the free throw tips in the excerpt from *Basketball for Women*. Discuss why the authors used a list format instead of including the tips in a paragraph.

   Think of some sport or other activity with which you are very familiar. Write a set of instructions similar to the free throw tips for performing an action or specific skill from this activity.

### A LAST WORD

Many young, talented sports players dream of being successful in professional sports. Is there more to life than sports? What can our sports achievements teach us about succeeding in life?

## CONNECTING

1.  Research local training schools and colleges for people like Flick. As a class, develop a pamphlet on the opportunities for post–high school training and education in your area. For each school or college, include prerequisites, admission standards, costs, areas of study, and job placement opportunities. *Workshop 20*

2. Interview the coaches of several sports. Ask them to describe the qualities and traits a successful athlete must possess. Write a feature article based on your interviews, including accurate quotations from each coach you interviewed. Have a peer editor check your article, and then submit your article to the school newspaper for publication. *Workshops 19 and 27*

# The Fruits of Labor

- *A True Money Tree*
- *Birdfoot's Grampa*

## EXPLORING

In the fable "The Grasshopper and the Ants," the lazy grasshopper played all day in the summer while the ants worked. In winter, of course, the ants had plenty to eat, and the grasshopper froze and starved. The Little Red Hen worked hard to plant, grow, and harvest the wheat, and no one helped. When the bread was baked, however, everyone lined up to help eat it. These tales illustrate the moral that good workers are secure, comfortable, and successful. What other stories do you know with the same moral?

## THEME CONNECTION... LABOR PAYS OFF

Nearly everyone in today's world must work. This Chinese tale describes how even those who start with little can get ahead if they work hard. The lesson is that laziness has no rewards. In "Birdfoot's Grampa," the toads, too, are working hard. The old man understands that both people and nature must work hard to co-exist.

## TIME & PLACE

"A True Money Tree" comes from the Chinese province of Shantung, home of the sage Confucius (551–479 B.C.). The story teaches the Confucian lesson of respecting one's parents as well as the lesson of hard work.

The Abenaki tribe is part of Five Nations (which include the Iroquois) of upper New York. It is part of the Abenaki tradition for fathers to pass down stories to their sons. Bruchac carries on that tradition as well as the Native American respect for nature in "Birdfoot's Grampa."

## THE WRITER'S CRAFT

### SYMBOLISM

Writers use symbols to help readers understand ideas, character traits, and larger concepts. Symbols give deeper meaning to a poem or story. The "money tree" in the story stands for the person whose hard work brings him riches. The tree's branches are arms and hands that dig, plant, and harvest.

In the poem, the grandfather's efforts to help the toads cross the road symbolize people living in harmony with nature. The grandfather believes nothing should interfere with the order of nature.

# A True Money Tree

M. A. Jagendorf and Virginia Weng

In years gone by, there lived an old Chinese man by the name of Li. He had two sons, Long Life and Good Life.

Long Life's mother had died when he was a young boy, and Li had been lonely without a wife in the house. So he had married again, and when she gave him a son, he named him Good Life, for life in his house was good. But alas! The new wife did not like Long Life, so she made him do all the hard work in the house and in the fields and garden. But Long Life was an obedient son and did not complain. He did all that had to be done while his stepmother and brother looked on.

When he was seventeen years old, his father died, and his life with his stepmother was made even harder than it had been before. Although he did all the work in the house and fields, he was scolded all the time. No matter how much he tried to please his stepmother, she was always finding fault with him. She was always thinking of ways to get rid of him.

So one day she said, "You are old enough to be on your own now. We should divide the land your father left. Your brother is still young, and he can stay with me. We should each live in our own home, then there will be no quarrel between us."

Long Life agreed to this and left the division of property to his stepmother. She took the house and the best fields around it for herself and her son. To Long Life she gave a barren piece of land on a hill far from the village.

Long Life did not complain. He built himself a little hut and began clearing the land and plowing and planting on it. He cut some firewood, and little by little he grew enough food to support himself nicely.

With Long Life gone from the house and land where he had done all the work, there was no one to do it. Good Life and his mother were lazy and careless, so they became poorer and poorer. One day the mother said to her son, "Look we have a fine house and good land, and your brother lives in a hut on a piece of barren and hilly land, but he is getting richer and we are getting poorer. I am sure your father left him something of which we did not get our share. Son, go to your brother and make him tell you the truth, and ask him why he is getting rich and we are becoming poor. Tell him if he got something from his father we don't know about, he must give us at least half of it."

Good Life came to his brother in his little hut and said, "Brother, did our father give you some treasure we don't know about? We have fine land and you have a rocky barren piece—-how is it that you are doing so well and we so

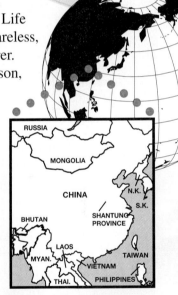

RUSSIA
MONGOLIA
CHINA
N.K.
S.K.
SHANTUNG PROVINCE
BHUTAN
LAOS
MYAN.
VIETNAM
TAIWAN
THAI.
PHILIPPINES

## About the Authors

Born in Austria, Moritz Jagendorf (1888–1981) came to the United States when he was fifteen years old. He worked as a dentist in New York City for 40 years while he pursued his interest in American, European, and Asian folklore. Jagendorf has written numerous books on folklore. With Virginia Weng—a writer, editor, and film producer of Chinese descent—Jagendorf wrote *The Magic Boat and Other Chinese Folk Stories*.

poorly? You have plenty of everything and we have nothing. Did our father leave something you are hiding from us? We want our share of it."

"Brother, you are right. Our wise father left me a wonderful treasure—a money tree. It has two trunks and there are five branches on each trunk. All my food and clothing depend on that wonderful tree. From that tree I will always get enough money to live in good health and pleasure . . . . It—"

Good Life broke in, "Where is that tree? Where are you hiding it?"

"I am not hiding it. It is with me all the time on my little piece of land, in my garden, and I am always there working at it. It gives me food, drink, and clothes and anything else I need, and if you—"

Before he could finish his words, Good Life rushed out and ran to his home. "Mother, Mother," he cried, "you were right. My father left a money tree that will give us money for all we need, but Long Life took it. He told me. It will give money for food, clothes, and everything else we need."

"I knew we were cheated," she cried. "Run to Long Life's orchard and dig up that money tree and plant it in our garden. It should be here."

Good Life did not need any coaxing. He found a spade and ran to Long Life's garden. He searched for a long time until he found a tree with two trunks and ten branches. He worked hard digging it up. Then he dragged it to his mother's garden and there he dug a deep hole and planted the tree, watering it well. Day after day he watered the tree and shook it hard—but no money fell from it.

Then Good Life went back to his brother in anger and cried, "I took a tree with two trunks and ten branches from your garden, and I planted it in our garden, watered it and took care of it, but no money falls from it. Did you tell me the truth?"

"Dear brother, I told you the truth—but you did not wait to hear the end of what I had to say. My money tree can never be stolen. It is my two arms and hands. The arms are the trunks and the fingers are the branches. Use them for planting trees and crops and to do all other work. Then money will come from them, and that will get you everything you need. My arms and hands are my fortune and I call them my money tree. You have a money tree, too. Put it to work as I do, and you will have all the money you need to buy whatever you want."

Good Life went home to his mother. On the way he had been thinking of his brother's words. "Mother," he said, "now I have the true money tree and . . ." He put his hands to work and soon he and his mother reaped money from that tree for food and everything else, just as his brother did. ❖

# Birdfoot's Grampa

Joseph Bruchac

## About the Author

Joseph Bruchac (b. 1942) is a well-known storyteller. Also known as *Sozap,* his Abenaki name, Bruchac often draws on his Native American heritage in his writing and storytelling. A poet and novelist as well, Bruchac has won national awards for his writing, including one for a storytelling tape of traditional Abenaki tales. His books of folktales include *Native American Stories* and *Thirteen Moons on Turtle's Back.*

The old man
must have stopped our car
two dozen times to climb out
and gather into his hands
the small toads blinded
by our lights and leaping,
live drops of rain.

The rain was falling,
a mist about his white hair
and I kept saying
you can't save them all,
accept it, get back in
we've got places to go.

But, leathery hands full
of wet brown life,
knee deep in the summer
roadside grass,
he just smiled and said
they have places to go to
too. ❖

## ACCENT ON...
### ENVIRONMENTAL SCIENCE

Both Long Life and Birdfoot's grandfather appreciate and respect the natural world around them. The field of environmental science seeks to preserve the natural environment. Study an area in your neighborhood or community that is in need of preservation or protection. Write a one- to two-page proposal suggesting ways in which the area would benefit from such care.

## UNDERSTANDING

1. Find evidence in the text of the differences between the two brothers. What is the significance of their names?

   Consult a baby name book to discover the meaning of your own name. Consider whether the meaning of your name fits your personality. In a short personal essay, explain why your name does or does not "fit" your personality.

2. Find evidence in "A True Money Tree" that Li's wife favors Good Life over Long Life. Consider the phrase, "When life gives you lemons, make lemonade." How does it apply to the theme of the story? Write a phrase that promotes the same feeling and design a poster to illustrate it. Share your work with the class.

3. In "Birdfoot's Grampa," the grandfather's instinct is not to interfere with the orderly progress of the toads. What does he understand that the narrator of the poem does not? How does the statement "they have places to go to, too" symbolize the coexistence of humans and animals? Write a letter of advice from this old man to his grandson about how best to live life. ***Workshop 16***

## A LAST WORD

How do we benefit by living in balance with the natural world around us? What can we do to maintain that balance?

## CONNECTING

1. Favoring one child over another can be a problem in families that include stepchildren. In groups, research in libraries and bookstores for information on being a member of a stepfamily and how to be a good stepparent. Using this information, write a 12- to 16-page children's book that helps children understand their feelings as they become a stepchild or get a new stepsister or stepbrother. Include a book plan that has rough sketches or descriptions of the illustrations.

2. Choose a type of bird, insect, lizard, or small mammal to research. Find out about the lifestyle of your chosen subject in relation to the movement of civilization into the countryside. Discover how, if at all, your subject has adapted to human growth. Prepare an oral report with maps, charts, and drawings to illustrate your research. ***Workshops 22 and 25***

# Hobbyist

## EXPLORING

Poison, a deadly chemical or drug, has been used for centuries as a weapon in mystery stories. Nearly every household contains poisonous chemicals that are used to kill insects or vegetation. Because these poisons are in our homes, small children are especially susceptible to accidental poisoning. What poisons does your family have around the house? How do you protect yourself and others from these chemicals?

## THEME CONNECTION...
## SURPRISE REACTION

One person's actions trigger a reaction from another, but even carefully thought-out actions do not always bring about the reactions we expect. In this unusual tale, a quiet little pharmacy becomes the setting for an evil scheme that backfires. The calm and very clever pharmacist injects a surprising element into a story that already seems intriguing.

## TIME & PLACE

The pharmacist in "Hobbyist" charges his "customer" one thousand dollars. In the 1950s, this was quite a sum. For comparison, the author, Fredric Brown, had begun his career by writing for sensational, or "pulp," magazines. He was paid one or two cents a word for the stories the magazines published.

## THE WRITER'S CRAFT

### DIALOGUE

Writers use dialogue carefully to create scenes and portray characters in a way that description alone cannot equal. "Hobbyist" centers around dramatic and serious conversation between a pharmacist and a customer. The dialogue helps us learn about the characters and creates suspense. Through the dialogue, both Mr. Sangstrom and the reader discover the serious consequences of the pharmacist's scheme.

# *Hobbyist*

## Fredric Brown

"I heard a rumor," Sangstrom said, "to the effect that you—" He turned his head and looked about him to make absolutely sure that he and the druggist were alone in the tiny prescription pharmacy. The druggist was a gnome-like **gnarled** little man who could have been any age from fifty to a hundred. They were alone, but Sangstrom dropped his voice just the same. "—to the effect that you have a completely undetectable poison."

The druggist nodded. He came around the counter and locked the front door of the shop, then walked toward a doorway behind the counter. "I was about to take a coffee break," he said. "Come with me and have a cup."

Sangstrom followed him around the counter and through the doorway to a back room ringed by shelves of bottles from floor to ceiling. The druggist plugged in an electric percolator, found two cups and put them on the table that had a chair on either side of it. He motioned Sangstrom to one of the chairs and took the other

## About the Author

Fredric Brown (1906–1972) worked as a proofreader and then as a writer for the Milwaukee *Journal.* During that time, he wrote and sold the first of more than 300 published short stories. In 1948, his first mystery novel, *The Fabulous Clipjoint,* received the Edgar Allan Poe Award for best first mystery novel. Brown wrote many science fiction stories and novels, including *What Mad Universe* and *Martians, Go Home.* For a brief time, he also wrote scripts for the Alfred Hitchcock television series.

gnarled—twisted

antidote—a remedy to counteract the effects of poison

virulent—extremely poisonous

● ● ● ● ● ● ●

"I must be convinced that you deserve what I can give you."

● ● ● ● ● ● ●

himself. "Now," he said. "Tell me. Whom do you want to kill, and why?"

"Does it matter?" Sangstrom asked. "Isn't it enough that I pay for—"

The druggist interrupted him with an upraised hand. "Yes, it matters. I must be convinced that you deserve what I can give you. Otherwise—" He shrugged.

"All right," Sangstrom said. "The *whom* is my wife. The *why*—" He started the long story. Before he had quite finished the percolator had finished its task and the druggist briefly interrupted to get the coffee for them. Sangstrom finished his story.

The little druggist nodded. "Yes, I occasionally dispense an undetectable poison. I do so freely; I do not charge for it, if I think the case is deserving. I have helped many murderers."

"Fine," Sangstrom said. "Please give it to me, then."

The druggist smiled at him. "I already have. By the time the coffee was ready I had decided that you deserved it. It was, as I said, free. But there is a price for the **antidote**."

Sangstrom turned pale. But he had anticipated—not this, but the possibility of a double-cross or some form of blackmail. He pulled a pistol from his pocket.

The little druggist chuckled. "You daren't use that. Can you find the antidote"—he waved at the shelves—"among those thousands of bottles? Or would you find a faster, more **virulent** poison? Or if you think I'm bluffing, that you're not really poisoned, go ahead and shoot. You'll know the answer within three hours when the poison starts to work."

"How much for the antidote?" Sangstrom growled.

"Quite reasonable. A thousand dollars. After all, a man must live. Even if his hobby is preventing murders, there's no reason why he shouldn't make money at it, is there?"

Sangstrom growled and put the pistol down, but within reach, and took out his wallet. Maybe after he had the antidote, he'd still use that pistol. He counted out a thousand dollars in hundred-dollar bills and put it on the table.

The druggist made no immediate move to pick it up. He said: "And one other thing—for your wife's safety and mine. You will write a confession of your intention—your former intention, I trust—to murder your wife. Then you will wait till I go out and mail it to a friend of mine on the homicide detail. He'll keep it as evidence in case you ever *do* decide to kill your wife. Or me, for that matter.

"When that is in the mail it will be safe for me to return here and give you the antidote. I'll get you the paper and pen . . .

"Oh, one other thing—although I do not absolutely insist on it. Please help spread the word about my undetectable poison, will you? One never knows, Mr. Sangstrom. The life you save, if you have any enemies, just might be your own. ❖

## ON THE JOB

### PHARMACEUTICAL TECHNICIAN

Pharmaceutical technicians assist scientists and engineers in the pharmaceutical, or drug, industry. Most technicians work for private companies that make finished drugs such as vitamin pills, antiseptics, antibiotics, and veterinary medicines. Good communication skills and attention to detail are essential in this kind of work. In addition to high school courses in biology and chemistry, a two-year technical degree with course work in engineering or veterinary science is highly recommended.

# UNDERSTANDING

1. Why does the author call the pharmacist's activities his hobby? Find evidence in the text that the pharmacist enjoys his hobby.

   Interview someone who has a hobby. Find out how he or she came to have that hobby, what amount of time is spent on it, how much it costs, and what its rewards are. Write a feature article on this person and his or her hobby. ***Workshops 19 and 26***

2. Find evidence in the story that the pharmacist has participated in a similar activity before. What is the basic philosophy or goal of the pharmacist, and how does he use the elements of his occupation in his hobby?

   Brainstorm other occupations that have another side that could become a person's hobby. For example, a fruit grower who raises apples might also carve apple wood dolls to sell in craft shops. Then consider the occupations you might like to pursue. What opportunities for a hobby could this occupation offer on the side?

3. While the pharmacist is preventing a crime, he also is committing a crime. Prove or disprove this statement with evidence from the story. Write an argumentative paper to make your point. ***Workshop 13 and 23***

4. Suppose that Sangstrom's wife somehow overhears the conversation between the pharmacist and her husband. Rewrite the story, including this new detail. What will be the outcome now? ***Workshop 1***

## A LAST WORD

Do you think the druggist's reaction to Sangstrom's request was justifiable? How would you define a justifiable action or reaction?

# CONNECTING

1. Work with several classmates to prepare a radio play of this story. Include background music and sound effects for the door closing and locking, the coffee pot percolating, the cups filling, and so on. Tape the play and play it for the rest of the class.

2. Most hobbies or activities involve some knowledge of certain processes. For example, in tennis it is necessary to know the steps involved in serving. Write the steps of a process you are familiar with so that someone else can learn it. Arrange your instructions in logical order, use clear language, and include details. *Workshop 12*

3. Consider the options Sangstrom has rather than murder. If a marriage is in trouble, where in your community can a couple find help? What private and public agencies or services are available? Prepare a pamphlet listing each service or program, its address and telephone number, fees, and any particular methods of counseling that are used. *Workshop 20*

# WRAP IT UP

1. In "A True Money Tree," Long Life explains that his arms and hands are his fortune, and he calls them his "money tree." In other words, Long Life understands that he will reap success only through his own labors and efforts. Think about the characters in "The Necklace," "The Colt," "Ex-Basketball Player," and the excerpt from *Farewell to Manzanar*. How do they react to the situations facing them? Do they understand and share Long Life's philosophy?

2. Birdfoot's grandfather takes the time and care to rescue small toads from the path of oncoming cars. Think of the many other characters in the selections in this unit. Which characters perform tasks that others don't want to bother with? What motivates them to do so? Explain the differences in the motives for their actions.

# UNIT
## ④
# COURAGE AND CONVICTION

*In some people's minds, having courage means being fearless and ready to try anything. However, people who are truly courageous may be full of fear. They recognize the dangers but choose to act, certain it's the right thing to do. This belief, or conviction, gives them courage to face the dangers.*

*This quiet kind of courageousness hardly ever makes headlines in the newspaper. Yet our world is a far better place because some people have the courage to confront the problems around them and the conviction to do what they think is right.*

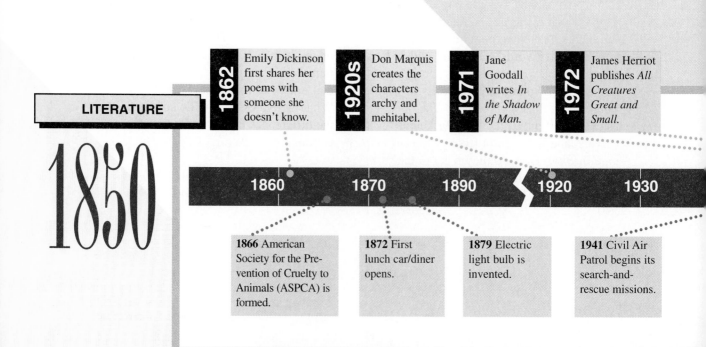

**LITERATURE**

**1850**

**1862** Emily Dickinson first shares her poems with someone she doesn't know.

**1920s** Don Marquis creates the characters archy and mehitabel.

**1971** Jane Goodall writes *In the Shadow of Man.*

**1972** James Herriot publishes *All Creatures Great and Small.*

1860    1870    1890    1920    1930

**1866** American Society for the Prevention of Cruelty to Animals (ASPCA) is formed.

**1872** First lunch car/diner opens.

**1879** Electric light bulb is invented.

**1941** Civil Air Patrol begins its search-and-rescue missions.

**1981** Toni Bambara receives an award for her literary achievement.

**1983** Alice Walker receives Pulitzer Prize for *The Color Purple.*

**1985** Jim Daniels receives a National Endowment for the Arts Creative Writing Fellowship.

**1993** Maya Angelou writes and recites "On the Pulse of Morning."

2000

1950    1960    1970    1980    1990

**1954** "Separate-but-equal" schools are ruled unconstitutional.

**1960** Jane Goodall begins her research on chimpanzees.

**1963** Eunice Kennedy Shriver organizes first Special Olympics.

**1972** Senate approves the Equal Rights Amendment.

**LIFE and WORK**

# *Raymond's Run*

## EXPLORING

● ● ● ● ● ● ● ● ● ● ● ● ● ● ● ● ● ● ● ● ● ●

Competition among friends can be healthy. A competitive spirit can help each person rise to new heights. But too much competitiveness can hurt a friendship. Do you compete with a friend in sports, school, or other areas? What are the benefits of this competition? Discuss examples of how competition has been positive or negative in your life.

## THEME CONNECTION...
## THE COMPETITIVE EDGE

As a competitive runner, Squeaky is a girl with a mission. She is fearless, strong, and determined, but she is also obstinate and stubborn. All these qualities drive her forward, but she has to be careful not to damage friendships or miss opportunities for the friendship she needs so much.

Through Squeaky's voice, we catch a glimpse of her life with her brother Raymond, for whom she is responsible. She has learned only one way to deal with the kids who pick on Raymond; she fights back. Her strength, however, can sometimes be her weakness.

## TIME & PLACE

The setting of "Raymond's Run" is a section of New York City called Harlem. The author, Toni Cade Bambara, spent part of her childhood there. The main character practices for her races along Broadway and Amsterdam, two of the major thoroughfares running north and south through New York City.

## THE WRITER'S CRAFT
### AUTHENTIC VOICE

Squeaky's personality jumps right off the page. The author has allowed us to see what is going on in Squeaky's head. Squeaky will not allow anyone to get in her way. She believes that she is the best, that she will win the race, and that she should show people who she really is. Squeaky's sarcastic and scornful voice is authentic to us because we probably have known someone like this, or we would like to be independent and headstrong just as she is.

● ● ● ● ● ● ● ● ● ● ● ● ● ● ● ● ● ● ● ● ● ● ● ● ● ● ● ● ● ●

# Raymond's Run

Toni Cade Bambara

don't have much work to do around the house like some girls. My mother does that. And I don't have to earn my pocket money by working; George runs errands for the big boys and sells Christmas cards. And anything else that's got to get done, my father does. All I have to do in life is mind my brother Raymond, which is enough.

Sometimes I slip and say my little brother Raymond. But as any fool can see he's much bigger and he's older too. But a lot of people call him my little brother 'cause he needs looking after 'cause he's not quite right. And a lot of smart mouths got lots to say about that too, especially when George was minding him. But now, if anybody has anything to say to Raymond, anything to say about his big head, they have to come by me. And I don't play the dozens or believe in standing around with somebody in my face doing a lot of talking. I'd much rather just knock you down and take my chances even if I am a little girl with skinny arms and a squeaky voice, which is how I got the name Squeaky. And if things get too tough, I run. And as anybody can tell you, I'm the fastest thing on two feet.

There is no track meet that I don't win the first-place medal. I used to win the twenty-yard dash when I was a little kid in kindergarten. Nowadays, it's the fifty-yard dash. And tomorrow I'm **subject** to run the quarter-mile relay all by myself and come in first, second, and third. The big kids call me **Mercury** 'cause I'm the swiftest thing in the neighborhood. Everybody knows that—except two people who know better, my father and me. He can beat me to Amsterdam Avenue with me having a two fire-hydrant head start and him running with his hands in his pockets and whistling. But that's private information. 'Cause can you imagine some thirty-five-year-old man stuffing himself into shorts to race little kids? So as far as everyone's concerned, I'm the fastest and that goes for Gretchen, too, who has put out the tale that she is going to win the first-place medal this year. Ridiculous. In the second place, she's got short legs. In the third place, she's got freckles. In the first place, no one can beat me and that's all there is to it.

I'm standing on the corner admiring the weather and about to take a stroll down Broadway so I can practice my breathing exercises, and I've got Raymond walking on the inside close to the buildings, 'cause he's subject to fits of fantasy and starts thinking he's a circus performer and that the curb is a tightrope strung high in the air. And sometimes after a rain he likes to step down off his tightrope right into the gutter and slosh around getting his shoes and cuffs wet. Then I get it when I get

## About the Author

Born in New York City, Toni Cade Bambara (1939–1995) received her bachelor's degree from Queens College and her master's degree from City College of New York. The short-story writer and novelist took the name Bambara from a signature on a sketchbook she found in her great-grandmother's trunk.

Bambara described herself as "a writer since childhood who nevertheless planned to be a doctor, lawyer, artist, musician, and everything else."

subject—likely

Mercury—in Roman mythology, the messenger god, who flew by means of a winged cap and sandals

prodigy—a highly talented child

home. Or sometimes if you don't watch him he'll dash across the traffic to the island in the middle of Broadway and give the pigeons a fit. Then I have to go behind him apologizing to all the old people sitting around trying to get some sun and getting all upset with the pigeons fluttering around them, scattering their newspapers and upsetting the wax-paper lunches in their laps. So I keep Raymond on the inside of me, and he plays like he's driving a stagecoach which is O.K. by me so long as he doesn't run me over or interrupt my breathing exercises, which I have to do on account of I'm serious about my running and I don't care who knows it.

Now some people like to act like things come easy to them, won't let on that they practice. Not me. I'll high-prance down 34th Street like a rodeo pony to keep my knees strong even if it does get my mother uptight so that she walks ahead like she's not with me, doesn't know me, is all by herself on a shopping trip, and I am somebody else's crazy child. Now you take Cynthia Procter for instance. She's just the opposite. If there's a test tomorrow, she'll say something like, "Oh, I guess I'll play handball this afternoon and watch television tonight," just to let you know she isn't thinking about the test. Or like last week when she won the spelling bee for the millionth time, "A good thing you got 'receive,' Squeaky, 'cause I would have got it wrong. I completely forgot about the spelling bee." And she'll clutch the lace on her blouse like it was a narrow

● ● ● ● ● ● ● ●
## "Some people like to act like things come easy to them."
● ● ● ● ● ● ●

escape. Oh, brother. But of course when I pass her house on my early morning trots around the block, she is practicing the scales on the piano over and over and over and over. Then in music class she always lets herself get bumped around so she falls accidentally on purpose onto the piano stool and is so surprised to find herself sitting there that she decides just for fun to try out the ole keys. And what do you know—Chopin's waltzes just spring out of her fingertips and she's the most surprised thing in the world. A regular **prodigy**. I could kill people like that. I stay up all night studying the words for the spelling bee. And you can see me any time of the day practicing running. I never walk if I can trot, and shame on Raymond if he can't keep up. But of course he does, 'cause if he hangs back someone's likely to walk up to him and get smart, or take his allowance from him, or ask him where he got that great big pumpkin head. People are so stupid sometimes.

So I'm strolling down Broadway breathing out and breathing in on counts of seven, which is my lucky number, and here comes Gretchen and her sidekicks: Mary Louise, who used to be a friend of mine when she first moved to Harlem from Baltimore and got beat up by everybody 'till I took up for her on account of her mother and my mother used to sing in the same choir when they were young girls, but people aren't grateful, so now she hangs out with the new girl, Gretchen, and talks about me like a dog; and Rosie, who is as fat as I am skinny and has a big mouth where Raymond is concerned and is too stupid to know that there is not a big deal of difference between herself and Raymond and that she can't afford to throw stones. So they are steady coming up Broadway and I see right away that it's going to be one of those Dodge City scenes 'cause the street isn't that big and they're close to the buildings just as we are. First I think I'll step into the candy store and look over the new comics and let them pass. But that's chicken and I've got a reputation to consider. So then I think I'll just walk straight on through them or even over them if necessary. But as they get to me, they slow down. I'm ready to fight, 'cause like I said I don't **feature** a whole lot of chit-chat, I much prefer to just knock you down right from the jump and save everybody a lotta precious time.

"You signing up for the May Day races?" smiled Mary Louise, only it's not a smile at all. A dumb question like that doesn't deserve an answer. Besides, there's just me and Gretchen standing there really, so no use wasting my breath talking to shadows.

"I don't think you're going to win this time," says Rosie, trying to **signify** with her hands on her hips all salty, completely forgetting that I have whupped her behind many times for less salt than that.

"I always win 'cause I'm the best," I say straight at Gretchen who is, as far as I'm concerned, the only one talking in this ventriloquist-dummy routine. Gretchen smiles, but it's not a smile, and I'm thinking that girls never really smile at each other because they don't know how and don't want to know how and there's probably no one to teach us how,

'cause grown-up girls don't know either. Then they all look at Raymond who has just brought his mule team to a standstill. And they're about to see what trouble they can get into through him.

"What grade you in now, Raymond?"

"You got anything to say to my brother, you say it to me, Mary Louise Williams of Raggedy Town, Baltimore."

"What are you, his mother?" sasses Rosie.

"That's right, Fatso. And the next word out of anybody and I'll be *their* mother too." So they just stand there and Gretchen shifts from one leg to the other and so do they. Then Gretchen puts her hands on her hips and is about to say something with her freckle-face self but doesn't. Then she walks around me looking me up and down but keeps walking up Broadway, and her sidekicks follow her. So me and Raymond smile at each other and he says "Gidyap" to his team and I continue with my breathing exercises, strolling down Broadway toward the ice man on 145th with not a care in the world 'cause I am Miss **Quicksilver** herself.

I take my time getting to the park on May Day because the track meet is the last thing on the program. The biggest thing on the program is the May Pole dancing, which I can do without, thank you, even if my mother thinks it's a shame I don't take part and "act like a girl for a change." You'd think my mother'd be grateful not to have to make me

feature—prefer

signify—send a signal

Quicksilver—another reference to Mercury; quick-silver is another name for the element mercury

Raymond's Run

parkees—slang;
people who
spend time in
the park

glockenspiel—
an instrument
similar to a
xylophone

a white organdy dress with a big satin sash and buy me new white baby-doll shoes that can't be taken out of the box 'till the big day. You'd think she'd be glad her daughter isn't out there prancing around a May Pole getting the new clothes all dirty and sweaty and trying to act like a flower or whatever you're supposed to be when you should be trying to be yourself, whatever that is, which is, as far as I am concerned, a poor black girl who really can't afford to buy shoes and a new dress you only wear once a lifetime 'cause it won't fit next year.

I was once a strawberry in a Hansel and Gretel pageant when I was in nursery school and didn't have no better sense than to dance on tiptoe with my arms in a circle over my head doing umbrella steps and being a perfect fool just so my mother and father could come dressed up and clap. You'd think they'd know better than to encourage that kind of nonsense. I am not a strawberry. I do not dance on my toes. I run. That is what I am all about. So I always come late to the May Day program, just in time to get my number pinned on and lay in the grass 'till they announce the fifty-yard dash.

I put Raymond in the little swings, which is a tight squeeze this year and will be impossible next year. Then I look around for Mr. Pearson, who pins the numbers on. I'm really looking for Gretchen if you want to know the truth, but she's not around. The park is jam-packed. Parents in hats and corsages and breast-pocket handkerchiefs peeking up. Kids in white dresses and light-blue suits. The **parkees** unfolding chairs and chasing the rowdy kids from Lenox as if they had no right be there. The big guys with their caps on backwards, leaning against the fence swirling the basketballs on the tips of their fingers, waiting for all these crazy people to clear out the park so they can play. Most of the kids in my class are carrying bass drums and **glockenspiels** and flutes. You'd think they'd put in a few bongos or something for real like that.

Then here comes Mr. Pearson with his clipboard and his cards and pencils and whistles and safety pins and fifty million other things he's always dropping all over the place with his clumsy self. He sticks out in a crowd because he's on stilts. We used to call him Jack and the Beanstalk to get him mad. But I'm the only one that can outrun him and get away, and I'm too grown for that silliness now.

"Well, Squeaky," he says, checking my name off the list and handing me number seven and two pins. And I'm thinking he's got no right to call me Squeaky, if I can't call him Beanstalk.

"Hazel Elizabeth Deborah Parker," I correct him and tell him to write it down on his board.

"Well, Hazel Elizabeth Deborah Parker, going to give someone else a break this year?" I squint at him real hard to see if he is seriously thinking I should lose the race on purpose just to give someone else a break. "Only six girls running this time," he continues, shaking his head sadly like it's my fault all of New York didn't turn out in sneakers. "That new girl should give you a run for your money." He looks around the park for Gretchen like a periscope in a submarine movie. "Wouldn't it be a nice gesture if you were . . . to ahhh . . ."

I give him such a look he couldn't finish putting that idea into words.

Squeaky runs different races, including the quarter-mile relay. Although the metric system is used to measure distances in most countries in the world, the United States uses the metric system for only some purposes, such as in science and in some track and field sports. The basic unit of measure in the metric system is the meter, which equals 39.37 inches. Find a conversion chart and compare U.S. standard units of measurement to those used in the metric system. Then convert the distances of these races into metric units: 20-yard dash, 30-yard dash, 50-yard dash, and quarter-mile relay.

Grown-ups got a lot of nerve sometimes. I pin number seven to myself and stomp away. I'm so burnt. And I go straight for the track and stretch out on the grass while the band winds up with "Oh, the Monkey Wrapped His Tail Around the Flag Pole," which my teacher calls by some other name. The man on the loud-speaker is calling everyone over to the track and I'm on my back looking at the sky, trying to pretend I'm in the country, but I can't because even grass in the city feels hard as a sidewalk, and there's just no pretending you are anywhere but in a "concrete jungle" as my grand-father says.

The twenty-yard dash takes all of two minutes 'cause most of the little kids don't know no better than to run off the track or run the wrong way or run smack into the fence and fall down and cry. One little kid, though, has got the good sense to run straight for the white ribbon up ahead so he wins. Then the second-graders line up for the thirty-yard dash and I don't even bother to turn my head to watch 'cause Raphael Perez always wins. He wins before he even begins by psyching the runners, telling them they're going to trip on their shoelaces and fall on their faces or lose their shorts or some-thing, which he doesn't really have to do since he is very fast, almost as fast as I am. After that is the forty-yard dash which I used to run when I was in first grade. Raymond is hollering from the swings 'cause he knows I'm about to do my thing 'cause the man on the loud-speaker has just announced the fifty-yard dash, although he might just as well be giving a recipe for angel food cake 'cause you can hardly make out what he's saying for the static. I get up and slip off my sweatpants and then I see Gretchen stand-ing at the starting line, kicking her legs out like a pro. Then as I get into place I see that ole Raymond is on line on the other side of the fence, bending down with his fingers on the ground just like he knew what he was doing. I was going to yell at him but then I didn't. It burns up your energy to holler.

Every time just before I take off in a race, I always feel like I'm in a dream, the kind of dream you have when you're sick with fever and feel all hot and weightless. I dream I'm flying over a sandy beach in the early morning sun, kissing the leaves of the trees as I fly by. And there's always the smell of apples, just like in the country when I was little and used to think I was a choo-choo train, running through the fields of corn and chugging up the hill to the orchard. And all the time I'm dreaming this, I get lighter and lighter until I'm flying over the beach again, getting blown through the sky like a feather that weighs nothing at all. But once I spread my fingers in the dirt and crouch over the Get on Your Mark, the dream goes and I am solid again and am telling myself, Squeaky you must win, you must win, you are the fastest thing in the world, you can even beat your father up Amsterdam if you really try. And then I feel my weight coming back just behind my knees then down to my feet then into the earth and the pistol shot explodes in my blood and I am off and weightless again, flying past the other runners, my arms pumping up and down and the whole world is quiet except for the crunch as I zoom over the gravel in the track. I glance to my left

> ● ● ● ● ● ● ● ●
>
> "I dream I'm flying over a sandy beach in the early morning sun . . ."
>
> ● ● ● ● ● ● ● ●

and there is no one. To the right, a blurred Gretchen, who's got her chin jutting out as if it would win the race all by itself. And on the other side of the fence is Raymond with his arms down to his side and the palms tucked up behind him, running in his very own style, and it's the first time I ever saw that and I almost stop to watch my brother Raymond on his first run. But the white ribbon is bouncing toward me and I tear past it, racing into the distance 'till my feet with a mind of their own start digging up footfulls of dirt and brake me short. Then all the kids standing on the side pile on me, banging me on the back and slapping my head with their May Day programs, for I have won again and everybody on 151st Street can walk tall for another year.

"In first place . . ." the man on the loudspeaker is clear as a bell now. But then he pauses and the loudspeaker starts to whine. Then static. And I lean down to catch my breath and here comes Gretchen walking back, for she's overshot the finish line too, huffing and puffing with her hands on her hips, taking it slow, breathing in steady time like a real pro and I sort of like her a little for the first time. "In first place . . ." and then three or four voices get all mixed up on the loudspeaker and I dig my sneaker into the grass and stare at Gretchen who's staring back, we both wondering just who did win. I can hear old Beanstalk arguing with the man on the loudspeaker and then a few others running their mouths about what the stopwatches say. Then I hear Raymond yanking at the fence to call me and I wave to shush him, but he keeps rattling the fence like a gorilla in a cage like in them gorilla movies, but then like a dancer or something he starts climbing up nice and easy but very fast. And it occurs to me, watching how smoothly he climbs hand over hand and remembering how he looked running with his arms down to his side and with the wind pulling his mouth back and his teeth showing and all, it occurred to me that Raymond would make a very fine runner. Doesn't he always keep up with me on my trots? And he surely knows how to breathe in counts of seven 'cause he's always doing it at the dinner table, which drives my brother George up the wall. And I'm smiling to beat the band 'cause if I've lost this race, or if me and Gretchen tied, or even if I've won, I can always retire as a runner and begin a whole new career as a coach with Raymond as my champion. After all, with a little more study I can beat Cynthia and her phony self at the spelling bee. And if I bugged my mother, I could get piano lessons and become a star. And I have a big **rep** as the baddest thing around. And I've got a roomful of ribbons and medals and awards. But what has Raymond got to call his own?

So I stand there with my new plans, laughing out loud by this time as Raymond jumps down from the fence and runs over with his teeth showing and his arms down to the side, which no one before him has quite mastered as a running style. And by the time he comes over I'm jumping up and down so glad to see him—my brother Raymond, a great runner in the family tradition. But of course everyone thinks I'm jumping up and down because the men on the loudspeaker have finally gotten themselves together and compared notes and are announcing "In first place—Miss Hazel Elizabeth Deborah Parker." (Dig that.) "In second place Miss Gretchen P. Lewis." And I look over at Gretchen wondering what the "P" stands for. And I smile. 'Cause she's good, no doubt about it. Maybe she'd like to help me coach Raymond; she obviously is serious about running, as any fool can see. And she nods to congratulate me and then smiles. And I smile. We stand there with this big smile of respect between us. It's about as real a smile as girls can do for each other, considering we don't practice real smiling every day, you know, 'cause maybe we are too busy being flowers or strawberries instead of something honest and worthy of respect . . . you know . . . like being people. ❖

rep—short for "reputation"

## ACCENT ON...
### EDUCATION

The Parker family's answer to Raymond's well-being is to have Squeaky watch out for him. What forms of education are available for people with mental or developmental disabilities? What can family members and society in general expect from people who are mentally challenged? Do they always have to be "watched out for?" Find out how people with developmental disabilities are taught, and what they can learn. Examine the issue from the point of view of a teacher to see if this type of career would appeal to you.

# UNDERSTANDING

1. Squeaky believes in loyalty to her family. Make a list of other beliefs she has. Next to each belief, write evidence from the text that illustrates it.

   Squeaky is straightforward and blunt. In her case, what you see is what you get. Write a one-page paper on your own personality and behaviors. How do you show others who you really are? *Workshop 7*

2.  Cynthia seems to be Squeaky's opposite. Squeaky does not respect Cynthia because their personalities are so different. Find evidence in the text that this is true.

   In the workplace, people with different attitudes, beliefs, and qualities must work together. In groups, develop a list of skills and behaviors that serve as rules for getting along with people. Compare your group's list with those of other groups. Create a class list and post a copy in the room for reference.

3. At the race's end, Squeaky changes her thinking considerably. Find evidence that illustrates the causes of her change, the process, and the results. For clues, reread the last sentence of the story. Write a descriptive essay about the change in Squeaky.

   Being able to write an observation report that describes the details of a situation or event is an important skill in the workplace. Write an observation report on something you can look at and describe, such as the condition of the locker rooms in your school, the state of a run-down building, the nature of a piece of equipment with which you work, and so on. *Workshop 10*

## A LAST WORD

Why does it take courage to be yourself, rather than a flower or a fairy or a strawberry, as Squeaky would say? What can be learned from Squeaky's honesty?

# CONNECTING

1. Research the subject area of running or track and field events. When and where did these events start? How did they progress to what they are today? Choose one specific topic in this area, write a report on it, and give an oral presentation. *Workshops 21 and 25*

2. Suppose Raymond had the opportunity to run in the Special Olympics. Write a letter to the Special Olympics headquarters asking for information. Find out when your state is organizing local events, who is sponsoring them, how to enter, and how to become a volunteer. Design posters to be placed around your community advertising the Special Olympics. *Workshop 17*

# from *Hey, I'm Alive!*

## EXPLORING

Being lost in a wilderness or surviving a plane crash in a remote area brings up horrible images for most of us. We wonder if we would have the stamina and determination necessary to survive. What *does* it take to live in the wild? What survival techniques do you know? How could a person prepare for such a frightening experience?

## THEME CONNECTION...
## COURAGE TO SURVIVE

A small-aircraft wreck in Alaska was given up as lost, but the passenger and pilot had not died. Their task was to survive days and nights without food and with very little hope. As you read their intense and moving story, imagine your own response had you been with them.

## TIME & PLACE

On February 4, 1963, Helen Klaben, 21, and Ralph Flores, 42, took off from Fairbanks, Alaska, in a small plane owned and piloted by Flores. They were bound for San Francisco; Klaben was planning to move to California. As a result of bad weather, the plane crashed, and the two were stranded in the Alaskan wilderness for seven weeks. Both were injured. For five of the weeks they ate only snow.

## THE WRITER'S CRAFT

### JOURNALS

Journals are a very personal form of literature. Stories of true-life adventure unfold in daily logs kept by ships' captains, explorers such as Lewis and Clark, pioneer women in log cabins, people fighting illnesses, and ordinary people living their lives. Journals give us insight into feelings as well as events, inviting us into the inner soul of the writer. This journal was written after the events described took place; however, its account is very intense.

# from *Hey, I'm Alive!*

Helen Klaben with Beth Day

## The First Week

"Don't cry, Helen," Ralph said.

"I have to cry. I have to cry," I sobbed. It was the third day since the crash. I couldn't stop crying. Planes kept passing over us, but we couldn't see them through the low gray clouds. They couldn't see us or our smoke signals through the trees. It was terribly cold—40 below—and dark. My foot and arm hurt awfully. For the first time, I was really hungry. I felt no one knew we were lost and alive except for God. I couldn't understand why He had put me here.

Ralph tried to comfort me. He said the search would go on until we were found. He tried to set my broken arm. Ralph made rough splints out of pieces of the plane's wing, and we tore up a dress of mine for bandages.

That morning Ralph had built a fire and melted snow for breakfast. I stayed in the plane, covered by parkas and canvas. His broken jaw was so painful he couldn't even swallow water. Despite his pain, Ralph dressed my injured foot with strips from one of my dresses. Then he covered it with a sweater and made

## About the Authors

Since Helen Klaben (b. 1942) was in the sixth grade, she had wanted to write an autobiography. She told her wish to a friend, who replied, "What ever happened to *you*?" A few years later, after surviving a wilderness plane crash, plenty had happened and she had plenty to tell. With Beth Day, she relates her story of survival and rescue. Day has written many books, including *Glacier Pilot* and *Grizzlies in Their Back Yard*.

me foot coverings out of canvas and string.

We were still sure we were going to be rescued at any minute, so we squandered our food and ate two meals. Really, *I* ate twice. For lunch, Ralph just sipped the warm juice from one of the cans of fruit he warmed over the fire. I ate the whole can. I also ate half a can of tuna fish. At dinner, I finished the tuna fish while Ralph opened a can of sardines. He mashed them up, mixed the mash with water, and, using a twig for a spoon, got some of the mess painfully into his mouth. That night I was hungrier than ever, and slept very badly.

## Hunger

On the seventh day I found two small chicken legs in the back of the plane. They were the remains of a chicken dinner we had bought in Fairbanks to eat on our flight to Whitehorse. They were good for a whole day's food for the two of us. And I mean good! Ralph cut the chicken into little pieces. Then he boiled it in melted snow water and made a delicious soup.

On the ninth day we were down to the last of the crackers and canned fruit. I was so hungry that I hoped Ralph would only be able to sip the juice, as he had done before. But his jaw was improved enough so that he could eat as much of the warm fruit as I did.

On the twelfth day I had a bad attack of stomach pains. I was in such pain that Ralph tried to help by patting my back like a baby. Finally the cramps went away. I didn't know what had caused them. I thought, "Maybe I'm starving to death. Maybe this is what it feels like."

The first three days after the food was all gone, I felt hunger pains. Then they went away, and I was seldom hungry again. It was as if my stomach went to sleep. But I did want water. In the morning I'd wake up thinking, "I wish Ralph would hurry with that water!" At breakfast we pretended the water was coffee or hot milk. At supper we imagined it was tea and different kinds of soup: one day tomato soup, then beef, another day mushroom and chicken and all the other kinds.

I found a new supply of food. I was brushing my teeth and by mistake swallowed some of the toothpaste. It tasted good. Ralph squeezed out an inch of the toothpaste and ate it. I was horrified at first, then gave it a second thought. What could be wrong with toothpaste? I put some on my tongue and let it melt slowly. It was almost like food. After that, I stopped brushing my teeth and we ate what was left of my large tube and Ralph's small tube. Just a little each day, to make it last. Sometimes we stirred it into our hot water. It tasted delicious. The toothpaste lasted almost two weeks.

## False Hopes

On February 25, three weeks after the crash, we saw a plane. It flew down so low over our little clearing that we were sure it had spotted us. We screamed and yelled and danced around, waving and hugging each other. We were certain we were about to be rescued.

That plane did not return. We looked for it all that day. And all the following day. When another day had passed, we realized it was never coming back.

We heard a few others far away during the next two days . . . then nothing. Slowly we realized that the air search had been given up. Now we were really on our own.

## The Move

*Helen and Ralph moved away from the crash site to a clearing in the woods, perhaps a mile down the mountain. They thought the open clearing would make them more visible. Ralph pushed Helen on a sled made from a piece of the plane. They set up camp, which consisted of a tent and a fire. They could hear a noise in the distance, a machine-like noise. In spite of being very weak, Ralph walked in the direction of the noise.*

When the next day dawned clear, I knew Ralph would leave, no matter what I said. It was as if he were determined to spend his last bit of strength—or perhaps use a strength he didn't have himself but came through his faith in God.

I didn't say anything more about not wanting to be left alone. I'd got along before. I would have to make my own peace again.

I sat by the fire, watching and calling after him. My eyes were filled with tears. He was so weak now. It was, I thought, March 20. I wrote in my notebook: "Ralph left . . . please, God, be with him."

The weather stayed fair. It was more comfortable in the canvas tent, with the fire right in front of the opening, than it had been in the plane. And I didn't have

**"We were certain we were about to be rescued."**

# SPOTLIGHT ON...
# UNDERSTANDING ORDER

When explaining events or a process, the order in which you present information is essential to your readers' understanding. Here are some different ways of ordering information in your thinking and writing processes.

1. Chronological order—Present events in the order in which they happen.
2. Order of cause and effect—Start with the cause of an event and end with its result.
3. Order of importance—Begin with the most important detail or fact and work to the least important, or reverse the order, depending on your purpose.
4. Spatial order—Organize information from top to bottom, side to side, inside out, or by some other spatial relationship.

◆ ◆ ◆ ◆ ◆ ◆ ◆ ◆ ◆ ◆ ◆ ◆ ◆ ◆ ◆ ◆ ◆ ◆ ◆ ◆ ◆ ◆

to worry about wood because there were plenty of fallen trees and branches lying around the edge of the clearing. I lay in the sun with my blanket around me, close enough to the fire to be warm, a can of water close by, and the sun and blue sky overhead. I couldn't ask for anything more, except my family.

**Ralph's Journey**

Ralph's plan was to go down to the lake—which turned out to be four miles away—tramp an S.O.S. in the snow, then walk in the direction of the noise, and try to find its source or a highway. Ralph thought the noise must come from a lumber or mining camp. He was certain someone was bound to spot the S.O.S. The last thing he said to me before he left was, "When they come for you, Helen, don't let them give up the search until they have found me, too." Ralph had saved my life a dozen times in the

weeks gone by. I was not about to leave him out there to die.

Ralph left on Thursday. It took him about six hours to get down to the lake, which turned out to be a frozen swamp. He stamped out a big S.O.S.—each letter about 75 feet long. Then he stamped out a long arrow pointing back in the direction where I was. That night he made a fire, boiled some water, and went to sleep on my coat on top of some branches.

The next day, Friday, Ralph started walking in the direction of the noise. He walked all day, and slept that night in the hollow of a tree. Saturday he climbed to the top of a tall tree, hoping to find some landmarks, but he saw nothing recognizable. He was so tired that he slept in the tree hollow the rest of the day and all through the night. On Sunday he started walking again. That afternoon, as he was crossing a frozen stream, he saw an

Unit 4:  Courage and Conviction

airplane. Ralph had one of our mirrors and he started signaling with it. The plane circled low around him and then flew away. But Ralph knew he had been sighted.

## Help Arrives

I read the Bible all day Thursday and Friday. Saturday was a beautiful day, and in the morning I heard a plane flying nearby. I stumbled out of the tent and stood in the clearing. But the plane was on the other side of the mountain and I couldn't see it. Then it was gone.

Sunday the weather was still fair. I was sitting by the fire around one in the afternoon, when I heard another plane. I put an armload of pine on the fire to raise smoke. By now the plane was right above me. I grabbed the piece of canvas with the identification number of the plane on it—N5886—and pulled it away from the fire into the center of the clearing where I hoped it could be seen from the sky. Then I got my mirror and began signaling.

The plane circled overhead. The smoke was billowing up in thick puffs. I stood up, waving my arms and flashing the mirror. By now I was crying from pain and joy. I couldn't bear to stand another second. "So rescue me already!" I shouted at the plane. "I can't stand."

The plane flew away, yet I was sure the pilot must have seen me. When he flew away I told myself he was going back for a helicopter that could come down in the clearing—as I had always dreamed would happen. I forced myself to lie down on my blanket and wait.

The pilot was Chuck Hamilton and he *had* seen me. That Sunday, March 24,

Chuck had been flying an Indian hunting guide named Jack George, and a load of mail and supplies, out to a distant ranch. Both Chuck and Jack had seen Ralph's S.O.S. and the arrow. They thought it had been put there by Indian trappers as a signal that they needed supplies.

Chuck picked up the trail of Ralph's homemade snowshoes. He followed the trail until he finally saw Ralph, who had just suffered a terrible stomach cramp. It had left him so weak that he could go no farther. He was just standing in the snow, leaning on his spear, using all his strength to stay up. Chuck and Jack thought Ralph was an Indian out trapping. They also thought he seemed to be in trouble.

Chuck's plane was too heavily loaded to land. So he returned to the S.O.S. and started following the arrow. It was then that I had heard the plane overhead. They saw the tent and me through the pine smoke. They thought it was an Indian camp, and that I needed supplies.

Chuck flew to the ranch. He dropped off Jack George and the supplies, then flew back, looking for me.

As Chuck flew over the campsite again, he saw the identification numbers from the plane that I had put out in the clearing. He read them with a growing sense of shock. He recognized N5886 as the number of the long-lost plane that had disappeared with pilot Flores and passenger Klaben seven weeks before.

Chuck located Ralph along the stream, and then landed on Airplane Lake near an Indian trapper's cabin that had been occupied all the time. It was only 12 miles from our wrecked plane. It was the trapper's chain saw we'd been hearing.

Chuck told the two trappers about Ralph and asked them to go out and find him. They set out immediately by dog sled. Chuck then flew on to Watson Lake Airport and told the Royal Canadian Mounted Police of what he had seen and done.

By eight o'clock that night I realized that it was too dark for a plane to come in. Maybe tomorrow . . . I lay there and prayed.

### Rescue

I awoke to the sound of an airplane. A small plane came into sight, then circled directly over me. I waved. The pilot dropped a red balloon with a little package tied to it. Then he waved and flew on. I crawled to the balloon, then dragged myself back to the tent. There was a note wrapped around the package. "Good morning," it said. "There are two other planes on the way." The package contained two candy bars, some gum, and cigarettes.

● ● ● ● ● ● ● ●
"I awoke to the sound of an airplane."
● ● ● ● ● ● ● ●

Soon a man on snowshoes came walking out of the woods. I didn't know who he was, but it didn't matter. I was too tired to get up, but when he came over to where I was sitting, I grabbed him around the neck and hugged and kissed him. I was crying, too, and I kept saying, "Thank God, thank God," over and over again. After seven weeks, I just sort of let go.

The first rescuer was Jack McCallum, who had flown over from Watson Lake. Chuck Hamilton soon followed, landing his plane near Jack's, about three miles from the campsite. When Chuck finally found us, he realized that he had flown over us many times without ever spotting the wrecked plane. If Ralph had not decided to move down to the clearing, and then make the S.O.S. out in the open, we would not have been seen until spring when the snows melted.

Chuck carried me on his back to his plane. He flew to Airplane Lake, near the trapper's cabin. It was a snug little cabin, and Ralph was inside, looking pale and sick, but smiling. The trappers fixed us a meal of moose steak and hot tea. The moose steak was delicious and the tea the best I ever drank. But eating made me so tired I had to lie down and rest before I could face the next part of our journey.

Then the men loaded Ralph and me into a plane, and Chuck took off for Watson Lake Airport. It was still a beautiful day when we landed at the airport that afternoon, the nicest day in months. But that night it began to snow. It was a terrible storm, a real blizzard. The snow completely wiped out Ralph's S.O.S.

### Aftermath

*Helen and Ralph were hospitalized in Whitehorse. Helen had lost 40 pounds; Ralph 58. Ralph's broken jaw needed repair, and the frostbitten toes on Helen's right foot would need to be amputated. News of their survival spread across the country. Within a few days, Helen flew back to her family in New York. She and Ralph said good-bye at the hospital; they never saw each other again.*

I did a lot of thinking while I was lying in a hospital bed in New York, recovering from the operation on my foot. There is no single magic ingredient that enabled me to survive seven weeks in the wilderness. I did not survive—as so many newspapers would have it—because of Ralph's strength and his Bible. They were part of it, but it wasn't as simple as all that.

I think that everything that happened in my life before the crash, the total of all my experiences, added up to 49 days of survival. I believe that everything that happens to us has a meaning, even if we cannot understand it.

I learned a lot. I learned—to my surprise—that I did not fear death when it was close to me. I learned I could overcome my fears of darkness and wild animals. I learned to be patient, when being patient was the only way to stay alive.

Finally, I want to say that I think everything that has happened to me in my life is wonderful. Particularly those seven weeks in the wilderness with Ralph. I owe my life to him. And I learned so much from him—about faith and courage, and strength, and persistence, and endurance. I don't kid myself for a minute that I would have made it down off that mountain alive without him.

My experiences in Alaska were wonderful because they enabled me to make a big discovery. I learned for the first time how much I love my family. And I learned something else I never knew before: I love life. ❖

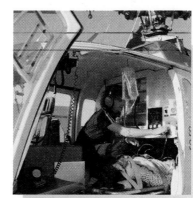

## ON THE JOB

### EMERGENCY MEDICAL TECHNICIAN

Emergency medical technicians (EMTs) provide immediate aid to victims of accidents or critical illnesses. EMTs are often the victim's first source of medical help, and they must be quick to determine the problem and treat it. Completion of a standard training program is mandatory for each of the four levels of EMT registration. Requirements vary by state, but most EMT trainees are required to take 100 hours of classroom training in basic emergency care.

# UNDERSTANDING

1. Outline the major points of "Hey, I'm Alive!" as if it were a captain's log. Use the column headings Date, Activity, Success/Failure, and Comments. You may need to invent or infer some information.

   Businesspeople and officials such as police officers often must write incident reports, or descriptions of events that occur. Write an incident report of something you have witnessed in person or in the news. ***Workshop 10***

2. Make a list of the exact chain of events that led to the eventual rescue. Next to each action, write the reason for it and how it led to the next event.

   Recognizing cause-and-effect relationships is an important thinking skill. When you read, look for words and phrases that signal causes and effects, such as *because, for, since, so, consequently, so that, in order that, if-then, thus,* and *therefore.* Write five sentences constructed to show the cause-effect relationship of an event, either from the story or from your own life. ***Workshop 14***

3. Find statements in the text that describe Klaben's relief at the time of rescue, and what she learned about herself.

   Choose a particular event in your life that taught you valuable lessons and moved you to a new understanding of what it means to be alive or free or happy. Write a journal entry similar to Klaben's that discusses your feelings.

**A LAST WORD**

Why does it sometimes take a threatening or extremely difficult situation to make us realize how much we love life? What causes us to forget this important lesson while living our daily lives?

# CONNECTING

1.  Invite a guest speaker to discuss survival techniques. Speakers might be military personnel, Boy or Girl Scouts, or paramedics. Research books and manuals for details on the subject. With a group, design a poster for younger students, and give a demonstration speech on a specific technique for the class. ***Workshops 21 and 25***

2. In the workplace, you may be asked to explain the reasons a particular situation occurred. In such situations, you know the effect, so you must infer or guess the cause. Choose a major historical event, such as the sinking of the Titanic, the explosion of the space shuttle *Challenger,* or the Gulf War. Research the causes of the event. In an essay, identify the causes and explain how they brought about the end result. List three or four major causes in a thesis statement. Then argue or present the facts and evidence in logical order. Conclude with an answer to "So what?" or "If only . . . ." ***Workshops 14 and 23***

# Personal Reflections

- *from Wouldn't Take Nothing for My Journey Now*
- *When I Think about Myself*

## EXPLORING

Some people see not what they have but what they lack. Others see what they have and then explore what they can make of it. Look closely at your own thinking. What attitude do you have toward what you have been given in life? How might a new attitude improve your life? How can a change of heart bring about a change in events?

## THEME CONNECTION...
## COURAGE TO MAKE CHANGES

Compared to the lives of those who came before us, our lives look pretty easy. Our ancestors toiled long and hard to provide a future for us, and now we are living that future. The grandmother in the essay would say that our life is as good as we think it is, that many would gladly change places with us.

## TIME & PLACE

In the 1930s, at a very young age, Maya Angelou experienced many traumas: parental divorce, separation from her parents, rape, poverty, and racial hatred. After her parents split, three-year-old Maya was sent with her older brother to live in Stamps, Arkansas, where race relations hadn't improved much since the Civil War. Angelou draws from these and other experiences to create the rich, strong, often mournful characters of her essays and poems.

## THE WRITER'S CRAFT

### STANZA

Just as we use a new paragraph in prose (ordinary) writing to indicate a change of topic, poets use stanzas to divide a poem. Often, the stanzas in a poem follow the same rhythmic pattern, like the verses in a song. Maya Angelou's poem "When I Think about Myself" has both stanzas and repeating rhythm. Listen to the musical beat that repeats in each stanza of her poem.

# from *Wouldn't Take Nothing for My Journey Now*

Maya Angelou

## About the Author

Maya Angelou was born Marguerita Johnson in St. Louis in 1928. After going to school in Arkansas and California, Angelou eventually moved to New York, where she studied dance and performed both on and off Broadway. Angelou spent four years in Ghana, Africa, working as an editor and teacher. Back in the United States, she began writing poetry, songs, screenplays, and a television series. Angelou wrote the acclaimed autobiography *I Know Why the Caged Bird Sings*, which tells of her life up to age 16.

conspiratorially —schemingly, secretly

stoically— showing no response or emotion

lamentation—an expression of sorrow or mourning

mewl—whimper

 hen my grandmother was raising me in Stamps, Arkansas, she had a particular routine when people who were known to be whiners entered her store. Whenever she saw a known complainer coming, she would call me from whatever I was doing and say **conspiratorially**, "Sister, come inside. Come." Of course I would obey.

My grandmother would ask the customer, "How are you doing today, Brother Thomas?" And the person would reply, "Not so good." There would be a distinct whine in the voice. "Not so good today, Sister Henderson. You see, it's this summer. It's this summer heat. I just hate it. Oh, I hate it so much. It just frazzles me up and frazzles me down. I just hate the heat. It's almost killing me." Then my grandmother would stand **stoically**, her arms folded, and mumble, "Uh-huh, uh-huh." And she would cut her eyes at me to make certain that I had heard the **lamentation**.

At another time a whiner would **mewl**, "I hate plowing. That packed-down dirt ain't got no reasoning, and mules ain't got good sense . . . Sure ain't. It's killing me. I can't ever seem to get done. My feet and my hands stay sore, and I get dirt in my eyes and up my nose. I just can't stand it." And my grandmother, again stoically with her arms folded, would say, "Uh-huh, uh-huh," and then look at me and nod.

As soon as the complainer was out of the store, my grandmother would call me to stand in front of her. And then she would say the same thing she had said at least a thousand times, it seemed to me. "Sister, did you hear what Brother So-and-So or Sister Much to Do complained about? You heard that?" And I would nod. Mamma would continue, "Sister, there are people who went to sleep all over the world last night, poor and rich and white and black, but they will never wake again. Sister, those who expected to rise did not, their beds became their cooling boards, and their blankets became their winding sheets. And those dead folks would give anything, anything at all for just five minutes of this weather or ten minutes of that plowing that person was grumbling about. So you watch yourself about complaining, Sister. What you're supposed to do when you don't like a thing is change it. If you can't change it, change the way you think about it. Don't complain."

It is said that persons have few teachable moments in their lives. Mamma seemed to have caught me at each one I had between the age of three and thirteen. Whining is not only graceless, but can be dangerous. It can alert a brute that a victim is in the neighborhood. ❖

FOCUS ON...
ART

In the excerpt from *Wouldn't Take Nothing for My Journey Now,* Angelou describes her grandmother, who caught her at many "teachable moments" in her life. In a medium of your choice, create a portrait of someone who has taught you a memorable life lesson. You may choose to make a watercolor, painting, sculpture, or collage, using traditional or other materials, that illustrates the qualities of your subject's personality.

# When I Think about Myself

Maya Angelou

When I think about myself,
I almost laugh myself to death,
My life has been one great big joke,
A dance that's walked
A song that's spoke,
I laugh so hard I almost choke
When I think about myself.

Sixty years in these folks' world
The child I works for calls me girl
I say "Yes ma'am" for working's sake.
Too proud to bend
Too poor to break,
I laugh until my stomach ache,
When I think about myself.

My folks can make me split my side,
I laughed so hard I nearly died,
The tales they tell, sound just like lying,
They grow the fruit,
But eat the rind,
I laugh until I start to crying,
When I think about my folks. ❖

# UNDERSTANDING

1.  Maya Angelou's grandmother was a small-business owner. As both owner and clerk, she knew how to treat her customers. Find evidence in the text of the way she treated customers.

   Working with a partner, imagine you are co-owners of a small store. Develop six to eight statements that describe the behaviors you expect your employees to exhibit as they relate to customers. Incorporate the key words or ideas into a collage or graphic design that will become a symbol of your service policy.

2. Look up the word *whine* in a thesaurus. What are some synonyms? Note the tone of these words. What are some antonyms for *whine?* What is the difference in tone among these words? Write a story for elementary school children to teach the lesson that Mamma taught Maya in the essay. Use the synonyms and antonyms in the story.

3. The narrator of "When I Think about Myself" says her life is a joke. What evidence does she give for this?

   The ideas in the poem could be expressed in essay format. Write the poet's thesis statement. Then write in essay form the arguments she gives. Conclude with a summary of what the speaker is feeling. *Workshop 8*

## A LAST WORD

Angelou's grandmother taught her a valuable life lesson. Why do you suppose it is easy to complain? What qualities are needed to live life without making complaints?

# CONNECTING

1.  Interview three clerks, waiters, or other service industry employees. Ask them (a) what undesirable behaviors they have seen customers display and (b) what behaviors they *wish* for from customers. In groups, combine your data and prepare a poster-sized graph that shows the data you collected.

   Design a clever paper placemat or lapel button to remind customers diplomatically and gently that they have a responsibility to be considerate and good natured. *Workshops 22 and 26*

2.  Parents are the first teachers children have. In magazines on parenting and books on child rearing, find out how parents can and should model positive behaviors. Take notes on specific ways parents influence children.

   With a partner, role-play a scene between a parent and a young child to show the possible negative effects of parental influence. Then change the scene, showing, instead, positive parental behavior and its effects on the child.

# Mrs. Donovan

## EXPLORING

Self-confident people display their strong beliefs and act with confidence. They know their strengths, and use them to move forward. What strengths do you have? What are your talents? What skills have you mastered? Describe yourself in terms of your abilities, no matter how small they may seem. Give an example of a time you used your strengths to accomplish something.

## THEME CONNECTION...
## SELF-ESTEEM AND CONFIDENCE

No one in the British village knew Mrs. Donovan's age, but everyone knew she gave competent advice on pet care. However, the loss of her beloved dog sent her into a despair that no human could comfort. Her self-esteem returned when she adopted an abused dog and restored him to health.

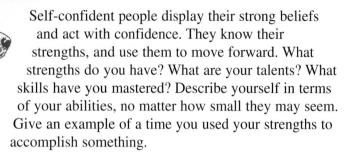

## TIME & PLACE

James Herriot, a veterinary surgeon, lived and worked in the Yorkshire Dales in Northern England. When he moved there from Scotland in 1937, there weren't many veterinarians in that wild and beautiful part of the country. Dr. Herriot traveled far and wide at all hours of the day and night to take care of animals.

## THE WRITER'S CRAFT

### NARRATOR

James Herriot was a masterful narrator of his experiences as a country veterinarian. In any story, even in movies and television programs, a narrator is usually involved in a minor way in the events, but the action focuses on some other character. In this case, Mrs. Donovan is the central figure, the character in whose personality and development we are interested. A skillful narrator moves the action along, helping readers untangle details of time and place.

# Mrs. Donovan

James Herriot

he silvery-haired old gentleman with the pleasant face didn't look the type to be easily upset but his eyes glared at me angrily and his lips quivered with indignation.

"Mr. Herriot," he said. "I have come to make a complaint. I strongly object to your callousness in subjecting my dog to unnecessary suffering."

"Suffering? What suffering?" I was mystified.

"I think you know, Mr. Herriot. I brought my dog in a few days ago. He was very lame and I am referring to your treatment on that occasion."

I nodded. "Yes, I remember it very well . . . but where does the suffering come in?"

"Well, the poor animal is going around with his leg dangling and I have it on good authority that the bone is fractured and should have been put in plaster immediately." The old gentleman stuck his chin out fiercely.

"All right, you can stop worrying," I said. "Your dog has a radial paralysis caused by a blow on the ribs and if you are patient and follow my treatment he'll gradually improve. In fact I think he'll recover completely."

"But he trails his leg when he walks."

"I know—that's typical, and to the layman it does give the appearance of a broken leg. But he shows no sign of pain, does he?"

"No, he seems quite happy, but this lady seemed to be absolutely sure of her facts. She was adamant."

"Lady?"

"Yes," said the old gentleman. "She is clever with animals and came round to see if she could help in my dog's **convalescence.** She brought some excellent condition powders with her."

"Ah!" A blinding shaft pierced the fog in my mind. All was suddenly clear. "It was Mrs. Donovan, wasn't it?"

"Well . . . er, yes. That was her name."

Old Mrs. Donovan was a woman who really got around. No matter what was going on in Darrowby—weddings, funerals, house-sales—you'd find the dumpy little figure and walnut face among the spectators, the darting, black-button eyes taking everything in. And always, on the end of its lead, her terrier dog.

When I say "old," I'm only guessing, because she appeared ageless; she seemed to have been around a long time but she could have been anything between fifty-five and seventy-five. She certainly had the vitality of a young woman because she must have walked vast distances in her dedicated quest to keep abreast of events. Many people took an uncharitable view of her **acute** curiosity but whatever the motivation, her activities took her into almost every channel of life in the town. One of these channels was our veterinary practice.

## About the Author

For more than 25 years, James Herriot (pen name of James Alfred Wight, 1916–1995) charmed readers around the world with memoirs of his life as a country animal doctor in Yorkshire, England. At an early age, Herriot was fascinated by animals, particularly dogs. He wrote, "I could never quite take dogs for granted. Why were they so devoted to the human race? Why should their greatest pleasure lie in being with us in our homes? . . . As a vet I could be with dogs all the time."

Because Mrs. Donovan, among her other widely ranging interests, was an animal doctor. In fact I think it would be safe to say that this facet of her life transcended all the others.

She could talk at length on the ailments of small animals and she had a whole **armory** of medicines and remedies at her command, her two specialties being her miracle-working condition powders and a dog shampoo of unprecedented value for improving the coat. She had an uncanny ability to sniff out a sick animal and it was not uncommon when I was on my rounds to find Mrs. Donovan's dark gypsy face poised intently over what I had thought was my patient while she administered calf's foot jelly or one of her own patent **nostrums**.

I suffered more than Siegfried because I took a more active part in the small animal side of our practice. I was anxious to develop this aspect and to improve my image in this field and Mrs. Donovan didn't help at all. "Young Mr. Herriot," she would confide to my clients, "is all right with cattle and such like, but he don't know nothing about dogs and cats."

And of course they believed her and had **implicit** faith in her. She had the irresistible mystic appeal of the amateur and on top of that there was her habit, particularly endearing in Darrowby, of never charging for her advice, her medicines, her long periods of diligent nursing.

Older folk in the town told how her husband, an Irish farmworker, had died many years ago and how he must have had a bit put away because Mrs. Donovan had apparently been able to indulge all her interests over the years without financial strain. Since she inhabited the streets of Darrowby all day and every day I often encountered her and she always smiled up at me sweetly and told me how she had been sitting up all night with Mrs. So-and-so's dog that I'd been treating. She felt sure she'd be able to pull it through.

There was no smile on her face, however, on the day when she rushed into the surgery while Siegfried and I were having tea.

"Mr. Herriot!" she gasped. "Can you come? My little dog's been run over!"

I jumped up and ran out to the car with her. She sat in the passenger seat with her head bowed, her hands clasped tightly on her knees.

"He slipped his collar and ran in front of a car," she murmured. "He's lying in front of the school half way up Cliffend Road. Please hurry."

I was there within three minutes but as I bent over the dusty little body stretched on the pavement I knew there was nothing I could do. The fast-glazing eyes, the faint, gasping respirations, the ghastly **pallor** of the mucous membranes all told the same story.

"I'll take him back to the surgery and get some saline into him, Mrs. Donovan," I said. "But I'm afraid he's had a massive internal hemorrhage. Did you see what happened exactly?"

She gulped. "Yes, the wheel went right over him."

> ● ● ● ● ● ● ● ●
> **"She had the irresistible mystic appeal of the amateur."**
> ● ● ● ● ● ● ● ●

convalescence —recovery

acute—sharp

armory—supply

nostrum—a medicine of unknown makeup, recommended by its maker but with no scientific proof of its effectiveness

implicit— unquestioning

pallor—paleness

boot—trunk of a car (in Britain)

R.S.P.C.A.— Royal Society for the Prevention of Cruelty to Animals

Ruptured liver, for sure. I passed my hands under the little animal and began to lift him gently, but as I did so the breathing stopped and the eyes stared fixedly ahead.

Mrs. Donovan sank to her knees and for a few moments she gently stroked the rough hair of the head and chest. "He's dead, isn't he?" she whispered at last.

"I'm afraid he is," I said.

She got slowly to her feet and stood bewilderedly among the little group of bystanders on the pavement. Her lips moved but she seemed unable to say any more.

I took her arm, led her over to the car and opened the door. "Get in and sit down," I said. "I'll run you home. Leave everything to me."

I wrapped the dog in my calving overall and laid him in the **boot** before driving away. It wasn't until we drew up outside Mrs. Donovan's house that she began to weep silently. I sat there without speaking till she had finished. Then she wiped her eyes and turned to me.

"Do you think he suffered at all?"

"I'm certain he didn't. It was all so quick—he wouldn't know a thing about it."

She tried to smile. "Poor little Rex, I don't know what I'm going to do without him. We've traveled a few miles together, you know."

"Yes, you have. He had a wonderful life, Mrs. Donovan. And let me give you a bit of advice—you must get another dog. You'd be lost without one."

She shook her head. "No, I couldn't. That little dog meant too much to me. I couldn't let another take his place."

"Well I know that's how you feel just now but I wish you'd think about it. I don't want to seem callous—I tell everybody this when they lose an animal and I know it's good advice."

"Mr. Herriot, I'll never have another one." She shook her head again, very decisively. "Rex was my faithful friend for many years and I just want to remember him. He's the last dog I'll ever have."

I often saw Mrs. Donovan around the town after this and I was glad to see she was still as active as ever, though she looked strangely incomplete without the little dog on its lead. But it must have been over a month before I had the chance to speak to her.

It was on the afternoon that Inspector Halliday of the **R.S.P.C.A.** rang me.

"Mr. Herriot," he said, "I'd like you to come and see an animal with me. A cruelty case."

"Right, what is it?"

"A dog, and it's pretty grim. A dreadful case of neglect." He gave me the name of a row of old brick cottages down by the river and said he'd meet me there.

Halliday was waiting for me, smart and businesslike in his dark uniform, as I pulled up in the back lane behind the houses. He was a big, blond man with cheerful blue eyes but he didn't smile as he came over to the car.

"He's in here," he said, and led the way towards one of the doors in the

> "He's the last dog I'll ever have."

long, crumbling wall. A few curious people were hanging around and with a feeling of inevitability I recognized a gnomelike brown face. Trust Mrs. Donovan, I thought, to be among those present at a time like this.

We went through the door into the long garden. I had found that even the lowliest dwellings in Darrowby had long strips of land at the back as though the builders had taken it for granted that the country people who were going to live in them would want to occupy themselves with the pursuits of the soil: with vegetable and fruit growing, even stock keeping in a small way. You usually found a pig there, a few hens, often pretty beds of flowers.

But this garden was a wilderness. A chilling air of desolation hung over the few gnarled apple and plum trees standing among a tangle of rank grass as though the place had been forsaken by all living creatures.

Halliday went over to a ramshackle wooden shed with peeling paint and a rusted corrugated iron roof. He produced a key, unlocked the padlock and dragged the door partly open. There was no window and it wasn't easy to identify the jumble inside; broken gardening tools, an ancient mangle, rows of flower pots and partly used paint tins. And right at the back, a dog sitting quietly.

I didn't notice him immediately because of the gloom and because the smell in the shed started me coughing, but as I drew closer I saw that he was a big animal, sitting very upright, his collar secured by a chain to a ring in the wall. I had seen some thin dogs but this advanced **emaciation** reminded me of

my textbooks on anatomy; nowhere else did the bones of pelvis, face and rib cage stand out with such horrifying clarity. A deep, smothered out hollow in the earth floor showed where he had lain, moved about, in fact lived for a very long time.

The sight of the animal had a stupefying effect on me; I only half took in the rest of the scene—the filthy shreds of sacking scattered nearby, the bowl of scummy water.

"Look at his back end," Halliday muttered.

I carefully raised the dog from his sitting position and realized that the stench in the place was not entirely due to the piles of excrement. The hindquarters were a welter of pressure sores which had turned gangrenous and strips of **sloughing** tissue hung down from them. There were similar sores along the sternum and ribs. The coat, which seemed to be a dull yellow, was matted and caked with dirt.

The Inspector spoke again. "I don't think he's ever been out of here. He's only a young dog—about a year old—but I understand he's been in this shed since he was an eight-week-old pup. Somebody out in the lane heard a whimper or he'd never have been found."

I felt a tightening of the throat and a sudden nausea which wasn't due to the smell. It was the thought of

emaciation— thinness; wasting away

sloughing— dead and separating

## SPOTLIGHT ON...
## GIVING DIRECTIONS

In his work as a veterinarian, Dr. Herriot often gave directions to his clients for giving medicine to or caring for their animals. When you give someone instructions, keep the following suggestions in mind:

1. Identify the task to be performed.
2. Keep your directions as short, simple, and clear as you can. Do not include any unnecessary information.
3. Provide a written copy of the directions, broken down into easy-to-follow steps.

◆◆◆◆◆◆◆◆◆◆◆◆◆◆◆◆◆◆◆◆◆◆◆◆◆◆◆◆◆

interminably—
seemingly
without end

this patient animal sitting starved and forgotten in the darkness and filth for a year. I looked again at the dog and saw in his eyes only a calm trust. Some dogs would have barked their heads off and soon been discovered, some would have become terrified and vicious, but his was one of the totally undemanding kind, the kind which had complete faith in people and accepted all their actions without complaint. Just an occasional whimper perhaps as he sat **interminably** in the empty blackness which had been his world and at times wondered what it was all about.

"Well, Inspector, I hope you're going to throw the book at whoever's responsible," I said.

Halliday grunted. "Oh, there won't be much done. It's a case of diminished responsibility. The owner's definitely simple. Lives with an aged mother who hardly knows what's going on either. I've seen the fellow and it seems he threw in a bit of food when he felt like it

and that's about all he did. They'll fine him and stop him keeping an animal in the future but nothing more than that."

"I see." I reached out and stroked the dog's head and he immediately responded by resting a paw on my wrist. There was a pathetic dignity about the way he held himself erect, the calm eyes regarding me, friendly and unafraid. "Well, you'll let me know if you want me in court."

"Of course, and thank you for coming along." Halliday hesitated for a moment. "And now I expect you'll want to put this poor thing out of his misery right away."

I continued to run my hand over the head and ears while I thought for a moment. "Yes . . . yes, I suppose so. We'd never find a home for him in this state. It's the kindest thing to do. Anyway, push the door wide open will you so that I can get a proper look at him."

In the improved light I examined him more thoroughly. Perfect teeth, well-proportioned limbs with a fringe of yellow hair. I put my stethoscope on his chest and as I listened to the slow, strong thudding of the heart the dog again put his paw on my hand.

I turned to Halliday. "You know, Inspector, inside this bag of bones there's a lovely healthy Golden Retriever. I wish there was some way of letting him out."

As I spoke I noticed there was more than one figure in the door opening. A pair of black pebble eyes were peering intently at the dog from behind the Inspector's broad back. The other spectators had remained in the lane but Mrs. Donovan's curiosity had been too much for her. I continued conversationally as though I hadn't seen her.

"You know, what this dog needs first of all is a good shampoo to clean up his matted coat."

"Huh?" said Halliday.

"Yes. And then he wants a long course of some really strong condition powders."

"What's that?" The Inspector looked startled.

"There's no doubt about it," I said. "It's the only hope for him, but where are you going to find such things? Really powerful enough, I mean." I sighed and straightened up. "Ah well, I suppose there's nothing else for it. I'd better put him to sleep right away. I'll get the things from my car."

When I got back to the shed Mrs. Donovan was already inside examining the dog despite the feeble **remonstrances** of the big man.

"Look!" she said excitedly, pointing to a name roughly scratched on the collar. "His name's Roy." She smiled up at me. "It's a bit like Rex, isn't it, that name."

"You know, Mrs. Donovan, now you mention it, it is. It's very much like Rex, the way it comes off your tongue." I nodded seriously.

She stood silent for a few moments, obviously in the grip of a deep emotion, then she burst out.

"Can I have 'im? I can make him better, I know I can. Please, please let me have 'im!"

"Well I don't know," I said. "It's really up to the Inspector. You'll have to get his permission."

Halliday looked at her in bewilderment, then he said: "Excuse me, Madam," and drew me to one side. We walked a few yards through the long grass and stopped under a tree.

"Mr. Herriot," he whispered," I don't know what's going on here, but I can't just pass over an animal in this condition to anybody who has a casual whim. The poor beggar's had one bad break already—I think it's enough. This woman doesn't look a suitable person . . ."

I held up a hand. "Believe me, Inspector, you've nothing to worry about. She's a funny old stick but she's been sent from heaven today. If anybody in Darrowby can give this dog a new life it's her."

Halliday still looked very doubtful. "But I still don't get it. What was all that stuff about him needing shampoos and condition powders?"

"Oh never mind about that. I'll tell you some other time. What he needs is lots of good grub, care and affection and that's just what he'll get. You can take my word for it."

remonstrances —protests, usually ineffective

necrotic—dead

granulating—a stage in the healing of a wound when new capillaries form on the surface of the wound

"All right, you seem very sure." Halliday looked at me for a second or two then turned and walked over to the eager little figure by the shed.

I had never before been deliberately on the look out for Mrs. Donovan; she had just cropped up wherever I happened to be, but now I scanned the streets of Darrowby anxiously day by day without sighting her. I didn't like it when Gobber Newhouse got drunk and drove his bicycle determinedly through a barrier into a ten foot hole where they were laying the new sewer and Mrs. Donovan was not in evidence among the happy crowd who watched the council workmen and two policemen trying to get him out; and when she was nowhere to be seen when they had to fetch the fire engine to the fish and chip shop the night the fat burst into flames, I became seriously worried.

Maybe I should have called round to see how she was getting on with that dog. Certainly I had trimmed off the **necrotic** tissue and dressed the sores before she took him away, but perhaps he needed something more than that. And yet at the time I had felt a strong conviction that the main thing was to get him out of there and clean him and feed him and nature would do the rest. And I had a lot of faith in Mrs. Donovan—far more than she had in me—when it came to animal doctoring; it was hard to believe I'd been completely wrong.

It must have been nearly three weeks and I was on the point of calling her at home when I noticed her stumping

• • • • • • • •
## "Haven't I made a difference to this dog!"
• • • • • • • •

briskly along the far side of the market-place, peering closely into every shop window exactly as before. The only difference was that she had a big yellow dog on the end of the lead.

I turned the wheel and sent my car bumping over the cobbles till I was abreast of her. When she saw me getting out she stopped and smiled impishly but she didn't speak as I bent over Roy and examined him. He was still a skinny dog but he looked bright and happy—his wounds were healthy and **granulating** and there was not a speck of dirt in his coat or on his skin. I knew then what Mrs. Donovan had been doing all this time; she had been washing and combing and teasing all that filthy tangle till she had finally conquered it.

As I straightened up she seized my wrist in a grip of surprising strength and looked up into my eyes.

"Now Mr. Herriot," she said. "Haven't I made a difference to this dog!"

"You've done wonders, Mrs. Donovan," I said. "And you've been at him with that marvelous shampoo of yours, haven't you?"

She giggled and walked away and from that day I saw the two of them frequently but at a distance and something like two months went by before I had a chance to talk to her again. She was passing by the surgery as I was coming down the steps and again she grabbed my wrist.

"Mr. Herriot," she said, just as she had done before. "Haven't I made a difference to this dog!"

I looked down at Roy with something akin to awe. He had grown and filled out and his coat, no longer yellow but a rich gold, lay in luxurious shining swathes over the well-fleshed ribs and back. A new, brightly studded collar glittered on his neck and his tail, beautifully fringed, fanned the air gently. He was now a Golden Retriever in full magnificence. As I stared at him he reared up, plunked his forepaws on my chest and looked into my face, and in his eyes I read plainly the same calm affection and trust I had seen back in that black, **noisome** shed.

"Mrs. Donovan," I said softly, "he's the most beautiful dog in Yorkshire." Then, because I knew she was waiting for it, "It's those wonderful condition powders. Whatever do you put in them?"

"Ah, wouldn't you like to know!" She bridled and smiled up at me **coquettishly** and indeed she was nearer being kissed at that moment than for many years.

I suppose you could say that that was the start of Roy's second life. And as the years passed I often pondered on the beneficent **providence** which had decreed that an animal which had spent his first twelve months abandoned and unwanted, staring uncomprehendingly into that unchanging, stinking darkness, should be whisked in a moment into an existence of light and movement and love. Because I don't think any dog had it quite so good as Roy from then on.

His diet changed dramatically from odd bread crusts to best stewing steak and biscuit, meaty bones and a bowl of warm milk every evening. And he never missed a thing. Garden fetes, school sports, evictions, **gymkhanas**—he'd be there. I was pleased to note that as time went on Mrs. Donovan seemed to be clocking up an even greater daily mileage. Her expenditure on shoe leather must have been phenomenal, but of course it was absolute pie for Roy—a busy round in the morning, home for a meal then straight out again; it was all go.

Mrs. Donovan didn't confine her activities to the town center; there was a big stretch of common land down by the river where there were seats, and people used to take their dogs for a gallop and she liked to get down there fairly regularly to check on the latest developments on the domestic scene. I often saw Roy loping majestically over the grass among a pack of assorted canines, and when he wasn't doing that he was submitting to being stroked or patted or generally fussed over. He was handsome and he just liked people; it made him irresistible.

It was common knowledge that his mistress had bought a whole selection of brushes and combs of various sizes with which she labored over his coat. Some people said she had a little brush for his teeth, too, and it might have been true, but he certainly wouldn't need his nails clipped—his life on the roads would keep them down.

Mrs. Donovan, too, had her reward; she had a faithful companion by her side every hour of the day and night. But there was more to it than that; she had always had the compulsion to help and heal animals and the salvation of Roy was the high point of her life—a blazing triumph which never dimmed.

I know the memory of it was always fresh because many years later I was

noisome—
unhealthy;
offensive to
the senses

coquettishly—
shyly;
flirtatiously

providence—
divine guidance

gymkhana—an
athletic sports
event

sitting on the sidelines at a cricket match and I saw the two of them; the old lady glancing keenly around her, Roy gazing placidly out at the field of play, apparently enjoying every ball. At the end of the match I watched them move away with the dispersing crowd; Roy would be about twelve then and heaven only knows how old Mrs. Donovan must have been, but the big golden animal was trotting along effortlessly and his mistress, a little more bent, perhaps, and her head rather nearer the ground, was going very well.

When she saw me she came over and I felt the familiar tight grip on my wrist.

"Mr. Herriot," she said, and in the dark probing eyes the pride was still as warm, the triumph still as bursting new as if it had all happened yesterday.

"Mr. Herriot, haven't I made a difference to this dog!" ❖

## ON THE JOB
### VETERINARY ASSISTANT

Veterinary assistants perform a variety of tasks, including giving medicine, treating minor wounds, preparing animals for surgery, and caring for them after surgery. They generally work at animal hospitals or in veterinarians' offices. Veterinary assistants need to know about animals' eating and sleeping habits. They must also enjoy working with animals and be able to follow directions carefully. High school courses in science and math are a helpful preparation, and a two-year college or technical school program in animal care is strongly suggested.

## ACCENT ON...
### PROFESSIONAL DOG TRAINING

Roy, the dog in Herriot's memoir, is a Golden Retriever. This loyal and intelligent breed is always eager to learn and is favored by many professional trainers and service-dog organizations. One such organization, Canine Companions for Independence, places Golden Retriever and Labrador puppies with families who raise them to be obedient and well socialized. Then, at 15 months, the puppies are placed with professional trainers who prepare them for lives as constant helping companions to physically challenged individuals. Find out about Canine Companions for Independence. What special techniques do the trainers use? Could those techniques be used to train *any* dog to perform helpful tasks?

## UNDERSTANDING

1. The veterinarian narrator is the foil, or opposite, of Mrs. Donovan. What he does with science, she does with her "powders" and caregiving. Divide a sheet of paper into two columns labeled "Mr. Herriot" and "Mrs. Donovan." In the columns, list actions and statements that illustrate the characters' differences.

   We often must work with people who are different from us in their attitudes and behaviors. On another chart, label the columns with your name and that of another person. What differences exist between you? What is good about the fact that people *do* differ? Explain in several paragraphs how you could make a good team *because* of your differences. ***Workshop 8***

2. Find evidence in the text that shows how Mrs. Donovan persuades the Inspector to let her have the Golden Retriever. How does Mr. Herriot support her? Write a letter from Mrs. Donovan to the Inspector requesting ownership of the dog. Include her plan for rehabilitating the dog. ***Workshop 13***

3. Study the change in Mrs. Donovan. How did the loss of her dog affect her, and how does the new animal change her life?

   A crisis can change a person's outlook and focus. Perhaps you have had an experience that changed your thinking, or perhaps you know someone who has. Was the change for the better or did it have a negative effect? Write an essay on such an experience and its effect on you. ***Workshop 9***

**A LAST WORD**

Dogs are well known for their faith in humans. Do we deserve their trust? How can we better appreciate all that they give to us?

## CONNECTING

1. Research people in your community who are "making a difference" in a specific area of caregiving, such as care providers for the elderly, the physically or mentally challenged children, and so on. Interview one of these people. In your interview, focus on the personal characteristics needed by those in caregiving professions. Then write a newspaper employment ad for a caregiver in a specific setting, such as a day-care worker or a hospice volunteer. ***Workshop 26***

2. Mrs. Donovan virtually had her own small business within the community. What small-business enterprise would you like to develop? Write a business plan that explains why you think the business is needed in your community and how you propose to run it. Include information you feel is vital to an understanding of what your business will be and how you will make it succeed.

# Interview with the Chimp Lady

## EXPLORING

• • • • • • • • • • • • • • • • • • • • • • • • •

A scientist investigates, observes, analyzes, and forms scientifically based guesses, or hypotheses. Have you ever wondered what an octopus feels like? Or perhaps how a squirrel cares for its young in the nest? Maybe you have asked other questions about animals. About what animals would you like to know more? Why?

## THEME CONNECTION...
## COURAGE TO SEEK ANSWERS

Jane Goodall wanted to learn. She had the courage and conviction to give up the comforts of her life and move into the jungle to live with the chimpanzees. She is a true research scientist, and her struggles and patience have paid off in the great satisfaction and insight she has gained from her experiences.

## TIME & PLACE

Chimpanzees are the apes most closely related to humans, sharing 99 percent of our genetic material. Jane Goodall has studied generations of chimpanzees in Gombe for more than 30 years. Gombe is in Tanzania, in the Eastern Highlands of Africa. Goodall was the first person to observe a chimp making and using a tool, a skill previously thought mastered only by humans.

## THE WRITER'S CRAFT
### INTERVIEW

Interviews are a major source of information and data. Successful interviewers prepare open-ended questions or statements that move the conversation toward revealing the knowledge desired. Interviewers must study the topic so that they can ask useful, educated questions. When the results of interviews are printed in magazines and other periodicals, they must be complete—the interviewer cannot distort or omit data. Reading an account of an interview should feel like being in the room at the time.

# Interview with the Chimp Lady

## Jane Goodall with Vicki Gabereau

Sometimes you have to wonder what it is that scientists do, research scientists especially. I haven't talked to a great many and I guess there is an obvious reason for that. Often their fields are beyond my comprehension. Not so with Jane Goodall. It doesn't matter if we don't understand all the **implications** and intricate details of a **primatologist**'s work, because we all love stories about chimpanzees. Jane Goodall is a science star, which is dandy for her, because she has been able to raise funds for continued work at her encampment at Gombe in Tanzania. Mind you, there can never be enough money, and there is a foundation that works full time to keep her projects going, the Jane Goodall Institute in San Francisco. I spoke to her in person in May 1984.

VICKI GABEREAU: Your last "National Geographic" special had an outrageous number of people viewing it.

JANE GOODALL: It was 17.9 million. Isn't that staggering?

VG: People don't seem to be able to get enough of it.

JG: It is interesting, isn't it? I sometimes wonder why it is. I think it's partly because chimps are so like us and I also think that there is a strange myth around me because I was the first person to do this sort of thing.

VG: At a time when it was odd for a young girl to do such a thing. Did you have this life in mind from childhood, that you would eventually rush off to the jungle?

JG: Apparently, when I was two I began watching animals and when I was four I disappeared. I was staying with my mother's family in the English countryside and I was gone so long that my mother called the police. After four and a half hours I appeared and I was so happy. I can still remember the moment. I'd been hiding in a hot, stuffy, little, dark hen-house because I could not understand where there was a hole big enough in the chicken for the egg to come out. So I waited. I waited for the chicken to come in and settle down in her nest and I can still see that egg coming out.

VG: Well, there's the basis of all your research—great patience.

JG: Exactly.

VG: The patience has been the key. You actually sat in that jungle for nearly two years before you could really get next to those chimps.

JG: That's right, it did take patience. But as I loved the life and I loved the forest—and I just loved being there—it didn't require as much patience as

implications—
consequences,
involved
meanings

primatologist—
one who studies
primates, an
order of
mammals
including
humans, apes,
and monkeys

amoral—without
moral sense or
principles

anthropologist—
one who studies
human origins,
cultures, races,
and social
relations

return fare—
round-trip fare

you might think. I didn't have to rush out and get a Ph.D. and earn my living, you know.

VG: But how did you keep up your enthusiasm and interest when there appeared to be no breakthroughs?

JG: Well, there were, because all the time I was sitting there I could see those chimps from a distance and little pieces of the puzzle began to fit together. But I've always liked being alone. It doesn't mean I'm antisocial; I'm not. I love being with people, too.

VG: How alone were you?

JG: All day, from the time I got up to the time I got back to the camp in the evening, when the authorities said I had to be with somebody. But even then I would climb up to some point and say, "You wait here, and I'll go over there."

VG: You are a rare breed, aren't you? Not too many do this kind of thing.

JG: There are far more now, let me tell you. I get so many letters from children and young people saying, "What do I do to get to do what you do?" This is a big responsibility, because these days it's getting very difficult to do what I did. The economic situation has changed and the political situation, too. More and more field stations are being closed down.

VG: You said that the Tanzanian officials didn't want you to be alone out there. Were they scratching their heads about you?

JG: They surely thought it was peculiar. Louis Leakey, who got the money for me to start off, was accused of being **amoral**. Sending a young girl off into the bush like that, it just wasn't done in those days.

VG: How did you get to Leakey in the first place? You didn't just march up to him, a legendary **anthropologist** and all.

JG: It wasn't quite that easy. I think when I was about eighteen my desire to be with animals really crystallized and I wanted to go to Africa. Eventually, I began to save enough money; in fact, I worked as a waitress to save up my fare. I had to get a **return fare**, you see. Finally I got to Africa. I had a temporary job, so I wasn't dependent on anyone. And I had heard about Dr. Leakey. People told me, "If you are interested in animals, you should go to see him." So I did.

VG: Was he thrilled to meet you or did he think you a bit odd?

JG: Oh, no. Almost immediately he offered me a job as his assistant. While I was working with him at the Olduvai Gorge where Zinjanthropus [the ancient human skeleton] was found, he started to talk to me about this little group of chimps on a wild lake shore. I thought he was teasing, but one day he said, "Why do you think I'm talking to you about this? This is what I want you to do, to study those chimps there." It really was

● ● ● ● ● ● ● ● ● ●

"He started to talk to me about this little group of chimps on a wild lake shore."

● ● ● ● ● ● ● ● ● ●

fantastic. But then he had to wait a whole year before he could find any money for me to go. Because it was so unique, nobody wanted to give any money, and I had no qualifications. At least no academic qualifications.

VG: Did he want you to have or get a degree?

JG: No, he didn't want me to. He wanted me to have an unbiased mind. He wanted me to go because I wanted to find out.

VG: Do you remember the arrival at your camp in the bush?

JG: I certainly remember the moment I arrived and looked up at that rugged country, thinking, "It is going to be difficult, but how exciting. And I'm jolly well going to do it."

VG: Who was with you?

JG: My mother. This was the amazing thing. She is fantastic and an adventuress and she wanted to come. She lives in England, but when I was working with Dr. Leakey in Nairobi she came for a visit. When it came time for me to go in, and I told you I had to be with somebody, I chose her. She stayed for three months and she set up this clinic with the local fishermen, which put me in such a good position with them.

VG: Is she a doctor or nurse?

JG: No, neither, but we have a medical family and my uncle was a surgeon. He gave us masses of medicine and instructions as to how to use it. Do you know it is nearly a quarter of a century ago?

VG: And I suppose some of the chimps that you encountered originally are still alive?

JG: Oh, sure they are, they live till they are fifty. And I am still working and now I have ten Tanzanian field assistants and they are there all the time collecting data, even as I talk to you.

VG: Throughout your studies there, it seems to me that the only **encroachment** you made upon them was the institution of the banana station. Apart from that, you introduced nothing into the chimps' lives that would be foreign to them.

JG: That's right. But we did it very badly at one time, right at the beginning before I had any idea that this research could carry on in the way it has been. I wanted to find out as much as I could. I kept thinking, "Golly, this is the end, I have to go back and write my thesis and write my degree." So we gave bananas every day and this had the most dramatic effect on the social structure, on the levels of aggression. When I realized that I could continue the study and have students, then we had to change the feeding altogether.

VG: From bananas to what?

JG: We still feed bananas, but, say, six every ten days, whereas a chimp can eat fifty at one sitting. So six is a very tiny amount. We only give bananas if a chimp comes by himself or in a small group.

VG: So as to not create a party atmosphere?

JG: Just enough so that if they're in the neighborhood, they'll drop by to see if there's anything going.

VG: At the local **pub**?

JG: That's right.

VG: Are they **gluttonous**? Will they eat till they burst?

encroachment—going beyond proper limits

pub—short for "public house"; a restaurant or gathering place

gluttonous—given to excessive eating

## FOCUS ON...
## GEOGRAPHY

Goodall lives outside Dar es Salaam, the capital of Tanzania, and conducts her research at a camp in the Gombe Stream National Park. Where in Africa is Tanzania? What ocean is nearby? What unique geographic features, such as mountains and lakes, are located there? Research the country of Tanzania and write a report. Include in your report an illustrated map of Tanzania, highlighting Dar es Salaam, Gombe Stream National Park, and Tanzania's unique geographic features.

◆ ◆ ◆ ◆ ◆ ◆ ◆ ◆ ◆ ◆ ◆ ◆ ◆ ◆ ◆ ◆ ◆ ◆ ◆ ◆ ◆

intimidate—to frighten with threats

"sex"—distinguish between human males and females

JG: They'll eat till they really can't eat any more. They will stuff themselves. They do enjoy their food, and they make these lovely oo-oo-ah chimp noises. They're happy when they get food.

VG: It must be a temptation to try and communicate, but you don't?

JG: Oh, I don't. It is very important not to try and interact. One could. You could be right in there, part of the group. But we specifically don't.

VG: What is your reaction to people who do the reverse to what you do—make attempts to communicate through sign language or whatever?

JG: It certainly doesn't upset me. It's not so much another world as it is the other side of the coin. It is an attempt to find out about the chimp intellect in a way that I can't do in the wild. It could make for a very good collaborative attempt to understand this very complex creature. In fact, I was just visiting the original chimp who learned sign language. That chimp has now adopted a baby and she's teaching the baby sign language, in the lab.

VG: Isn't that a remarkable thing, that what she learned, she is now teaching?

JG: In the wild, although a young one learns from the mother by observing and imitating and practicing, we now find that if a chimp is taught by humans, then she is capable of teaching. That is fascinating.

VG: Has any one of them ever become aggressive with you?

JG: Yes. The worst are the adolescent males, because they are out to **intimidate** the females of the community. And they can **"sex"** humans into males and females, too. Those adolescent males will treat me rather as they treat the females of the community. In other words, I must be intimidated. I don't think they'd ever really hurt one, but they jump up and they pound on you and hit you, and it does hurt. But once they've intimidated all the females, they work their way through the male hierarchy. Then they finally sort of grow up, as it were.

They don't bother the females any more, and they don't bother with me.

VG: In your opinion, do you think that they think about you in any way?

JG: I don't think I could ever answer that. They basically pay very little attention to us, which is nice. It is the young ones who watch more carefully, though. The most intelligent female there today once watched me drink a cup of coffee, and then I set it down. I didn't even know what she was doing, but she came over and picked up that cup and tried to drink it as we would. But of course it was hot, and she didn't put her lip touching the cup, but she poured it just as we would. That is pretty incredible for a wild animal. And that is the only example I have ever seen of a chimp trying to imitate something we've done. They imitate each other, but not us, fortunately. Otherwise we would really have trouble.

VG: What are your living circumstances in Gombe?

JG: Well, in 1975 I had a large research station with many foreign students, that is, non-Tanzanian students, mostly Americans. I lived there all the year round with my son, except when I was teaching over here. Then four of those students were kidnapped by a rebel group from Zaire. And although they were safely returned to their families in the end, unharmed, this area was then considered a sensitive one and it was deemed not wise to have foreign students there any more. So today I actually live in Dar es Salaam, the capital of Tanzania, and I visit Gombe for about three weeks every two months.

VG: Would you say you are living a city life?

JG: I wouldn't exactly call it that. I am outside the city, and the house is on the beach. I seldom see people. It is a beautiful place for working, and I have so much analysis to do, so much writing.

VG: And on occasion the "National Geographic" specials. It must be wonderful to have all those photos and the film footage of you romping around with these creatures.

JG: Yes, it is a bit like watching your family grow up, isn't it?

VG: Do the chimps rejoice in any way when you visit?

JG: No, thank goodness. But sometimes you feel a bit hurt. After all, I am so pleased to see them. Fifi, let's say, doesn't even look at me. But that is what I have been striving for, that is what I wanted, and that's what I've got.

## ACCENT ON...
### INFORMATION MANAGEMENT

Goodall and her field assistants study and research the chimpanzees of Gombe. As in most scientific research, a tremendous amount of information is collected. It must then be organized, maintained, analyzed, and presented. How does modern technology help in the management of scientific data? Discuss how computers can help in *each* step—information collection, organization, maintenance, analysis, and presentation.

VG: And what of your son? He goes to school in England. Does he have a similar passion to yours?

JG: No, he dislikes chimps intensely. And it is not really surprising, because chimps are hunters, and most of their prey is other primates, and this does include human infants. So when he was very tiny we had a cage made so that he'd be really safe. I think he probably resents the time that I've spent with the chimps, even though until he was nine he had one-half of every single day of my life, and when he was smaller he had the whole day virtually. But anyway, it turns out that very quietly, and unknown to anyone, he's been observing the behavior of the boys at his school. And he has come up with some shrewd insights. So, to answer your question: sort of. I think he may share a passion, but it will be human psychology.

VG: What are his observations?

JG: They are to do with why boys are aggressive to each other, and why some of them can turn the aggression off more easily than others, and why some are picked on and others are not. I've only just learned about this in the last few weeks and I think they are super insights. I would love it if he went into human psychology. If you are interested in the chimp because it's the most complex of creatures, then there is only one creature that is more fascinating, and that is us. ❖

## UNDERSTANDING

1.  Outline the main questions that Vicki Gabereau asks of Jane Goodall. Include any follow-up questions under each main question. From this outline, infer the objectives Gabereau had for her interview.

   Choose someone famous whom you would like to interview. Write three objectives, or main things you want to learn in the interview. Then write 15 questions to ask. With a partner, critique each other's questions on the basis of how effectively they will draw out the information needed to meet your objectives. *Workshop 26*

2. Take notes on the Goodall-Gabereau interview on notecards, making sure to have only one topic per card. Write the general topic—such as Initial Research, Techniques, or Lifestyle—at the top of each card. Then group the cards by general topic. Organize the cards within each topic and write an outline for a paper on Jane Goodall's experiences.

3.  Interviewing is an important skill; it is the major step in getting a job. Develop a list of questions you think might be asked during an employment interview. Some likely examples are "Why did you apply for this job?" and "What are your qualifications?" Pool your list with those of your classmates. Then choose 15 questions from the class list, and write out the answers as if you were applying for your "dream job."

## CONNECTING

1. Assume you are the interviewer in the text. You are asked to introduce Jane Goodall, who is the featured speaker at a banquet. Write your remarks. Include an introduction and information on her background, research, and lifestyle. Add an interesting anecdote about chimpanzees, then ask for a warm round of applause for Jane Goodall. Deliver your speech. *Workshop 25*

2. Suppose you are the public relations officer of a university. Jane Goodall has just signed a contract to teach the course, Behavior of Chimps and Humans: A Comparison. You must prepare a press release to let the public know about the university's association with this important scientist. Write the text of the press release, using computer technology, if possible. *Workshop 19*

# Women of Courage

- *Grandmother and the Workmen*
- *Women*

## EXPLORING

Americans expect service from service providers—clerks, mechanics, repairpersons, and others. We get impatient when we have to wait for an appointment, or for a return call from a serviceperson. In the case of government services, we insist that workers deliver a full day's work for their wages. What experiences have you had with poor service or with workers who seemed indifferent or inefficient? Describe your reaction and feelings.

## THEME CONNECTION...
## COURAGE TO TAKE CHARGE

The women in "Grandmother and the Workmen" and "Women" are take-charge individuals who set high standards for themselves and others. These women believe in the value of hard work and in personal responsibility. They are not afraid to speak out or to do the work themselves, if that is what must be done.

## TIME & PLACE

In his autobiography, Anthony Quinn speaks of struggling to be a Mexican-American teenager in Los Angeles during the 1920s. Though the 1920s was considered a time of prosperity in the U.S., members of the Mexican-American community may not have shared in the abundance. Quinn, his mother, and his Mexican grandmother would have been accustomed to hard work from living in poverty in El Paso before moving to California.

## THE WRITER'S CRAFT
### ANECDOTE

An anecdote is a short, generally amusing story that is often biographical or personal. Like biographies and essays, anecdotes are a form of narration. As we go through life, we collect many interesting, unusual, and amusing anecdotes about our experiences, our friends, our relatives, and our colleagues. This anecdote is told by a famous Hispanic actor whose opinion about his grandmother is shown by the warm and personal way he characterizes her. Readers share his feelings of admiration, amazement, and amusement at her behavior toward the workmen.

# Grandmother and the Workmen

Anthony Quinn

 randmother had been watching the men digging out on the street for five days. At first there had been an army of engineers surveying with their **transits** and **levels**. The neighborhood had been excited by the rumor that we would finally get a sewer pipe, which would spell the end of the backyard **two-holers**.

The men had marked the street with red and yellow chalk marks, put pegs down, and then had disappeared. After two or three months, the only memory of their having been there was that Widow Alonzo's daughter had been jilted by the head engineer.

Then one day three trucks arrived, unloaded men and equipment, and the digging began. Grandmother kept close check on their progress. They dug about a cubic foot and a half per man in one week. According to my grandmother, she dug more than that an hour in the vegetable garden surrounding our **privy**.

Every night as she prepared our **frijoles** and mustard greens, she cursed the injustice that we should be starving while those men out in the street were getting the enormous wage of three dollars a day, enough money to feed our family for a month.

One morning she couldn't stand it any longer and went out and **accosted** the fat foreman.

"I want a job!"

"Doing what, lady?"

"Digging like these men."

"Are you kidding, lady? That's man's work."

"Look, mister, I can lean on a shovel as good as they can. I've been watching them all week. A dog can dig faster."

"Look, you got any complaints, go to City Hall."

"I just want a job. I've got two hungry kids to feed."

"Go and do some sewing or washing."

Feeling challenged, my grandmother pulled a pick from the hands of a stunned workman and began to tear up the street.

The foreman tried to wrest the pick out of her hand, but she threatened him with it.

"I'm going to dig here all day. If you don't think I've earned my money at the end of the day you won't have to pay me."

The foreman shrugged and walked away. All the men, who had gathered around to watch the **spectacle**, laughed **uproariously** at her. An hour later, when she was still furiously swinging the pick, the men started to gather off to one side and mutter about going on strike. Meanwhile, various spectators had gathered on the side, cheering.

● ● ● ● ● ● ●

"I just want a job. I've got two hungry kids to feed."

● ● ● ● ● ● ●

**About the Author**

Anthony Quinn—actor, painter, sculptor, and author—was born in 1915 in Chihuahua, Mexico when his father was off fighting in the Mexican revolution. About a year later, Quinn and his mother moved to El Paso, Texas, buried in a coal truck because they had to pass through revolutionary lines of fighting. His childhood was one of extreme poverty. After a number of attempted careers, Quinn began acting at age 20 and went on to make nearly 300 motion pictures in a 60-year period.

transit—a surveyor's instrument for measuring angles

level—an instrument that indicates when something is perfectly horizontal

two-holers—outhouses

privy—another word for outhouse

frijoles—beans (Spanish)

accosted—approached and spoke in a challenging way

spectacle—sight

uproariously—heartily

The men finally went back to their work, at the insistence of the foreman, who seemed to hope the old lady would disappear and that it was all just a bad dream—a nightmare. After a while, the superintendent showed up and was amazed at the sight that greeted him. The foreman rushed up to him and explained. The superintendent looked at the other workers and said, "From what I can see, this is the first time these bums have done any work. Maybe she's right. Maybe we should let her work."

He walked over to Grandmother and said, "Lady, stop a minute. I want to talk to you."

She went on digging.

"Lady, listen to me. You can't work like a common laborer."

"Why not?"

## ON THE JOB
## CONSTRUCTION LABORER

Construction laborers work in every phase of building activity. They work on the construction sites of homes, high-rise buildings, airports, highways, dams and bridges, and water and sewer projects. The work demands physical strength and an alert mind. Some laborers specialize in certain kinds of work, such as bricklaying, and many contractors offer training programs. Laborers with any specific skill or training to offer have a strong advantage in this keenly competitive area.

"I don't know," he said, "but it don't look right. Besides," he smiled, "you're making them all look bad. You're right, they are bums, but this would start a revolution, lady. My business is to get this street done. I don't want to be involved in any crazy revolution by women picking and shoveling like ordinary laborers."

The old lady stopped for a second and considered.

"All you want is this street done, right? I promise you, with me among them, you will get it done in half the time."

"I don't doubt it, lady, but there'd be an awful lot of explaining to do. I beg you to leave the men alone. Look, tell you what I'll do. I understand you've worked three hours already. I'll pay you for the whole day. We'll be around for some time and you can bring the men water. I'll pay you for a full day's work."

For the rest of the month, the men had the best water carrier of their lives. My grandmother took her job very seriously. In the morning she would make ice-cold lemonade for the men working out on the street. Sometimes she would vary it and put in strawberry. No group of pick-and-shovel workers ever drank such nectar as she made. I think they were a little sad when they finished the job and had to move to another neighborhood. But that month my grandmother made a grand total of sixty dollars, which kept us in three square meals a day for a long time. ❖

## Food Basket, 1920–1922

| Product | Year | New York | Atlanta | Chicago | Denver | Los Angeles |
|---|---|---|---|---|---|---|
| Beans, navy, per pound | 1920 | 12.0¢ | 13.5¢ | 11.6¢ | 12.7¢ | 9.9¢ |
| | 1921 | 8.9¢ | 10.0¢ | 7.9¢ | 9.1¢ | 8.0¢ |
| | 1922 | 10.0¢ | 11.1¢ | 9.8¢ | 10.1¢ | 9.1¢ |
| Beef, rib roasts, per pound | 1920 | 40.5¢ | 30.7¢ | 33.5¢ | 28.4¢ | 30.0¢ |
| | 1921 | 36.4¢ | 27.4¢ | 30.2¢ | 23.6¢ | 29.3¢ |
| | 1922 | 35.3¢ | 26.7¢ | 28.8¢ | 22.9¢ | 28.3¢ |
| Beef, steaks (round), per pound | 1920 | 47.3¢ | 36.7¢ | 34.7¢ | 34.2¢ | 32.4¢ |
| | 1921 | 41.3¢ | 32.8¢ | 31.0¢ | 27.2¢ | 29.9¢ |
| | 1922 | 39.6¢ | 31.2¢ | 29.1¢ | 25.8¢ | 28.2¢ |
| Bread, per loaf | 1920 | 11.7¢ | 12.2¢ | 11.6¢ | 11.8¢ | 10.1¢ |
| | 1921 | 10.3¢ | 11.1¢ | 10.3¢ | 10.3¢ | 9.3¢ |
| | 1922 | 9.5¢ | 9.9¢ | 9.7¢ | 8.3¢ | 9.0¢ |
| Butter, per pound | 1920 | 70.5¢ | 73.3¢ | 63.4¢ | 64.8¢ | 68.9¢ |
| | 1921 | 52.4¢ | 54.1¢ | 48.9¢ | 47.0¢ | 52.4¢ |
| | 1922 | 48.0¢ | 49.1¢ | 45.2¢ | 42.6¢ | 51.8¢ |

SOURCE: Derks, Scott. From *The Value of a Dollar, 1860–1989*, edited by Scott Derks. Copyright © Gale Research, Inc. Reproduced by permission.

## FOCUS ON... ECONOMICS

Quinn's grandmother earns $60 in one month working as a water carrier for construction laborers. The narrator explains that the money kept the family well fed "for a long time." How much food does $60 buy today? Could it feed a family of four for one week? Make a one-week meal plan for a family of four, including three balanced meals a day. Then find out the cost of the food items needed. Create a computer-generated chart of the meal plan and the food-item cost.

## Income, Standard Jobs, 1920–1924

| Job Type | (Dollar figures are annual pay, unless otherwise noted.) | | | | |
|---|---|---|---|---|---|
| | 1920 | 1921 | 1922 | 1923 | 1924 |
| Average of all industries, excluding farm labor | $1,489 | $1,349 | $1,305 | $1,393 | $1,402 |
| Average of all industries, including farm labor | $1,407 | $1,233 | $1,201 | $1,299 | $1,303 |
| Building trades, union workers Average hours/week | $1.08/hr 43.80 hrs | $1.01/hr 43.80 hrs | $1.11/hr 43.90 hrs | $1.19/hr 43.80 hrs | $1.05/hr 43.80 hrs |
| Domestics | $665 | $649 | $649 | $711 | $732 |
| Farm labor | $810 | $522 | $508 | $572 | $574 |
| Finance, insurance, and real estate | $1,758 | $1,860 | $1,932 | $1,896 | $1,944 |
| Gas and electricity workers | $1,432 | $1,364 | $1,343 | $1,339 | $1,417 |
| Lower-skilled labor | $1,207 | $780 | $807 | $984 | $1,128 |
| Manufacturing, union workers Average hours/week | 88¢/hr 45.70 hrs | 92¢/hr 46.10 hrs | 87¢/hr 46.20 hrs | 91¢/hr 46.30 hrs | 97¢/hr 46.10 hrs |
| Medical/health services workers | $752 | $983 | $912 | $845 | $845 |
| Public school teachers | $970 | $1,109 | $1,206 | $1,239 | $1,269 |
| State and local government workers | $1,164 | $1,296 | $1,316 | $1,336 | $1,346 |
| Street railway workers | $1,608 | $1,539 | $1,436 | $1,493 | $1,544 |
| Telegraph industry workers | $1,159 | $1,145 | $1,110 | $1,133 | $1,150 |

SOURCE: Derks, Scott. From *The Value of a Dollar*, *1860–1989*, edited by Scott Derks. Copyright © Gale Research, Inc. Reproduced by permission.

# Women

## Alice Walker

**About the Author**

Alice Walker was born in Eatonton, Georgia, in 1944 and educated at Spelman College and Sarah Lawrence College. She writes poetry, essays, short stories, and novels. Walker's early work draws on her Southern childhood experiences, her civil rights activism, and her experiences in Africa. She describes herself as a "womanist," an African-American feminist whose work explores issues of race, gender, liberation, and cultural tradition. Her novel *The Color Purple* received a Pulitzer Prize and in 1985 was made into a movie.

headragged—
wearing head-
rags, or scarves
wrapped around
their heads

They were women then
My mama's generation
Husky of voice—Stout of
Step
With fists as well as
Hands
How they battered down
Doors
And ironed
Starched white
Shirts
How they led
Armies
**Headragged** Generals
Across mined
Fields
Booby-trapped
Kitchens
To discover books
Desks
A place for us
How they knew what we
*Must* know
Without knowing a page
Of it
Themselves. ❖

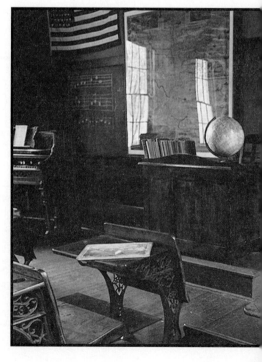

# UNDERSTANDING

1. Note the irony in the anecdote about the old woman who outworks the men. Find examples of the reactions she gets when she joins the work crew. How are the men threatened by her presence?

   On the job today, men are entering professions that used to be considered "women's work." List five professions that used to be filled by only men or only women but are now becoming more gender balanced.

2. Grandmother earned $60 a month working full time. If she worked 43.5 hours a week, as was common at that time, what was she earning per hour? If she had held the job for a year, how much money would she have made? Using the table "Income, Standard Jobs, 1920–1924," on page 203, determine in which category of worker the woman was. If the story took place in 1921, how does her salary compare? In 1924?

   Now examine the table "Food Basket, 1920–1922." How do the prices of staple foods compare to those today? Research today's prices for the five items listed. Develop a comparative graph to show the differences. *Workshop 22*

3.  It is unlikely that the women in the poem actually did batter down doors, but the narrator wants to emphasize how solidly the doors were closed against the education of the women's children. So she uses a literary device called hyperbole—an exaggeration to make a point. In groups, develop a list of phrases using hyperbole that are commonly heard. For instance, your parents may say they've told you "a million times" to clean your room.

A LAST WORD

How would you respond to a situation you believed to be unjust? Would you have the conviction to challenge the situation as the grandmother did? As the women did?

# CONNECTING

1. Conduct a survey on how people feel about work and how hard they work. As a class, design a questionnaire with five questions. Conduct the survey and compile your data, listing responses on separate sheets labeled with the question asked. Write a report that summarizes the results.

2. Careful and exact writing is called for in the workplace, as in poetry. This is especially true in product descriptions. In groups, develop and design a sales catalog. Decide on a category of products you will sell, for example sports equipment, clothing, gift items, etc. Then, write catalog descriptions for six to ten items. Include a drawing of each product.

# Conviction Comes in All Sizes

- *Short-Order Cook*
- *If I can stop one Heart*
- *the lesson of the moth*

## EXPLORING

Knowing what we desire in life, what challenges we want to undertake, and how we want to be remembered is difficult. Just knowing what profession to pursue and what skills we'll need is hard because the choices are so numerous. What do you dream of becoming? What do you believe strongly? When you attend your 20th high school reunion, what do you hope to have accomplished?

## THEME CONNECTION...
## STRENGTH OF ONE'S CONVICTION

In these poems, a proud cook, a caring poet, and a thrill-seeking moth express their central beliefs about what matters in life. The three different philosophies have an underlying similarity: strong conviction and courage. The important things are to set goals, meet them with energy, and believe in oneself.

## TIME & PLACE

The setting of "Short-Order Cook" is the blue-collar world of Detroit, Michigan. Jim Daniels says most of his poems "come out of various minimum-wage jobs that I have worked." Emily Dickinson wrote "If I can stop one Heart" during the mid-1800s, from her home in Amherst, Massachusetts. In the 1920s, "archy the cockroach" was invented in Don Marquis's New York office and became a comic character in his newspaper column. As shown in "the lesson of the moth," archy was a philosophical poet.

## THE WRITER'S CRAFT
### POETIC DEVICES

Poetry readers gain meaning from a poem's *images*. Images are words or phrases that appeal to one or more of the five senses. Devices used to create images in these three poems are *rhyme* (repetition of sounds at the ends of words), *rhythm* (the pattern of beats in the lines), *personification* (giving a nonhuman subject human characteristics), *onomatopoeia* (words that imitate sounds), and *alliteration* (repetition of beginning consonant sounds). Try to find examples of these devices as you read the poems.

## Short-Order Cook

Jim Daniels

An average joe comes in
and orders thirty cheeseburgers and thirty fries.

I wait for him to pay before I start cooking.
He pays.
He ain't no average joe.

The grill is just big enough for ten rows of three.
I slap the burgers down
throw two buckets of fries in the deep frier
and they pop pop spit spit . . .
psss . . .
The counter girls laugh.
I concentrate.
It is the crucial point—
they are ready for the cheese:
my fingers shake as I tear off slices
toss them on the burgers/fries
    done/dump/
refill buckets/burgers ready/flip into
    buns/
beat that melting cheese/wrap burgers in
    plastic/
into paper bags/fries done/dump/fill
    thirty bags/
bring them to the counter/wipe sweat on
    sleeve
and smile at the counter girls.
I puff my chest out and bellow:
"Thirty cheeseburgers, thirty fries!"
They look at me funny.
I grab a handful of ice, toss it in my mouth
do a little dance and walk back to the grill.
Pressure; responsibility, success,
thirty cheeseburgers, thirty fries. ❖

**About the Author**

Jim Daniels (b. 1956) was born in Detroit, Michigan. In his poems, Daniels draws on his experiences living and working in Detroit. He received a 1985 National Endowment for the Arts Creative Writing Fellowship and his first book of poems, *Places/Everyone,* received the Brittingham Prize in Poetry. Daniels currently lives in Pittsburgh.

## ON THE JOB
### CHEF

Chefs work in hotels, restaurants, and cafeterias. In large restaurants, cooks or chefs become experts in one kind of food, such as pastry, soup, or vegetables. Chefs oversee the kitchen, decide on serving sizes, set prices, plan menus, and order supplies. Strong skills in math are necessary for such calculations. Chefs also create new food dishes and improve familiar ones. No formal education is necessary, but a cooking diploma from a vocational or culinary school is helpful.

# If I can stop one Heart

Emily Dickinson

If I can stop one Heart from breaking
I shall not live in vain
If I can ease one Life the Aching
Or cool one Pain

Or help one fainting Robin
Unto his Nest again
I shall not live in Vain. ❖

## About the Author

Unknown as a poet during her lifetime, Emily Dickinson (1830–1886) is now famous worldwide. She was born in Amherst, Massachusetts. After attending college for one year, Dickinson returned to her family home in Amherst, where she filled her days with domestic chores. At night, she wrote poems about nature, life, and death. Dickinson's solitary life offered her little world experience, yet her poems show an intense understanding of life and human feelings. In 1955, 69 years after her death, all of her poems finally were published in one volume.

## ON THE JOB

### HOME HEALTH AIDE

Home health aides provide services in the home for people who cannot take care of themselves. They assist in a variety of ways, including giving baths and massages, helping patients exercise, and instructing patients and their families in health care. Patience and understanding are key qualities for success in this job, and it is essential that aides be in good health. Most employers prefer to hire high school graduates, especially those with volunteer or part-time hospital experience.

## the lesson of the moth

Don Marquis

i was talking to a moth
the other evening
he was trying to break into
an electric light bulb
and fry himself on the wires

why do you fellows
pull this stunt i asked him
because it is the **conventional**
thing for moths or why
if that had been an uncovered
candle instead of an electric
light bulb you would
now be a small unsightly cinder
have you no sense

plenty of it he answered
but at times we get tired
of using it
we get bored with the routine
and crave beauty
and excitement
fire is beautiful
and we know that if we get
too close it will kill us
but what does that matter
it is better to be happy
for a moment
and be burned up with beauty

than to live a long time
and be bored all the while

so we wad all our
    life up
into one little
    roll
and then we
    shoot the roll
that is what life
    is for
it is better to be a
    part of beauty
for one instant and
    then cease to
exist than to exist
    forever
and never be a part of
    beauty
our attitude toward life
is come easy go easy
we are like human beings
used to be before they became
too civilized to enjoy themselves

and before i could argue him
out of his philosophy
he went and **immolated** himself
on a patent cigar lighter
i do not agree with him
myself i would rather have
half the happiness and twice
the **longevity**

but at the same time i wish
there was something i wanted
as badly as he wanted to fry himself

**archy** ❖

**About the Author**

Don Marquis (1878–1937) was a columnist in New York for the *Sun* and *Tribune* newspapers. Born in Illinois, Marquis held a variety of jobs before he became a successful writer. One day, while Marquis worked at the *New York Sun,* the "biggest cockroach you ever saw" skittered across his desk. This incident gave Marquis the idea for a comic character named archy, a philosophical cockroach. His stories and verse about archy are still read today.

conventional—usual

immolate—kill or destroy as a sacrifice

longevity—length of life

archy—the philosophical cockroach poet who wrote "the lesson of the moth" for Don Marquis. The poem has no capitalization or punctuation because archy couldn't reach those keys on the typewriter.

*From* Theodore Roosevelt's Address at the Sorbonne,
Paris, France, April 23, 1910

It is not the critic who counts; not the man who points out
how the strong man stumbles, or where the doer of deeds
could have done them better. The credit belongs to the man
who is actually in the arena, whose face is marred by dust
and sweat and blood; who strives valiantly; who errs, and
comes short again and again, because there is no effort
without error and shortcoming; but who does actually strive
to do the deeds; who knows the great enthusiasms, the
great devotions; who spends himself in a worthy cause; who
at the best knows in the end the triumph of high achievement, and who at the worst, if he fails, at least fails while
daring greatly, so that his place shall never be with those
cold and timid souls who know neither victory nor defeat. ❖

# UNDERSTANDING

1. Emily Dickinson's poem states a principle by which she believes she should
   live. Examine the poem for Dickinson's beliefs.

   What is your credo, the belief that governs how you treat others? Write it
   and list examples of how you follow your credo. Then write a paragraph on
   how your beliefs influence your relationships at home, school, and work.

2. In the cockroach's conversation with the moth, we discover the difference in
   their philosophies. Write the philosophy of the moth. Then write the comments
   of the cockroach in response.

   Locate three advertisements in a magazine read by the general public. Make
   a three-column chart in which you record the following for each advertisement: the product name, a description of pictures or images, and the ad's
   underlying message. Then, for each advertisement, finish this statement: "If
   you use ____(product), you will ____." ***Workshop 24***

3. What message do the actions of the short-order cook give readers about his credo?

   Assume you are the manager of the restaurant. When you evaluate your
   employees, you look at the following criteria: job knowledge, quantity of
   work, quality of work, personal initiative, leadership, and interpersonal skills.
   Make a chart and rate the cook on a scale from 1 to 5. Comment on specific
   positive or negative aspects of his job performance.

## A LAST WORD

Each day offers
hope. Why does it
take conviction and
courage to make
the most of each
day? How can we
look beyond the
routine of our daily
lives to find beauty
and happiness?

**210**
Unit 4:  Courage and Conviction

## CONNECTING

1. Setting goals and meeting them is a lifetime skill. The first step is to identify your goals—they should be specific. Then place them in order of importance. Establish a time line for each goal, revise the goal if needed, and evaluate your progress. Design a form for personal goal setting and evaluation. Include each of the steps mentioned here and others that you feel may help you. Explain your form to a peer editing group for feedback on design and effectiveness.

2. Consider Emily Dickinson's message in your own life. Identify a group of people in your neighborhood who need assistance. In groups, establish an organization through which teens can help people after school. Name your organization, write its central goal, and define the people it will help. Write an action plan for the organization and design an application form. Give an oral presentation that outlines your organization and its project and encourages teens to join. ***Workshops 11 and 25***

# WRAP IT UP

### UNIT 4

1. In "Raymond's Run," Squeaky delights in her brother Raymond's running talent. In "Mrs. Donovan," Mrs. Donovan saves Roy. The women in Alice Walker's poem fight for the rights of their children. According to the poem, "If I can stop one Heart," which of these characters best comprehends the need and reward of helping others? Think of a time when you were able to help a person or animal. What did you learn about yourself in the process? Did you feel that your life had purpose? Prepare a speech describing your experience and how it helped you to understand the meaning of living a worthwhile life.

2. In "the lesson of the moth," the moth has a passionate desire for living life to the fullest; archy, the cockroach envies that desire. Think of Squeaky, Angelou's grandmother, Mrs. Donovan, Jane Goodall, the grandmother who challenges the workmen, and the short-order cook. In what ways do their approaches to life agree with that of the moth? Why is courage and conviction needed to live each day to the fullest? Are some people born with a passionate desire while others are not? Write an inspirational essay that attempts to persuade readers to live each day with courage and conviction.

# UNIT
## ⑤
# TURNING
# POINTS

We can predict certain significant events in our lives, such as entering high school and getting a driver's license. However, sometimes we recognize turning points only after they have occurred. We are suddenly different in some way. Only later do we realize that a certain conversation or even an event entirely outside our control has changed our lives forever.

Not all turning points are welcome occurrences. Receiving a disappointing gift or being caught stealing are painful experiences at the time. Yet, these events can become important turning points. The selections in this unit explore turning points that changed people's lives unexpectedly, in large ways and in small.

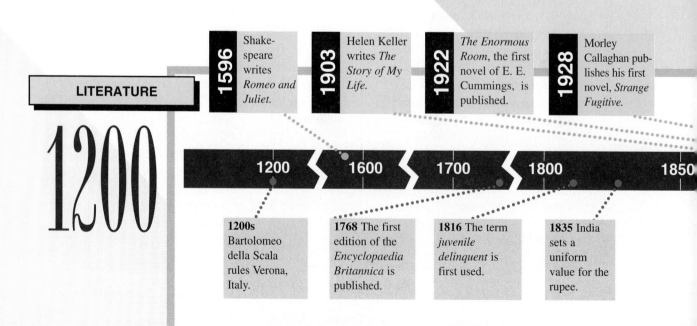

**LITERATURE**

**1596** Shakespeare writes *Romeo and Juliet.*

**1903** Helen Keller writes *The Story of My Life.*

**1922** *The Enormous Room*, the first novel of E. E. Cummings, is published.

**1928** Morley Callaghan publishes his first novel, *Strange Fugitive.*

1200

1200 — 1600 — 1700 — 1800 — 1850

**1200s** Bartolomeo della Scala rules Verona, Italy.

**1768** The first edition of the *Encyclopaedia Britannica* is published.

**1816** The term *juvenile delinquent* is first used.

**1835** India sets a uniform value for the rupee.

*from* **Romeo and Juliet**
—William Shakespeare

**Three Wise Guys**
—Sandra Cisneros

**All the Years of Her Life**
—Morley Callaghan

**A Rupee Earned**
—I. F. Bulatkin

**On Being Seventeen, Bright, and Unable to Read**
—David Raymond

*from* **The Story of My Life**
—Helen Keller

**Who Needs It?**
—Vilas Manivat

**A Young Lady of Property**
—Horton Foote

*in Just-*
—E. E. Cummings

1920   1940   1960   1990

2000

**1927** Clara Bow becomes a star in the silent movies.

**1973** The Rehabilitation Act provides help for children with learning problems.

**1977** The first mechanical hand finger-spells for deaf-blind people.

**1993** The "Brady Bill" requires a background check on gun buyers.

**LIFE and WORK**

# *from* Romeo and Juliet

## EXPLORING

Sometimes we sense danger before anything bad actually happens. Some call this feeling intuition, but others perceive that our sense of danger is based on concrete facts and conditions that warn us. Do you respond to your own intuition? Or do you ignore your feelings and move forward recklessly?

## THEME CONNECTION... CONSEQUENCES THAT COST

Our decisions, at times, can lead to very serious consequences. Sometimes the consequences cannot be imagined; sometimes the consequences *can* be imagined, but we choose not to consider them. In this scene from *Romeo and Juliet,* quick tempers lead to decisions affecting life, death, and exile.

## TIME & PLACE

In the first two acts of the play, we learn that the prominent Montague and Capulet families of Verona, Italy, are sworn enemies, with an "ancient grudge." Romeo, a member of the Montague family, disguises himself and attends a feast at the Capulet house. There he meets and falls in love with Juliet Capulet. They profess their love to each other in the famous "balcony scene" after the feast. Romeo and Juliet elope and marry the next day. Romeo is just returning from their secret marriage as the action in Act III, scene i, begins. Tybalt, a Capulet, is infuriated that Romeo had been at the feast the night before.

## THE WRITER'S CRAFT

### TRAGEDY

*Romeo and Juliet* is a tragedy. A tragedy is a drama that ends disastrously for the main characters and sometimes for the supporting characters as well (as in this play). The tragic ending can be death or devastation. In the case of *Romeo and Juliet,* a number of deaths leave the survivors grieving over the waste of young lives and its senseless cause—the feud between two families.

# from *Romeo and Juliet*

## William Shakespeare

### Characters

Mercutio, kinsman to the Prince and friend of Romeo
Benvolio, nephew to Montague and friend of Romeo
Tybalt, nephew to Lady Capulet
Romeo, son of Montague
Citizens of Verona
Escalus, Prince of Verona
Lady Capulet
Montague

### About the Author

English poet and playwright William Shakespeare (1564–1616) is the most widely known author in all of English literature. Born in Stratford-upon-Avon, he later lived in London, where he pursued a career in the theater as both an actor and a playwright. He wrote at least 37 plays, including histories, tragedies, comedies, and romances. In 1596, Shakespeare wrote his second tragedy, *Romeo and Juliet.*

Act III, scene i. A public place in Verona

*Enter* Mercutio, Benvolio, *and* Men.

BENVOLIO. I pray thee, good Mercutio, let's **retire**.
   The day is hot, the Capulets abroad,
   And, if we meet, we shall not 'scape a brawl,
   For now, these hot days, is the **mad blood** stirring.

MERCUTIO. Thou art like one of these fellows that, when he   5
   enters the confines of a tavern, claps me his sword upon the
   table and says 'God send me no need of thee!' and by the
   **operation** of the second cup draws him on the **drawer,** when
   indeed there is no need.

BENVOLIO. Am I like such a fellow?   10

MERCUTIO. Come, come, thou art as hot a Jack in thy mood
   as any in Italy; and as soon moved to be moody, and as soon
   moody to be moved.

BENVOLIO. And what to?

MERCUTIO. Nay, and there were two such, we should have none   15
   shortly, for one would kill the other. Thou! why, thou wilt quarrel
   with a man that hath a hair more or a hair less in his beard than thou
   hast. Thou wilt quarrel with a man for cracking nuts, having no other
   reason but because thou hast hazel eyes. What eye but such an eye
   would spy out such a quarrel? Thy head is as full of quarrels as an   20
   egg is full of meat; and yet thy head hath been beaten as addle as an
   egg for quarrelling. Thou hast quarrelled with a man for coughing in

retire—go back inside

mad blood—men's tempers

operation . . . drawer—by the time his second drink has affected him (**operation**), he draws his sword on the barman (**drawer**)

the street, because he hath wakened thy dog that hath lain asleep in the sun. Didst thou not fall out with a tailor for wearing his new **doublet** before Easter? with another for tying his new shoes with old **riband**? And yet thou wilt **tutor** me from quarrelling!

BENVOLIO. An I were so apt to quarrel as thou art, any man should buy the **fee simple** of my life for an hour and a quarter.

MERCUTIO. The fee simple? O **simple**!

*Enter* Tybalt *and others.*

BENVOLIO. By my head, here come the Capulets.

MERCUTIO. By my heel, I care not.

TYBALT. Follow me close, for I will speak to them.

Gentlemen, **good-den**. A word with one of you.

MERCUTIO. And but one word with one of us? Couple it with something; make it a word and a blow.

TYBALT. You shall find me apt enough to that, sir, an you will give me **occasion**.

MERCUTIO. Could you not take some occasion without **giving**?

TYBALT. Mercutio, thou **consortest** with Romeo.

MERCUTIO. **Consort**? What, dost thou make us minstrels? An thou make minstrels of us, look to hear nothing but discords. Here's my **fiddlestick**; here's that shall make you dance. Zounds, consort!

BENVOLIO. We talk here in the public haunt of men.
Either withdraw unto some private place,
Or **reason coldly** of your grievances,                    45
Or else depart. Here all eyes gaze on us.

MERCUTIO. Men's eyes were made to look, and let them gaze.
I will not budge for no man's pleasure, I.

*Enter* Romeo.

TYBALT. Well, peace be with you, sir. Here comes my man.

MERCUTIO. But I'll be hanged, sir, if he **wear your livery**.          50

Marry, go before to field, he'll be your follower!
**Your worship** in that sense may call him man.

TYBALT. Romeo, the love I bear thee can **afford**
No better term than this: thou art a villain.

ROMEO. Tybalt, the reason that I have to love thee                                  55
Doth much excuse the appertaining rage
To such a greeting. Villain am I none.
Therefore farewell. I see thou knowest me not.

TYBALT. Boy, this shall not excuse the **injuries**
That thou hast done me; therefore turn and draw.                                   60

ROMEO. I do protest I never injured thee,
But love thee better than thou canst **devise**
Till thou shalt know the reason of my love;
And so, good Capulet, which name I **tender**
As dearly as mine own, be satisfied.                                               65

MERCUTIO. O calm, dishonorable, vile submission!
**Alla stoccata** carries it away.                                    [*Draws.*]
Tybalt, you **ratcatcher**, will you walk?

TYBALT. What wouldst thou have with me?

MERCUTIO. Good King of Cats, nothing but one of your nine lives. That              70
I mean to **make bold withal**, and, as you shall use me hereafter, **dry-beat**
the rest of the eight. Will you pluck your sword out of his **pilcher** by the ears?
Make haste, lest mine be about your ears ere it be out.

TYBALT. I am **for** you.                                              [*Draws.*]

ROMEO. Gentle Mercutio, put thy rapier up.                                         75

MERCUTIO. Come, sir, your **passado**!                             [*They fight.*]

ROMEO. Draw, Benvolio; beat down their weapons.
Gentlemen, for shame! forbear this outrage!
Tybalt, Mercutio, the Prince expressly hath
Forbid this **bandying** in Verona streets.                                        80
Hold Tybalt! Good Mercutio!
         [Tybalt *under* Romeo's *arm thrusts* Mercutio *in,
              and flies with his* Followers.]

MERCUTIO.                        I am hurt.
A **plague** a both your houses! I am **sped**.
Is he gone and **hath nothing**?

---

Your worship—
a respectful
phrase used
here with great
sarcasm

afford—allow

line 55—Romeo
refers to his
secret marriage
to Juliet, which
prevents him
from being
angry

injuries—insults,
referring to
Romeo's pres-
ence at the
Capulet feast

devise—imagine

tender—offer or
speak

Alla stoccata—
the sword gets
away with it; the
stoccado is a
thrust in fencing

ratcatcher—
Tybalt was a
name often
given to cats;
Mercutio invites
Tybalt to go
somewhere else
to fight ("will you
walk?").

line 71–73—
Mercutio means
to take one of
Tybalt's nine
lives. Then
depending on
how he feels
after the fight,
he may take the
other eight

pilcher—the
sword scabbard
or case

for—ready for

passado—
forward thrust
with the sword

bandying—
exchanging
blows

**BENVOLIO.** What, art thou hurt?

**MERCUTIO.** Ay, ay, a scratch, a scratch. Marry, 'tis enough.
Where is my page? Go, **villain**, fetch a surgeon. [*Exit* Page.] 85

**ROMEO.** Courage, man. The hurt cannot be much.

**MERCUTIO.** No, 'tis not so deep as a well, nor so wide as a church door;
but 'tis enough, 'twill serve. Ask for me to-morrow, and you shall find
me a grave man. I am **peppered**, I warrant, for this world. A plague a
both your houses! Zounds, a dog, a rat, a mouse, a cat, to scratch a man 90
to death! A braggart, a rogue, a villain, that fights **by the book of
arithmetic**! Why the devil came you between us? I was hurt under
your arm.

**ROMEO.** I thought all for the best.

**MERCUTIO.** Help me into some house, Benvolio, 95
Or I shall faint. A plague a both your houses!
They have made worms' meat of me. **I have it**,
And soundly too. Your houses!
[*Exit, supported by* Benvolio.]

**ROMEO.** This gentleman, the Prince's near **ally**,
My very friend, hath got this mortal hurt 100
In my behalf—my reputation stained
With Tybalt's slander—Tybalt, that an hour
Hath been my cousin. O sweet Juliet,
Thy beauty hath made me effeminate
And in my temper soft'ned valor's steel! 105

*Enter* Benvolio.

**BENVOLIO.** O Romeo, Romeo, brave Mercutio is dead!
That gallant spirit hath **aspired** the clouds,
Which too untimely here did scorn the earth.

**ROMEO.** This day's black fate on **moe days** doth depend;
This but begins the woe others must end. 110

*Enter* Tybalt.

**BENVOLIO.** Here comes the furious Tybalt back again.

**ROMEO.** Alive in triumph, and Mercutio slain?
Away to heaven **respective lenity**,
And fire-eyed fury be my **conduct** now!

---

plague . . .— Mercutio curses the Montague and Capulet families

sped—finished

hath nothing— has no injuries

villain—here, an affectionate use of the term

peppered— done for

by the book of arithmetic— according to a set plan; in a very measured way

I have it—I've had it

ally—kinsman

aspired— risen to

moe days . . .— The terrible events of this day will hang down over other days

respective lenity— reasonable gentleness

conduct—guide

FOCUS ON...
ARTS AND HUMANITIES

How do you think Shakespeare staged this scene from *Romeo and Juliet?* Working in small groups, create a staging plan, including set design, props, costumes, and sound effects. Then enact the scene with Benvolio, Mercutio, Romeo, Tybalt, and their followers. As soon as your group feels prepared, present your scene in front of the class.

◆ ◆ ◆ ◆ ◆ ◆ ◆ ◆ ◆ ◆ ◆ ◆ ◆ ◆ ◆ ◆ ◆ ◆

Now, Tybalt, **take** the 'villain' back again          115
That late thou gavest me; for Mercutio's soul
Is but a little way above our heads,
**Staying** for thine to keep him company.
Either thou or I, or both, must go with him.

TYBALT. Thou, wretched boy, that didst consort him here,          120
Shalt with him hence.

ROMEO.                    This shall determine that.
                    [*They fight.* Tybalt *falls.*]

BENVOLIO. Romeo, away, be gone!
The citizens are **up**, and Tybalt slain.
Stand not amazed. The Prince will doom thee death
If thou art taken. Hence, be gone, away!          125

ROMEO. O! I am **fortune's fool**!

BENVOLIO.                    Why dost thou stay?
                    [*Exit* Romeo.]

*Enter* Citizens.

CITIZEN. Which way ran he that killed Mercutio?
Tybalt, that murderer, which way ran he?

BENVOLIO. There lies that Tybalt.

CITIZEN.                    Up, sir, go with me.
I charge thee in the Prince's name obey.          130

take . . . —
take back the
word 'villain'

Staying—waiting

up—up in arms

fortune's fool—a
victim of luck, in
this case bad
luck

*Enter* Prince, *attended, old* Montague, Capulet, *their* Wives, *and all.*

PRINCE. Where are the vile beginners of this fray?

BENVOLIO. O noble Prince, I can **discover** all
    The unlucky **manage** of this fatal brawl.
    There lies the man, slain by young Romeo,
    That slew thy kinsman, brave Mercutio.        135

LADY CAPULET. Tybalt, my cousin! O my brother's child!
    O Prince! O husband! O, the blood is spilled
    Of my dear kinsman! Prince, as thou art true,
    For blood of ours shed blood of Montague.
    O cousin, cousin!        140

PRINCE. Benvolio, who began this bloody fray?

BENVOLIO. Tybalt, here slain, whom Romeo's hand did slay.
    Romeo, that spoke him fair, bid him bethink
    How **nice** the quarrel was, and urged **withal**
    Your high displeasure. All this—uttered        145
    With gentle breath, calm look, knees humbly bowed—
    Could not take truce with the **unruly spleen**
    Of Tybalt deaf to peace, **but that he tilts**
    With piercing steel at bold Mercutio's breast;
    Who, all as hot, turns deadly point to point,        150
    And, with a martial scorn, with one hand beats
    **Cold death** aside and with the other sends
    It back to Tybalt, whose dexterity
    **Retorts it**. Romeo he cries aloud,
    'Hold, friends! Friends, part!' and swifter than his tongue,    155
    His agile arm beats down their fatal points,
    And 'twixt them rushes; underneath whose arm
    An **envious** thrust from Tybalt hit the life
    Of stout Mercutio, and then Tybalt fled;
    But by and by comes back to Romeo,        160
    Who had but **newly entertained** revenge,
    And to't they go like lightning; for, ere I
    Could draw to part them, was stout Tybalt slain;
    And, as he fell, did Romeo turn and fly.
    This is the truth, or let Benvolio die.        165

LADY CAPULET. He is a kinsman to the Montague;
    Affection makes him false, he speaks not true.

---

**Glossary (margin notes):**

discover—reveal

manage—course

nice—trivial

withal—in addition

unruly spleen—uncontrolled anger

but that he tilts—so still he [Tybalt] thrust his sword

Cold death—Tybalt's sword

Retorts it—turns it back

envious—malicious

newly entertained—just thought of

Who . . . doth owe—Who must pay for Tybalt's death?

concludes—brings to an end; Romeo, by killing Tybalt, has done what the law would have done.

hate's proceeding—The Prince refers to the consequences of the two families' feud

Some twenty of them fought in this black strife,
And all those twenty could but kill one life.
I beg for justice, which thou, Prince, must give.
Romeo slew Tybalt; Romeo must not live.

PRINCE. Romeo slew him; he slew Mercutio.
   **Who** now the price of his dear blood **doth owe?**

MONTAGUE. Not Romeo, Prince; he was Mercutio's friend;
   His fault **concludes** but what the law should end,
   The life of Tybalt.

PRINCE.             And for that offense
   Immediately we do exile him hence.
   I have an interest in your **hate's proceeding,**
   **My blood** for your rude brawls doth lie a-bleeding;
   But I'll **amerce** you with so strong a fine
   That you shall all repent the loss of mine.
   I will be deaf to pleading and excuses;
   Nor tears nor prayers shall **purchase out** abuses.
   Therefore use none. Let Romeo **hence** in haste,
   Else, when he is found, that hour is his last.
   Bear hence this body, and attend our will.
   **Mercy** but murders, pardoning those that kill.

170

175

180

185

My blood—my kinsman

amerce—penalize; the families will pay a large fine so that they will be sorry about the death of the Prince's kinsman.

purchase out—buy a pardon for

hence—go away

Mercy . . . kill—Showing mercy to or pardoning those that kill only leads to more murders.

[*Exit, with others.*] ◆

# ACCENT ON...
## HOSPITALITY AND TOURISM

Stratford-upon-Avon is the birthplace of Shakespeare. Each year, millions of tourists visit his gravesite at Stratford Church. Research locations in Stratford and London where Shakespeare lived and worked. Plan a weeklong group tour for your class. Prepare a pamphlet describing the tour's itinerary and briefly explaining the significance of each site to be visited. Through your tour preparations, try to make Shakespeare's life and times come alive for your class.

# UNDERSTANDING

1. When Mercutio and Benvolio arrive in the square, Benvolio thinks it may be dangerous to linger and advises leaving. What is Mercutio's response to Benvolio's advice to "retire"? Rewrite this portion of the scene in modern language. Imagine two boys arriving in a dangerous neighborhood. How would they talk to each other? ***Workshop 4***

2. Create a diagram that illustrates the sequence of events in this scene. Examine the text to discover the actions of Tybalt, Mercutio, Benvolio, and Romeo. All of the action is strong, and it moves toward a very serious climax. Indicate that climax on your diagram. ***Workshop 1***

3. The concept of honor is a motivator in this scene. What actions are taken for the sake of honor? List examples from the text.

    In what sorts of situations does honor drive our behavior today? Write a persuasive essay presenting your views on the role of honor in teenage relationships. ***Workshop 13***

4. Describe in a few words the philosophy of these young men on handling conflict. What other options do young people have in modern conflicts? In groups, research conflict resolution techniques, and design a poster that depicts young people using one of the techniques. Your poster should appeal to young people. You may want to use speech balloons (like the ones cartoonists use) to help communicate your message.

A LAST WORD

The long-harbored feelings of hatred between the Montagues and the Capulets profoundly affect all of their lives—and the love between Romeo and Juliet. What might cause such deep hatred? What does it take for hatred to be replaced with feelings of love or forgiveness?

# CONNECTING

1. Using your library as a resource, locate reports of gang violence in your community or state. Identify themes or motivations for the conflicts. Design a project to benefit the needy that two rival gangs could work on cooperatively. Write a proposal, keeping in mind that your audience includes the gang members as well as the needy people who will benefit from the project. ***Workshop 13***

2. The Prince sentences Romeo to exile. In light of the events of the afternoon, is this fair punishment? What would happen to Romeo in today's court system? Write a news article relating the day's events for your local newspaper. ***Workshop 19***

# Three Wise Guys
## *Un Cuento de Navidad*
## *(A Christmas Story)*

## EXPLORING

Holidays and birthdays are occasions that inspire expectations, hopes, and dreams about gifts to be received. Did you ever expect or wait for a special gift with great excitement and then have your hopes dashed when you didn't receive it? Write about your disappointment in a journal. Or tell about a time when you waited excitedly for something that never happened.

## THEME CONNECTION...
## EXPECTATIONS AND REALITY

A special Christmas gift arrives and a whole family waits impatiently to open it on the special day. Each family member imagines that the box contains something that will improve his or her life. After the gift is opened, however, they are disappointed for the moment and life continues as before. Reality, it seems, can be less exciting than expectations. Surprisingly, the gift changes reality for the son in ways he does not expect.

## TIME & PLACE

Though the family in this story now lives in Texas, they continue to celebrate Christmas according to traditions learned in Mexico. These customs were influenced by the practices of Spanish missionaries who came to the Americas in the 1500s. According to the Bible, three kings or Wise Men arrived to give gifts to the infant Jesus on January sixth, the Day of the Three Kings. On the evening of January fifth, Mexican children leave out shoes or boxes to be filled with gifts. Sometimes they stuff the shoes with grass for the Wise Men's camels to munch.

## THE WRITER'S CRAFT
### FORESHADOWING

Weaving hints into a story about what is to come is called foreshadowing. Writers use this technique to draw readers into the plot and entice them to continue reading. In "Three Wise Guys," the climax occurs late in the story but the author foreshadows earlier that the gift will be something special. She also foreshadows the nature of the gift by revealing that it is from the principal at the children's school.

# Three Wise Guys

## Un Cuento de Navidad
## (A Christmas Story)

Sandra Cisneros

## About the Author

A poet and novelist, Sandra Cisneros (b. 1954) grew up in Chicago in a large Mexican-American family that includes her mother, father, and six brothers. She began writing at the age of 10. For Cisneros, writing is a way of dealing with the poverty and loneliness she experienced as a child. Cisneros is a graduate of Loyola University in Chicago and the University of Iowa's prestigious Writer's Workshop. Her first novel, *The House on Mango Street,* was widely acclaimed. "Three Wise Guys" appears in Cisneros's story collection *Woman Hollering Creek.*

*chicharras*— Spanish for cicadas or locusts

*urracas*— Spanish for magpies, noisy black-and-white feathered birds related to crows and jays

The big box came marked DO NOT OPEN TILL XMAS, but the mama said not until the Day of the Three Kings. Not until El Día de los Reyes, the sixth of January, do you hear? That is what the mama said exactly, only she said it all in Spanish. Because in Mexico where she was raised, it is the custom for boys and girls to receive their presents on January sixth and not Christmas, even though they were living on the Texas side of the river now. Not until the sixth of January.

Yesterday the mama had risen in the dark same as always to reheat the coffee in a tin saucepan and warm the breakfast tortillas. The papa had gotten up coughing and spitting up the night, complaining how the evening before the buzzing of the **chicharras** had kept him from sleeping. By the time the mama had the house smelling of oatmeal and cinnamon, the papa would be gone to the fields, the sun already tangled in the trees and the *urracas* screeching their rubber-screech cry. The boy Rubén and the girl Rosalinda would have to be shaken awake for school. The mama would give the baby Gilberto his bottle, and then she would go back to sleep before getting up again to the chores that were always waiting. That is how the world had been.

But today the big box had arrived. When the boy Rubén and the girl Rosalinda came home from school, it was already sitting in the living room in front of the television set that no longer worked. Who had put it there? Where had it come from? A box covered with red paper with green Christmas trees and a card on top that said: *Merry Christmas to the González Family. Frank, Earl, and Dwight Travis. P.S. DO NOT OPEN TILL XMAS.* That's all.

Two times the mama was made to come into the living room, first to explain to the children and later to their father how the brothers Travis had arrived in the blue pickup and how it had taken all three of those big men to lift the box off the back of the truck and bring it inside and how she had had to nod and say thank-you thank-you thank-you over and over because those were the only words she knew in English. Then the brothers Travis had nodded as well the way they always did when they came and brought the boxes of clothes or the turkey each November or the canned ham on Easter ever since the children had begun to earn high grades at the school where Dwight Travis was the principal.

But this year the Christmas box was bigger than usual. What could be in a box so big? The boy Rubén and the girl Rosalinda begged all afternoon to be allowed to open it, and that is when the mama had said the sixth of January, the Day of the Three Kings. Not a day sooner.

It seemed the weeks stretched themselves wider and wider since the arrival of the big box. The mama got used to sweeping around it because it was too heavy for her to push in a corner, but since the television no longer worked ever since the afternoon the children had poured iced tea through the little grates in the back, it really didn't matter if it obstructed the view. Visitors that came inside the house were told and told again the story of how the box had arrived, and then each was made to guess what was inside.

It was the *comadre* Elodia who suggested over coffee one afternoon that the big box held a portable washing machine that could be rolled away when not in use, the kind she had seen in her Sears, Roebuck catalog. The mama said she hoped so, because the wringer washer she had used for the last ten years had finally gotten tired and quit. These past few weeks she had to boil all the clothes in the big pot she used for cooking the Christmas tamales. Yes. She hoped the big box was a portable washing machine. A washing machine, even a portable one, would be good.

But the neighbor man Cayetano said, What foolishness, *comadre*. Can't you see the box is too small to hold a washing machine, even a portable one? Most likely God has heard your prayers

and sent a new color TV. With a good antenna you could catch all the Mexican soap operas, the neighbor man said. You could distract yourself with the complicated troubles of the rich and then give thanks to God for the blessed simplicity of your poverty. A new TV would surely be the end to all your miseries.

Each night when the papa came home from the fields, he would spread newspapers on the cot in the living room where the boy Rubén and the girl Rosalinda slept, and sit facing the big box in the center of the room. Each night he imagined the box held something different. The day before yesterday he guessed a new record player. Yesterday an ice chest . . . . Today the papa sat . . . fanning himself with a magazine, and said in a voice as much a plea as a prophecy: air conditioner.

But the boy Rubén and the girl Rosalinda were sure the big box was filled with toys. They had even punctured a hole in one corner with a pencil when their mother was busy cooking, although they could see nothing inside but blackness.

Only the baby Gilberto remained uninterested in the contents of the big box and seemed each day more fascinated with the exterior of the box rather than the interior. One afternoon he tore off a fistful of paper, which he was chewing when his mother scooped him up with one arm, rushed him to the kitchen sink, and forced him to swallow handfuls of lukewarm water in case the red dye of the wrapping paper might be poisonous.

> ●●●●●●●●
> **"Each night he imagined the box held something different."**
> ●●●●●●●●

*comadre*—pronounced koh MA dray; Spanish for godmother

When Christmas Eve finally came, the family González put on their good clothes and went to midnight **mass**. They came home to a house that smelled of tamales and **atole,** and everyone was allowed to open one present before going to sleep, but the big box was to remain untouched until the sixth of January.

On New Year's Eve the little house was filled with people, some related, some not, coming in and out. The friends of the papa came with bottles, and the mama set out a bowl of grapes to count off the New Year. That night the children did not sleep in the living-room cot as they usually did, because the living room was crowded with big-fannied ladies and fat-stomached men **sashaying** to the accordion music of the Midget Twins from McAllen. Instead the children fell asleep on a lump of handbags and crumpled suit jackets on top of the mama and the papa's bed, dreaming of the contents of the big box.

Finally the fifth of January. And the boy Rubén and the girl Rosalinda could hardly sleep. All night they whispered last-minute wishes. The boy thought perhaps if the big box held a bicycle, he would be the first to ride it, since he was the oldest. This made his sister cry until the mama had to yell from her bedroom on the other side of the plastic curtains, Be quiet or I'm going to give you each the stick, which sounds worse in Spanish than it does in English. Then no one said anything. After a very long time, long after they heard the mama's wheezed breathing and their papa's piped snoring, the children closed their eyes and remembered nothing.

The papa was already in the bathroom coughing up the night before from his throat when the *urracas* began their clownish chirping. The boy Rubén awoke and shook his sister. The mama frying the potatoes and beans for breakfast nodded permission for the box to be opened.

With a kitchen knife the boy Rubén cut a careful edge along the top. The girl Rosalinda tore the Christmas wrapping with her fingernails. The papa and the mama lifted the cardboard flaps, and everyone peered inside to see what it was the brothers Travis had brought them on the Day of the Three Kings.

There were layers of balled newspaper packed on top. When these had been cleared away, the boy Rubén looked inside. The girl Rosalinda looked inside. The papa and the mama looked.

This is what they saw: the complete *Encyclopaedia Britannica Junior,* twenty-four volumes in red imitation leather with gold embossed letters beginning with volume 1, Aar–Bel, and ending with volume 24, Yel–Zyn. The girl Rosalinda let out a sad cry as if her hair was going to be cut again. The boy Rubén pulled out volume 4, Ded–Fem. There were many pictures and many words, but there were more words than pictures. The papa flipped through volume 22, but because he could not read English words, simply put the book back and grunted. What can we do with this? No one said anything and shortly after, the screen door slammed.

Only the mama knew what to do with the contents of the big box. She withdrew volumes 6, 7, and 8, marched off to the dinette set in the kitchen, placed two on Rosalinda's chair so she could better reach the table, and put one underneath the plant stand that danced.

# FOCUS ON...
# GEOGRAPHY

In the story, the mama was raised on the Mexican side of the Rio Grande River, but the González family now lives on the Texas side of the river. Using an atlas, prepare a map of the Rio Grande River valley that shows the important land formations, towns and cities, climate, and anything else that characterizes the area for your audience.

When the boy and the girl returned from school that day, they found the books stacked into squat pillars against one livingroom wall and a board placed on top. On this were arranged several plastic doilies and framed family photographs. The rest of the volumes the baby Gilberto was playing with, and he was already rubbing his sore gums along the corners of volume 14.

The girl Rosalinda also grew interested in the books. She took out her colored pencils and painted blue on the lids of all the illustrations of women, and with a red pencil dipped in spit she painted their lips and fingernails red-red. After a couple of days, when all the pictures of women had been colored in this manner, she began to cut out some of the prettier pictures and paste them on loose-leaf paper.

One volume suffered from being exposed to the rain when the papa improvised a hat during a sudden shower. He forgot it on the hood of the car when he drove off. When the children came home from school, they set it on the porch to dry. But the pages puffed up and became so fat, the book was impossible to close.

Only the boy Rubén refused to touch the books. For several days he avoided the principal because he didn't know what to say in case Mr. Travis were to ask how they were enjoying the Christmas present.

On the Saturday after New Year's, the mama and the papa went into town for groceries and left the boy in charge of watching his sister and baby brother. The girl Rosalinda was stacking books into spiral staircases and making her paper dolls descend them in a fancy manner.

Perhaps the boy Rubén would not have bothered to open the volume left on the kitchen table if he had not seen his mother wedge her **name-day** corsage in its pages. On the page where the mama's carnation lay pressed between two pieces of kleenex was a picture of a dog in a spaceship. FIRST DOG IN SPACE the caption said. The boy turned to another page and read where cashews came from. And then about the man who

name-day—Catholics are often named after a saint. The name-day is the church's special day for the saint after whom one is named.

Three Wise Guys

**227**

invented the guillotine. And then about Bengal tigers. And about clouds. All afternoon the boy read, even after the mama and the papa came home. Even after the sunset, until the mama said time to sleep and put the light out.

In their bed on the other side of the plastic curtain the mama and the papa slept. Across from them in the crib slept the baby Gilberto. The girl Rosalinda slept on her end of the cot. But the boy Rubén watched the night sky turn from violet. To blue. To gray. And then from gray. To blue. To violet once again. ❖

## ACCENT ON...
### ADVERTISING
• • • • • • • • • • • • • • • • • • • • • •

For Rubén, the encyclopedia opens up a whole new world of knowledge. Working in small groups, create an advertising campaign to promote and sell encyclopedias. Create a slogan for your campaign. If possible, present your materials in a multimedia format of video, audio, and print.

## UNDERSTANDING

1. The principal has given the family gifts before. In the text, find examples of his gifts. What do these gifts reflect about his understanding of these people? Write a letter from the principal to Rubén telling him what he hopes Rubén and his family will do with the books. Focus on each member of the family. For instance, the principal might suggest ways for the parents to learn from the books and improve their English at the same time. *Workshop 16*

2.  How do the instructions on the package and those added by the mother heighten the family's anticipation? Find and bring to class examples of instructions from products you have in your home. Divide the instructions into categories, such as cleaning instructions, cooking instructions, assembly instructions, and so on. In groups, choose a category and outline the most important points that type of instruction should include. *Workshop 12*

3. Find in the text ideas from each character about what is in the box. How does the anticipation lead to disappointment?

    The poet Alice Walker wrote a poem that starts, "Expect nothing. Live frugally on surprise." Write a letter to a young person to teach him or her the lesson of "Three Wise Guys" and of these words by Walker. Use concrete examples from the story and from your own experience. *Workshop 16*

### A LAST WORD

In "Three Wise Guys," a gift gives a boy the opportunity to discover new worlds and satisfy his own curiosity. How might you help someone discover the wider world of knowledge?

## CONNECTING

1.  Research the Christmas customs of Mexican Catholics. What is the extent of Spanish influence? As a class, plan and prepare a Mexican/Spanish Christmas celebration day. Then form groups of four to five students. Each group should be responsible for one part of the celebration: food research and preparation, gift ideas (acquire the gifts if possible), dances, songs, and so on. Display all items found or created for the occasion.

2. The *Encyclopaedia Britannica* is a unique gift. Invite your school's librarian to come to class and show and talk about the *Britannica* and other encyclopedias in print and on CD-ROM. Submit questions to a student planning committee that will manage the question-and-answer session. Write a clear, simple set of instructions on where to find and how to use the library's encyclopedias. Ask students who speak or are learning Spanish to translate the instructions. Display the instructions in the library. *Workshop 12*

# All the Years of Her Life

## EXPLORING

● ● ● ● ● ● ● ● ● ● ● ● ● ● ● ● ● ● ● ●

What is a good parent? Is it one who gets a child out of trouble? Or is it one who keeps a child from getting into trouble in the first place? In many areas of the country, lawmakers are debating these questions. Perhaps the question should be as follows: Who is responsible when a child gets into trouble—the child or the parent? Discuss your answer to this question.

## THEME CONNECTION...
## RECOGNIZING EPIPHANIES

At some point, most of us will have an epiphany—a moment when we suddenly understand something. For one person, an epiphany might involve a mathematical concept. For another, it might relate to human nature. What each person does following his or her epiphany is a matter of individual choice—we can act on our new knowledge, or we can ignore it.

## TIME & PLACE

The story takes place in a large city, such as New York City, as indicated when the characters pass under the "Sixth Avenue elevated." Some large cities still have mass transport railway systems that run not just *on* the ground (as opposed to underground subways) but *above* the ground. These elevated trains make a great deal of noise as they pass through a neighborhood.

## THE WRITER'S CRAFT
### LIMITED OMNISCIENT
### POINT OF VIEW

Morley Callaghan uses the limited omniscient point of view in this story. That is, the author provides an external view of all characters and events, and gives *some* information about one or more characters' thoughts and feelings. Specifically, Callaghan occasionally lets the reader know what Alfred is thinking.

# All the Years of Her Life

## Morley Callaghan

hey were closing the drug-store, and Alfred Higgins, who had just taken off his white jacket, was putting on his coat and getting ready to go home. The little grey-haired man, Sam Carr, who owned the drugstore, was bending down behind the cash register, and when Alfred Higgins passed him, he looked up and said softly, "Just a moment, Alfred. One moment before you go."

The soft, confident, quiet way in which Sam Carr spoke made Alfred start to button his coat nervously. He felt sure his face was white. Sam Carr usually said, "Good night," brusquely, without looking up. In the six months he had been working in the drugstore Alfred had never heard his employer speak softly like that. His heart began to beat so loud it was hard for him to get his breath. "What is it, Mr. Carr?" he asked.

"Maybe you'd be good enough to take a few things out of your pocket and leave them here before you go," Sam Carr said.

"What things? What are you talking about?"

"You've got a **compact** and a lipstick and at least two tubes of toothpaste in your pocket, Alfred."

"What do you mean? Do you think I'm crazy?" Alfred blustered. His face got red and he knew he looked fierce with indignation. But Sam Carr, standing by the door with his blue eyes shining brightly behind his glasses and his lips moving underneath his grey mustache, only nodded his head a few times, and then Alfred grew very frightened and he didn't know what to say. Slowly he raised his hand and dipped it into his pocket, and with his eyes never meeting Sam Carr's eyes, he took out a blue compact and two tubes of toothpaste and a lipstick, and he laid them one by one on the counter.

"Petty thieving, eh, Alfred?" Sam Carr said. "And maybe you'd be good enough to tell me how long this has been going on."

"This is the first time I ever took anything."

"So now you think you'll tell me a lie, eh? What kind of a sap do I look like, huh? I don't know what goes on in my own store, eh? I tell you you've been doing this pretty steady," Sam Carr said as he went over and stood behind the cash register.

Ever since Alfred had left school he had been getting into trouble wherever he worked. He lived at home with his mother and his father, who was a printer. His two older brothers were married and his sister had got married last year, and it would have been all right for his parents now if Alfred had only been able to keep a job.

While Sam Carr smiled and stroked the side of his face very delicately with

## About the Author

Morley Callaghan (1903–1990), a novelist and short-story writer, was born in Toronto, Canada. While working summers for the *Toronto Star,* Callaghan met Ernest Hemingway, who encouraged him in fiction writing. He was educated at the University of Toronto but gave up a legal career when his stories began to appear in magazines. In 1928, after publishing his first novel, Callaghan left for Paris. He recorded his trip in his memoir, *That Summer in Paris.*

compact—a small container of cosmetics or makeup

the tips of his fingers, Alfred began to feel that familiar terror growing in him that had been in him every time he had got into trouble.

"I like you," Sam Carr was saying. "I liked you and would have trusted you, and now look what I got to do." While Alfred watched with his alert, frightened blue eyes, Sam Carr drummed with his fingers on the counter. "I don't like to call a cop in point-blank," he was saying as he looked very worried. "You're a fool, and maybe I should call your father and tell him you're a fool. Maybe I should let them know I'm going to have you locked up."

"My father's not home. He's a printer. He works nights," Alfred said.

"Who's at home?"

"My mother, I guess."

"Then we'll see what she says." Sam Carr went to the phone and dialed the number. Alfred was not so much ashamed, but there was the deep fright growing in him, and he blurted out arrogantly, like a strong, full-grown man, "Just a minute. You don't need to draw anybody else in. You don't need to tell her." He wanted to sound like a swaggering, big guy who could look after himself, yet the old, childish hope was in him, the longing that someone at home would come and help him. "Yeah, that's right, he's in trouble," Mr. Carr was saying. "Yeah, your boy works for me. You'd better come down in a hurry." And when he was finished Mr. Carr went over to the door and looked out at the street and

> ●●●●●●●●●●
> ## "Yet the old, childish hope was in him, the longing that someone at home would come and help him."
> ●●●●●●●●●●

watched the people passing in the late summer night. "I'll keep my eye out for a cop," was all he said.

Alfred knew how his mother would come rushing in; she would rush in with eyes blazing, or maybe she would be crying, and she would push him away when he tried to talk to her, and make him feel her dreadful contempt; yet he longed that she might come before Mr. Carr saw the cop on the beat passing the door.

While they waited—and it seemed a long time—they did not speak, and when at last they heard someone tapping on the closed door, Mr. Carr, turning the latch, said crisply, "Come in, Mrs. Higgins." He looked hard-faced and stern.

Mrs. Higgins must have been going to bed when he telephoned, for her hair was tucked in loosely under her hat, and her hand at her throat held her light coat tight across her chest so her dress would not show. She came in, large and plump, with a little smile on her friendly face. Most of the store lights had been turned out and at first she did not see Alfred, who was standing in the shadow at the end of the counter. Yet as soon as she saw him she did not look as Alfred thought she would look: she smiled, her blue eyes never wavered, and with a calmness and dignity that made them forget that her clothes seemed to have been thrown on her, she put out her hand to Mr. Carr and said politely, "I'm Mrs. Higgins. I'm

Alfred's mother." Mr. Carr was a bit embarrassed by her lack of terror and her simplicity, and he hardly knew what to say to her, so she asked, "Is Alfred in trouble?"

"He is. He's been taking things from the store. I caught him redhanded. Little things like compacts and toothpaste and lipsticks. Stuff he can sell easily," the proprietor said.

As she listened Mrs. Higgins looked at Alfred sometimes and nodded her head sadly, and when Sam Carr had finished she said gravely, "Is it so, Alfred?"

"Yes."

"Why have you been doing it?"

"I been spending money, I guess."

"On what?"

"Going around with the guys, I guess," Alfred said.

Mrs. Higgins put out her hand and touched Sam Carr's arm with an understanding gentleness, and speaking as though afraid of disturbing him, she said, "If you would only listen to me before doing anything." Her simple earnestness made her shy; her **humility** made her falter and look away, but in a moment she was smiling gravely again, and she said with a kind of patient dignity, "What did you intend to do, Mr. Carr?"

"I was going to get a cop. That's what I ought to do."

"Yes, I suppose so. It's not for me to say, because he's my son. Yet I sometimes think a little good advice is the

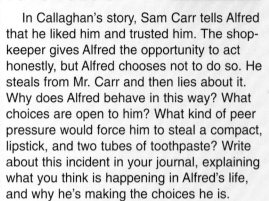

# FOCUS ON... PSYCHOLOGY

In Callaghan's story, Sam Carr tells Alfred that he liked him and trusted him. The shopkeeper gives Alfred the opportunity to act honestly, but Alfred chooses not to do so. He steals from Mr. Carr and then lies about it. Why does Alfred behave in this way? What choices are open to him? What kind of peer pressure would force him to steal a compact, lipstick, and two tubes of toothpaste? Write about this incident in your journal, explaining what you think is happening in Alfred's life, and why he's making the choices he is.

◆ ◆ ◆ ◆ ◆ ◆ ◆ ◆ ◆ ◆ ◆ ◆ ◆ ◆ ◆

best thing for a boy when he's at a certain period in his life," she said.

Alfred couldn't understand his mother's quiet **composure**, for if they had been at home and someone had suggested that he was going to be arrested, he knew she would be in a rage and would cry out against him. Yet now she was standing there with that gentle, pleading smile on her face, saying, "I wonder if you don't think it would be better just to let him come home with me. He looks a big fellow, doesn't he? It takes some of them a long time to get any sense," and they both stared at Alfred, who shifted away with a bit of light shining for a moment on his thin face and the tiny pimples over his cheekbone.

But even while he was turning away uneasily Alfred was realizing that Mr. Carr had become aware that his mother was really a fine woman; he knew that Sam Carr was puzzled by his mother, as

humility—the state of being humble; not arrogant or assertive

composure—calmness

if he had expected her to come in and plead with him tearfully, and instead he was being made to feel a bit ashamed by her vast tolerance. While there was only the sound of the mother's soft, assured voice in the store, Mr. Carr began to nod his head encouragingly at her. Without being alarmed, while being just large and still and simple and hopeful, she was becoming dominant there in the dimly lit store. "Of course, I don't want to be harsh," Mr. Carr was saying, "I'll tell you what I'll do. I'll just fire him and let it go at that. How's that?" and he got up and shook hands with Mrs. Higgins, bowing low to her in deep respect.

There was such warmth and gratitude in the way she said, "I'll never forget your kindness," that Mr. Carr began to feel warm and genial himself.

"Sorry we had to meet this way," he said. "But I'm glad I got in touch with you. Just wanted to do the right thing, that's all," he said.

"It's better to meet like this than never, isn't it?" she said. Suddenly they clasped hands as if they liked each other, as if they had known each other a long time. "Good night, sir," she said.

"Good night, Mrs. Higgins. I'm truly sorry," he said.

The mother and son walked along the street together, and the mother was taking a long, firm stride as she looked ahead with her stern face full of worry. Alfred was afraid to speak to her, he was afraid of the silence that was between them, so he only looked ahead too, for the excitement and relief was still pretty strong in him; but in a little while, going along like that in silence made him terribly aware of the strength and the sternness in her; he began to wonder what she was thinking of as she stared ahead so grimly; she seemed to have forgotten that he walked beside her; so when they were passing under the Sixth Avenue elevated and the rumble of the train seemed to break the silence, he said in his old, bluster-way, "Thank God it turned out like that. I certainly won't get in a jam like that again."

"Be quiet. Don't speak to me. You've disgraced me again and again," she said bitterly.

"That's the last time. That's all I'm saying."

"Have the decency to be quiet," she snapped. They kept on their way, looking straight ahead.

When they were at home and his mother took off her coat, Alfred saw that she was really only half-dressed and she made him feel afraid again when she said, without even looking at him, "You're a bad lot. God forgive you. It's one thing after another and always has been. Why do you stand there stupidly? Go to bed, why don't you?" When he was going, she said, "I'm going to make myself a cup of tea. Mind, now, not a word about tonight to your father."

While Alfred was undressing in his bedroom, he heard his mother moving around the kitchen. She filled the kettle and put it on the stove. She moved a chair. And as he listened there was no shame in him, just wonder and a kind of admiration of her strength and repose. He could still see Sam Carr nodding his head encouragingly to her; he could hear her talking simply and earnestly, and as he sat on his bed he felt a pride in her strength. "She certainly was smooth," he thought. "Gee, I'd like to tell her she sounded swell."

Unit 5: Turning Points

And at last he got up and went along to the kitchen and when he was at the door he saw his mother pouring herself a cup of tea. He watched and he didn't move. Her face, as she sat there, was a frightened, broken face utterly unlike the face of the woman who had been so assured a little while ago in the drugstore. When she reached out and lifted the kettle to pour hot water in her cup, her hand trembled and the water splashed on the stove. Leaning back in the chair, she sighed and lifted the cup to her lips, and her lips were groping loosely as if they would never reach the cup. She swallowed the hot tea eagerly, and then she straightened up in relief, though her hand holding the cup still trembled. She looked very old.

It seemed to Alfred that this was the way it had been every time he had been in trouble before, that this trembling had really been in her as she hurried out half-dressed to the drugstore. He understood why she had sat alone in the kitchen the night his young sister had kept repeating **doggedly** that she was getting married. Now he felt all that his mother had been thinking of as they walked along the street together a little while ago. He watched his mother, and he never spoke, but at that moment his youth seemed to be over; he knew all the years of her life by the way her hand trembled as she raised the cup to her lips. It seemed to him that this was the first time he had ever looked upon his mother. ❖

doggedly—stubbornly, determinedly

# ACCENT ON...
## CRIMINOLOGY
• • • • • • • • • • • • • • • • • • • • •

Alfred has an opportunity to learn about honesty, respect, and self-responsibility. Do you think he learns from his experience, or do you think he will shoplift again? What kind of crime-prevention program could you design to help kids realize the serious consequences of some actions? Consult local outreach or teen support programs to get ideas for your own proposal.

## ON THE JOB
• • • • • • • • • • • • • • • •
## RETAIL CLERK
• • • • • • • • • • • • • • • •

Retail clerks sell merchandise to customers. They work in department, discount, and variety stores, as well as specialty shops. Their duties vary depending on the store. Some clerks, for example, may mostly handle exchanged or returned merchandise; others may work exclusively with customers. Clerks must practice excellent personal hygiene and grooming. High school classes in business education, merchandising, and marketing are helpful preparation.

# UNDERSTANDING

1. What does Sam Carr accuse Alfred of having done? What proof does he have and what does he do about it? Write a carefully worded letter from Carr *not* recommending Alfred for his next job because Alfred was caught stealing in his store when employed there. ***Workshop 17***

2. The story contains three characters: Alfred, his mother, and Sam Carr. Each has a very different point of view. Write a paragraph from each character's viewpoint describing Alfred's crime and the situation in general. Have each character predict Alfred's future. ***Workshop 8***

3. The mother does not want to talk with Alfred on the way home from Carr's. She says, "Be quiet. Don't speak to me. You've disgraced me again and again." Is Alfred moved by his mother's words?

   Write a note from Alfred to his mother to be left on the kitchen table later that night. What does he say to her?

4. The author writes that the mother's "hand trembled and the water splashed on the stove." What does this information indicate? Write a short essay explaining your views. Consider why Mrs. Higgins continued to get Alfred out of trouble and whether her actions did him any good. Use examples from the story to support your points. ***Workshop 7***

**A LAST WORD**

Parents can sometimes protect their children from the consequences of their actions. Do you think parental protection helps or hurts a child? What happens to people who are always bailed out of problem situations they have created?

# CONNECTING

1. Research the policy of several local businesses concerning employee theft. Organize your findings in some kind of visual presentation—perhaps a graph or a chart—and display your final product for the class. ***Workshop 22***

2.  If Sam Carr had called the police, what would have happened to Alfred in your community? With a partner, write a letter inviting a local law enforcement official to talk to your class about this type of employer-employee relationship problem. In your letter, include a sample of the questions you would like to ask during the class interview. ***Workshops 17 and 26***

3. Suppose that 10 years have gone by and you now own your own business. Write an entry for your employee policy manual that pertains to employee theft. Prepare a special section of the classroom bulletin board and post every student's entry.

# A Rupee Earned

## EXPLORING

Sometimes we have to work for something in order to appreciate it. Which do you value more—something received as a gift or something earned? Consider the things you have earned. Now, compare them with the items given to you as gifts. How do you treat the two? Is there a difference?

## THEME CONNECTION...
## LEARNING FROM EXPERIENCE

If someone has never *earned* anything, he or she has missed the satisfaction of the experience. We might think that it is better just to receive something than to have to work for it, but perhaps this is not the case. Whether a person earns money, praise, or recognition, the experience of earning it is irreplaceable. In this story, the father tries to teach his son the value of work.

## TIME & PLACE

Because this story is a parable, there is no distinct time or place described in the text. We know that the action takes place at a time when blacksmiths are able to earn a good living by making horseshoes and forging iron tools. We also know that the story takes place in or near India due to the money and coin references.

## THE WRITER'S CRAFT

### PARABLE

This story is a parable—a short story written to point out a moral truth. As is often true with such tales, a main character is required to take a journey or to complete a task. Within the course of the story, there are usually several opportunities to learn the intended lesson, giving the character—and the reader—a chance to learn from his or her mistakes.

# A Rupee Earned

## I. F. Bulatkin

nce upon a time, in a land to the north, there lived a blacksmith who had worked hard all his life to provide for the needs of his family. So diligently had he labored and so carefully had he saved that his wife and his children never knew want, and he even managed to **put by** a small store of wealth.

But unlike his father, the son of this industrious man was such a lazybones that in the whole wide world there was none to equal him. Although he was healthy and strong he did not know how to do anything but eat, drink, and sleep in the shade. In all the twenty years of his life he had not earned a single **anna**, and he never gave a thought to the fact that he was living on his father's bread.

Now the time came when the blacksmith grew old and no longer had the strength to raise a spark from his anvil. Finally the old man took to his bed, and when he realized that death was near, he called his son to his side.

"I do not know why you are so lazy," the aged blacksmith lamented. "You cannot take after me, for I have been on friendly terms with work my whole life long. Little by little I acquired my household goods by toil and honest sweat. How can it be that a son of mine cannot earn even one **rupee**?"

"Well, to earn just a rupee is not such a magnificent thing," the youth replied.

● ● ● ● ● ● ● ● ● ●
## "How can it be that a son of mine cannot earn even one rupee?"
● ● ● ● ● ● ● ● ● ●

"My son," said the father, "show me that you can earn one rupee and all that I own will be yours when I die. Yes, you must prove to me now that you can earn something by the labor of your hands; otherwise, when I am gone you will not receive a rusty horseshoe nail. That is my will."

Now the blacksmith's son wanted very much to come into this inheritance, but he was so lazy he hated to **bestir** himself to perform the small task his father required. Besides, he did not know how. What a cruel thing, to have to earn a whole rupee when he had never earned a single anna since the day he was born! But a paternal word is a stone mountain, and as a stone mountain is not removed, a paternal word is not changed. His father had spoken.

The doting mother of this good-for-nothing youth could not bear to see him suffer. When she found a convenient moment, she said to him:

"Listen, little son, here is a rupee for you. Go and amuse yourself today, but when you come home in the evening, pretend you are returning from work and tell your father that you have earned the money."

The youth was so lazy he did not want to bother himself even this much, but he knew that something had to be done. So he took his mother's rupee, and with a bit of bread and cheese and a leather bag of wine he went off into the mountains. All day long he ate and drank and counted the birds in the sky. Then at

FOCUS ON...
MATH

How might the son have supported himself had his parents not continued to let him live at home? Do you know how much it would cost per month to house, feed, and clothe yourself? Estimate your monthly living costs, including rent, food, clothes, and transportation. Then figure out how many hours per week and for what wage you will need to work to meet these monthly costs.

nightfall he returned home and gave his father the rupee, saying:

"Here, Father, take it. It wasn't easy for me to earn this rupee. I cannot straighten my back, I worked so hard."

The father took the coin, looked at it from both sides, and tossed it from palm to palm. Then he threw it into the fire.

"No," he said, "you did not earn that rupee."

With a shrug of his shoulders the son replied: "Well, you don't have to believe me." And he went off to bed.

The next day the worried mother gave her son a second rupee, but this time she instructed him:

"Sleep all day if you wish, little son, but before you come home in the evening, run one mile. You will perspire, you will be tired, and then your father will believe that you have been at work, and that you did his bidding and earned the money by your labor."

The lazybones cared for his legs, but he cared still more to inherit his father's fortune. So he took his mother's rupee, and with food and drink he set out for the mountains as before. From dawn to dusk he ate and drank and warmed himself in the sun, but when it came time to go home he ran a mile, and then for good measure he ran another.

And when he arrived at the threshold he was so tired he could hardly draw a breath. Perspiration poured from him in streams. He toppled onto a bench and held out the rupee.

"It surely was hard for me to earn this rupee!" he gasped. "I worked like an ox the livelong day. I am falling over my feet with fatigue."

The father took the coin from his son, turned it over again and again in his hand, then threw it into the fire.

"No," he said, "you are deceiving me, my son. This rupee was given to you. It was useless for you to run from the mountains."

What could the lazy youth say? "You don't wish to believe me," he shrugged, smiling. "To be sure, it's not true." And forthwith he lay down by the fire and went to sleep.

A Rupee Earned

The good-for-nothing youth dreamed sweet dreams, but sleep did not come to his dear mother. She realized now that in deceiving her husband they only lost their hard-earned money, and she also knew that all this brought no profit to her son.

So the next day she instructed differently:

"Come now, little son. If you want to inherit your father's property, you must take yourself off and really go to work. If you only earn one or two annas a day, in a week you can make a whole rupee."

It seemed there was nothing else to do; the time had come to obey. The lazy-bones worked for a whole week. He carried something for one man; he helped with something for another. One man gave him one anna; another gave him two. Bit by bit he accumulated a whole rupee.

Then he went to his father and poured a handful of coins before him. Again the old man turned over the money, weighed it in his hand, and held some pieces up to the light. Then he said:

"No, my son. You have deceived me again. You did not earn this money." And he seized all the coins and threw them into the fire like so much rubbish.

But this time the son was in a frenzy. He hurled himself into the fireplace, separated the burning coals with his bare hands, and snatched the money out of the very fire itself. "Why did you do that?" he cried. "I haven't straightened up my back for a whole week and you want to burn my money in the fire!"

The father looked at his son and said:

"Now I believe that you earned this rupee yourself. Someone else's money you do not care about—that is cheap. But the money you earn by your own labor—ah, that you make a big fuss over! So it is, my son. Remember my words: As long as you work, you will have money and contentment, and all things will be yours. But if you will not work, another person's money cannot help you, for someone else's rupee is not worth one anna."

Then the father willed all his property to his son and went to the land from which no man ever returns. ❖

## ACCENT ON...
### CHILD CARE
### AND GUIDANCE

In the parable, the son does not learn the value of earning money by his own labor until he is 20 years old. How might parents guide their children to become responsible for themselves? Research different approaches toward child rearing and guidance. In a class presentation, compare and contrast the different methods and explain which method you prefer and why.

## UNDERSTANDING

1. Find passages in the story's opening paragraphs that describe the differences between father and son. Later, what does the son *say* to reveal his lack of understanding about work? Write the father's request as if it were an assignment for class. Indicate the reward if the task is completed correctly. ***Workshop 12***

2. Does the mother understand what the father is trying to teach their son? Find evidence in the text.

   Create a three-column chart. Label the columns "Son's Thoughts and Feelings," "Mother's Thoughts and Feelings," and "Outcome." Now review the story and complete the chart for each of the three attempts the son makes to carry out the father's task. Compare your chart with those of several classmates. Discuss whether you think the son will continue to work after receiving his inheritance.

3. The son wants to inherit his father's wealth. But the father wants his son to understand what wealth really means. How does the youth finally demonstrate his understanding of his father's lesson? Select a line from the story that reveals its theme and create a poster to illustrate the lesson. Display the poster in class.

## CONNECTING

1. Define the term *work ethic*. In groups, examine the work ethic of two different cultures. Present your material in a panel discussion for the class. In an opinion essay, explain your feelings about the importance of work and its rewards, whether in the form of money, praise, or self-respect.

2. Parents, grandparents, and other family members give advice that may help or harm children. Have you ever been given poor advice from a member of your family? Write a letter of advice to a younger brother, sister, or classmate on how to discern between good and bad advice. ***Workshop 16***

3. Imagine that you have saved up enough money to remodel your bedroom completely. You pay half of the money up front to the remodeling firm. Once the workers start, they work slowly and sloppily. Your new shelves are crooked, and the workers even ask you to go to the store to buy them some doughnuts. In the end, your room is unfinished and the bill is huge. Write a letter of complaint explaining to the owner of the business your feelings about the quality of work. ***Workshop 17***

> ### A LAST WORD
> Children learn from the behavior of adults, usually their parents. Do you think that children acquire definite attitudes toward work and money from their parents and other adults around them? Consider the attitudes toward work and money that you have learned from your own family.

# On Being Seventeen, Bright, and Unable to Read

## EXPLORING

People learn in different ways. One person may learn most effectively by doing, another by hearing, and another by seeing. How do you learn best? Are some things easier for you to learn than others? What things do other people learn more quickly than you, and what do you learn more quickly than others?

## THEME CONNECTION...
## LEARNING TO LEARN

Sometimes learning takes a lot of hard work. Other times it comes easily. Most people have little tricks to help them learn—ways to remember historical events or people's names, for example. In this essay, a young man discusses the difficulty he has with learning and how he has come to cope with it.

## TIME & PLACE

People with dyslexia have difficulty learning to read in spite of the fact that they have clear vision and often high intelligence. Dyslexia causes people to see words in reverse (*rat* for *tar*) or upside down. Dyslexia comes in many forms. Dyslexics can have trouble reading, writing, and/or spelling. This learning disability was first described by an English doctor in 1896. He called the condition "word blindness." Famous people who are thought to have had dyslexia include Winston Churchill, Thomas Edison, and Nelson Rockefeller.

## THE WRITER'S CRAFT
### INFORMATIVE ESSAY

In an informative essay, the author writes about a topic of interest to a specific audience. The author writes to inform, obviously, but there may be a purpose beyond that. In the case of David Raymond's essay, the purpose is to share information so that it might help others.

# On Being Seventeen, Bright, and Unable to Read

David Raymond

ne day a substitute teacher picked me to read aloud from the textbook. When I told her, "No, thank you," she came unhinged. She thought I was acting smart and told me so. I kept calm, and that got her madder and madder. We must have spent 10 minutes trying to solve the problem, and finally she got so red in the face I thought she'd blow up. She told me she'd see me after class.

Maybe someone like me was a new thing for that teacher. But she wasn't new to me. I've been through scenes like that all my life. You see, even though I'm 17 and a junior in high school, I can't read because I have **dyslexia.** I'm told I read "at a fourth-grade level," but from where I sit, that's not reading. You can't know what that means unless you've been there. It's not easy to tell how it feels when you can't read your homework assignments or the newspaper or a menu in a restaurant or even notes from your own friends.

My family began to suspect I was having problems almost from the first day I started school. My father says my early years in school were the worst years of his life. They weren't so good for me, either. As I look back on it now, I can't find the words to express how bad it really was. I wanted to die. I'd come home from school screaming, "I'm dumb. I'm dumb—I wish I were dead!"

I guess I couldn't read anything at all then—not even my own name—and they tell me I didn't talk as good as other kids. But what I remember about those days is that I couldn't throw a ball where it was supposed to go, I couldn't learn to swim, and I wouldn't learn to ride a bike, because no matter what anyone told me, I knew I'd fail.

Sometimes my teachers would try to be encouraging. When I couldn't read the words on the board, they'd say, "Come on, David, you know that word." Only I didn't. And it was embarrassing. I just felt dumb. And dumb was how the kids treated me. They'd make fun of me every chance they got, asking me to spell *cat* or something like that. Even if I knew how to spell it, I wouldn't; they'd only give me another word. Anyway, it was awful, because more than anything I wanted friends. On my birthday when I blew out the candles I didn't wish I could learn to read; what I wished for was that the kids would like me.

With the bad reports coming from school, and with me moaning about wanting to die and how everybody hated me, my parents began looking for help. That's when the testing started. The school tested me, the child-guidance center tested me, private psychiatrists tested me. Everybody knew something was wrong—especially me.

## About the Author

David Raymond was born in Norwalk, Connecticut, in 1958. He attended college in a program for students with learning disabilities and graduated with honors. Raymond listened to his college lectures and books on tape, which enabled him to complete his assignments. He now lives in Connecticut and works in real estate development and design. Recently, Raymond completed an architectural program at Harvard University and plans to do more work in the field of design.

dyslexia—a condition that causes a disturbance in the ability to read

## FOCUS ON...
## SCIENCE

For people with dyslexia, difficulties in processing sounds, especially fast sounds, show up at a young age. How does the brain process speech? What happens after a sound hits the ear? How does the brain make sense of spoken words? Research this process and then, using a computer program, create a flow chart or diagram that illustrates the hearing process.

◆ ◆ ◆ ◆ ◆ ◆ ◆ ◆ ◆ ◆ ◆ ◆ ◆ ◆ ◆

It didn't help much when they stuck a fancy name onto it. I couldn't pronounce it then—I was only in second grade—and I was ashamed to talk about it. Now it rolls off my tongue, because I've been living with it for a lot of years—dyslexia.

Elementary School

All through elementary school it wasn't easy. I was always having to do things that were "different," things the other kids didn't have to do. I had to go to a child psychiatrist, for instance.

One summer my family forced me to go to a camp for children with reading problems. I hated the idea, but the camp turned out pretty good, and I had a good time. I met a lot of kids who couldn't read and somehow that helped. The director of the camp said I had a higher IQ than 90 percent of the population. I didn't believe him.

About the worst thing I had to do in fifth and sixth grade was go to a special education class in another school in our town. A bus picked me up, and I didn't like that at all. The bus also picked up emotionally disturbed kids and retarded kids. It was like going to a school for the retarded. I always worried that someone I knew would see me on that bus. It was a relief to go to the regular junior high school.

Junior High School

Life began to change a little for me, then, because I began to feel better about myself. I found the teachers cared; they had meetings about me and I worked harder for them for a while. I began to work on the potter's wheel, making vases and pots that the teachers said were pretty good. Also, I got a letter for being on the track team. I could always run pretty fast.

## High School

At high school the teachers are good and everyone is trying to help me. I've gotten honors some **marking periods,** and I've won a letter on the cross-country team. Next quarter I think the school might hold a show of my pottery. I've got some friends. But there are still some embarrassing times. For instance, every time there is writing in the class, I get up and go to the special education room. Kids ask me where I go all the time. Sometimes I say, "to Mars."

Homework is a real problem. During free periods in school I go into the special ed room, and staff members read assignments to me. When I get home, my mother reads to me. Sometimes she reads an assignment into a tape recorder, and then I go into my room and listen to it. If we have a novel or something like that to read, she reads it out loud to me. Then I sit down with her and we do the assignment. She'll write, while I talk my answers to her. Lately I've taken to dictating into a tape recorder, and then someone—my father, a private tutor, or my mother—types up what I've dictated. Whatever homework I do takes someone else's time, too. That makes me feel bad.

We had a big meeting in school the other day—eight of us, four from the guidance department, my private tutor, my parents and me. The subject was me. I said I wanted to go to college, and they told me about colleges that have facilities and staff to handle people like me. That's nice to hear.

As for what happens after college, I don't know and I'm worried about that. How can I make a living if I can't read?

Who will hire me? How will I fill out the application form? The only thing that gives me any courage is the fact that I've learned about well-known people who couldn't read or had other problems and still made it. Like Albert Einstein, who didn't talk until he was 4 and flunked math. Like Leonardo da Vinci, who everyone seems to think had dyslexia.

I've told this story because maybe some teacher will read it and go easy on a kid in the classroom who has what I've got. Or, maybe some parent will stop nagging his kid and stop calling him lazy. Maybe he's not lazy or dumb. Maybe he just can't read and doesn't know what's wrong. Maybe he's scared, like I was. ❖

marking periods—grading periods; usually quarters or semesters

## ACCENT ON...
## COMPUTER TECHNOLOGY

Dyslexia affects nearly 15 percent of the population. Recent experimental programs have shown that computer exercises help children with learning disabilities such as dyslexia to develop key mental and auditory, or hearing, skills. Children with dyslexia frequently confuse sounds, especially those that begin with hard consonants, such as *b, d, p,* and *t.* Design a computer software program or game that helps children differentiate between these sounds. If possible, include sound in your program or game that emphasizes the hard consonants and makes them easier to hear and process in the brain.

# UNDERSTANDING

1. Raymond opens his essay with a surprising response to a teacher. What is it? List the ideas introduced in the opening paragraph that are explained later in the essay. Share your list with several classmates. Now summarize the essay. Be sure to identify the main points of the essay in the order they appear.

2. Find evidence in the essay that Raymond begins to experience some success in junior high. How does success affect how he feels about himself?

   What activity do you do well that makes you feel good about yourself? Jot down a description of it. Share your experience in small groups. What do such things have in common?

3. Raymond occasionally responds to questions with sarcasm. Locate Raymond's sarcastic answers in the essay. How does sarcasm help him cope with the pain of feeling dumb?

   Write a letter from Raymond's point of view to a prospective employer. Explain the condition of dyslexia and how it might affect job performance. Include suggestions for altering the work situation to accommodate Raymond's dyslexia. Consider communication with co-workers as well as with customers or clients. ***Workshop 17***

## A LAST WORD

Learning abilities differ from student to student. How might you be more understanding of students whose abilities differ from yours?

# CONNECTING

1. Form teams and research two or three types of reading and/or learning disorders. Learn one diagnostic technique used to identify such disorders that you can explain and demonstrate to the rest of the class. ***Workshops 21 and 25***

2. In the last paragraph Raymond tells the reader why he has written this essay. He appeals to (tries to arouse sympathy in) parents and teachers. How does he appeal to students? Write a short informative essay describing a learning experience you have had. Relate what you learned, in an attempt like Raymond's to make a similar experience easier for someone else. ***Workshops 3 and 9***

3. Plan a half-day conference for parents of preschoolers on what to watch for as their children begin to read. Who would be qualified to speak to parents? What topics should be covered? Develop a detailed agenda for the conference, including names of speakers and topics of speeches or discussion groups.

# *from* The Story of My Life

## EXPLORING
● ● ● ● ● ● ● ● ● ● ● ● ● ● ● ● ● ● ● ● ●

For most of us who use labels or names to identify sights, sounds, and other sensations, it is nearly impossible to imagine not having the use of those labels. But try to imagine touching objects and understanding not that they are sharp or soft or round, but only that they are pleasant or unpleasant. Discuss the importance of sight and sound and of being able to express yourself in words.

## THEME CONNECTION...
## HELPING OTHERS

Some people face challenges that seem impossible to overcome. For them, or for anyone, the key to success may be the help of one special person at just the right time. The benefits to both are likely to be invaluable. Until she met Annie Sullivan, Helen Keller had an overwhelming challenge in her life. Sullivan discovered the key that unlocked the world for Helen.

## TIME & PLACE

Helen Keller was a child in the 1880s, a time when girls played with dolls and prepared to become good wives and housekeepers. How fortunate she was to have parents who understood the value of education. They contacted the Perkins Institution for the Blind in Boston. The Institution sent a teacher—Anne Sullivan—who was herself partially blind. Miss Sullivan used a system of "touch teaching" and was a pioneer in using this type of instruction for the sensory impaired.

## THE WRITER'S CRAFT
### SPECIFIC EXAMPLES

A strong essay contains specific examples to show or prove the accuracy of each point. Helen Keller uses many specific examples to communicate the importance of Sullivan's teaching methods. The specific examples of "d-o-l-l" and "w-a-t-e-r" help readers understand how basic Keller's need for language was.

● ● ● ● ● ● ● ● ● ● ● ● ● ● ● ● ● ● ● ● ● ● ● ● ● ● ● ● ● ●

# from *The Story of My Life*

Helen Keller

## About the Author

Helen Keller was born in Tuscumbia, Alabama, in 1880. At the age of 19 months, scarlet fever left Keller blind and deaf. Just before she turned seven, Keller was introduced to Anne Sullivan, her teacher. Through sign language, Sullivan taught the child to communicate for the first time in her life. When Keller was 10 years old, she asked Sullivan to teach her to speak. At the age of 24, Keller graduated from Radcliffe College. She later became an author and lecturer and lived to be 88 years old.

The most important day I remember in all my life is the one on which my teacher, Anne Mansfield Sullivan, came to me. I am filled with wonder when I consider the immeasurable contrast between the two lives which it connects. It was the third of March, 1887, three months before I was seven years old.

On the afternoon of that eventful day, I stood on the porch, dumb, expectant. I guessed vaguely from my mother's signs and from the hurrying to and fro in the house that something unusual was about to happen, so I went to the door and waited on the steps. The afternoon sun penetrated the mass of honeysuckle that covered the porch, and fell on my upturned face. My fingers lingered almost unconsciously on the familiar leaves and blossoms which had just come forth to greet the sweet southern spring. I did not know what the future held of marvel or surprise for me. Anger and bitterness had preyed upon me continually for weeks and a deep languor had succeeded this passionate struggle.

Have you ever been at sea in a dense fog, when it seemed as if a tangible white darkness shut you in, and the great ship, tense and anxious, groped her way toward the shore with **plummet** and **sounding-line**, and you waited with beating heart for something to happen? I was like that ship before my education began, only I was without compass or sounding-line, and had no way of knowing how near the harbor was. "Light! Give me light!" was the wordless cry of my soul, and the light of love shone on me in that very hour.

I felt approaching footsteps. I stretched out my hand as I supposed to my mother. Someone took it, and I was caught up and held close in the arms of her who had come to reveal all things to me, and, more than all things else, to love me.

The morning after my teacher came she led me into her room and gave me a doll. The little blind children at the Perkins Institution had sent it and **Laura Bridgman** had dressed it; but I did not know this until afterward. When I had played with it a little while, Miss Sullivan slowly spelled into my hand the word "d-o-l-l." I was at once interested in this finger play and tried to imitate it. When I finally succeeded in making the letters correctly, I was flushed with childish pleasure and pride. Running downstairs to my mother I held up my hand and made the letters for *doll*. I did not know that I was spelling a word or even that words existed; I was simply making my fingers go in monkey-like imitation. In the days that followed, I learned to spell in this uncomprehending way a great many words, among them

**plummet**—a tool used by carpenters to determine a straight, usually vertical line; in this case, Keller uses it to mean a straight line toward shore

**248**          Unit 5: Turning Points

*pin*, *hat*, *cup* and a few verbs like *sit*, *stand*, and *walk*. But my teacher had been with me several weeks before I understood that everything has a name.

One day, while I was playing with my new doll, Miss Sullivan put my big rag doll into my lap also, spelled "d-o-l-l" and tried to make me understand that "d-o-l-l" applied to both. Earlier in the day we had had a tussle over the words "m-u-g" and "w-a-t-e-r." Miss Sullivan had tried to impress it upon me that "m-u-g" is *mug* and that "w-a-t-e-r" is *water*, but I persisted in confounding the two. In despair she had dropped the subject for the time, only to renew it at the first opportunity. I became impatient at her repeated attempts and, seizing the new doll, I dashed it upon the floor. I was keenly delighted when I felt the fragments of the broken doll at my feet. Neither sorrow nor regret followed my passionate outburst. I had not loved the doll. In the still, dark world in which I lived there was no strong sentiment or tenderness. I felt my teacher sweep the fragments to one side of the hearth, and I had a sense of satisfaction that the cause of my discomfort was removed. She brought me my hat, and I knew I was going out into the warm sunshine. This thought, if a wordless sensation may be called a thought, made me hop and skip with pleasure.

We walked down the path to the well-house, attracted by the fragrance of the honeysuckle with which it was covered. Someone was drawing water and my teacher placed my hand under the spout. As the cool stream gushed over one hand, she spelled into the other the word *water* first slowly, then rapidly. I stood

Helen Keller as a young girl

still, my whole attention fixed upon the motions of her fingers. Suddenly I felt a misty consciousness as of something forgotten—a thrill of returning thought; and somehow the mystery of language was revealed to me. I knew then that "w-a-t-e-r" meant that wonderful cool something that was flowing over my hand. That living word awakened my soul, gave it light, hope, joy, set it free! There were barriers still, it is true, but barriers that could in time be swept away.

I left the well-house eager to learn. Everything had a name, and each name gave birth to a new thought. As we returned to the house, every object which I touched seemed to quiver with life. That was because I saw everything with the strange, new sight that had come to me. On entering the door, I remembered the doll I had broken. I felt my way to

sounding-line— an instrument used to measure the depth of water

Laura Bridgman— Helen's mother had read about Laura, a blind and deaf girl who had learned to communicate at the Perkins Institution; it was this article that led her to contact the Institution about a teacher for Helen.

the hearth and picked up the pieces. I tried vainly to put them together. Then my eyes filled with tears; for I realized what I had done, and for the first time I felt repentance and sorrow.

I learned a great many new words that day. . . . It would have been difficult to find a happier child than I was as I lay in my crib at the close of that eventful day and lived over the joys it had brought me, and for the first time longed for a new day to come. ❖

Helen Keller, 1955

# ACCENT ON...
## COMMUNICATIONS TECHNOLOGY

Helen Keller dedicated her autobiography to Alexander Graham Bell who, in her words, "taught the deaf to speak and enabled the listening ear to hear speech from the Atlantic to the Rockies." Find out about the modern technology used in creating telecommunication systems for the deaf and hard of hearing. You may want to contact a representative from your local telephone company to explain specific services offered.

## UNDERSTANDING

1. Compare the opening three paragraphs of the excerpt with the last paragraph, in which Helen leaves the well-house. How does her concept of anticipation and hope change? Write a diary entry from Anne Sullivan's point of view telling of Helen's breakthrough.

2. Anne Sullivan begins by spelling very simple words into Helen's hand. It is the word *water* that finally brings recognition and understanding. This word is richly symbolic because of all the things that water can stand for. Make a T-chart and list all of the things water can represent on the left. Then, in the right column, indicate the relationship of that thing to the excerpt. Write an essay explaining both the literal and symbolic uses of the word in Keller's autobiography.

3. It is clear that the arrival of Anne Sullivan is an important event. Review the text and select at least three examples that illustrate this importance. In a short summary paragraph, describe the events of Sullivan's arrival and state the theme of this excerpt.

   Summarizing is an important skill in the workplace, too. Read an article in any professional journal or trade magazine and write a brief summary. Be sure to paraphrase all the main points of the article in the same order. Do not add any information to your summary that was not in the original article.

## A LAST WORD

Helen Keller's discovery of language freed her from a life of isolation. How aware are you of the extraordinary role language plays in your life? To whom and to what does language connect you?

## CONNECTING

1. Helen Keller was blind and deaf. Investigate modern-day opportunities for people who face similar challenges. Where do they go to school? Do public schools participate in their education? What technologies exist to allow blind and deaf people to have experiences similar to those of seeing and hearing people? Prepare an oral report and present it to your class. *Workshop 25*

2. Invite a blind or deaf person to address the class. Prepare well-thought-out questions to ask your guest. Keep in mind that this person may experience the world very differently from the way you do. At the same time, this person has likes and dislikes, needs and preferences, just as you do. *Workshop 26*

3. Read the play *The Miracle Worker*. Make a chart of the similarities and differences between Keller's version of Sullivan's arrival and the play's version. How much did the playwright change the facts? Present an oral report in which you compare and contrast Sullivan's arrival in the two works. *Workshops 15 and 25*

The Story of My Life

# Who Needs It?

## EXPLORING

● ● ● ● ● ● ● ● ● ● ● ● ● ● ● ● ● ●

Throughout history, men and women have sought wealth, beauty, and fame—things they thought would bring them happiness. What will bring you happiness? What *is* happiness? Is it having everything you need? Consider the difference between the things you need and the things you want. What will you do to acquire the things you need? How will you get the things you want?

## THEME CONNECTION...
## THE GOODNESS OF GIVING

The main character in this story has a reputation for being generous. He can see that the man robbing his store thinks he *needs* money badly. As is his custom, the shopkeeper gives freely, not out of fear. His generosity alters the other man significantly and unexpectedly.

## TIME & PLACE

This story takes place in Thailand in a small shop. Approximately 95 percent of the Thai population is of the Buddhist religion. The shopkeeper seems to follow Buddhist practices in dealing with the thief. Buddhism teaches meditation and the importance of moral actions. One of the basic beliefs of Buddhism is that the cause of suffering is desire.

## THE WRITER'S CRAFT

### IRONY

Irony presents a sharp contrast between appearance and reality. There are three types of irony: verbal, situational, and dramatic. Verbal irony occurs when one thing is said but another is meant. In situational irony, the reader expects a certain event or outcome but something else happens. Dramatic irony occurs when readers know something that the characters do not. In "Who Needs It?" the reader expects Nai Phan to be afraid of the man with the gun. The irony is that Nai Phan changes the man's view on life. This is an example of situational irony.

# Who Needs It?

Vilas Manivat

Translated by Jennifer Draskau

ai Phan was one of the neighborhood celebrities. Not because he was a dancer with feet as light as stardust; nor had he distinguished himself in the fields of politics or literature. Perhaps a talent for concocting a good dish of fried rice was his claim to immortality, but even if his culinary gifts had not been outstanding, he would have been famous, for he was ready to allow his customers unlimited credit.

He liked to give children sweets without asking for money. Of course this always caused his wife to complain, but he would reply: "Twenty **satangs** worth of sweets won't reverse the family fortunes." The Than Khun, a high official who lived in the lane, used to say to his boy when he fancied a good cup of coffee: "Go and bring coffee from Nai Phan's. He puts in plenty of milk; you'd think he kept a cow for the purpose!"

There lived in the same lane a drunkard who loved to turn up at the cook shop and recite verses from the **tale of Khun Chang and Khun Phaen;** Nai Phan would listen with **rapt** attention. After the performance the drunkard would ask for a glass of free iced tea, which Nai Phan would gladly supply, with a doughnut thrown in for good measure.

During the rains Nai Phan would say to the young girl students, "Young ladies, you have been wading in mud with difficulty. From now on you can carry your shoes to my shop to put them on." He would always give them clean water to wash their feet.

But at eight p.m. sharp every night, he would shut up his shop. His friends would say to him, "You should start serving at night; business is good then, and you will get rich quicker."

Nai Phan would laugh good-humoredly saying, "It's better to go to bed than to get rich quick!"

This retort touched something in the hearts of listeners who were richer than Nai Phan, yet were still not satisfied with their wealth, but were struggling to **amass** even greater fortunes.

People who lived in the lane, returning home late at night after a long day spent chasing money, would see Nai Phan reclining in his little deck chair, chatting contentedly with his wife. Then they would think to themselves: "How happy they look, free from **hankering** after wealth. They are better off than us."

One evening his wife went to a cinema, and Nai Phan was alone. It was getting dark and he was preparing to close his shop, when a young man rushed in.

## About the Author

Vilas Manivat was born in Thailand. Manivat has written many travel books about the United States and England, for which he is well known in Thailand. A famous television personality, Manivat has also taught journalism in Thailand.

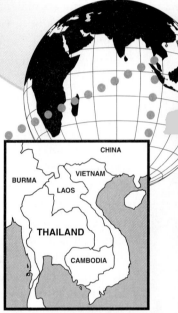

CHINA
VIETNAM
BURMA
LAOS
THAILAND
CAMBODIA

satang—the primary unit of money in Thailand

tale of Khun Chang and Khun Phaen— Thai legends

rapt—wholly absorbed; engrossed

amass—collect, store up

hankering— longing for

"What can I do for you, sir?" Nai Phan asked.

Instead of replying, the stranger produced a gun and leveled it at his heart. Nai Phan did not understand, but he felt that matters were getting out of hand.

"Hand over your cash," the young man snapped roughly, "all of it; whatever you have. Murder seems to be the fashion nowadays; people shoot each other every day. If I kill you, it will not be anything special, and if you kill me, that would not be very strange either, so be quick about it. If I don't get the money, I'll let you have a taste of bullets."

Nai Phan did not tremble. He stood quite calmly and said in a conversational tone: "I'll give you the money, but not because of your gun, I'll give it to you because you seem to need it so badly. Perhaps it is a matter of life and death. Here . . . all the money I have is here. Take it and hurry home. Who knows? Perhaps your mother is ill; perhaps she has not touched food for days. Hurry home; perhaps many people are waiting there, wondering whether you will bring back money or not. Many lives may depend on your return with this money. I won't tell the police. There is about nine hundred here in cash; there may be more . . . take it."

He placed the money on the table but the young gunman did not seem able to get up enough courage to touch it.

"Why don't you take it?" Nai Phan asked. "Look here, why would I trick you? I know you're hard up. We're all hard up these days. I don't believe you are a bad man. Who would choose to be a thief if he could afford not to? Perhaps your father has had a stroke and you have to look after him. Take him this money, but don't spend it all on medicine. Believe me, a doctor can cure the body, but a man needs a cure for his mind and soul as well. Buy some sweet-smelling flowers, a garland for your mother to place before the sacred image at home. That's what I do every night. You don't have to know what holiness is or where it lives. It is enough to feel at peace with yourself. That's heaven. Oh!—and put away your gun—you will feel better at once. A man who carries a gun cannot know peace, his heart is tortured with fear and doubt, and the scent of danger. We cannot be happy as long as our hands are cluttered with weapons."

● ● ● ● ● ● ● ●

"We cannot be happy as long as our hands are cluttered with weapons."

● ● ● ● ● ● ● ●

The young man put the gun in his pocket, obedient as a child. He raised his hands in the wai salute to Nai Phan, who was famous for his fried rice and coffee and his generosity.

"I ought to shoot myself instead of shooting you," he said.

"Don't speak like a crazy man," said the shopkeeper, handing the young man the money. "This is all there is. Take it, it is yours. It is not a gift made in anger. I know that the prisons are full, but not of criminals. You are a man like myself, like any other man; any man, even a minister, would do the same if he were desperate."

Nai Phan promotes an extremely healthy mental attitude toward life. A healthy mental attitude is usually a sign of good physical and social health as well. You, too, can apply good habits toward each aspect of your overall health. Keep in mind the following:

1. *Physical health:* Take good care of your body by exercising, eating a balanced diet, and getting plenty of rest.
2. *Mental health:* Take good care of your inner self by accepting who you are, expressing your emotions, and learning how to handle difficult situations.
3. *Social health:* Take good care of your social health by getting along well with family members, making and keeping friends, and working cooperatively in groups.

The young gunman sat down. "I have never met you, and I have never met anyone who speaks like you. I will not take your money, but I have put away my gun. Now I'll go home to my mother like you said." He coughed a few times and continued: "I am a bad son. All the money my mother gave me I spent on the horses; the little I had left I spent on drink—"

"Everyone makes mistakes. What is life but a mixture of experiments, mistakes, and failures?" said Nai Phan.

"I'm not strong, you know," the young man went on. "Did you hear my cough? I'm afraid I've got **T.B.** I deserve it, I suppose, because I've done bad things— I ought really to die as soon as possible. I should not live on, burdening the earth. Thank you, and goodbye."

"You don't have to go right away. Stay on for a bit and let's talk. I'd like to get to know you. Where do you live?

What are your interests? I mean, what do you believe in?"

The young man shook his head hopelessly. "I don't know where to go now. Where can I go? What do I believe in? I don't know. There seems to be nothing in this world worth believing in. I have been a miserable wretch since the day I was born; no wonder I don't like my fellow man. Sometimes I think everyone must be responsible for my bad luck. I don't want to be around people. I don't trust anyone. I hate the way men talk to each other, the way they spend their lives, the way they love and praise each other, the way they laugh and smile."

Nai Phan nodded understandingly. "Everyone feels like that sometimes."

"Can you believe me? I'm not interested in anything any more. I'm tired of everything. The whole world seems empty. There's no substance, nothing a

T.B.— abbreviation for tuberculosis, a disease that affects the lungs

Who Needs It?

man can hold on to or respect. If I really wanted to work I suppose I could always look for a job. But I hate the sight of humankind, I don't want any favors from them. I stay one week in one job, two weeks in another—I never stay long anywhere."

"Do you read books?"

"I used to. But I've given up. I don't even read newspapers now. Why should I? I know too well what's in them. Only shooting, robbery, murder! They change the places and the names, but the stories are always the same."

The young man rubbed his chin and squinted thoughtfully at Nai Phan. "Lucky for you you did not show any fear or anger when I threatened you with the gun. I would have killed you for sure. This world is full of men who like to show anger, mean-spirited men who are always crying out that civilization and morality are deteriorating. I don't believe it. I don't believe that because hundreds or thousands have gone bad all men must do the same. I know now that I did not come here for money but to prove to myself that my own belief is right. I used to think that although the world is losing hope and is sinking into an abyss, dirty and soiled by the sins of men, there would remain at least one man who is not a man just because he looks like one, but a real human being. He must know how to love others, how to win the respect of other men. But I could not quite believe it because I had never met anyone like that. For years I have been thinking, 'Let me meet a man who has not grown evil with the world's evil, so that I can believe that there is still goodness, so that I can have the strength to go on living.' Now I have met such a man. You have given me everything I wanted. There is nothing more to give. I am going home now. Certainly in my mind, I shall never hate the world again. I have discovered at last the sort of life I want to lead."

The stranger seemed more cheerful. He got up to leave and then, remembering, he brought out his gun. He handed it to the shopkeeper.

"Please take this. I no longer need it. It is the brand of the savage. Any man who carries a gun has no compassion or respect for others, he only respects the gun. Bandits may live by their guns, but their lives will be troubled always by the fact that their enemies may come upon them unawares. They have no time to look at the sunset or to sing. When a man has no time to sing, it is better to be a cricket or a mynah bird."

## ACCENT ON...
### SOCIAL SERVICES
• • • • • • • • • • • • • • • • • • • •

Nai Phan assumes that the stranger needs money desperately because of a life and death matter, such as a terrible illness in his family. If this had been the case, where might the stranger have gone for help? Research local social service agencies. Then describe one that could help a family struggling to eat and pay bills because of illness or a job layoff. Explain the purpose, goals, and day-to-day functions of such a service, as well as how such an organization is financed and staffed.

The gunman smiled happily, and waving in farewell, he added: "I'll come back to see you again, but don't let me see the gun again. It is the enemy of the pure life. Goodbye."

The stranger vanished in the darkness. Nai Phan, the shopkeeper, bent his head to inspect his newest acquisition. He was thinking that tomorrow he would sell it. He badly needed a new coffee strainer. ❖

## ON THE JOB
### STORE MANAGER

Store managers are responsible for running stores at a profit. The duties vary depending on the size and kind of store, but there are four major divisions in the operation of any store: merchandising, controlling store operations, accounting and bookkeeping, and advertising and promoting. Preparatory high school courses include merchandising, accounting, and advertising. Many chain stores offer management training programs.

## UNDERSTANDING

1. Find evidence in the story of Nai Phan's generosity. How do his wife and the rest of the community feel about his habits? Find statements in the text that illustrate their feelings. Why does it "touch their hearts"? Research famous people who have touched the hearts of others through their generosity. Report orally to the class about their accomplishments and character. *Workshops 21 and 25*

2. What does the thief think he wants? What does he get from Nai Phan? In your journal, describe a time when you set out to do one thing, but something very different actually happened. How did you feel about the unexpected outcome? Did it change your life? How?

3. What characteristics does the thief think belong to "a real human being"? What characteristics would you add or remove from that list?

   Write a list of characteristics of a good employee for a business you may own in the future. Think about the lists you just made. Prepare your list to be placed in an employee manual.

### A LAST WORD

"Who Needs It?" raises questions about what it means to be a real human being. What does it take to make you happy? How might feelings of personal contentment affect your behavior toward others?

## CONNECTING

1. People today have become driven to earn money, sometimes at the expense of satisfying other human needs. Find out what companies in your area seem to pay close attention to human needs in the workplace—for example, companies that have on-site child care; workout rooms; flex-time scheduling; clean, well-lit work areas; and so on. Invite a company executive or a human resources employee to talk to the class about what the company offers and why. Prepare questions on how these workplace benefits affect worker attitudes and production. Also, inquire about the costs of the benefits and whether they place a burden on the company. *Workshop 26*

2.  Work benefits are currently a bargaining issue in most jobs. Like Nai Phan, many have discovered that the money earned is not the only reward for working. With a group, create a benefits manual for the small business of your dreams. Include items that you feel would make the workplace enjoyable, manageable, and productive.

# A Young Lady of Property

## EXPLORING

• • • • • • • • • • • • • • • • • • • • •

Being honest with yourself and others about your feelings can have a profoundly positive effect on your outlook. We learn about honesty when we are very young children. But sometimes no one teaches us to be honest with *ourselves.* *Not* being honest with ourselves can lead to unwise decisions. Have you ever bought something and then realized you never really wanted it in the first place? How can you avoid such misjudgments in the future?

## THEME CONNECTION...
### SELF-EVALUATION

Glamour and fame are appealing, especially to some people. But would you *really* want to live that kind of life? What about the more common pursuits of home and family and friends?

Whatever your goal, it is important to be honest with yourself about your abilities and your desires. Honest self-evaluation is the best way to ensure that you make good decisions.

## TIME & PLACE

The first years following World War I were fairly grim; prices rose and wages stayed low. In 1922, however, the economy began to turn around. The automobile became affordable and, therefore, almost common among American families. There were also new forms of entertainment. Radio caught hold right at the beginning of the decade. American jazz seized the whole world with its rhythms and passion. And silent moving pictures drew great crowds at movie "palaces." In 1927 the first "talking picture" was released.

## THE WRITER'S CRAFT
### ELEMENTS OF DRAMA

Drama is literature that tells a story through action and dialogue. Plays are intended to be performed in front of an audience in a series of acts, each of which has several scenes. Each scene typically depicts a specific place and time. *A Young Lady of Property* is a one-act play divided into scenes that are indicated in the stage directions. (See Workshop 4.)

• • • • • • • • • • • • • • • • • • • • • • • • • • • • • • • •

# A Young Lady of Property

Horton Foote

## Characters

Miss Martha Davenport
Mr. Russell Walter Graham
Wilma Thompson
Arabella Cookenboo
Lester Thompson    Mrs. Leighton
Minna Boyd    Miss Gert
Man

**About the Author**

Horton Foote's (b. 1916) first encounter with a one-act play was as an actor in high school. By then, Foote already had been listening for years to the stories of the "good talkers" in Wharton, Texas, his hometown. At 16, Foote left Texas to study acting in California. He then moved to New York City to continue acting and to begin writing. He has written plays for radio, TV, film, and stage. He wrote the screenplay for the Academy Award–winning film *The Trip to Bountiful* and won Oscars for his screenplays for *To Kill a Mockingbird* and *Tender Mercies*.

**Place:** *Harrison, Texas*
**Time:** *Late spring, 1925*

*The stage is divided into four areas. Area one, directly across the front of the stage, is a sidewalk. Area two, just above the sidewalk left of center. is part of a kitchen. A table, with a portable phonograph on it, and four chairs are placed here. Area three is above the sidewalk right of center, it has a yard swing in it. Area four is directly upstage center. In it is a post office window.*

*The lights are brought up on the post office window. It is attended by two people,* Miss Martha Davenport, *who is inside the window, and* Mr. Russell Walter Graham, *who is leaning on the outside ledge of the window. It is about three-thirty of a late spring day.* Miss Martha *and* Mr. Russell Walter *look very sleepy. Two girls around fifteen come in with schoolbooks in their arms. They are* Wilma Thompson *and* Arabella Cookenboo. Wilma *is a handsome girl with style and spirit about her.* Arabella *is gentle looking, so shy about growing into womanhood that one can't really tell yet what she is to look like or become. She is Wilma's shadow and obviously her adoring slave. They go up to the window.* Mr. Russell Walter *sees them and punches* Miss Martha.

RUSSELL. Look who's here, Miss Martha. The Bobbsey twins.

(Miss Martha *gives a peal of laughter that sounds as if she thinks* Mr. Russell Walter *the funniest man in five counties.*)

MISS MARTHA (*again giggling*). Now, Mr. Russell Walter, don't start teasing the young ladies. How are you, girls?

WILMA *and* ARABELLA. Fine.

RUSSELL. Can I sell you any stamps? We have some lovely special deliveries today. Our ones and twos are very nice too.

MARTHA (*giggling*). Isn't he a tease, girls?

WILMA. Mr. Russell Walter, when's the next train in from Houston?

RUSSELL. Why? Going on a trip?

MARTHA (*rolling at his wit*). Now, Mr. Russell Walter, stop teasing the young ladies. The next mail doesn't come in on the train, dear ones; it comes in on the bus. And that will be at six. Although the Houston mail is usually very light at that time, there are a few special deliveries. Do you think your letter might come by special delivery, Wilma?

WILMA. No ma'am. Regular.

MARTHA. Oh. Well in that case I don't hold out much hope for it on that delivery. It's usually mostly second-class mail. You know, seed catalogs and such. The next Houston mail heavy with first-class is delivered at five tomorrow morning.

RUSSELL. Which she knows better than you.

MARTHA (*giggling*). Now, Mr. Russell Walter, stop teasing the young ladies.

WILMA. Arabella and I were discussing coming here from school, Mr. Russell Walter, that the mail sometimes gets in the wrong box.

RUSSELL. Rarely, Miss Wilma. Rarely.

WILMA. Arabella says that once a Christmas card meant for her got put by mistake in Box 270, instead of her box, which is 370, and she didn't get it back until the third of January.

RUSSELL. Well, if that happens, nothing we can do about it until the person whose box it got into by mistake returns it.

WILMA. Yes, sir. (*a pause*) I don't suppose any mail has been put in my box since my Aunt Gert was here last.

RUSSELL. Well, seeing as she was here just a half hour ago, I don't think so.

MARTHA. Who are you expecting a letter from, young lady?

WILMA. Somebody very important. Come on, Arabella. (*They start out.*

*They pause. She goes back to the window.*) Mr. Russell Walter, once I had a movie star picture, Ben Lyons I think, that was addressed to Wilma Thomas instead of Thompson, and if you remember, Mr. Peter was new at the time and put it into General Delivery, and it wasn't until two weeks later that you discovered it there and figured it belonged to me.

RUSSELL. Well, Mr. Peter isn't new here now.

WILMA. But I thought maybe accidentally someone put my letter in General Delivery.

RUSSELL. Nope.

MARTHA. Oh, Mr. Walter. Go ahead and look. It won't hurt you.

RUSSELL. Now, Miss Martha . . .

MARTHA. Now just go ahead . . . (*She hands him a stack of letters.*)

RUSSELL. All right. . . . Anything to please the ladies. (*He goes over to the letters and starts looking into them.*)

MARTHA. Wilma, I saw your daddy and Mrs. Leighton at the picture show together again last night. Maybe you'll be having a new mother soon.

WILMA. Well, I wouldn't hold my breath waiting if I were you.

MARTHA. I was saying to Mr. Russell Walter, I see the tenants have left the Thompson house. Maybe they were asked to leave so Mr. Thompson might move in with a bride.

WILMA. They were asked to leave because they were tearing it to pieces. They had weeds growing in the yard and had torn off wallpaper. My Aunt Gert asked them to leave. . . .

MARTHA. Oh, of course. They didn't take any pride in it at all. Not like when your mother was living. Why, I remember your mother always had the yard filled with flowers, and . . . (*The phone rings.*) Excuse me. (Miss Martha *answers it.*) Post office. Yes. Yes. She's here. Yes, I will. (*She puts the phone down.*) That was your Aunt Gertrude, Wilma. She said you were to come right home.

WILMA. All right.

MARTHA. Found any mail for Wilma, Mr. Russell Walter?

RUSSELL. Nope, Miss Wilma. No mail and no female either.

MARTHA (*giggling*). Isn't he a sight? You come back at six, Wilma. Maybe we'll have something then.

WILMA. Yes ma'm. Come on, Arabella.

(*They go outside the area and walk directly down the center of the stage and pause at the apron, looking up and down. They are now on the sidewalk area.*)

WILMA. I'd like to scratch that old cat's eyes out. The idea of her saying old lady Leighton is going to be my mother. She's so nosy. I wonder how she'd like it if I asked her if Mr. Russell Walter was going to ask her to marry him after she's been chasing him for fifteen years.

ARABELLA. Well, just ignore her.

WILMA. I intend to.

ARABELLA. What are you going to do now, Wilma?

WILMA. Fool around until the six o'clock mail.

ARABELLA. Don't you think you ought to go home like your aunt said?

WILMA. No.

ARABELLA. Have you told your Aunt Gert about the letter you're expecting yet?

WILMA. No.

ARABELLA. When are you going to tell her?

WILMA. Not until it comes. I think I'll go over and see my house. Look at how those tenants left it. I may have to sell it yet to get me to Hollywood. . . .

ARABELLA. Wilma, is that house really yours?

WILMA. Sure it's mine. My mother left it to me.

ARABELLA. Well, do you get the rent for it and tell them who to rent to like Papa does his rent houses?

WILMA. No. But it's understood it's mine. My mother told Aunt Gert it was mine just before she died. Daddy had put it in her name because he was gambling terrible then, and Aunt Gert says Mama was afraid they'd lose it. I let Daddy rent it and keep the money now. Aunt Gert says I should, as he is having a very hard time. His job at the cotton gin doesn't pay hardly anything. Of course, I feel very lucky having my own house.

ARABELLA. Well, I have a house.

WILMA. Do you own it yourself?

ARABELLA. No. But I live in it.

WILMA. Well, that's hardly the same thing. I own a house, which is very unusual, Aunt Gert says, for a girl of fifteen. I'm a young lady of property,

Aunt Gert says. Many's the time I thought I'll just go and live in it all by myself. Wouldn't Harrison sit up and take notice then? Once when I was thirteen and I was very fond of my Cousin Neeley I thought I'd offer it to him to get through law school. But I'm glad I didn't, since he turned out so hateful. (*a pause*) Do you remember when I used to live in my house?

ARABELLA. No.

WILMA. Well, it's a long time ago now, but I still remember it. My mama and I used to play croquet in the yard under the pecan trees. We'd play croquet every afternoon just before sundown and every once in a while she'd stop the game and ask me to run to the corner without letting the neighbors know what I was doing, to see if my father was coming home. She always worried about his getting home by six, because if he wasn't there by then she knew it meant trouble. My mother always kept me in white starched dresses. Do you remember my mother?

ARABELLA. No. But my mother does. She says she was beautiful, with the **disposition** of a saint.

WILMA. I know. Her name was Alice. Isn't that a pretty name?

ARABELLA. Yes. It is.

WILMA. There's a song named "Sweet Alice Ben Bolt." Aunt Gert used to sing it all the time. When Mama died, she stopped. My mama died of a broken heart.

ARABELLA. She did?

WILMA. Oh, yes. Even Aunt Gert

disposition— temperament, personality

admits that. Daddy's gambling broke her heart. Oh, well. What are you going to do about it? Boy, I used to hate my daddy. I used to dream about what I'd do to him when I grew up. But he's sorry now and reformed. So I've forgiven him.

ARABELLA. Oh, sure. You shouldn't hate your father.

WILMA. Well, I don't know. Do you know something I've never told another living soul?

ARABELLA. What?

WILMA. Swear you won't tell?

ARABELLA. I swear.

WILMA. I love him now. Sometimes I think I'd give up this whole movie-star business if I could go back to our house and live with Daddy and keep house for him. But Aunt Gert says under the circumstances that's not practical. I guess you and everybody else know what the circumstances are, Mrs. Leighton. She's got my daddy hogtied. Aunt Gert say she isn't good enough to shine my mother's shoes, and I think she's right.

(Miss Martha *comes out of the post office area upstage center. She walks halfway down the center of the stage.*)

MARTHA. Are you girls still here?

WILMA. Yes ma'am.

MARTHA. Minna called this time, Wilma. She said you were to come home immediately. (Miss Martha *goes back inside the post office area and into her window upstage center.*)

ARABELLA. Now come on, Wilma. You'll just get in trouble.

## FOCUS ON... GEOGRAPHY

*A Young Lady of Property* is set in the fictional town of Harrison, a Gulf Coast town in southeast Texas. Research the Gulf Coast region of southeast Texas and write three or four paragraphs describing the region, its major cities, and its unique geographical features. Then prepare a map illustrating the region and the location of these features.

◆ ◆ ◆ ◆ ◆ ◆ ◆ ◆ ◆ ◆ ◆ ◆ ◆ ◆ ◆ ◆

WILMA. Yes sir.

LESTER. Say hello to Mrs. Leighton.

WILMA (*most ungraciously*). Hello, Mrs. Leighton.

MRS. LEIGHTON (*most graciously*). Hello, Wilma.

WILMA. All right. (*They start off right. Wilma stops. She looks panicky.*) Wait a minute, Arabella. Yonder comes my daddy walking with that fool Mrs. Leighton. I'd just as soon I didn't have to see them. Let's go the other way. (*They turn around and start left. A man's voice calls in the distance:* "Wilma, Wilma." Wilma *and* Arabella *stop.* Wilma *whispers:*) That's the kind of luck I have. He saw me. Now I'll have to speak to old lady Leighton.

ARABELLA. Don't you like her?

WILMA. Do you like snakes?

ARABELLA. No.

WILMA. Well, neither do I like Mrs. Leighton and for the same reason.

(Lester Thompson *and* Mrs. Leighton *enter from downstage right.* Lester *is a handsome, weak man in his forties.* Mrs. Leighton *is thirty-five or so, blond, pretty, and completely unlike* Wilma's *description. There is a warmth about her that we should wish that* Wilma *might notice.* Lester *goes over to* Wilma.)

LESTER (*as he leaves* Mrs. Leighton). Excuse me, Sibyl. Wilma . . .

LESTER. What are you doing hanging around the streets, Wilma?

WILMA. Waiting to see if I have a letter.

LESTER. What kind of letter, Wilma?

WILMA. About getting into the movies. Arabella and I saw an ad in the *Houston Chronicle* about a Mr. Delafonte who is a famous Hollywood director.

LESTER. Who is Mr. Delafonte?

WILMA. The Hollywood director I'm trying to tell you about. He's giving screen tests in Houston to people of beauty and talent, and if they pass they'll go to Hollywood and be in the picture shows.

LESTER. Well, that's all a lot of foolishness, Wilma. You're not going to Houston to take anything.

WILMA. But, Daddy . . . I . . .

LESTER. You're fifteen years old and you're gonna stay home like a fifteen-year-old girl should. There'll be plenty of time to go to Houston.

WILMA. But, Daddy, Mr. Delafonte won't be there forever.

LESTER. Go on home, Wilma.

WILMA. But, Daddy . . .

LESTER. Don't argue with me. I want you to march home just as quick as you can, young lady. I'm going to stand right here until you turn that corner, and if I ever catch you hanging around the streets again, it will be between you and me.

WILMA. Yes sir. Come on, Arabella.

(She *and* Arabella *walk out left.* Lester *stands watching.* Sibyl Leighton *comes up to him.*)

MRS. LEIGHTON. Have you told her we're getting married, Lester?

LESTER. No, I'm telling Gert tonight.

MRS. LEIGHTON. Aren't you going to tell Wilma?

LESTER. No. Gert's the one to tell her. Wilma and I have very little to say to each other. Gert has her won over completely.

MRS. LEIGHTON. They must be expecting it. Why would they think you're selling your house and quitting your job?

LESTER. I don't think they know that either. I'll explain the whole thing to Gert tonight. Come on. She's turned the corner. I think she'll go on home now.

(*They walk on and off. The lights are brought up downstage left in area 2. It is part of the kitchen in* Gertrude Miller's *house.* Minna Boyd, *a thin, strong Negro woman in her middle forties, is seated at the table. She has a portable, hand-winding* **Victrola** *on the table. She is listening to a jazz recording.* Wilma *and* Arabella *come in upstage center of the kitchen area.*)

MINNA. Well, here's the duchess. Arrived at last. Where have you been, Wilma? What on earth do you mean aggravating us this way? Your Aunt Gert was almost late for her card party worrying over you.

WILMA. You knew where I was. You called often enough. I was at the post office waiting for the mail.

MINNA. How many times has Miss Gert told you not to hang around there? Where's your pride? You know Mr. Russell Walter called and told her you were about to drive them crazy down at the post office. He said when you get your letter, he's gonna be so relieved he'll deliver it in person. Your aunt says you're to get right to your room and study.

WILMA. We're just going. Come on, Arabella.

MINNA. And without Arabella. I know how much studying you and Arabella will do. You'll spend your whole time talking about Hollywood and picture shows. **Clara Bow** this and Alice White that. You go in there and learn something. The principal called your auntie this morning and told her you were failing in your typing and shorthand.

WILMA (very *bored*). Well, I don't care. I hate them. I never wanted to take them anyway.

MINNA. Never mind about that. You just get in there and get to it. (Wilma *pays no attention. She goes deliberately and sits in a chair, scowling.*) Wilma . . .

beau—boyfriend

Pola Negri . . .— Negri, Compson, and Lee were all silent film actresses

WILMA. What?

MINNA. Now why do you want to act like this?

WILMA. Like what?

MINNA. So ugly. Your face is gonna freeze like that one day and then you're gonna be in a nice how-do-you-do.

ARABELLA. I'd better go, Wilma.

WILMA. All right, Arabella. Someday soon I'll be established in my own house, and then you won't be treated so rudely.

MINNA. You come back some other time.

ARABELLA. Thank you, I will.

WILMA. I'll never get out of the house again today, Arabella, so will you check on the six o'clock mail?

ARABELLA. All right.

WILMA. Come right over if I have a letter.

ARABELLA. All right. Goodbye.

(Arabella *goes out upstage center of the kitchen area and goes offstage.* Wilma *plucks an imaginary guitar and sings, in an exaggerated hillbilly style,* "Write me a Letter. Send it by mail. Send it in care of Birmingham jail.")

MINNA. Wilma, what is that letter about you're expectin'? Have you got a **beau** for yourself?

WILMA. Don't be crazy.

MINNA. Look at me.

WILMA. I said no, and stop acting crazy. I'm expecting a letter from Mr. Delafonte.

MINNA. Mr. who?

WILMA. Mr. Delafonte, the famous movie director.

MINNA. Never heard of him.

WILMA. Well. I wouldn't let anyone know if I was that ignorant. The whole world has heard of Mr. Delafonte. He has only directed **Pola Negri** and Betty Compson and Lila Lee and I don't know who all.

MINNA. What are you hearing from Mr. Delafonte about?

WILMA. A Hollywood career.

MINNA. What are you going to do with a Hollywood career?

WILMA. Be a movie star, you goose. First he's going to screen-test me, and then I'll go to Hollywood and be a Wampus baby star.

MINNA. A what?

WILMA. A Wampus baby star. You know. That's what you are before you are a movie star. You get chosen to be a Wampus baby star and parade around in a bathing suit and get all your pictures in the papers and the movie magazines.

MINNA. I want to see Miss Gert's face when you start parading around in a bathing suit for magazines. And what's all this got to do with a letter?

WILMA. Well, I read in a Houston paper where Mr. Delafonte was in Houston interviewing people at his studio for Hollywood screen tests. So Arabella and I wrote him for an appointment.

MINNA. And that's what your letter is all about? No gold mine. No oil well. Just Mr. Delafonte and a movie test.

WILMA. Yes. And if you be nice to me, after I win the screen test and sell my house I might take you out with me.

MINNA. Sell your what?

WILMA. My house.

MINNA. Wilma . . . why don't you stop talking like that? . . .

WILMA. Well, it's my house. I can sell it if I want to.

MINNA. You can't.

WILMA. I can.

MINNA. That house wasn't given to you to sell. A fifteen-year-old child. Who do you think is gonna let you sell it?

WILMA. Haven't you told me the house was mine? Hasn't Aunt Gert?

MINNA. Yes, but not to sell and throw the money away. And besides, it looks like to me the house is gonna be having permanent visitors soon.

WILMA. Who?

MINNA. What you don't know won't hurt you.

WILMA. If you mean my daddy and old lady Leighton, I'd burn it down first.

MINNA. Wilma.

WILMA. I will, I'll burn it down right to the ground.

(Miss Gert *comes in downstage left of the kitchen area. She is in her forties, handsome and tall.*)

MINNA. Hello. Miss Gert. . . .

GERT. Hello, Minna. Hello, Wilma.

MINNA. How was the party?

GERT. All right. Minna, Neeley is going to be away tonight, so don't fix any supper for him, and we had refreshments at the party, so I'm not hungry. (*She suddenly bursts out crying and*

*has to leave the room. She goes running out downstage left of the kitchen area.*)

WILMA. Now what's the matter with her?

MINNA. Sick headache likely. You stay here, I'll go see.

WILMA. All right. If she wants any ice, I'll crack it.

(Minna *goes out downstage left of the kitchen area. Wilma turns on the phonograph and plays a popular song of the 1920s.*)

MINNA (*comes back in*). We better turn that off. She's got a bad one. First sick headache she's had in three years. I remember the last one.

WILMA. Does she want any cracked ice? . . .

MINNA. No.

WILMA. Did she hear any bad news?

MINNA. I don't know.

WILMA. Can I go in to see her?

MINNA. Nope. You can please her, though, by getting into your studying.

WILMA. If you won't let me sell my house and go to Hollywood, I'll just quit school and move over there and rent out rooms. Support myself that way.

MINNA. You won't do nothin' of the kind. You go in there now and study.

WILMA. Why do I have to study? I have a house . . . and . . .

MINNA. Wilma, will you stop talking crazy?

> ● ● ● ● ● ● ●
> "Well, it's my house. I can sell it if I want to."
> ● ● ● ● ● ●

WILMA. I'm not talking crazy. I could think of worse things to do. I'll rent out rooms and sit on the front porch and rock and be a lady of mystery, like a lady I read about once that locked herself in her house. Let the vines grow all around. Higher and higher until all light was shut out. She was eighteen when the vines started growing, and when she died and they cut the vines down and found her she was seventy-three, and in all that time she had never put her foot outside once. All her family and friends were dead. . . .

MINNA. I know you're crazy now.

WILMA. Minna . . . Minna . . . (*She runs to her.*) I'm scared. I'm scared.

MINNA. What in the name of goodness are you scared of?

WILMA. I'm scared my daddy is going to marry Mrs. Leighton.

MINNA. Now . . . now . . . (*holds her*)

WILMA. Minna, let me run over to my house for just a little bit. I can't ever go over there when there's tenants living in it. I feel the need of seeing it. I'll come right back.

MINNA. Will you promise me to come right back?

WILMA. I will.

MINNA. And you'll get right to your studying and no more arguments?

WILMA. No more.

MINNA. All right, then run on.

WILMA. Oh. Minna. I love you. And you know what I'm going to do? I'm going to be a great movie star and send my chauffeur and my limousine to Harrison and put you in it and drive you all the way to Hollywood.

MINNA. Thank you.

WILMA. H.O.B.

MINNA. H.O.B.? What's H.O.B.?

WILMA. Hollywood or bust! . . . (*She goes running out upstage center of the kitchen area.* Minna *calls after her:*)

MINNA. Don't forget to get right back.

(*We hear* Wilma's *voice answering in the distance:* "All right." *The lights are brought down. The lights are brought immediately up in the kitchen, a half-hour later.* Aunt Gert *comes in downstage left of the area. She has on a dressing gown. Twilight is beginning. She switches on a light. She looks around the room. She calls:*)

GERT. Minna, Minna. (*A pause. She calls again:*) Minna. Minna.

(*In comes* Arabella *upstage center of the area. She is carrying two letters.*)

ARABELLA. Hello, Miss Gertrude.

GERT. Hello, Arabella.

ARABELLA. Where's Wilma?

GERT. I don't know. The door to her room was closed when I went by. I guess she's in there studying.

ARABELLA. Yes'm. (*She starts out of the room downstage left of the area.*)

GERT. Arabella.

(Arabella *pauses.*)

ARABELLA. Yes'm.

GERT. Wilma's gotten behind in her schoolwork, so please don't ask her to go out anyplace tonight, because I'll have to say no, and . . .

ARABELLA. Oh, no ma'am. I just brought her letter over to her. She asked me to get it if it came in on the six o'clock mail, and it did.

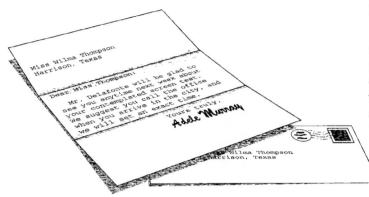

GERT. Is that the letter she's been driving us all crazy about?

ARABELLA. Yes ma'am, I got one too. (*She holds two letters up. Puts one on the table.*)

GERT. Oh. Well . . . (Arabella *starts out again downstage left of the area.*) Arabella, what is in that letter?

ARABELLA. Hasn't Wilma told you yet?

GERT. No.

ARABELLA. Then you'd better find out from her. She might be mad if I told you.

GERT. All right. (Arabella *starts out of the room.*) You didn't see Minna out in the backyard as you were coming in, did you?

ARABELLA. No.

GERT. I wonder where she can be. It's six-fifteen and she hasn't started a thing for supper yet.
(Arabella *goes out downstage left of the area and looks out an imaginary window right center. She comes back in the room.*)

ARABELLA. Wilma isn't in the bedroom.

GERT. She isn't?

ARABELLA. No ma'am. Not in the front room either. I went in there.

GERT. That's strange. Isn't that strange? (Minna *comes in upstage center of the area. She has a package in her hand.*) Oh, there you are, Minna.

MINNA. I had to run to the store for some baking soda. How do you feel? (*Minna puts the package on the table.*)

## FOCUS ON... DRAMATIC ARTS

Early in the play, Wilma dreams of being a Hollywood actress. Try out your own acting skills by enacting part of the play. Working in small groups, select a portion of the play to perform. If possible, create or locate props and costumes to use in your performance. After rehearsing, perform your enactment for the rest of the class.

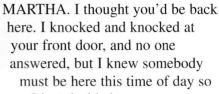

GERT. Better. Where's Wilma?

MINNA. You don't mean she's not back yet?

GERT. Back? Where did she go?

MINNA. She swore to me if I let her go over to her house for a few minutes she'd be back here and study with no arguments.

GERT. Well, she's not here.

MINNA. That's the trouble with her. Give her an inch and she'll take a mile.

GERT. Arabella, would you run over to Wilma's house and tell her to get right home?

ARABELLA. Yes ma'am.

(*She picks the letter up off the table and takes it with her as she goes out downstage left of the area. A knock is heard offstage.*)

GERT (*calling*). Come in. (Miss Martha *comes in upstage center of the area.*) Oh, hello, Miss Martha.

MARTHA. Hello, Gert. Hello, Minna.

MINNA. Hello, Miss Martha. . . .

MARTHA. I thought you'd be back here. I knocked and knocked at your front door, and no one answered, but I knew somebody must be here this time of day so I just decided to come on back.

GERT. I'm glad you did. We can't hear a knock at the front door back here. Sit down, won't you?

MARTHA. I can't stay a second. I just wanted to tell Wilma that her letter arrived on the six o'clock bus.

GERT. She knows, thank you, Miss Martha. Arabella brought it over to her.

MARTHA. Oh, the address on the back said the Delafonte Studio. I wonder what that could be?

GERT. I don't know.

MINNA. I knows. It's the moving pictures. She wrote about getting into them.

GERT. I do declare. She's always up to something.

MARTHA. Well, I never heard of moving pictures in Houston. I just heard the news about Lester. Was I surprised! Were you?

GERT. Yes, I was.

MARTHA. When's the wedding taking place?

GERT. I don't know.

MARTHA. Oh, I see. Well, I have to run on now.

GERT. All right, thank you, Miss Martha, for coming by. I know Wilma will appreciate it.

MARTHA. I'll just go out the back way, if you don't mind. It'll save me a few steps.

GERT. Of course not.

MARTHA. Good night.

GERT. Good night. Miss Martha. (*She goes out upstage center of the area.*)

MINNA. What news is this?

GERT. Oh, you must know, Minna. Lester and Mrs. Leighton are getting married at last. That's why I came home from the party all upset. I had to hear about my own brother's marriage at a bridge party. And I know it's true. It came straight from the county clerk's office. They got their license this morning.

MINNA. Well, poor Wilma. She'll take this hard.

GERT. She's going to take it very hard. But what can you do? What can you do?

(*They both sit dejectedly at the table. The lights fade in the area downstage left as they come up on the area downstage right.* Wilma *comes in from upstage center of the downstage right area. It is the yard of her house. She sits in the swing rocking back and forth, singing "Birmingham Jail" in her hillbilly style.* Arabella *comes running in right center of the yard area.*)

WILMA. Heh, Arabella. Come sit and swing.

ARABELLA. All right. Your letter came.

WILMA. Whoopee. Where is it?

ARABELLA. Here. (*She gives it to her.* Wilma *tears it open. She reads:*)

WILMA. "Dear Miss Thompson: Mr. Delafonte will be glad to see you anytime next week about your contemplated screen test. We suggest you call the office when you arrive in the city, and we will set an exact time. Yours truly, Adele Murray." Well . . . Did you get yours?

ARABELLA. Yes.

WILMA. What did it say?

ARABELLA. The same.

WILMA. Exactly the same?

ARABELLA. Yes.

WILMA. Well, let's pack our bags. Hollywood, here we come.

ARABELLA. Wilma . . .

WILMA. Yes?

ARABELLA. I have to tell you something . . . Well . . . I . . .

WILMA. What is it?

ARABELLA. Well . . . promise me you won't hate me, or stop being my friend. I never had a friend, Wilma, until you began being nice to me, and I couldn't stand it if you weren't my friend any longer. . . .

WILMA. Oh, my cow. Stop talking like that. I'll never stop being your friend. What do you want to tell me?

ARABELLA. Well . . . I don't want to go to see Mr. Delafonte, Wilma. . . .

WILMA. You don't?

ARABELLA. No. I don't want to be a movie star. I don't want to leave Harrison or my mother or father. . . . I just want to stay here the rest of my life and get married and settle down and have children.

WILMA. Arabella . . .

ARABELLA. I just pretended like I wanted to go to Hollywood because I knew you wanted me to, and I wanted you to like me. . . .

WILMA. Oh, Arabella . . .

ARABELLA. Don't hate me, Wilma.
You see, I'd be afraid . . . I'd die if I
had to go to see Mr. Delafonte. Why,
I even get faint when I have to recite
before the class. I'm not like you.
You're not scared of anything.

WILMA. Why do you say that?

ARABELLA. Because you're not. I know.

WILMA. Oh, yes, I am. I'm scared of
lots of things.

ARABELLA. What?

WILMA. Getting lost in a city. Being
bitten by dogs. Old lady Leighton
taking my daddy away. . . . (*a pause*)

ARABELLA. Will you still be my
friend?

**W**ILMA. Sure. I'll always be your
friend.

ARABELLA. I'm glad. Oh, I almost
forgot. Your Aunt Gert said for you to
come on home.

WILMA. I'll go in a little. I love to swing
in my front yard. Aunt Gert has a swing
in her front yard, but it's not the same.
Mama and I used to come out here and
swing together. Some nights when
Daddy was out all night gambling, I
used to wake up and hear her out here
swinging away. Sometimes she'd let
me come and sit beside her. We'd
swing until three or four in the
morning. (*A pause. She looks out into
the yard.*) The pear tree looks sickly,
doesn't it? The fig trees are doing
nicely though. I was out in back and the
weeds are near knee high, but fig trees
just seem to thrive in the weeds. The
freeze must have killed off the banana
trees. . . . (*A pause.* Wilma *stops*

*swinging—she walks around the yard.*)
Maybe I won't leave either. Maybe I
won't go to Hollywood after all.

ARABELLA. You won't?

WILMA. No. Maybe I shouldn't. That
just comes to me now. You know
sometimes my old house looks so
lonesome it tears at my heart. I used
to think it looked lonesome just
whenever it had no tenants, but now
it comes to me it has looked lonesome ever since Mama died and we
moved away, and it will look lonesome until some of us move back
here. Of course, Mama can't, and
Daddy won't. So it's up to me.

ARABELLA. Are you gonna live here
all by yourself?

WILMA. No. I talk big about living here
by myself, but I'm too much of a
coward to do that. But maybe I'll
finish school and live with Aunt Gert
and keep on renting the house until I
meet some nice boy with good habits
and steady ways, and marry him.
Then we'll move here and have children, and I bet this old house won't
be lonely anymore. I'll get Mama's
old croquet set and put it out under
the pecan trees and play croquet with
my children, or sit in this yard and
swing and wave to people as they
pass by.

ARABELLA. Oh, I wish you would.
Mama says that's a normal life for a
girl, marrying and having children.
She says being an actress is all right,
but the other's better.

WILMA. Maybe I've come to agree with
your mama. Maybe I was going to
Hollywood out of pure lonesomeness.

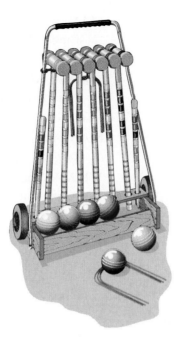

I felt so alone with Mrs. Leighton getting my daddy and my mama having left the world. Daddy could have taken away my lonesomeness, but he didn't want to or couldn't. Aunt Gert says nobody is lonesome with a house full of children, so maybe that's what I just ought to stay here and have. . . .

ARABELLA. Have you decided on a husband yet?

WILMA. No.

ARABELLA. Mama says that's the bad feature of being a girl; you have to wait for the boy to ask you and just pray that the one you want wants you. Tommy Murray is nice, isn't he?

WILMA. I think so.

ARABELLA. Jay Godfrey told me once he wanted to ask you for a date, but he didn't dare because he was afraid you'd turn him down.

WILMA. Why did he think that?

ARABELLA. He said the way you talked he didn't think you would go out with anything less than a movie star.

WILMA. Maybe you'd tell him different. . . .

ARABELLA. All right. I think Jay Godfrey is very nice. Don't you?

WILMA. Yes, I think he's very nice and Tommy is nice. . . .

ARABELLA. Maybe we could double-date sometimes.

WILMA. That might be fun.

ARABELLA. Oh. Wilma. Don't go to Hollywood. Stay here in Harrison and let's be friends forever. . . .

WILMA. All right. I will.

ARABELLA. You will?

WILMA. Sure, why not? I'll stay here. I'll stay and marry and live in my house.

ARABELLA. Oh, Wilma. I'm so glad. I'm so very glad.

(Wilma *gets back in the swing. They swing vigorously back and forth. . . . A man comes in right center of the yard area.*)

MAN. I beg your pardon. Is this the Thompson house?

(*They stop swinging.*)

WILMA. Yes sir.

MAN. I understand it's for sale. I'd like to look around.

WILMA. No sir. It's not for sale. It's for rent. I'm Wilma Thompson. I own the house. My daddy rents it for me. . . .

MAN. Oh, well, we were told by Mr. Mavis . . .

WILMA. I'm sure. Mr. Mavis tries to sell everything around here. He's pulled that once before about our house, but this house is not for sale. It's for rent.

MAN. You're sure?

WILMA. I'm positive. We rent it for twenty-seven fifty a month. You pay lights, water, and keep the yard clean. We are very particular over how the yard is kept. I'd be glad to show it to you. . . .

MAN. I'm sorry. I was interested in buying. There must have been a mistake.

WILMA. There must have been.

MAN. Where could I find your father, young lady?

WILMA. Why do you want to see him?

MAN. Well, I'd just like to get this straight. I understood from Mr. Mavis . . .

WILMA. Mr. Mavis has nothing to do with my house. My house is for rent, not for sale.

MAN. All right. (*The* Man *leaves. He goes out right center of the yard area.*)

WILMA. The nerve of old man Mavis putting out around town that my house is for sale. Isn't that nervy, Arabella?

(Arabella *gets out of the swing.*)

ARABELLA. We'd better go. It'll be dark soon. The tree frogs are starting.

WILMA. It just makes me furious. Wouldn't it make you furious?

ARABELLA. Come on. Let's go.

WILMA. Wouldn't it make you furious?

ARABELLA. Yes.

WILMA. You don't sound like you mean it.

ARABELLA. Well . . .

WILMA. Well . . . what? . . .

ARABELLA. Nothing. . . . Let's go.

WILMA. Arabella, you know something you're not telling me.

ARABELLA. No, I don't. Honest, Wilma . . .

WILMA. You do. Look at me, Arabella . . .

ARABELLA. I don't know anything. I swear . . .

WILMA. You do. I thought you were my friend.

ARABELLA. I am. I am.

WILMA. Well, then why don't you tell me?

ARABELLA. Because I promised not to.

WILMA. Why?

ARABELLA. Well . . . I . . .

WILMA. What is it? Arabella, please tell me.

ARABELLA. Well . . . Will you never say I told you?

WILMA. I swear.

ARABELLA. Well, I didn't tell you before because in all the excitement in telling you I wasn't going to Hollywood and your saying you weren't going, I forgot about it . . . until that man came . . .

WILMA. What is it, Arabella? What is it?

ARABELLA. Well, I heard my daddy tell my mother that Mr. Lester had taken out a license to marry Mrs. Leighton.

WILMA. Oh, well. That doesn't surprise me too much. I've been looking for that to happen.

ARABELLA. But that isn't all. Wilma. . . .

WILMA. What else?

ARABELLA. Well . . .

WILMA. What else?

ARABELLA. Well . . .

WILMA. What else, Arabella? What else? . . .

ARABELLA. Well . . . My daddy heard that your daddy had put this house up for sale. . . .

WILMA. I don't believe you. . . .

ARABELLA. That's what he said, Wilma. . . . I . . . He said Mr. Lester came to him and wanted to know if he wanted to buy it. . . .

WILMA. Well. He won't do it. Not my house. He won't do it! (Wilma *has jumped out of the swing and runs out of the yard upstage center.*)

ARABELLA. Wilma . . . Wilma . . . Please . . . don't say I said it. . . . Wilma . . .

(*She is standing alone and frightened as the lights fade. The lights are brought up in the area left of center.* Minna *is mixing some dough on the table.* Miss Gert *comes in.*)

GERT. She's not back yet?

MINNA. No. I knew when Arabella took that letter over there she wouldn't be here until good dark.

GERT. I just put in a call for Lester. . . . He is going to have to tell her about the marriage. It's his place. Don't you think so?

MINNA. I certainly do. I most certainly do.

(Wilma *comes running in upstage center of the kitchen area.*)

WILMA. Aunt Gert, do you know where I can find my daddy?

GERT. No, Wilma . . . I . . .

WILMA. Well, I've got to find him. I went over to the **cotton gin,** but he'd left. I called out to his boardinghouse and he wasn't there. . . .

GERT. Well, I don't know, Wilma. . . .

WILMA. Is he gonna sell my house?

GERT. Wilma . . .

WILMA. Is he or isn't he?

GERT. I don't know anything about it. . . .

● ● ● ● ● ● ●
## "Is he gonna sell my house?"
● ● ● ● ● ● ●

**cotton gin**—a machine that separates seeds, hulls, and foreign material from cotton

WILMA. Well, something's going on. Let me tell you that. I was sitting in the swing with Arabella when a man came up and said he wanted to buy it, and I said to rent, and he said to buy, that Mr. Mavis had sent him over, and I told him he was mistaken, and he left. Well, I was plenty mad at Mr. Mavis and told Arabella so, but she looked funny, and I got suspicious, and I finally got it out of her that Daddy was going to marry old lady Leighton and was putting my house up for sale. . . . (Gert *is crying.*) Aunt Gert. Isn't that my house?

GERT. I'd always thought so. . . .

WILMA. Then he can't do it. Don't let him do it. It's my house. It's all in this world that belongs to me. Let Mrs. Leighton take him if she wants to but not my house. Please, please, please. (*She is crying.* Minna *goes to her.*)

MINNA. Now, come on, honey. Come on, baby. . . .

WILMA. I wouldn't sell it, not even to get me to Hollywood. I thought this afternoon, before the letter from Mr. Delafonte came, I'd ask Aunt Gert to let me sell it, and go on off, but when I went over there and sat in my yard and rocked in my swing and thought of my mama and how lonesome the house looked since we moved away . . . I knew I couldn't . . . I knew I never would. . . . I'd never go to Hollywood before I'd sell that house, and he can't. . . . I won't let him. I won't let him.

MINNA. Now, honey . . . honey . . . Miss Gert, do you know anything about this?

GERT. (*wiping her eyes*). Minna, I don't. I heard at the card party that he was marrying Mrs. Leighton . . . but I heard nothing about Lester's selling the house. . . .

MINNA. Well, can he? . . .

GERT. I don't know. I just never thought my brother, my own brother . . . Oh, I just can't stand things like this. You see, it's all so mixed up. I don't think there was anything said in writing about Wilma's having the house, but it was clearly Alice's intention. She called me in the room before Lester and made him promise just before she died that he would always have the house for Wilma. . . .

MINNA. Well, why don't we find out? . . .

GERT. Well . . . I don't know how. . . . I left a message for Lester. I can't reach him.

MINNA. I'd call Mr. Bill if I were you. He's a lawyer.

GERT. But, Minna, my brother.

MINNA. I'd call me a lawyer, brother or no brother. If you don't, I will. I'm not gonna have what belongs to this child stolen from her by Mr. Lester or anybody else. . . .

GERT. All right. I will. I'll go talk to Bill. I'll find out what we can do legally.

(*She starts out downstage left of the area.* Lester *comes in upstage center of the area.* Minna *sees him coming.*)

MINNA. Miss Gert.

(Gert *turns and sees him just as he gets inside the area.*)

LESTER. Hello, Gert.

GERT. Hello, Lester.

LESTER. Hello, Wilma.

WILMA. Hello . . .

GERT. Wilma. I think you'd better leave. . . .

WILMA. Yes'm. . . . (*She starts out.*)

LESTER. Wait a minute, Gert. I've something to tell you all. I want Wilma to hear. . . .

GERT. I think we know already. Go on, Wilma.

WILMA. Yes'm.

(Wilma *leaves downstage left of the area.* Minna *follows after her. A pause.*)

GERT. We've heard about the marriage, Lester.

LESTER. Oh, well. I'm sorry I couldn't be the one to tell you. We only decided this morning. There was a lot to do, a license and some business to attend to. I haven't told anyone. I don't know how the news got out.

GERT. You didn't really expect them to keep quiet about it at the courthouse?

LESTER. Oh. Well, of course I didn't think about that. (*a pause*) Well, the other thing is . . . You see . . . I've decided to sell the house.

GERT. I know. Wilma just found out about that, too.

LESTER. Oh. Well, I'll explain the whole thing to you. You see, I felt . . . (Gert *starts to cry.*) Now what's the matter with you, Gert?

GERT. To think that my brother, my own brother, would do something like this.

LESTER. Like what? After all it's my house, Gert.

GERT. There's some dispute about that. The least I think you could have done, the very least, was come to tell your own child.

LESTER. Well, I'm here now to do that. I only put it up for sale at noon today. I've nothing to hide or be ashamed of. The house is in my name. Sibyl, Mrs. Leighton, doesn't like Harrison. You can't blame her. People have been rotten to her. We're moving to Houston. I'm selling this house to pay down on one in Houston. That'll belong to Wilma just the same, someday. Sibyl's agreed to that, and Wilma will really get a better house in time. And we always want her to feel like it's her home, come and visit us summers . . . and like I say when something happens to me or Sibyl, the house will be hers. . . .

GERT. That's not the point, Lester. . . .

LESTER. What do you mean?

GERT. You know very well.

LESTER. I can't make a home for her over there, can I? She'll be grown soon and marrying and having her own house. I held on to this place as long as I could. . . . Well, I'm not going to feel guilty about it. . . .

GERT. I'm going to try to stop you, Lester. . . .

LESTER. Now look, Gert. For once try and be sensible. . . .

GERT. Legally I'm going to try and stop you. I'm going . . .

LESTER. Please, Gert . . .

GERT. . . . to call Bill and tell him the whole situation and see what we can do. If we have any rights I'll take it to every court I can. Brother or no brother. . . .

LESTER. Now look, don't carry on like this. Maybe I've handled it clumsily, and if I have I'm sorry. I just didn't think. . . . I should have, I know . . . but I . . .

GERT. That's right. You didn't think. You never do. Well, this time you're going to have to. . . .

LESTER. Can't you look at it this way? Wilma is getting a better house and . . .

GERT. Maybe she doesn't want a better house. Maybe she just wants this one. But that isn't the point either. The sickening part is that you really didn't care what Wilma thought or even stopped for a moment to consider if she had a thought. You've never cared about anyone or anything but yourself. Well, this time I won't let you without a fight. I'm going to a lawyer.

LESTER. Gert . . .

GERT. Now get out of my house. Because brother or no, I'm through with you.

LESTER. All right. If you feel that way.

(*He leaves upstage center of the area. Gert stands for a moment, thinking what to do next. Minna comes in downstage left of the area.*)

MINNA. I was behind the door and I heard the whole thing.

GERT. Did Wilma hear?

MINNA. No, I sent her back to her room. Now you get right to a lawyer.

GERT. I intend to. He's gotten me mad now. I won't let him get by with it if I can help it. I think I'll walk over to Bill's. I don't like to talk about it over the telephone.

MINNA. Yes'm.

GERT. You tell Wilma to wait here for me.

MINNA. Yes'm. Want me to tell her where you've gone?

GERT. I don't see why not. I'll be back as soon as I finish.

MINNA. Yes'm. (Gert *leaves upstage center of the area.* Minna *goes to the door and calls:*) Wilma. Wilma. You can come here now. (*She fills a plate with food and puts it on the table.* Wilma *comes in downstage left of the area.*) You better sit down and try to eat something.

WILMA. I can't eat a thing.

MINNA. Well, you can try.

WILMA. No. It would choke me. What happened?

MINNA. Your aunt told him not to sell the house, and he said he would, and so she's gone to see a lawyer.

WILMA. Does she think she can stop him?

MINNA. She's gonna try. I know she's got him scared. . . .

WILMA. But it's my house. You know that. He knows that. . . . Didn't she tell him?

MINNA. Sure she told him. But you know your daddy. Telling won't do any good; we have to prove it.

WILMA. What proof have we got?

MINNA. Miss Gert's word. I hope that's enough. . . .

WILMA. And if it isn't?

MINNA. Then you'll lose it. That's all. You'll lose it.

WILMA. I bet I lose it. I've got no luck.

MINNA. Why do you say that?

WILMA. What kind of luck is it takes your mama away, and then your daddy, and then tries to take your house? Sitting in that yard swinging I was the happiest girl in the world this afternoon. I'd decided not to go in the movies and to stay in Harrison and get married and have children and live in my house. . . .

MINNA. Well, losing a house won't stop you from staying in Harrison and getting married. . . .

WILMA. Oh, yes. I wouldn't trust it with my luck. With my kind of luck I wouldn't even get me a husband. . . . I'd wind up like Miss Martha working at the post office chasing Mr. Russell Walter until the end of time. No mother and no father and no house and no husband and no children. No, thank you. I'm just tired of worrying over the whole thing. I'll just go on into Houston and see Mr. Delafonte and get on out to Hollywood and make money and get rich and famous. (*She begins to cry.*)

MINNA. Now, honey. Honey . . .

WILMA. Minna, I don't want to be rich and famous. . . . I want to stay here. I want to stay in Harrison. . . .

MINNA. Now, honey. Try to be brave.

WILMA. I know what I'm gonna do. (*She jumps up.*) I'm going to see old

> ● ● ● ● ● ● ●
> ### "I bet I lose it. I've got no luck."
> ● ● ● ● ● ● ●

lady Leighton. She's the one that can stop this. . . .

MINNA. Now, Wilma. You know your aunt don't want you around that woman.

WILMA. I can't help it. I'm going. . . .

MINNA. Wilma . . . you listen to me . . .

(Wilma *runs out upstage center of the area.*) Wilma . . . Wilma . . . you come back here. . . .

(*But* Wilma *has gone.* Minna *shakes her head in desperation. The lights fade. When the lights are brought up, it is two hours later.* Minna *is at the kitchen table reading the paper.* Gert *comes in upstage center of the area.*)

GERT. Well, we've won.

MINNA. What do you mean?

GERT. I mean just what I say. Lester is not going to sell the house.

MINNA. What happened?

GERT. I don't know what happened. I went over to see Bill and we talked it all through, and he said legally we really had no chance, but he'd call up Lester and try to at least bluff him into thinking we had. And when he called Lester, he said Lester wasn't home, and so I suggested his calling you know where.

MINNA. No. Where?

GERT. Mrs. Leighton's. And sure enough he was there, and then Bill told him why he was calling, and Lester said, well, it didn't matter as he'd decided not to sell the house after all.

## FOCUS ON... SOCIAL STUDIES

The play is set in the year 1925. During the 1920s, prior to the Great Depression that began in 1929, the United States experienced an economic boom. In Houston, Texas, oil was discovered in the early 1900s, which spawned considerable industrial development, expansion, and prosperity. Many people left their jobs in small towns to work in the booming oil industry. Find out about this time period in Texas history. What effect did the oil boom in Houston have on smaller towns, such as the fictional Harrison? Share your findings with the class in a multimedia presentation.

◆ ◆ ◆ ◆ ◆ ◆ ◆ ◆ ◆ ◆ ◆ ◆

MINNA. You don't mean it?

GERT. Oh, yes, I do. Where's Wilma?

MINNA. She's over there with them.

GERT. Over where with them?

MINNA. At Mrs. Leighton's.

GERT. Why, Minna . . .

MINNA. Now don't holler at me. I told her not to go, but she said she was going, and then she ran out that door so fast I couldn't stop her.

(Wilma *comes running in upstage center of the area.*)

WILMA. Heard the news? House is mine again.

MINNA. Do you know what happened?

WILMA. Sure. Mrs. Leighton isn't so bad. Boy, I went running over there expecting the worst . . .

GERT. Wilma, what do you mean going to that woman's house? Wilma, I declare . . .

WILMA. Oh, she's not so bad. Anyway we've got her to thank for it.

MINNA. Well, what happened? Will somebody please tell me what happened?

WILMA. Well, you know I was sitting here and it came to me. It came to me just like that. See Mrs. Leighton. She's the one to stop it and it's got to be stopped. Well, I was so scared my knees were trembling the whole time going over there, but I made myself do it, walked in on her, and she looked more nervous than I did.

GERT. Was your father there?

WILMA. No ma'am. He came later. Wasn't anybody there but me and

Mrs. Leighton. I'm calling her Sibyl now. She asked me to. Did Arabella come yet?

MINNA. Arabella?

WILMA. I called and asked her to come and celebrate. I'm so excited. I just had to have company tonight. I know I won't be able to sleep anyway. I hope you don't mind, Aunt Gert. . . .

MINNA. If you don't tell me what happened . . .

WILMA. Well . . . Mrs. Leighton . . . I mean Sibyl . . . (Arabella *comes in upstage center of the area.* Wilma *sees her.*) Oh, come on in, Arabella.

ARABELLA. Hi. I almost didn't get to come. I told my mama it was life or death, and so she gave in. But she made me swear we'd be in bed by ten. Did you hear about Mr. Delafonte?

WILMA. No? What?

ARABELLA. He's a crook. It was in the Houston papers tonight. He was operating a business under false pretenses. He had been charging twenty-five dollars for those screen tests and using a camera with no film in it.

WILMA. My goodness.

ARABELLA. It was in all the papers. On the second page. My father said he mustn't have been very much not to even get on the front page. He wasn't a Hollywood director at all. He didn't even know Lila Lee or Betty Compson.

WILMA. He didn't?

ARABELLA. No.

MINNA. Wilma, will you get back to your story before I lose my mind?

WILMA. Oh. Yes . . . I got my house back, Arabella.

ARABELLA. You did?

WILMA. Sure. That's why I called you over to spend the night. A kind of celebration.

ARABELLA. Well, that's wonderful.

MINNA. Wilma . . .

WILMA. All right. Where was I?

GERT. You were at Mrs. Leighton's.

WILMA. Oh, yes. Sibyl's. I'm calling her Sibyl now, Arabella. She asked me to.

MINNA. Well . . . what happened? Wilma, if you don't tell me . . .

WILMA. Well, I just told her the whole thing.

MINNA. What whole thing?

WILMA. Well, I told her about my mother meaning for the house to always be mine, and how I loved the house, and how I was lonely and the house was lonely, and that I had hoped my daddy and I could go there and live someday but knew now we couldn't, and that I had planned to go to Hollywood and be a movie star but that this afternoon my friend Arabella and I decided we didn't really want to do that, and that I knew then that what I wanted to do really was to live in Harrison and get married and live in my house and have children so that I wouldn't be lonely anymore and the house wouldn't. And then she started crying.

GERT. You don't mean it.

WILMA. Yes ma'am. And I felt real sorry for her, and I said I didn't hold anything against her, and then Daddy came in, and she said why didn't he tell her that was my house, and he said because it wasn't. And then she asked him about what Mother told you, and he said that was true but now I was going to have a better house, and she said I didn't want to have a better house, but my own house, and that she wouldn't marry him if he sold this house, and she said they both had jobs in Houston and would manage somehow, but I had nothing, so then he said all right.

GERT. Well. Good for her.

MINNA. Sure enough, good for her.

WILMA. And then Mr. Bill called and Daddy told him the house was mine again, and then she cried again and hugged me and asked me to kiss her and I did, and then Daddy cried and I kissed him, and then I cried. And they asked me to the wedding and I said I'd go and that I'd come visit them this summer in Houston. And then I came home.

MINNA. Well. Well, indeed.

GERT. My goodness. So that's how it happened. And you say Mrs. Leighton cried?

WILMA. Twice. We all did. Daddy and Mrs. Leighton and me. . . .

GERT. Well, I'm glad, Wilma, it's all worked out.

WILMA. And can I go visit them this summer in Houston?

GERT. If you like.

WILMA. And can I go to the wedding?

GERT. Yes, if you want to.

WILMA. I want to.

MINNA. Now you better have some supper.

WILMA. No. I couldn't eat, I'm still too excited.

MINNA. Miss Gert, she hasn't had a bite on her stomach.

GERT. Well, it won't kill her this one time, Minna.

WILMA. Aunt Gert, can Arabella and I go over to my yard for just a few minutes and swing? We'll be home by ten. . . .

GERT. No, Wilma, it's late.

WILMA. Please. Just to celebrate. I have it coming to me. We'll just stay for a few minutes.

GERT. Well . . .

WILMA. Please . . .

GERT. Will you be back here by ten, and not make me have to send Minna over there?

WILMA. Yes ma'am.

GERT. All right.

WILMA. Oh, thank you. (*She goes to her aunt and kisses her.*) You're the best aunt in the whole world. Come on, Arabella.

ARABELLA. All right. (*They start upstage center of the area.* Gert *calls after them:*)

GERT. Now remember. Back by ten, Arabella has promised her mother. And you've promised me.

WILMA (*calling in distance*). Yes ma'am.

(Gert *comes back into the room.*)

GERT. Well, I'm glad it's ending this way.

MINNA. Yes ma'am.

GERT. I never thought it would. Well, I said hard things to Lester. I'm sorry I had to, but I felt I had to.

MINNA. Of course you did.

GERT. Well, I'll go to my room. You go on when you're ready.

MINNA. All right. I'm ready now. The excitement has wore me out.

GERT. Me too. Leave the light on for the children. I'll keep awake until they come in.

MINNA. Yes'm.

GERT. Good night.

MINNA. Good night.

(Gert *goes out downstage left of the area.* Minna *goes to get her hat. The lights fade. The lights are brought up in the downstage right area.* Wilma *and* Arabella *come in upstage center of the area and get in the swing.*)

WILMA. Don't you just love to swing?

ARABELLA. Uh huh.

WILMA. It's a lovely night, isn't it? Listen to that mockingbird. The crazy thing must think it's daytime.

ARABELLA. It's light enough to be day.

WILMA. It certainly is.

ARABELLA. Well, it was lucky we decided to give up Hollywood with Mr. Delafonte turning out to be a crook and all.

WILMA. Wasn't it lucky?

ARABELLA. Do you feel lonely now?

WILMA. No, I don't feel nearly so lonely. Now I've got my house and plan to get married. And my daddy and I are going to see each other, and I think Mrs. Leighton is going to make a nice friend. She's crazy about moving pictures.

ARABELLA. Funny how things work out.

WILMA. Very funny.

ARABELLA. Guess who called me on the telephone.

WILMA. Who?

ARABELLA. Tommy . . . Murray.

WILMA. You don't say.

ARABELLA. He asked me for a date next week. Picture show. He said Jay was going to call you.

WILMA. Did he?

ARABELLA. I asked him to tell Jay that you weren't only interested in going out with movie actors.

WILMA. What did he say?

ARABELLA. He said he thought Jay knew that. (*A pause.* Wilma *jumps out of the swing.*) Wilma. What's the matter with you? Wilma . . . (*She runs to her.*)

WILMA. I don't know. I felt funny there for a minute. A cloud passed over the moon and I felt lonely . . . and funny . . . and scared. . . .

ARABELLA. But you have your house now.

WILMA. I know . . . I . . . (*A pause. She points offstage right.*) I used to sleep in there. I had a white iron bed. I remember one night Aunt Gert woke me up. It was just turning light out, and she was crying. "I'm taking you

> ● ● ● ● ● ● ● ●
> "No, I don't feel nearly so lonely."
> ● ● ● ● ● ● ● ●

home to live with me." she said. "Why?" I said. "Because your mama's gone to heaven." she said. (*a pause*) I can't remember my mama's face anymore. I can hear her voice sometimes calling me far off: "Wilma, Wilma, come home." Far off. But I can't remember her face. I try and I try, but finally I have to go to my bureau drawer and take out her picture and look to remember. . . . Oh, Arabella. It isn't only the house I wanted. It's the life in the house. My mama and me and even my daddy coming in at four in the morning. . . .

ARABELLA. But there'll be life again in this house.

WILMA. How?

ARABELLA. You're gonna fill it with life again, Wilma. Like you said this afternoon.

WILMA. But I get afraid.

ARABELLA. Don't be. You will, I know you will.

• • • • • • •
"But there'll be life again in this house."
• • • • • • •

WILMA. You think I can do anything. Be a movie star . . . Go to Hollywood. (*a pause*) The moon's from behind the cloud. (*A pause. In the distance we can hear the courthouse clock strike ten.*) Don't tell me it's ten o'clock already. I'll fill this house with life again. I'll meet a young man with steady ways and nice habits. . . . (*Far off* Aunt Gert *calls:* "Wilma. Wilma." Wilma *calls back:*) We're coming. You see that pecan tree out there?

ARABELLA. Uh huh.

WILMA. It was planted the year my mother was born. It's so big now I can hardly reach around it. (Aunt Gert *calls again:* "Wilma. Wilma." Wilma *calls back:*) We're coming. (*She and* Arabella *sit swinging.* Wilma *looks happy and is happy as the lights fade.*) ❖

ACCENT ON...
ARCHITECTURE
• • • • • • • • • • • • • • • • • • • • • • •

Wilma's dream home is the house of her childhood. It is her hope to fill that house with life once again. What would your dream home be like? Where would it be located? Create a detailed floor plan of your dream house. To accompany your floor plan, write a brief essay describing why this is the perfect home for you and what hopes you have for your life there.

# UNDERSTANDING

1. Plays are about relationships—including misunderstandings—between characters. If you were to give the characters a piece of advice early in this play, what would it be? How would it resolve the conflicts earlier?

    In a letter from Wilma to a friend who has moved away, describe the continued relationship between Wilma and her father and his new wife, Mrs. Leighton. Through the letter, predict the future of Wilma's relationship with Mrs. Leighton. *Workshop 16*

2. Wilma has the admirable quality of being honest with herself and others. Find examples of this honesty. What if she were dishonest or deceitful? Rewrite a scene to show Wilma displaying these characteristics. How does the outcome of the play change? *Workshop 4*

3. Wilma and Arabella were able to accept the truth about Mr. Delafonte because they had already changed their plans. But what if they had discovered this information *before* their change of heart? Role-play their reaction in class. Discuss the effect of this change on the play.

## A LAST WORD

Wilma's professional and personal goals change as she matures and learns what it means to be grown up. What kinds of risks does being grown up require? What does growing up mean to you?

# CONNECTING

1. Create a T-chart. On one side, list ideas about your dream home, no matter how far-fetched. On the other side, list the realities—things you need to do before you could own your dream home. Research what it takes to buy a home in your community. Write an action plan on purchasing a home. Consider design, cost, and financing in your plan. *Workshop 11*

2. Witnesses are important. They can clarify situations by telling what they saw or heard. Miss Gert was a witness to Wilma's mother's dying wish. How is this important in the play? In small groups research the meaning of *witness*.

    Write an incident report of something important you have personally witnessed, such as a car accident or a fight. Pay close attention to details. *Workshop 10*

# *in Just-*

## EXPLORING

In spring, we celebrate new beginnings as life is reborn after the cold of winter. Children of all ages enjoy the change in weather by spending time outside and playing games. Can you recall a best friend who joined you in springtime activities? Does your family have seasonal traditions, like summer picnicking or autumn kite-flying? Share with the class your memories of special friends and family traditions.

## THEME CONNECTION...
## THE TURNING SEASONS

The joy of spring permeates the mood of this poem. It is difficult for most of us *not* to be affected by the changing of the seasons—particularly the change from winter to spring. In the poem, the cheerful activities of inseparable friends reflect the song of the balloonman as he softly whistles.

## TIME & PLACE

Even though the ground is muddy as a result of springtime showers, the children of "in Just-" are able to play games. The setting of the poem is a modern-day park with marble games and hopscotch grids painted on the asphalt. The balloonman whistles to get the attention of his potential customers.

## THE WRITER'S CRAFT

### FREE VERSE

Lineation is the way a poet places words in lines. In free verse, the poet freely selects where to start and stop each line, working carefully to extend the meanings of the words. The poet also has the freedom to defy the rules of spelling and punctuation to underscore his or her meaning. For example, Cummings writes "eddieandbill" and "bettyandisbel" to express the closeness of the children's friendships. Find other examples of unconventional punctuation and spacing in this poem. What do they mean?

# *in Just-*

E. E. Cummings

in Just-
spring          when the world is mud-
luscious the little
lame balloonman

whistles          far          and wee

and eddieandbill come
running from marbles and
piracies and it's
spring

when the world is puddle-wonderful

the queer
old balloonman whistles
far          and          wee
and bettyandisbel come dancing

from hop-scotch and jump-rope and

it's
spring
and
          the

                    goat-footed

balloonMan          whistles
far
and
wee ❖

## About the Author

Edward Estlin Cummings (1894–1962) was born in Cambridge, Massachusetts. During World War I, Cummings volunteered to serve as an ambulance driver in France. He was imprisoned by French authorities; this experience provided material for his first book, *The Enormous Room.* His unique poetic style breaks the rules of poetic form. He dropped the use of capital letters to begin each line of poetry in imitation of ancient Greek sentence style.

## FOCUS ON...
## LITERATURE

For as long as poets have been writing, spring has been a subject to explore and celebrate. Find a poem about spring written by another poet in a form or style that differs from Cummings's poem. Then compare and contrast the two poems. Identify the poems' main ideas and explain how their form and style reinforce their meaning.

## UNDERSTANDING

1. List the words in the poem that describe the balloonman. At what point does the poet use lineation to separate descriptive words from the balloonman's name? How does the spelling of his name change and why? What does the poet imply by these changes?

   Write an observation report describing the changes that take place in a specific, familiar location in spring. *Workshop 10*
2. Why are the games children play signs of spring? How do the games create images in your mind's eye? Draw an illustration of this poem, placing the appropriate lines by the images you create.
3. Notice how the poet freely adjusts the length of lines and the placement of words. For example, he separates the word "mud-luscious" onto two lines. What reasons are there for this manipulation? Find other examples of where the poet breaks words and lines to help the reader understand exactly what he means. Select two and explain them in a paragraph. *Workshop 8*
4. Titles are important in that they usually give the reader a hint about the most important point of a piece of literature. How does capitalization in the poem hint ironically at the underlying meaning of the poem?

   Think of a significant moment in your life. Give it an ironic title. Use capital and lowercase letters to emphasize the significance of the title.

### A LAST WORD

What makes the world different in spring? What hopes and emotions come alive?

## CONNECTING

1. Write a poem about your favorite season. Use free verse, altering line length and word placement to convey added meaning. Also, experiment with using capital letters to indicate change. Type your poem on a computer and print it out. If your computer has the capacity, create a symbol or other graphic to convey the meaning of your poem. The placement of the graphic near your poem should have significance.

2. Working with a partner, design a magazine advertisement for a small business that provides entertainment for children's parties. The advertisement will appear in parents' magazines as well as several magazines aimed at children. Create the advertisement on computer. Include graphics or provide descriptions of pictures or photographs you would include. *Workshops 20 and 24*

# WRAP IT UP

UNIT 5

1. Many of the characters and narrators in this unit's selections experience meaningful turning points in their lives. Romeo finds himself suffering serious consequences for his action against Tybalt. Young Rubén in "Three Wise Guys" suddenly becomes aware of his own desire to learn. What turning points are experienced by the main characters in the other selections in this unit? Write an essay in which you compare and contrast the turning points experienced by at least three of these characters and narrators.

2. In Horton Foote's play *A Young Lady of Property,* the main character, Wilma, changes and grows in many ways. In an essay, explain how the house she owns is a significant part of her growth and of her self-understanding. What crisis does Wilma face when she is threatened with losing the house? What does Wilma come to realize about herself and her independence? What does Wilma realize that the house really means to her? What does Wilma learn that being grown up requires?

in Just-

# UNIT
## ⟨6⟩
# LIFE'S LESSONS

*Every day young people spend hours learning information from their teachers and their textbooks. However, life's most important lessons occur both inside and outside the classroom. These lessons teach us to do our best and have confidence in ourselves. Sometimes we learn not to take life too seriously, to have fun and enjoy being alive. Occasionally, we learn not to expect too much from others.*

*No one ever stops learning life's lessons. In fact, no one ever learns them all. These lessons can come quickly or take years to sink in. We can miss them if we are too busy or distracted to pay attention. Like the characters in this unit's selections, we need to be ready for life's lessons.*

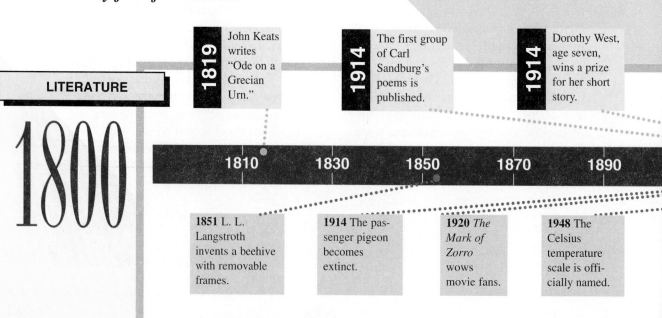

**LITERATURE**

**1800**

**1819** John Keats writes "Ode on a Grecian Urn."

**1914** The first group of Carl Sandburg's poems is published.

**1914** Dorothy West, age seven, wins a prize for her short story.

1810    1830    1850    1870    1890

**1851** L. L. Langstroth invents a beehive with removable frames.

**1914** The passenger pigeon becomes extinct.

**1920** *The Mark of Zorro* wows movie fans.

**1948** The Celsius temperature scale is officially named.

**1953** Ernest Hemingway wins Pulitzer Prize for *The Old Man and the Sea.*

**1960** Mai Vo-Dinh immigrates to the United States.

**1972** Gary Soto discovers poetry at college.

1910    1930    1950    1970    1990

2000

**1969** The Uniform Consumer Credit Code limits interest on loans.

**1973** Recession causes the highest unemployment since the 1940s.

**1994** A study shows that one-third of children under the age of 11 have bet money.

**1995** A new chemical is developed to preserve cut flowers.

**LIFE and WORK**

# Beauty Is Truth

## EXPLORING

Sometimes what you study in school seems far removed from what is important in your life. Have you ever wanted to ask a teacher, "When will you ask me about *my* world?" or "What does this have to do with *my* life?" Discuss a time when you felt like asking these questions. Have you experienced a time when your studies *did* connect with your life? Did you have to make an effort to connect the material to your life, or did it just happen?

## THEME CONNECTION...
## LEARNING THROUGH HONEST EXPRESSION

Honesty in art, literature, music—any form of human expression—helps give it timeless beauty. Through writing about the reality of her life, the main character in this story realizes that her family's love and loyalty are what really matter.

## TIME & PLACE

The setting of the story is Harlem, a section of New York City. In the early 1900s, Harlem became one of the largest African-American communities in the United States, but it has suffered economically since World War II.

This story takes place at a time when mild corporal punishment from teachers and parents was acceptable and expected. At home and at school, young people were likely to experience slapping or spanking if they broke the rules. Such punishment is strictly forbidden in schools today, and most parents have learned other ways to discipline their children.

## THE WRITER'S CRAFT

### MOTIVATION

Motivation is the force that drives a character to behave in a certain way. In "Beauty Is Truth," the main character demonstrates a love for her family that motivates her actions throughout the story. Ultimately, her description of the truth in her life reflects her deep love for her brother and mother.

# Beauty Is Truth

Anna Guest

A t 125th Street, they all got off, Jeanie and her friend Barbara and a crowd of other boys and girls who went to the same downtown high school. Through the train window, Jeanie thought she saw the remaining passengers look at them with relief and **disdain**. Around her, the boys and girls pressed forward with noisy gaiety. They were all friends now. They were home again in Harlem.

A tall boy detached himself from a group, bowed low and swept his cap before him in a courtly salute.

"Greetings, Lady Jeanie. Greetings, Barbara."

Jeanie bit her lip. Frowning, she pulled her coat closer and shrugged. Barbara smiled and dimpled, pleased for her friend.

"I told you he likes you," she whispered. "Look, he's waiting. Want me to go on ahead?"

Jeanie really was wasting an opportunity. Norman was keen. She saw Jeanie's head, slightly bowed and thrust forward. It was no use. She was an odd girl, but Barbara liked her anyway. The boy swung gracefully back to his group.

"Coming to the show tonight?" Barbara asked.

"No, I can't. I'm so far behind in my homework, I'd better try to do some before they decide to throw me out." Jeanie still frowned.

"Want a Coke or something?" asked Barbara as they passed the big ice-cream parlor window, cluttered with candy boxes and ornate with curly lettering. They could see the jukebox near the door and some boys and girls sitting down at a table. It looked warm and friendly.

Jeanie shook her head, one brief shake.

"I think I'll stop in. I'm awful thirsty," said Barbara.

Jeanie shrugged.

"So long, then."

"So long."

She walked along the busy street, aimlessly looking in the store windows, turned the corner, and walked the few blocks to her house. Though it was chilly, each brownstone or gray **stoop** had its cluster of people clinging to the iron railings. Some children on skates played a desperate game of hockey with sticks that were not hockey sticks. When a car approached, they did not interrupt their game until it was almost too late. Amid shouts from the driver and wild **jeers** from the children, the car passed, and the game was resumed in all its concentrated intensity.

Her little brother Billy was playing in front of the stoop with three or four other kids. They were bending over something on the sidewalk, in a closed circle. Pitching pennies again, she thought with **repugnance**. She was going to pass them and started up the three stone steps to the doorway. A window on the ground floor opened, and Fat Mary leaned out. . . .

"Now you're going to catch it, Billy Boy. Your sister's going to tell your mama you been pitching pennies again."

Jeanie did not pause.

disdain—dislike, scorn

stoop—a small porch or stepped platform by the door of an apartment building

jeers—comments meant to be rude or to ridicule

repugnance—strong dislike

Billy sprang up. "Hi, Jeanie. Jeanie, gimme a nickel. I need a nickel. A nickel, a nickel. I gotta have a nickel."

The other little boys took up the chant. "A nickel, a nickel. Billy needs a nickel."

She threw them a furious glance and went in. Two little girls sat on the second landing, playing house. They had a set of toy dishes spread out on the top stair and held dolls in their laps. She stepped over them, careful not to disturb their arrangements.

The kitchen smelled dank and unused, and the opening of the door dislodged a flake of green-painted plaster. It fell into the sink, with a dry powdering. A black dress someone had given her mother lay over the chair before the sewing machine. It reminded her that her sleeve had torn half out, dressing after gym. She really should sew it, but the sight of the black dress waiting to be made over made her dislike the thought of sewing. She would just have to wear her coat in school tomorrow. Lots of kids did. She did not like her shape anyway. . . .

She hung her coat on a hook in the room she shared with her mother and stood **irresolute**. Her mother would be coming in soon and would expect to find the potatoes peeled and the table laid. She caught sight of a comic book and, unwillingly attracted by the **garish** colors, read one side. "Ah!" she thought in disgust. "Billy!" She thought of her homework. She was so far behind in social studies that she could probably

never make it up. It was hardly worth trying. **Mercantilism**. The rise of the merchant class. She would probably fail. And gym, all those cuts in gym. Miss Fisher, her grade advisor, had called her down yesterday and warned her. "Ah!" she said again. Miss Fisher was all right. She had even been encouraging. "I know you can do it," she had said.

She sat down on the bed and opened her loose-leaf notebook at random. A page fell out. She was about to jam it back in, when the freshly inked writing caught her eye. Today's English. Some poem about a vase and youths and maidens. Miss Lowy had brought in some pictures of vases with people on them, dressed in togas or whatever they were, spinning and reading from scrolls. Why did everybody get so excited about the Greeks? It was so long ago. "Wonderful! Wonderful!" Miss Lowy had exclaimed. How could anybody get so stirred up over a poem? She meant it too. You could tell from her expression.

"Listen, boys and girls. Listen." A lifted arm **enjoined** them.

*"Beauty is truth, truth beauty,—that is all*
*Ye know on earth, and all ye need to know."*

There it was, copied into her notebook. Caught by something in the lines, she tried to find the poem in her tattered **anthology**, not bothering about the index but riffling the pages to and fro. John Keats, at last—"On First Looking into Chapman's Homer." More Greeks. Here

> "How could anybody get so stirred up over a poem?"

it *was*—"Ode on a Grecian Urn." The poem, all squeezed together in the middle of the page, looked dry and dusty, withered and far away, at the bottom of a dry well. She saw, not as much words, as an uninteresting, meandering pattern. The big THOU at the opening repelled her. She turned the page to find that the poem went on. Recognizing the last lines, she heard them again, falling so roundly, so perfectly, from the lips of Miss Lowy. She turned back to the beginning. Why "Grecian," why not "Greek"? With an effort, she began to dig the poem out of its **constricted** print.

*"Thou foster child of silence and slow times,"* its soft **susurrus** carried her on. She read the poem through to the end, trying to remember her teacher's **cadences**.

"Write about beauty and truth. Write about life," Miss Lowy had said.

She tore a page out of her notebook and opened her pen. Pulling over a chair, she rested her book on the sooty windowsill. She stared out at the dusk falling sadly, sadly, thickening into darkness over the coal yards.

A crash of the kitchen door caused a **reverberation** in the windowsill. The notebook slipped out of her hands.

"Where'd you get that bottle of pop?" she heard her mother's voice, hard and sounding more Southern than usual.

A high-pitched, wordless sniveling came in reply.

"I asked you. Where'd you get that pop? You better tell me."

"A lady gave me a nickel. A lady came down the street and ask me—"

"You lying. I know where you got that money. Gambling, that's what you was doing."

"I was only pitching pennies, Ma. It's only a game, Ma."

"Gambling and stealing and associating with bad friends. I told you to stay away from them boys. Didn't I? Didn't I?" Her mother's voice rose. "I'm going to give you a beating you ain't going to forget."

Billy wailed on a long descending note. Jeanie could hear each impact of the strap and her mother's heavy breathing.

"I want you to grow up good, not lying and gambling and stealing," her mother gasped, "and I'm going to make you good. You ain't never going to forget this." When it had been going on forever, it stopped. A final slap of the strap. "And you ain't going to get any supper either. You can go now. You can go to bed and reflect on what I told you."

He stumbled past her, whimpering, fists grinding into eyes, and into the dark little **alcove** which was his room. Jeanie heard the groan of the bed as he threw himself on it. She felt a pain in her fingers and saw them still pressed tightly around the pen.

Her mother appeared in the doorway. She wore her hat and coat.

"Come help me get supper, Jeanie. You should have got things started." Her voice was tired and **tremulous** and held no **reproach**.

"I don't want any supper, Ma."

Her mother came in and sat down heavily on the bed, taking off her hat and letting her coat fall open.

"I had a hard day. I worked hard every minute," she said. "I brought you

constricted— squeezed tightly together

susurrus— whispering or rustling sound

cadences—the rising and falling pitches of a voice

reverberation— vibration, as an echo

alcove—nook, a small part of a room set back from the rest of the room

tremulous— trembling, shaky

reproach— scolding, blame

FOCUS ON...
LITERATURE

Miss Lowy reads aloud John Keats's poem "Ode on a Grecian Urn" to Jeanie's class. Read this poem and reflect on the lines "Beauty is truth, truth beauty,—that is all/Ye know on earth, and all ye need to know." Then, in your own words, explain what Keats means in these lines.

◆ ◆ ◆ ◆ ◆ ◆ ◆ ◆ ◆ ◆ ◆ ◆ ◆

skylark—proba-bly a reference to Percy Bysshe Shelley's poem "To a Skylark"

sullen—gloomily silent

something extra nice for dessert. I stood on line to get some of them tarts from Sutter's."

Jeanie rose and silently put her mother's hat on the shelf. She held out her hand for her mother's coat and hung it up.

Together they opened the paper bags on the kitchen table. She set the water to boil.

As they ate in silence, the three tarts shone like subtle jewels on a plate at one end of the chipped porcelain table. Her mother looked tired and stern.

"You better fix your brother up a plate," she said, still stern. "Put it on a tray. Here, take this." And she put on the tray the most luscious, the most perfect of the tarts. "Wait." She went heavily over to her swollen black handbag, took out a small clasp purse, opened it, and carefully, seriously, deliberately, picked out a coin, rejected it, and took out another. "Give him this." It was a quarter.

After the dishes were washed, Jeanie brought her books into the kitchen and spread them out under the glaring over-head light. Billy had been asleep, huddled in his clothes. Tears had left dusty streaks on his face.

Her mother sat in the armchair, ripping out the sides of the black dress. Her spectacles made her look strange. *"Beauty is truth,"* Jeanie read in her notebook. Hastily, carelessly, defiantly disregarding margins and doubtful spellings, letting her pen dig into the paper, she began to write: "Last night my brother Billy got a ter-rible beating. . . .

Scramble to borrow the social studies homework from a girl in her homeroom, say hello to Barbara, undress for gym, dress again, the torn sleeve, bookkeep-ing—a blot, get another piece of ledger paper. "This is the third I've given you. You might say thank you." Get to English early. Slip her composition in under the others, sit in the last seat. Don't bother me. I am in a bad mood. Rows and rows of seats. Rows and rows of windows opposite. She could even read the writing on some of the black-boards, but who cared? A boy leaned far out of the window before closing it. Other heads turning. Would he fall? No, he was safe. Heads turned back. A poem about a **skylark**. From where she sat, she could see about a square foot of sky, drained of all color by the looming school walls. Miss Lowy read clearly, standing all alone at the front of the room in her clean white blouse and with her smooth blond hair.

Miss Lowy, maybe you see skylarks. Me, I'd be glad to see some sky, she thought and nearly uttered it. Around her, students were writing in their note-books. Miss Lowy was about to speak to her. Better start writing something. **Sullen**, Mr. MacIver had called her last week. She felt about for her notebook and pen. It had been a mistake to write as she had done about her brother's beating. They would laugh if they knew. Shirley, who was the class secretary, and Saul, with the prominent forehead. No, he would not laugh. He was always writing about spaceships and the end of the world. No danger, though, that her story would be read. Only the best manuscripts were read. She remembered keenly the blotched appearance of the paper, the lines crossed out, and the words whose spelling she could never be sure of. Oh, well, she didn't care. Only one more period and then the weekend. "Lady Jeanie's too proud to come to our party. Jeanie, what are you waiting for? Jeanie's waiting for a Prince Charming with a red Cadillac to come and take her away." If Barbara asked her again, she would go with her, maybe. There was going to be a party at Norma's Saturday night, with Cokes and sandwiches and records and dancing, everybody chipping in. "Jeanie, I need a nickel. Mama, I need a dollar. I need, I need."

The bell rang, and the pens dropped, the books were closed with a clatter. She slipped out ahead of the pushing, jostling boys and girls.

Monday, Miss Lowy had on still another perfect white blouse. She stood facing the class, holding a sheaf of papers in her hand. Most of the students looked at her expectantly. Marion, who nearly always got 90, whispered to her neighbor. Michael, who had but recently come from Greece—ah, but that was a different Greece—grumbled and shifted in his seat. He would have to do his composition over. He always did.

"I spent a very enjoyable time this weekend reading your work," said Miss Lowy, waiting for the class to smile.

"Seriously, though, many of your pieces were most interesting, even though they were a trifle unconventional about spelling and punctuation." A smile was obviously indicated here too, and the class obeyed. She paused. "Sometimes, however, a piece of writing is so honest and human that you forgive the technical weaknesses. Not that they aren't important," she said hastily, "but what the writer has to say is more significant."

The three best students in the class looked confused. It was their pride not to have technical errors. "When you hear this," Miss Lowy continued, "I think you'll agree with me. I know it brought tears to my eyes."

The class looked incredulous.

"It's called 'Evening Comes to 128th Street.'" Her face took on that rapt look.

Jeanie's heart beat painfully. She picked up a pencil but dropped it, so unsteady were her fingers. Even the back of Shirley's head was listening. Even the classes in the other wing of the building, across the courtyard, seemed fixed, row on row, in an attitude of listening. Miss Lowy read on. It was all there, the coal yards and Fat Mary, the stoop and the tarts from Sutter's, Billy asleep with the tears dried on his face, the clasp purse and the quarter.

"'The funny part of it was, when I woke him. Billy wasn't mad. He was glad about the quarter and ate his supper, dessert and all, but Mama never did eat her tart, so I put it away.'"

A **poignancy** of remembrance swept over Jeanie, then shame and regret. It was no business of theirs, these strange white people.

poignancy— painfully emotional quality

No one spoke. The silence was unbearable. Finally Marion, the incomparable Marion, raised her hand.

"It was so real," she said, "you felt you were right there in that kitchen."

"You didn't know who to feel sorry for," said another student. "You wanted to cry with the mother and you wanted to cry with Billy."

"With the girl too," said another. Several heads nodded.

"You see," said Miss Lowy. "It's literature. It's life. It's pain and truth and beauty."

Jeanie's heart beat so, it made a mist come before her eyes. Through the blur she heard Miss Lowy say it was good enough to be sent in to *Scholastic*. It showed talent; it showed promise. She heard her name called and shrank from the eyes turned upon her.

After school, she hurried out and caught the first train that you could catch only if you left immediately and did not stroll or stop the least bit to talk to someone. She did not want to meet anyone, not even Barbara.

Was that Billy among the kids on the stoop?

"Billy," she called, "Billy."

What would she say to him? Beauty is truth, truth beauty?

"Billy," she called again urgently.

Billy lifted his head and, seeing who it was, tore himself reluctantly away from his friends and took a step toward her. ❖

# ON THE JOB
## TEACHER

High school teachers instruct students from the ninth or tenth grade through the twelfth grade. Usually, high school teachers specialize in and teach one subject, such as language arts, math, science, social studies, or physical education. The best teachers pass on to their students an enthusiasm for learning. Because teachers work closely with students, they must have strong interpersonal and communication skills, patience, and creativity. A bachelor's degree and teaching certificate are required.

# ACCENT ON...
## WORD PROCESSING

Jeanie writes her story so quickly that she pays little attention to spelling and punctuation. If Jeanie had had a computer available, she could have entered her story and used software to check her spelling and grammar and to print out a clean, revised version. Find out what software programs are available that help writers learn or check grammar and spelling. Are any available on your school's computers? If possible, create your written assignments for this lesson using a word processing program and check for technical errors with an appropriate software program. Then proofread to make sure the computer programs did their jobs.

## UNDERSTANDING

1. Find examples of Jeanie's actions and words that reveal information about her personality. What do you learn about Jeanie as she goes home from school?

    Watch a television situation comedy or a movie. Study the behavior of one character. What do the character's actions reveal about his or her personality?

2.  Examine the scene between Jeanie and her mother. What does Jeanie do that tells you how she feels about her mother? About her brother? How would you characterize the mood of Jeanie's home?

    Working in a group, find examples of nonverbal communication in the story. Make a list of all the times when characters *show* anger, frustration, impatience, or other emotions through actions alone.

3. What was Miss Lowy's assignment for her students? What does Jeanie use as subject matter for her writing? Why is she successful? Write a one-page letter or send an e-mail message to a childhood friend describing the reality or truth in your life and how it is beautiful. ***Workshops 16 and 18***

## CONNECTING

1. Helen Keller said, "I love the beautiful truth." Truth is beautiful by virtue of its very existence. To tell the truth in prose, song, painting, or poetry strikes a chord in all of us. Find a recording of a song that, for you, tells something true about life. Play it to the class. Then describe for the class what seems true in the song for you.

2. Jeanie is under a lot of pressure. She has assignments due at school and considerable conflict at home. How does this make her feel? What does she do to relieve the stress?

    Interview four or five people of different ages. Find out how they cope with stress and make a list of their stress relief techniques. Then use the *Reader's Guide to Periodical Literature* or search the Internet to find an article on stress relief. Write a news article for the school newspaper about how students can relieve stress with the use of several stress relief techniques. ***Workshops 19 and 26***

---

### A LAST WORD

At certain times in your life, you may have difficulty dealing with stresses at home, school, or work. How might your own self-image affect the way in which you cope with stress? How might a clear understanding of your talents and skills help you in times of difficulty?

---

# Life and Death

- *Farewell*
- *Making a Fist*
- *A Day's Wait*

## EXPLORING

The concept of death is difficult to understand and describe. How can we describe what we have never experienced? How is death different from life? How do you explain a place if you have never been there? List where you will be in a week, a month, a year. Consider how you'll feel then and there. How will that differ from how you feel now?

## THEME CONNECTION...
## LEARNING NOT TO FEAR THE FUTURE

In "Farewell," the poet defines life as brief and difficult to grasp. "Making a Fist" emphasizes what it means to live; to be able to make a fist is to survive. In "A Day's Wait," ignorance keeps a boy from understanding the truth about his own medical condition, causing unnecessary anxiety.

## TIME & PLACE

The author of "Farewell," Isapo-muxika, is a member of the Crow Indian tribe, one of a number of tribes that formerly hunted buffalo on the Great Plains. The poet makes references to nature, a common element in Native-American writing.

The narrator in "Making a Fist" is taking a modern-day car trip to Tampico, an important port city in Mexico. The trip from Texas to Tampico would be a long day's ride.

Ernest Hemingway writes "A Day's Wait" from personal experience; his own son had fallen ill. The story is set in the 1940s.

## THE WRITER'S CRAFT
### SPARE DETAILS

Ernest Hemingway is the master of writing with strong, brief language, often implying relationships and images with a single word, such as *we* or *they*. His brevity packs power; the reader is left to focus on only the essential details.

In the same way, Isapo-muxika suggests the essence of life in a few brief metaphorical phrases. And the mother in "Making a Fist" delivers a brief answer to a child's question.

# *Farewell*

Isapo-muxika (Crowfoot)

A little while
and
I will be gone from among you,
whither I cannot tell.
From nowhere we come;
into nowhere we go.

What is life?
It is a flash of a firefly
in the night.
It is a breath of a buffalo
in the winter time.
It is the little shadow
that runs across the grass
and loses itself in the sunset. ❖

# Making a Fist

Naomi Shihab Nye

For the first time, on the road north of Tampico,
I felt the life sliding out of me,
a drum in the desert, harder and harder to hear.
I was seven, I lay in the car
watching palm trees swirl a sickening pattern past the glass.
My stomach was a melon split wide inside my skin.

"How do you know if you are going to die?"
I begged my mother.
We had been traveling for days.
With strange confidence she answered,
"When you can no longer make a fist."

Years later I smile to think of that journey,
the borders we must cross separately,
stamped with our unanswerable woes.
I who did not die, who am still living,
still lying in the backseat behind all my questions,
clenching and opening one small hand. ❖

**About the Author**

Naomi Shihab Nye grew up in St. Louis, Missouri; Jerusalem, Israel; and San Antonio, Texas, where she now lives. She travels to schools throughout the United States as a visiting writer. She has also traveled to the Middle East and Asia on several speaking tours. Her poems have appeared in many collections and anthologies.

# A Day's Wait

## Ernest Hemingway

He came into the room to shut the windows while we were still in bed and I saw he looked ill. He was shivering, his face was white, and he walked slowly as though it ached to move.

"What's the matter, **Schatz**?"

"I've got a headache."

"You better go back to bed."

"No. I'm all right."

"You go to bed. I'll see you when I'm dressed."

But when I came downstairs he was dressed, sitting by the fire, looking a very sick and miserable boy of nine years. When I put my hand on his forehead I knew he had a fever.

"You go up to bed," I said, "you're sick."

"I'm all right," he said.

When the doctor came he took the boy's temperature.

"What is it?" I asked him.

"One hundred and two."

Downstairs, the doctor left three different medicines in different colored capsules with instructions for giving them. One was to bring down the fever, another a **purgative**, the third to overcome an acid condition. The germs of influenza can only exist in an acid condition, he explained. He seemed to know all about influenza and said there was nothing to worry about if the fever did not go above one hundred and four degrees. This was a light epidemic of flu and there was no danger if you avoided pneumonia.

Back in the room I wrote the boy's temperature down and made a note of the time to give the various capsules.

"Do you want me to read to you?"

"All right. If you want to," said the boy. His face was very white and there were dark areas under his eyes. He lay still in the bed and seemed very detached from what was going on.

I read aloud from Howard Pyle's *Book of Pirates;* but I could see he was not following what I was reading.

"How do you feel, Schatz?" I asked him.

"Just the same, so far," he said.

I sat at the foot of the bed and read to myself while I waited for it to be time to give another capsule. It would have been natural for him to go to sleep, but when I looked up he was looking at the foot of the bed, looking very strangely.

"Why don't you try to go to sleep? I'll wake you up for the medicine."

"I'd rather stay awake."

After a while he said to me, "You don't have to stay in here with me, Papa, if it bothers you."

"It doesn't bother me."

"No, I mean you don't have to stay if it's going to bother you."

I thought perhaps he was a little lightheaded and after giving him the prescribed capsules at eleven o'clock I went out for a while.

## About the Author

The novelist and short-story writer Ernest Hemingway (1899–1961) was born in Oak Park, Illinois. He played football and began writing news columns and short stories in high school. His early short stories hint at the concise style for which he would later become famous. Hemingway decided against attending college and instead moved to Kansas City, where he found a job on the Kansas City *Star.* Through the years, Hemingway built his reputation on such honored novels as *A Farewell to Arms* and *For Whom the Bell Tolls.*

Schatz— German for "treasure"; a term of endearment

purgative—a medicine that causes a clearing of the intestines

## FOCUS ON... MATHEMATICS

The boy in "A Day's Wait" confuses the Fahrenheit and Celsius scales for temperature measurement. If everyone used the same system of measurement, confusions such as this could be avoided. Research the metric system. Why is it a logical system for all measurements in science, industry, and commerce? Why are people in the United States slow to accept and use this system? Debate the pros and cons of converting to the metric system.

◆ ◆ ◆ ◆ ◆ ◆ ◆ ◆ ◆ ◆ ◆ ◆ ◆ ◆ ◆ ◆ ◆ ◆ ◆ ◆ ◆ ◆ ◆ ◆ ◆ ◆ ◆ ◆ ◆ ◆ ◆ ◆ ◆ ◆ ◆ ◆ ◆ ◆ ◆ ◆ ◆ ◆

covey—small
flock

It was a bright, cold day, the ground covered with a sleet that had frozen so that it seemed as if all the bare trees, the bushes, the cut brush and all the grass and the bare ground had been varnished with ice. I took the young Irish setter for a little walk up the road and along a frozen creek, but it was difficult to stand or walk on the glassy surface and the red dog slipped and slithered and I fell twice, hard, once dropping my gun and having it slide away over the ice.

We flushed a **covey** of quail under a high clay bank with overhanging brush and I killed two as they went out of sight over the top of the bank. Some of the covey lit in trees, but most of them scattered into brush piles and it was necessary to jump on the ice-coated mounds of brush several times before they would flush. Coming out while you were poised unsteadily on the icy, springy brush they made difficult shooting and I killed two, missed five, and

started back pleased to have found a covey close to the house and happy there were so many left to find on another day.

At the house they said the boy had refused to let anyone come into the room.

"You can't come in," he said. "You mustn't get what I have."

I went up to him and found him in exactly the position I had left him, white-faced, but with the tops of his cheeks flushed by the fever, staring still, as he had stared, at the foot of the bed.

I took his temperature.

"What is it?"

"Something like a hundred," I said. It was one hundred and two and four tenths.

"It was a hundred and two," he said.

"Who said so?"

"The doctor."

"Your temperature is all right," I said. "It's nothing to worry about."

"I don't worry," he said, "but I can't keep from thinking."

"Don't think," I said. "Just take it easy."

"I'm taking it easy," he said and looked straight ahead. He was evidently holding tight onto himself about something.

"Take this with water."

"Do you think it will do any good?"

"Of course it will."

I sat down and opened the *Pirate* book and commenced to read, but I could see he was not following, so I stopped.

"About what time do you think I'm going to die?" he asked.

"What?"

"About how long will it be before I die?"

"You aren't going to die. What's the matter with you?"

"Oh, yes, I am. I heard him say a hundred and two."

"People don't die with a fever of one hundred and two. That's a silly way to talk."

"I know they do. At school in France the boys told me you can't live with forty-four degrees. I've got a hundred and two."

He had been waiting to die all day, ever since nine o'clock in the morning.

"You poor Schatz," I said. "Poor old Schatz. It's like miles and kilometers. You aren't going to die. That's a different thermometer. On that thermometer thirty-seven is normal. On this kind it's ninety-eight."

"Are you sure?"

"Absolutely," I said. "It's like miles and kilometers. You know, like how many kilometers we make when we do seventy miles in the car?"

"Oh," he said.

But his gaze at the foot of the bed relaxed slowly. The hold over himself relaxed too, finally, and the next day it was very slack and he cried very easily at little things that were of no importance. ❖

## ON THE JOB
### NURSE

Licensed practical nurses (LPNs) help doctors and registered nurses (RNs) care for patients in hospitals, nursing homes, and other health care facilities. They have the technical knowledge to perform routine nursing duties, such as taking patients' blood pressure. LPNs have a great deal of contact with patients, so it is important that they have good interpersonal skills. All nurses must be able to follow directions precisely. Useful high school courses include science, math, and health.

## UNDERSTANDING

1.   Find the exact line in "A Day's Wait" when the boy hints that he misunderstands the seriousness of his condition. What is the foundation for his misunderstanding? What comparison does the father use to teach the boy? Find evidence of the boy's change when he finally understands. In groups, brainstorm other comparisons that would help the boy understand. Rewrite the ending of the story using the best comparison.

2.  In "Making a Fist," how are the fist and the car ride symbols of larger concepts? Write a short narrative essay about a car ride you have taken. Identify the main points, then edit your essay to include only two or three of the main points. *Workshop 9*

3.  How does the subject of "Farewell" change from one stanza to the next? Organizing and separating ideas visually helps us communicate more clearly. Make a list of the things you need to do before a long trip, such as pack, purchase tickets, and take the dog to the kennel. Then organize the list and put it in order of priority.

## CONNECTING

1.  Misunderstandings can disrupt business. Choose an issue in your class, organization, or team that could cause confusion. Write a short memo to the teacher, coach, or advisor that will help to avoid misunderstandings among staff, faculty, team members, parents, and students. *Workshop 18*

2.  The writers in this lesson try to introduce us to the concept of death, something we've never experienced. Plan a trip to a place you've never been—a state park, another country. Gather information, pictures, brochures, and files from a travel agency and from the Internet. Collect the materials in a notebook. Speculate in a paragraph about what you think it will be like there. How will it compare to where you are? *Workshop 8*

3.   *Money* magazine publishes an annual list of the best places to live. Research the magazine's criteria for a healthy community. In small groups, rate your own community according to these criteria. Prepare a panel presentation for your class and share in a discussion. *Workshop 15*

### A LAST WORD

We do not live forever. How might an understanding and acceptance of our own mortality help us lead more courageous lives? How might we have a greater appreciation of life with each new day?

# The Savings Book

## EXPLORING

Poverty means different things to different people. The meaning of the term varies from town to town, country to country. Do you worry about being in poverty? Consider being truly poor—not having enough to eat, and no resources to *get* anything to eat. Do you have a plan for saving and spending that you trust will keep you out of poverty?

## THEME CONNECTION... LEARNING TO RECORD YOUR LIFE

A savings book records the transactions—deposits and withdrawals—of your bank account. It shows when you made, saved, and spent money. It is a journal of the comings and goings of your financial resources. The narrator of the essay learns that a savings book records not only his finances but his life.

| DATE | DEPOSIT | WITHDRAWAL | INTEREST | BALANCE |
|------|---------|------------|----------|---------|
| 5/27/69 | $14.00 | | | $14.00 |
| 6/9/69 | | $4.00 | | $10.00 |
| 6/20/69 | | $3.25 | | $6.75 |
| 6/30/69 | | | $.05 | $6.80 |
| 7/13/69 | | $5.80 | | $1.00 |
| 9/5/69 | $140.00 | | | $141.00 |
| 9/15/69 | | $15.00 | | $126.00 |
| 9/24/69 | | $6.00 | | $120.00 |

SAVINGS          PASSBOOK

## TIME & PLACE

During the 1970s, when the action in "The Savings Book" occurs, the United States experienced a recession—an overall decline in business activity. Buying, selling, and producing decreased. Therefore, the number of jobs decreased as well. High unemployment made poverty a fact of life for many families.

## THE WRITER'S CRAFT

### REPETITION

Repetition is the repeated use of words and phrases to create a specific effect on the reader. Speechwriters repeat phrases to emphasize points that are meant to impress audiences. Poets repeat more than words; they repeat sounds to produce rhythm. In "The Savings Book," the author repeats dates to emphasize the frequency of his transactions and to tie the story together.

# The Savings Book

Gary Soto

## About the Author

While growing up in Fresno, California, Gary Soto (b. 1952) couldn't decide whether he wanted to be a priest, a migratory worker, or a paleontologist. Then, in college, he discovered poetry. Soto says, "I don't think I had any literary aspirations when I was a kid. In fact, we didn't have books, and no one encouraged us to read. So my wanting to write poetry was a sort of fluke." Soto is best known for his poetry, though he also writes short stories and essays. Soto's work is often based on his own experiences growing up in a Mexican-American community.

rescinded— voided; taken back

My wife, Carolyn, married me for my savings: Not the double digit figures but the strange three or four dollar withdrawals and deposits. The first time she saw my passbook she laughed until her eyes became moist and then hugged me as she called "Poor baby." And there was truth to what she was saying: Poor.

I remember opening my savings account at Guarantee Savings May 27, 1969, which was a Monday. The previous Saturday my brother and I had taken a labor bus to chop cotton in the fields west of Fresno. We returned home in the back of a pickup with fourteen dollars each and a Mexican national who kept showing us watches and rings for us to buy. That day my brother and I wouldn't spring for Cokes or sandwiches, as most everyone else on our crew did when a vending truck drove up at lunch time, tooting a loud horn. The driver opened the aluminum doors to display his goods, and the workers, who knew better but couldn't resist, hovered over the iced Cokes, the cellophaned sandwiches, and the Hostess cupcakes.

We looked on from the shade of the bus, sullen and most certainly sensible. Why pay forty cents when you could get a Coke in town for half the price. Why buy a sandwich for sixty-five cents when you could have slapped together your own sandwich. That was what our mother had done for us. She had made us tuna sandwiches which by noon had grown suspiciously sour when we peeled back the top slice to peek in. Still, we ate them, chewing slowly and watching each other to see if he were beginning to double over. Finished, we searched the paper bag and found a broken stock of saltine crackers wrapped in wax paper. What a cruel mother, we thought. Dry crackers on a dry day when it was sure to rise into the nineties as we chopped cotton or, as the saying went, "played Mexican golf."

We had each earned fourteen dollars for eight hours of work, the most money I had ever made in one day. Two days later, on May 27, 1969, I deposited those dollars; on June 9th I made my first withdrawal—four dollars to buy a belt to match a pair of pants. I had just been hired to sell encyclopedias, and the belt was intended to dazzle my prospective clients when they opened the door to receive me. But in reality few welcomed my presence on their doorsteps and the only encyclopedias I sold that summer were to families on welfare who so desperately wanted to rise from their soiled lives. Buy a set, I told them, and your problems will disappear. Knowledge is power. Education is the key to the future, and so on. The contracts, however, were **rescinded** and my commissions with them.

On June 20 I withdrew three dollars and twenty-five cents to buy a plain white shirt because my boss had suggested that I should look more "professional." Still, I sold encyclopedias to the poor and again the contracts were thrown out. Finally I was fired, my briefcase taken away, and the company tie undone from my neck. I walked home in the summer heat despairing at the consequence: No new clothes for the fall.

On July 13 I took out five dollars and eighty cents which, including the five cents interest earned, left me with a balance of one dollar. I used the money for bus fare to Los Angeles to look for work. I found it in a tire factory. At summer's end I returned home and walked proudly to Guarantee Savings with my pockets stuffed with ten dollar bills. That was September 5, and my new balance jumped to one hundred and forty-one dollars. I was a senior in high school and any withdrawals from my account went exclusively to buy clothes, never for food, record albums, or con-

certs. On September 15, for instance, I withdrew fifteen dollars for a shirt and jeans. On September 24 I again stood before the teller to ask for six dollars. I bought a sweater at the Varsity Shop at Coffee's.

Slowly my savings dwindled that fall semester, although I did beef it up with small deposits: Twenty dollars on October 1, ten dollars on November 19, fifteen dollars on December 31, and so on. But by February my savings account balance read three dollars and twelve cents. On March 2 I returned to the bank to withdraw one crisp dollar to do God knows what. Perhaps it was to buy my mother a birthday gift. Seven days later, on March 10, I made one last attempt to bolster my savings by adding eight dollars. By March 23, however, I was again down to one dollar.

By the time I finally closed my account, it had fluctuated for five years, rising and falling as a barometer to my financial quandary. What is curious to me about this personal history are the kinds of

The Savings Book

testimony—evidence of a fact

transactions that took place—one day I would withdraw three dollars while on another day I would ask for six. How did it vanish? What did it buy? I'm almost certain I bought clothes but for what occasion? For whom? I didn't have a girlfriend in my senior year, so where did the money go?

To withdraw those minor amounts was no easy task. I had to walk or bicycle nearly four miles, my good friend Scott tagging along, and afterward we'd walk up and down the Fresno Mall in search of the elusive girlfriend or, if worse come to worst, to look for trouble.

My savings book is a **testimony** to my fear of poverty—that by saving a dollar here, another there, it would be kept at bay.

I admit that as a kid I worried about starving, although there was probably no reason. There was always something to eat; the cupboards were weighed down with boxes of this and that. But when I was older the remembrance of difficult times stayed with me: The time Mother was picking grapes and my brother ate our entire lunch while my sister and I played under the vines. For us there was nothing to eat that day. The time I opened the refrigerator at my father's (who was separated from our mother at the time) to stare at one puckered apple that sat in the conspicuous glare of the refrigerator's light. I recalled my uncle lying on a couch dying of cancer. I recalled my father who died from an accident a year later and left us in even more roughed up shoes. I had not been born to be scared out of my wits, but that is what happened. Through a set of experiences early in my life, I grew up fearful that some financial tragedy would strike at any moment, as

when I was certain that the recession of 1973 would lead to chaos—burned cars and street fighting. During the recession I roomed with my brother and I suggested that we try to become vegetarians. My brother looked up from his drawing board and replied: "Aren't we already?" I thought about it for a while, and it was true. I was getting most of my hearty meals from my girlfriend, Carolyn, who would later become my wife. She had a job with great pay, and when she opened her refrigerator I almost wept for the bologna, sliced ham, and drumsticks. I spied the cheeses and imported olives, tomatoes, and the artichoke hearts. I opened the freezer—chocolate ice cream!

At that time Carolyn put up with my antics, so when I suggested that we buy fifty dollars worth of peanut butter and pinto beans to store under her bed, she happily wrote out a check because she was in love and didn't know any better. I was certain that in 1974 the country would slide into a depression and those who were not prepared would be lost. We hid the rations in the house and sat at the front window to wait for something to happen.

What happened was that we married and I loosened up. I still fear the worst, but the worst is not what it once was. Today I bought a pair of shoes; tomorrow I may splurge to see a movie, with a box of popcorn and a large soda that will wash it all down. It's time to live, I tell myself, and if a five dollar bill flutters from my hands, no harm will result. I laugh at the funny scenes that aren't funny, and I can't think of any better life. ❖

## UNDERSTANDING

1.  Find evidence that the narrator is afraid of poverty. How does he avoid poverty? With a partner, make a list of safeguards you know to prevent poverty. Write a memo telling someone your own age about smart practices to avoid financial difficulties. **Workshop 18**

2. Who saves foods and provisions in the story? What organizations in your community help families in times of need? Write a letter of request to the Red Cross or some other organization. Ask for information about how to prepare for hard times or for disasters. **Workshop 17**

3. Find information in the text that tells why Carolyn married the narrator. From his financial record Carolyn inferred that he was going to be financially responsible. What can you infer from a person's bank records?

    Each issue of *Money* magazine features a family's financial situation. The article covers the family's saving and spending habits. Bring an issue to class and share the article with your classmates.

## A LAST WORD

What are some of the similarities between Soto's experience and poverty today? What might a person do to avoid poverty? How might a strong savings plan today benefit you in the future?

## CONNECTING

1. Investigate the savings plans at two or three banks in your area. Work as a group to write a pamphlet for teens to help them choose savings programs appropriate for their needs and goals. **Workshop 20**

2. Credit cards are being used by younger consumers every day. Research the credit card application process. Find out how a customer gets accepted by a card company. Put together a folder of application forms and brochures explaining the use and care of credit cards. Invite a banker to speak to your class. Prepare questions that focus on credit habits and how *bad* credit can become a problem. **Workshop 26**

## ON THE JOB
### BANK TELLER

Bank tellers handle customers' deposit and withdrawal transactions. Tellers are responsible for the money in their cash drawers and for all the checks, deposits, loan payments, and other money they receive during the day. After banking hours, tellers settle their accounts on a settlement sheet, which records the days' activities. To prepare in high school for a job as a bank teller, you can take business math courses and other courses in which you learn to use business machines.

# *Advice for All*

- *Advice to the Young*
- *The Secluded Lot*
- *Primer Lesson*

## EXPLORING

Teens and young people receive much advice from parents, neighbors, coaches, bosses, and others. It is difficult to sort out all the advice that is offered, especially because most of us learn best through experience. However, sometimes following advice helps prevent pain or embarrassment. Discuss a time when advice from others helped you. What advice have you *not* followed? List several pieces of advice you have received, who gave them, and why.

## THEME CONNECTION...
## LEARNING FROM ADVICE

Young people can benefit from the advice of those who are older and more experienced. They can learn from the successes and failures of family members, acquaintances, and public figures. Good advice might help a young person make a difficult decision, resolve a conflict, or avoid a danger.

## TIME & PLACE

As with all good advice, the advice in these selections is timeless. It is relevant to all people, regardless of age. None of the writers included any clues to give readers a sense of a particular time or place. The story and poems are set in modern times and could occur in any area.

## THE WRITER'S CRAFT

### MORAL

A moral is an instructive lesson about right and wrong, often told in fables or parables but also in short stories and poems. Each of the three pieces delivers a moral lesson to the reader. The narrator in "Advice to the Young" instructs young people to pursue simple work to discover life's truth. In "The Secluded Lot," the lesson is that appearances can be deceiving. In "Primer Lesson," the narrator warns against speaking words that we might later regret saying.

# Advice to the Young

Miriam Waddington

**1**
keep bees and
grow asparagus,
watch the tides
and listen to the
wind instead of
the politicians
make up your own
stories and believe
them if you want to
live the good life.

**2**
All rituals
are instincts
never fully
trust them
study to im-
prove biology
with reason.

**3**
Digging trenches
for asparagus
is good for the
muscles and
waiting for the
plants to settle
teaches patience
to those who are
usually in too
much of a hurry.

**4**
There is morality
in bee-keeping
it teaches how
not to be afraid
of the bee swarm
it teaches how
not to be afraid of
finding new places
and building them
all over again. ❖

# The Secluded Lot

## Elizabeth Morison Townshend

blazoned—dis-
played boldly

consecrated—
declared sacred

plaintive—sad

veritable—
actual, not
imaginary

"I'd like to inquire about a lot," the old man said, the effort of decision evident in his voice. "At my age you never know . . ."

"It's a good investment," Mr. Jerome replied. Through years of experience he knew these rather delicate matters must be handled with a businesslike approach. "Lots have gone up a good third in value over the past few years. That is, if you ever wanted to resell."

"No, I won't want to resell."

Mr. Jerome looked at the old man thoughtfully. The old-timer was difficult to bracket. *Don't be fooled by the frayed cuffs,* he told himself, *there's probably more life savings under his mattress than most people have in the bank.*

"This section was just opened up last year," he said, pointing to the large map on the wall. It might have been any map in any real estate office, except for the heading. The dreaded title was **blazoned** forth:

### REST HAVEN CEMETERY

"I'd prefer an older location." The old man looked down at his unpolished shoes, embarrassed. "I mean, where trees and shrubs have had a chance to grow."

"We've still a few left in the older sections—at various price ranges. The Avenue lots are more expensive, of course."

"Too much traffic," the old man said.

"There's one or two on Ridge Road and Cypress Hill—exclusive areas, many old families up there."

"I'd like a good view," the old man explained. "but more important, privacy."

"That will run the price up," Mr. Jerome warned. He was not sure how much price mattered.

"Haven't you something out of the way, sort of hard to find? I don't want relatives interfering—nosing about, you know."

Mr. Jerome studied the map thoughtfully. The blacked-in marks indicated which plots had been sold and occupied. With the exception of the new areas, there were few white vacancies left.

"There might be room for just one more off Willow Walk here," he said. "Needs a bit of clearing, though, and a proper entrance. It would be very private."

"Just the one?"

"Yes."

"Then I think I'd like to see it—if you have the time."

Mr. Jerome looked at his watch: "Yes, I will have the time."

"The size?"

"A little bigger than standard: one by two and a half yards—sets off the head-stone just right."

They entered a black limousine and drove slowly through the cemetery. The shade trees stretched their branches over the **consecrated** ground. A warbler began its **plaintive** melody. Others joined the chant, until a **veritable** choir filled the air. Through the open window came the fragrant smells of spring. Here were splashes of brilliant pink azaleas, extravagant dogwoods, forsythia with weeping golden blossoms. They passed prim beds of narcissi and tulips, clumps of bleeding-heart, drifts of daisies and forget-me-nots among the low-growing evergreens.

"Spring is kind of a promise," the old man was saying, obviously moved.

All winter Mr. Jerome, the head gardener and the men at the greenhouse had planned and anticipated just this impression. Now it all seemed so spontaneous and natural—worth hiring the extra clippers and cutters, seeders and transplanters. Yes, Mr. Jerome was pleased.

Where Willow Walk circled downhill again, the limousine came to a halt. Mr. Jerome guided the old man between chiselled, high-polish marbles, between tall and rectangular shafts of granite.

"That's Carrara marble," Mr. Jerome informed him. "This is Vermont. Nice color, that rose—specially imported Aberdeen granite—about the most durable there is." Carefully circling a slightly raised mound, Mr. Jerome continued: "Now don't let them fool you on synthetics—that new cement and marble chip mix—it won't hold up at all."

Parting the branches of the heavy thicket, Mr. Jerome led the way. Against a natural crag was just room for a bigger than standard lot. Covered with a tangle of unruly vines and underbrush, it was obviously an afterthought.

"Well, here we are," Mr. Jerome said brightly. It was in far worse condition than he remembered and quite inaccessible. Besides, a bramble had caught on the sleeve of his good suit and left a slight tear.

"Of course, it needs a little fixing."

"No, I like it the way it is—wild and secret and uncared-for—hidden by the thicket of branches."

For some time, the old man stood there, gazing off into the distance. "Am I allowed . . . " he hesitated, correcting himself. "Is the purchaser allowed to visit it at any time?"

"Come as often as you like," Mr. Jerome adjusted his black tie. "Perpetual care, you know, is included in the purchase price."

"I don't want perpetual care." The old gentleman was indignant. "As if you could make promises for the next generation and the next. I mean, with atomic and hydrogen bombs and goodness knows what else."

"Then in that case, we could give you a special price."

In Mr. Jerome's language this meant the highest possible figure at which the customer would buy. Shrewdly, he estimated the demand, the desire and upped the figure ten per cent.

"It's higher than I thought," the old man said sadly. "But it's just what I wanted."

"Then why not take it?" Mr. Jerome was an expert in these matters. "After all, it's for eternity."

"And eternity," the old man added, "is kind of a long time."

"Then it's settled." Mr. Jerome hastened to close the deal. "The contract can be worded to accord with your wishes."

"My last wishes," the old man said.

Mr. Jerome was glad to be back in the safety of his mahogany office again. Carefully he crossed out the *Perpetual Care* clause and instructed his secretary, Miss Jones, to type in the old man's name on the blank lines between the small print—*Mortimer Blake.*

cortège—a
funeral
procession

The old man adjusted his glasses, but the print was obviously too fine for him to read.

"No loans or mortgages may be raised on a burial lot, you understand—nor can they be seized for debt." Mr. Jerome recited the routine clauses with a let's-be-done-with-it indifference.

Waiting, embarrassed, the old man glanced at the file clerk—sorting a large stack of documents and correspondence. This particular one had her puzzled. Undecided, she slipped it into a box marked "Pending," and the old man wondered what, under the circumstances, *pending* might mean.

"Please sign here." Mr. Jerome pushed the document towards him. The old man signed in a shaky hand.

"Good afternoon, Rest Haven." Miss Jones used just the right intonation over the telephone. "Services tomorrow at eleven in the chapel."

The telephone rang again. "It's about that advertisement in the *Herald,* sir."

Mr. Jerome picked up the receiver. "The same ad—just a gentle reminder," he said, "and the usual space."

Slowly old Mr. Blake counted out his money. Yes he had brought the entire sum in cash. Between phone calls, Mr. Jerome made out a receipt and handed him his copy. "Good morning, Rest Haven," the efficient Miss Jones was saying. Then her voice took on that tone of practiced solemnity: "One minute, please . . ."

Fumbling with his hat, the old man started for the door.

During the ensuing year old man Blake made periodic visits to his lot. All the workmen in the cemetery knew him by name. But in this separate little world, where personal feelings were respected, nobody thought it odd that he went quite regularly to commune with nature and the life everlasting.

As a **cortège** neared Willow Walk, Mr. Jerome could see the old man in the distance, parting the bushes and disappearing from view. After the Committal Service—when everything possible had been done for the Departed and the Bereaved had gone their sorrowful ways—something prompted Mr. Jerome to intrude on the old man's privacy—perhaps a word or two of comfort, which he knew so well how to administer.

On the other side of the thicket he was surprised to find Mr. Blake stooping over a high, square, white box, intent on fixing something. A bee circled slowly overhead, then dove for its target.

"Ouch!" yelled Mr. Jerome. "That cursed bee stung me."

"I'm sorry," the old man said, "but that sting cost the bee its life."

Then it was that Mr. Jerome began to understand. The full implications left him aghast. There was no precedent for this in all cemetery history.

"How dare you operate a beehive in this cemetery?"

"It's on my property. I purchased it, did I not?"

"No business such as this is allowed within this sanctuary."

"I'm not soliciting business. The bees are just going about their normal and natural pursuits. Besides, Rose Haven Nectar brings a special price."

"You sell the honey?" Jerome was shocked.

"Maybe it was just beginner's luck," old man Blake replied modestly, "but those twenty-dollar Beginner's Beekeeping Outfits certainly work wonders. Like the advertisement said, I had over 100 pounds of surplus honey the first year."

## FOCUS ON...
## BIOLOGY

Mr. Blake takes great pleasure in bee-keeping and is quite successful at it. To Mr. Jerome's outcry of protest, Mr. Blake reminds him that bees pollinate the flowers. Research the process of plant pollination. Are there different methods? How are bees involved? How do bees make honey? Create a diagram illustrating the pollination process.

"This is preposterous!" Mr. Jerome exploded, his highly trained sensitivities deeply offended.

"Experienced beekeepers figure one to two **hectares** of heavy flowering plants for each colony of bees," the old man went on. "Of course, in my small rooming house it was out of the question. Then I saw this beautiful land and acquired property of my own."

"It's dreadful—unheard of," Jerome sputtered.

"You don't need much capital," the old man continued with enthusiasm. "Only queen-size cells with eggs inside and some royal jelly. The worker bees do the rest."

"All this time, a veritable factory." Mr. Jerome was beside himself. "All right under my very nose."

"With good beekeeping management, the colonies should increase to thirty in a few years."

"Oh, no!" Jerome's well-modulated voice rose to a shout: "Look here, I won't have it. You must stop this at once!"

"Why should you want me to stop?"

"For obvious reasons: we can't have the mourners stung. . . . "

"Mr. Jerome, I have done you a great service. Your flowers have never been so magnificent or plentiful."

"That's true," he was forced to admit.

"Why? Because of my bees. They pollinate your flowers. Now, if you could spare me a few moments."

At that particular second Mr. Jerome was fully occupied, easing another attacker gently off the lapel of his serge suit. All his spare time would be devoted to a solution of Mr. Blake's special problem. *It must be illegal,* he thought, with every intention of rushing back to the office to examine the small print.

The old man straightened and looked at him proudly.

"Mr. Jerome, I have reached an important decision: I should like to buy another lot." ❖

hectare—1 hectare equals 10,000 square meters, or approximately 2.5 acres

# Primer Lesson

Carl Sandburg

Look out how you use proud words.
When you let proud words go, it is
   not easy to call them back.
They wear long boots, hard boots; they
   Walk off proud; they can't hear you
   calling—
Look out how you use proud words. ❖

## SPOTLIGHT ON... ACCURACY

Carl Sandburg urges care and caution in the use of words. What would life be like if we didn't exercise caution? What would life be like if we acted without a care for accuracy? Here are a few extreme examples of what life would be like if we did our jobs accurately only 99.9 percent of the time.

- 50 newborn babies would be dropped at birth by doctors every day.
- 22,000 checks would be deducted from wrong bank accounts each hour.
- 16,000 pieces of mail would be lost by the U.S. Postal Service every hour.
- Two planes would not land safely at O'Hare International Airport in Chicago every day.

Source: *Inc. Magazine*, April 1989.

◆◆◆◆◆◆◆◆◆◆◆◆◆◆◆◆◆◆◆◆◆

# UNDERSTANDING

1. "The Secluded Lot" is told from a limited omniscient point of view. Readers see events primarily through Mr. Jerome's eyes and values. However, the details lead us to believe that a surprise is in store for us. Find the lines where you first began to suspect that the old man had a different plan for the property.

    Often land finds new uses. Have you had any property development in your area? Has land been used one way one year and a different way another year? Explain. Write a short news article describing such a situation. **Workshop 19**

2. The speaker in "Advice to the Young" says that the young need to learn patience. Do you agree? Write an essay examining the pace of life for today's teenagers. If you were to slow down, what would you do with the extra time? Create a week's calendar of your life's events now. Write down everything, including time spent viewing television and just relaxing. With a marker, indicate your free time.

3.  What "proud words"—brags, boasts, and self-congratulations—do you hear at school? List them. Manufacturers brag about their products all the time in advertising. Working in a group, find three print advertisements and mount them on paper. Circle the proud words in each. Are the words *too* proud? Decide whether your group thinks the company can live up to its words. **Workshop 24**

## A LAST WORD

Carl Sandburg advises against using proud words. Miriam Waddington and the character Mr. Blake advocate beekeeping. What advice might you offer to the young on living a good life?

# CONNECTING

1. What are your ideas about "the good life"? What sorts of things are there to be enjoyed? List all that seems good about life. Then divide the list into two categories: things that cost money (cars, homes, trips), and things that don't cost money (colorful sunsets, wildflowers, good conversation). Write a letter or poem of advice to a young child based on your observances.

2. Advertisers walk a fine line between telling the truth and boasting too much about a product's attributes or characteristics. When an advertisement does overstate a product's attributes, it is called false advertising. While viewing television, notice the commercials carefully. Select two that you think are accurate; then select two that seem to be simply empty bragging. Videotape the commercials, if possible, and show the tapes in class. Discuss the importance to society of truth in advertising. **Workshop 24**

# Translating Grandfather's House

## EXPLORING

● ● ● ● ● ● ● ● ● ● ● ● ● ● ●

When we translate, we change words, usually from one language to another, so that those who don't know the original language can understand a thought or idea. Have you ever needed to explain something over again in a different way in order for your listeners to understand your point? How did you find a way of telling your story so that others could understand?

## THEME CONNECTION...
## A LESSON IN ATTITUDES

If people in an audience are not receptive, a speaker might reach them by changing the way he or she delivers the message. Sometimes an audience is not ready or able to understand a message. The young child in this poem learns firsthand that some people have stereotypes or attitudes that are difficult to change.

## TIME & PLACE

Cuban Americans are one of the three largest Hispanic groups in the United States. Many Hispanic immigrant children go back and forth between speaking one language and another—Spanish at home and English at school or work. They are translating wherever they are, it seems. This and other poems by Hispanic Americans explore the process of translating between worlds, or between imagination and reality.

## THE WRITER'S CRAFT

### CONTENT LANGUAGE

Poetry is concentrated language. The concentration comes from the content words—words that are full of meaning, often creating vivid images in the mind. Phrases such as "rows of lemon and mango trees" or "shadow of a palomino" create images in the reader's mind. Rich content language conveys meaning effectively and efficiently.

# Translating Grandfather's House

E. J. Vega

According to my sketch,
Rows of lemon & mango
Trees frame the courtyard
Of Grandfather's stone
And clapboard home;
The shadow of a palomino
Gallops on the lip
Of the horizon.

The teacher says
The house is from
Some Zorro
Movie I've seen.

"Ask my mom," I protest.
"She was born there—
Right there on the second floor!"

Crossing her arms she moves on.

Memories once certain as rivets
Become confused as awakenings
In strange places and I question
The house, the horse, the wrens
Perched on the slate roof—
The roof Oscar Jartín
Tumbled from one hot Tuesday,
Installing a new weather vane;
(He broke a shin and two fingers).
Classmates finish drawings of New York City
Housing projects on Navy Street.
I draw one too, with wildgrass
Rising from sidewalk cracks like widows.
In big round letters I title it:

GRANDFATHER'S HOUSE

Beaming, the teacher scrawls
An A+ in the corner and tapes
It to the green blackboard.

To the green blackboard. ❖

**About the Author**

E. J. Vega, a poet of Cuban heritage, has had poems published in many anthologies and literary magazines, among them *River Styx, Parnassus,* and *American Review.* Vega received an M.F.A. degree in creative writing from Columbia University. He teaches writing at the State University of New York Maritime College.

## FOCUS ON...
## ART

The speaker in the poem fills his sketch with specific details he remembers about his grandfather's house: rows of lemon and mango trees, the stone and clapboard house, the palomino galloping on the horizon. In a painting or drawing, create your own visual memory of a specific place, such as the house of a grandparent. Then write a two- or three-paragraph explanation of why this place is special to you and what memories you have of it.

## UNDERSTANDING

1. Find the lines in the poem that tell how many sketches the child draws. What is the teacher's objection to the first drawing? Why does the boy draw another? What does he title it? How does the teacher respond?

    Paint a picture in which the sky is not blue, white, or gray and the trees are not green or brown. Choose colors you particularly like. Post all the pictures around the room; respond in writing to how they look to you.

2. Why does the child question his memory? What metaphor does he use to describe his memory? His picture changes from abstract (not factual) to concrete (based on the the real world and its objects). Write a letter to a friend describing what you remember about a house you lived in or visited as a young child. *Workshop 16*

3. The poem contains several characters. Which one delivers spoken words? Write a dialogue between the student and the teacher that takes place after the action of the poem has ended.

## CONNECTING

1. It is essential that language be accurate in certain situations. For example, when an airplane is landing and taking off, the pilot in the plane and the controller in the tower speak in a set pattern that is necessary for absolute clarity and understanding. However, when we describe the color of the moon on a summer night, inexact language probably won't have serious consequences.

     Create a T-chart. On one side list items that must be spoken about with utmost accuracy. On the other, speculate on items that could be discussed with creative flair. Choose one item from each side of your chart and write an appropriate description—one with accuracy and one with creativity.
     ***Workshop 10***

2.  Working with a group, create a poster in which you show several different interpretations of a single type of item. You might draw illustrations or cut pictures from old magazines. For example, you could show a variety of bicycles, including antique ones, large ones, small ones, and so on. Or you could use houses or horses. Try to include a range in terms of type, sophistication, and cost of the actual item. In an explanation on the poster, explain the type of variation you are featuring.

What happens when a person is denied recognition of his or her own heritage? How might we show respect and understanding toward one another and our diverse backgrounds?

# The Fly

## EXPLORING

If you always tell the truth, you never need to remember exactly what you have said. A lie can be difficult to remember word for word, in the event that it must be retold. Have you ever caught someone in a lie? Discuss times when you have had to decide whether to lie or to tell the truth. How important is telling the truth to you?

## THEME CONNECTION...
### A LESSON IN KEEPING PROMISES

When we give our word, before witnesses or not, a promise is sealed. In this tale, the villain thinks he can lie his way out of a promise, but he is caught by the details of his false story. The young person stands by the truth, and the man is obliged to keep his promise.

## TIME & PLACE

"The Fly" is an adaptation of an old Vietnamese folktale. Much of the mythology of Vietnam had its origins in Taoist traditions that came to Vietnam from China many hundreds of years ago. Taoism is a Chinese mystical philosophy founded by Lao-tzu in the 6th century B.C. It teaches simplicity and is concerned with obtaining long life and good fortune, often by magical means.

## THE WRITER'S CRAFT
### PROTAGONIST AND ANTAGONIST

The protagonist is the central character of a short story or novel. In "The Fly," the protagonist is the young boy who ultimately outsmarts the rich man. The rich man is the antagonist—the character or force that works *against* the protagonist. In this case, the rich man is trying to deceive the boy.

When using the terms protagonist and antagonist, remember that the prefix *pro-* means *for,* and the prefix *ant-* or *anti-* means *against.*

# The Fly
Mai Vo-Dinh

Everyone in the village knew the **usurer**, a rich and smart man. Having accumulated a fortune over the years, he settled down to a life of leisure in his big house surrounded by an immense garden and guarded by a pack of ferocious dogs. But still unsatisfied with what he had acquired, the man went on making money by lending it to people all over the county at exorbitant rates. The usurer reigned supreme in the area, for numerous were those who were in debt to him.

One day, the rich man set out for the house of one of his peasants. Despite repeated reminders, the poor laborer just could not manage to pay off his long-standing debt. Working himself to a shadow, the peasant barely succeeded in making ends meet. The moneylender was therefore determined that if he could not get his money back this time, he would proceed to **confiscate** some of his debtor's most valuable belongings. But the rich man found no one at the peasant's house but a small boy of eight or nine playing alone in the dirt yard.

"Child, are your parents home?" the rich man asked.

"No, sir," the boy replied, then went on playing with his sticks and stones, paying no attention whatever to the man.

"Then, where are they?" the rich man asked, somewhat irritated, but the little boy went on playing and did not answer.

When the rich man repeated his query, the boy looked up and answered, with deliberate slowness, "Well, sir, my father has gone to cut living trees and plant dead ones, and my mother is at the marketplace selling the wind and buying the moon."

"What? What in heaven are you talking about?" the rich man commanded. "Quick, tell me where they are, or you will see what this stick can do to you!" The bamboo walking stick in the big man's hand looked indeed menacing.

After repeated questioning, however, the boy only gave the same reply. Exasperated, the rich man told him, "All right, little devil, listen to me! I came here today to take the money your parents owe me. But if you tell me where they really are and what they are doing, I will forget all about the debt. Is that clear to you?"

"Oh, sir, why are you joking with a poor little boy? Do you expect me to believe what you are saying?" For the first time the boy looked interested.

"Well, there is heaven and there is earth to witness my promise," the rich man said, pointing up to the sky and down to the ground.

But the boy only laughed. "Sir, heaven and earth cannot talk and

usurer—one who lends money, usually at an exorbitant (higher than normal or proper) rate

confiscate—to seize with authority, often in exchange for unpaid moneys

## SPOTLIGHT ON...
## STRATEGIES FOR
## TAKING ESSAY TESTS

In "The Fly," the young boy is calm and confident when facing the usurer in court. Feelings of calmness and confidence are helpful not only when facing conflicts, but also when taking essay tests. When you take essay tests, remember the following tips.

1. Skim the entire test. Get a sense of the number of questions and the level of difficulty of each.
2. Plan how much time to allow for each question.
3. Make sure you listen to the teacher's oral directions as well as follow the written ones.
4. Answer all questions and do not stray from the topic.
5. Answer the questions you know first; then go back to address questions of which you are unsure.
6. Review to be sure you have answered all questions.

therefore cannot testify. I want some living thing to be our witness."

Catching sight of a fly alighting on a bamboo pole nearby, and laughing inside because he was fooling the boy, the rich man proposed, "There is a fly. He can be our witness. Now, hurry and tell me what you mean when you say that your father is out cutting living trees and planting dead ones, while your mother is at the market selling the wind and buying the moon."

Looking at the fly on the pole, the boy said, "A fly is a good enough witness for me. Well, here it is, sir. My father has simply gone to cut down bamboos and make a fence with them for a man near the river. And my mother . . . oh, sir, you'll keep your promise, won't you? You will free my parents of all their debts? You really mean it?"

"Yes, yes, I do solemnly swear in front of this fly here." The rich man urged the boy to go on.

"Well, my mother, she has gone to the market to sell fans so she can buy oil for our lamps. Isn't that what you would call selling the wind to buy the moon?"

Shaking his head, the rich man had to admit inwardly that the boy was a clever one. However, he thought, the little genius still had much to learn, believing as he did that a fly could be a witness for anybody. Bidding the boy goodbye, the man told him that he would soon return to make good his promise.

A few days had passed when the moneylender returned. This time he found the poor peasant couple at home, for it was late in the evening. A nasty scene ensued, the rich man claiming his money and the poor peasant apologizing and begging for another delay. Their argument awakened the little boy, who ran to his father and told him, "Father, Father, you don't have to pay your debt. This gentleman here has promised me that he would forget all about the money you owe him."

"Nonsense!" The rich man shook his walking stick at both father and son. "Nonsense! Are you going to stand there and listen to a child's inventions? I never spoke a word to this boy. Now, tell me, are you going to pay or are you not?"

The whole affair ended by being brought before the **mandarin** who governed the county. Not knowing what to believe, all the poor peasant and his wife could do was to bring their son with them when they went to court. The little boy's insistence about the rich man's promise was their only encouragement.

The mandarin began by asking the boy to relate exactly what had happened between himself and the moneylender. Happily, the boy hastened to tell about the explanations he gave the rich man in exchange for the debt.

"Well," the mandarin said to the boy, "if this man here has indeed made such a promise, we have only your word for it. How do we know that you have not invented the whole story yourself? In a case such as this, you need a witness to confirm it, and you have none." The boy remained calm and declared that naturally there was a witness to their conversation.

"Who is that, child?" the mandarin asked.

"A fly, Your Honor."

"A fly? What do you mean, a fly? Watch out, young man, fantasies are not to be tolerated in this place!" The man-

darin's **benevolent** face suddenly became stern.

"Yes, Your Honor, a fly. A fly which was alighting on this gentleman's nose!" The boy leaped from his seat.

"**Insolent** little devil, that's a pack of lies!" the rich man roared indignantly, his face like a ripe tomato. "The fly was *not* on my nose; *he was on the house-pole. . . .* " But he stopped dead. It was, however, too late.

The majestic mandarin himself could not help bursting out laughing. Then the audience burst out laughing. The boy's parents too, although timidly, laughed. And the boy, and the rich man himself, also laughed. With one hand on his stomach, the mandarin waved the other hand toward the rich man:

"Now, now that's all settled. You have indeed made your promises, dear sir, to the child. *Housepole or no housepole, your conversation did happen after all!* The court says you must keep your promise."

And still chuckling, he dismissed all parties. ❖

mandarin—any of numerous levels of Chinese public officials

benevolent— kindly

insolent—disre-spectful, rude

# UNDERSTANDING

1. What is the significance of the fly in the story? In a paragraph, speculate on the course of the story if there had not been a fly. *Workshop 8*

2. From the content of the second paragraph, what can you infer as the meaning of *usurer*? Compare your guess with a dictionary's definition. What does the phrase "exorbitant rate" mean? How do you know when something is too expensive? Research lending laws in your area and report orally to the class on your findings.

3. The mandarin comes to a conclusion based on one fact. Find that fact in the text. Do you think he is fair in basing his decision on this? Write a paragraph describing the mandarin's good qualities as a judge. *Workshops 8 and 10*

## A LAST WORD

What does it mean to give your word to someone? What honor is there in keeping one's word?

# CONNECTING

1. Numerous agencies and businesses loan money today at reasonable interest rates. Find out who loans money in your town. How do people qualify for loans? What is *principal?* How are interest rates figured and how do they affect the amount of a loan? Prepare a diagram or chart to explain how a loan works. *Workshop 22*

2. What are the criteria for a credible witness in a court of law? Interview an authority in your local courthouse. Ask him or her specifically about witnesses and their credibility. Based on what you learn, write a paragraph defining a good witness. *Workshops 8 and 26*

## ON THE JOB
### COURT REPORTER

Court reporters work for courts at all levels, from local traffic court to the United States Supreme Court. They record in shorthand all the words spoken during a legal proceeding. Because their records are official, speed and accuracy are essential. Not surprisingly, the major qualification for this type of work is exceptional stenographic skills. High school courses in typing, stenography, shorthand, and English grammar and punctuation are extremely useful.

# Say It with Flowers

## EXPLORING

An employer can create a serious problem for employees by requiring something that is impossible for them to do or is something they don't believe is right. When your instructions contradict your personal values, you encounter a dilemma. Should you maintain your values and possibly lose your job? In society, what does it mean to "play the game"? When would it be right not to play the game?

## THEME CONNECTION...
## LEARNING PERSONAL INTEGRITY

The human spirit is precious. We dull it by following someone else's values without considering our own sense of what is right. There are consequences to pay when we do not act with integrity. Teruo learns that when he acts according to his own values, he strengthens his spirit and builds personal integrity.

## TIME & PLACE

Toshio Mori has set a number of his stories, including this one, in Japanese-American communities in California. Certain expressions, such as "blockhead" and "sap," indicate that this story is set in the 1940s or 1950s.

## THE WRITER'S CRAFT
### INTERNAL AND EXTERNAL CONFLICT

When main characters have a problem with other characters or outside forces, we say the characters have external conflicts. If characters struggle with issues within themselves, we say they have internal conflicts. Teruo struggles with both internal and external conflicts in this story, so readers see him as a complex character. Not only must he face the outside forces, but he must struggle with his own feelings as he decides on a course of action.

# Say It with Flowers

Toshio Mori

He was a queer one to come to the shop and ask Mr. Sasaki for a job, but at the time I kept my mouth shut. There was something about this young man's appearance which I could not altogether **harmonize** with a job as a clerk in a flower shop. I was a delivery boy for Mr. Sasaki then. I had seen clerks come and go, and although they were of various sorts of **temperaments** and conducts, all of them had the technique of waiting on the customers or acquired one eventually. You could never tell about a new one, however, and to be on the safe side I said nothing and watched our boss readily take on this young man. Anyhow, we were glad to have an extra hand.

Mr. Sasaki undoubtedly remembered last year's rush when Tommy, Mr. Sasaki and I had to do everything and had our hands tied behind our backs for having so many things to do at one time. He wanted to be ready this time. "Another clerk and we'll be all set for any kind of business," he used to tell us. When Teruo came around looking for a job, he got it, and Morning Glory Flower Shop was all set for the year as far as our boss was concerned.

When Teruo reported for work the following morning, Mr. Sasaki left him in Tommy's hands. Tommy was our number one clerk for a long time.

"Tommy, teach him all you can," Mr. Sasaki said. "Teruo's going to be with us from now on."

"Sure," Tommy said.

"Tommy's a good florist. You watch and listen to him," the boss told the young man.

"All right, Mr. Sasaki," the young man said. He turned to us and said, "My name is Teruo." We shook hands.

We got to know one another pretty well after that. He was a quiet fellow with very little words for anybody, but his smile **disarmed** a person. We soon learned that he knew nothing about the florist business. He could identify a rose when he saw one, and gardenias and carnations too; but other flowers and materials were new to him.

"You fellows teach me something about this business, and I'll be grateful. I want to start from the bottom," Teruo said.

Tommy and I nodded. We were pretty sure by then he was all right. Tommy eagerly went about showing Teruo the florist game. Every morning for several days Tommy repeated the prices of the flowers for him. He told Teruo what to do on telephone orders, how to keep the greens fresh, how to make bouquets, corsages, and **sprays.** "You need a little more time to learn how to make big funeral pieces," Tommy said. "That'll come later."

In a couple of weeks, Teruo was just as good a clerk as we had had in a long

harmonize—to bring into line with

temperament—the distinguishing emotional traits of a person

disarmed—won over

time. He was curious almost to a fault and was a glutton for work. It was about this time our boss decided to move ahead his yearly business trip to Seattle. Undoubtedly he was satisfied with Teruo, and he knew we could get along without him for a while. He went off and left Tommy in full charge.

During Mr. Sasaki's absence I was often in the shop helping Tommy and Teruo with the customers and the orders. One day when Teruo learned that I once had worked in the nursery and had experience in flower growing, he became inquisitive.

"How do you tell when a flower is fresh or old?" he asked me. "I can't tell one from the other. All I do is follow your instructions and sell the ones you tell me to sell first, but I can't tell one from the other."

I laughed, "You don't need to know that, Teruo," I told him. "When the customers ask you whether the flowers are fresh, say yes firmly. 'Our flowers are always fresh, madam.'"

Teruo picked up a vase of carnations. "These flowers came in four or five days ago, didn't they?"

"You're right. Five days ago," I said.

"How long will they keep if a customer bought them today?" Teruo asked.

"I guess in this weather they'll hold a day or two," I said.

"Then they're old," Teruo almost gasped. "Why, we have fresh ones that last a week or so in the shop."

"Sure, Teruo. And why should you worry about that?" Tommy said. "You

talk right to the customers, and they'll believe you. Our flowers are always fresh? You bet they are! Just came in a little while ago from the market."

Teruo looked at us calmly. "That's a hard thing to say when you know it isn't true."

"You've got to get it over with sooner or later," I told him. "Everybody has to do it. You too, unless you want to lose your job."

"I don't think I can say it convincingly again," Teruo said. "I must've said yes forty times already when I didn't know any better. It'll be harder next time."

"You've said it forty times already, so why can't you say yes forty million times more? What's the difference?

> ● ● ● ● ● ● ● ●
> "You talk right to the customers, and they'll believe you."
> ● ● ● ● ● ● ● ●

Remember, Teruo, it's your business to live," Tommy said.

"I don't like it," Teruo said.

"Do we like it? Do you think we're any different from you?" Tommy asked Teruo. "You're just a green kid. You don't know any better, so I don't get sore, but you got to play the game when you're in it. You understand, don't you?"

Teruo nodded. For a moment he stood and looked curiously at us for the first time and then went away to water the potted plants.

In the **ensuing** weeks we watched Teruo develop into a slick salesclerk, but for one thing. If a customer forgot to ask about the condition of the flowers, Teruo did splendidly. But if someone should mention about the freshness of the flowers, he wilted right in front of the

spray—a decorative, flat arrangement of flowers and foliage

ensuing—following

customer's eyes. Sometimes he would sputter. On other occasions he would stand gaping speechless, without a comeback. Sometimes, looking embarrassedly at us, he would take the customers to the fresh flowers in the rear and complete the sale.

"Don't do that any more, Teruo," Tommy warned him one afternoon after watching him repeatedly sell the fresh ones. "You know we got plenty of the old stuff in the front. We can't throw all that stuff away. First thing you know the boss'll start losing money, and we'll all be thrown out."

"I wish I could sell like you," Teruo said. "Whenever they ask me, 'Is this fresh? How long will it keep?' I lose all sense about selling the stuff and begin to think of the difference between the fresh and the old stuff. Then the trouble begins."

"Remember, the boss has to run the shop so he can keep it going," Tommy told him. "When he returns next week, you better not let him see you touch the fresh flowers in the rear."

On the day Mr. Sasaki came back to the shop, we saw something unusual. For the first time I watched Teruo sell old stuff to a customer. I heard the man plainly ask him if the flowers would keep good, and very clearly I heard Teruo reply, "Yes, sir. These flowers'll keep good." I looked at Tommy, and he winked back. When Teruo came back to make it into a bouquet, he looked as if he had just discovered a snail in his mouth. Mr. Sasaki came back to the rear and watched him make the bouquet. When Teruo went up front to complete the sale, Mr. Sasaki looked at Tommy and nodded approvingly.

When I went out to the truck to make my last delivery for the day, Teruo followed me. "Gee, I feel rotten," he said to me. "Those flowers I sold won't last longer than tomorrow. I feel lousy. I'm lousy. The people'll get to know my word pretty soon."

"Forget it," I said. "Quit worrying. What's the matter with you?"

"I'm lousy," he said, and went back to the store.

Then one early morning the inevitable happened. While Teruo was selling the fresh flowers in the back to a customer, Mr. Sasaki came in quietly and watched the transaction. The boss didn't say anything at the time. All day Teruo looked sick. He didn't know whether to explain to the boss or shut up.

While Teruo was out to lunch, Mr. Sasaki called us inside. "How long has this been going on?" he asked us. He was pretty sore.

"He's been doing it off and on. We told him to quit," Tommy said. "He says he feels rotten selling the old flowers."

"Old flowers!" snorted Mr. Sasaki. "I'll tell him plenty when he comes back. Old flowers! Maybe you can call them old at the wholesale market, but they're not old in a flower shop."

"He feels guilty fooling the customers," Tommy explained.

The boss laughed impatiently. "That's no reason for a businessman."

When Teruo came back, he knew what was up. He looked at us for a moment and then went about cleaning the stems of the old flowers.

"Teruo," Mr. Sasaki called.

Teruo approached us as if steeled for an attack.

"You've been selling fresh flowers and leaving the old ones go to waste. I can't afford that, Teruo," Mr. Sasaki said. "Why don't you do as you're told? We all sell the flowers in the front. I tell you they're not old in a flower shop. Why can't you sell them?"

"I don't like it, Mr. Sasaki," Teruo said. "When the people ask me if they're fresh, I hate to answer. I feel rotten after selling the old ones."

"Look here, Teruo," Mr. Sasaki said. "I don't want to fire you. You're a good boy, and I know you need a job, but you've got to be a good clerk here or you're going out. Do you get me?"

"I get you," Teruo said.

In the morning we were all at the shop early. I had an eight o'clock delivery, and the others had to rush with a big funeral order. Teruo was there early. "Hello," he greeted us cheerfully, as we came in. He was unusually high-spirited, and I couldn't account for it. He was there before us and had already filled out the eight o'clock package for me.

He was almost through with the funeral frame, padding it with wet moss and covering it all over with brake fern, when Tommy came in. When Mr. Sasaki arrived, Teruo waved his hand and cheerfully went about gathering the flowers for the funeral piece. As he flitted here and there, he seemed as if he had forgotten our presence, even the boss. He looked at each vase, sized up the

## FOCUS ON... MARKETING

How might Mr. Sasaki have changed his thinking and benefited from Teruo's method of customer relations? Plan a marketing campaign in which you highlight the slogan "Say It with Flowers." Create a multimedia presentation, including print, television, and radio advertisements, to promote your campaign.

◆ ◆ ◆ ◆ ◆ ◆ ◆ ◆ ◆ ◆ ◆ ◆ ◆ ◆ ◆

flowers, and then cocked his head at the next one. He did this with great deliberation, as if he were the boss and the last word in the shop. That was all right, but when a customer soon after came in, he swiftly attended him as if he owned all the flowers in the world. When the man asked Teruo if he was getting fresh flowers, without batting an eye he escorted the customer into the rear and eventually showed and sold the fresh ones. He did it with so much grace, dignity and swiftness that we stood around like his **stooges.** However, Mr. Sasaki went on with his work as if nothing had happened.

Along toward noon Teruo attended his second customer. He fairly ran to greet an old lady who wanted a cheap bouquet around fifteen cents for a dinner table. This time he not only went back to the rear for the fresh ones but added three or four extras. To make it more irritating for the boss, who was watching every move, Teruo used an extra lot of **maidenhair** because the old lady was appreciative of his art of making bouquets. Tommy and I

stooge—someone who plays a subordinate, or inferior, role to someone else

maidenhair—a type of fern used as greenery in floral arrangements

asparagus—a
fernlike plant
whose leaves
are used as
greenery in
floral arrange-
ments

watched the boss fuming inside of his
office.

When the old lady went out of the
shop, Mr. Sasaki was furious. "You're a
blockhead. You have no business sense.
What are you doing here?" he said to
Teruo. "Are you crazy?"

Teruo looked cheerful enough. "I'm
not crazy, Mr. Sasaki," he said. "And I'm
not dumb. I just like to do it that way,
that's all."

The boss turned to Tommy and me.
"That boy's a sap," he said. "He's got
no head."

Teruo laughed and walked off to the
front with a broom. Mr. Sasaki shook his
head. "What's the matter with him? I
can't understand him," he said.

While the boss was out to lunch,
Teruo went on a mad spree. He waited
on three customers at one time, ignoring
our presence. It was amazing how he did
it. He hurriedly took one customer's
order and had him write a birthday
greeting for it, jumped to the second
customer's side and persuaded her to buy
roses because they were the freshest of
the lot. She wanted them delivered, so he
jotted the address down on the sales
book and leaped to the third customer.

"I want to buy that orchid in the
window," she stated without
deliberation.

"Do you have to have orchid, madam?"

"No," she said. "But I want something nice for tonight's ball, and I think
the orchid will match my dress. Why do
you ask?"

"If I were you I wouldn't buy that
orchid," he told her. "It won't keep. I
could sell it to you and make a profit,

but I don't want to do that and spoil your
evening. Come to the back, madam, and
I'll show you some of the nicest gardenias in the market today. We call them
Belmont, and they're fresh today."

He came to the rear with the lady. We
watched him pick out three of the
biggest gardenias and make them into a
corsage. When the lady went out with
her package, a little boy about eleven
years old came in and wanted a twenty-
five-cent bouquet for his mother's birthday. Teruo waited on the boy. He was
out in the front, and we saw him pick out
a dozen of the two-dollar-a-dozen roses
and give them to the kid.

Tommy nudged me. "If he was the
boss, he couldn't do those things," he said.

"In the first place," I said, "I don't
think he could be a boss."

"What do you think?" Tommy said.
"Is he crazy? Is he trying to get himself
fired?"

"I don't know," I said.

When Mr. Sasaki returned, Teruo was
waiting on another customer, a young lady.

"Did Teruo eat yet?" Mr. Sasaki asked
Tommy.

"No, he won't go. He says he's not
hungry today," Tommy said.

We watched Teruo talking to the
young lady. The boss shook his head.
Then it came. Teruo came back to the
rear and picked out a dozen of the very
fresh white roses and took them out to
the lady.

"Aren't they lovely!" we heard her
exclaim.

We watched him come back, take
down a box, place several maidenhairs
and **asparagus,** place the roses neatly
inside, sprinkle a few drops, and then

give it to her. We watched him thank her, and we noticed her smile and thanks. The girl walked out.

Mr. Sasaki ran excitedly to the front. "Teruo! She forgot to pay!"

Teruo stopped the boss on the way out. "Wait, Mr. Sasaki," he said. "I gave it to her."

"What!" the boss cried indignantly.

"She came in just to look around and see the flowers. She likes pretty roses. Don't you think she's wonderful?"

"What's the matter with you?" the boss said. "Are you crazy? What did she buy?"

"Nothing, I tell you," Teruo said. "I gave it to her because she admired it, and she's pretty enough to deserve beautiful things and I liked her."

"You're fired! Get out!" Mr. Sasaki spluttered. "Don't come back to the store again."

"And I gave her fresh ones too," Teruo said.

Mr. Sasaki rolled out several bills from his pocketbook. "Here's your wages for this week. Now get out," he said.

"I don't want it," Teruo said. "You keep it and buy some more flowers."

"Here, take it. Get out," Mr. Sasaki said.

Teruo took the bills and rang up the cash register. "All right, I'll go now. I feel fine. I'm happy. Thanks to you." He waved his hand to Mr. Sasaki. "No hard feelings."

On the way out Teruo remembered our presence. He looked back. "Goodbye. Good luck," he said cheerfully to Tommy and me.

He walked out of the shop with his shoulders straight, head high, and whistling. He did not come back to see us again. ❖

# ACCENT ON...
## COMMUNICATION TECHNOLOGY

At Mr. Sasaki's flower shop, and other flower shops around the world, modern communication technology has had a great impact on the way business is done. Find out how flower shops "communicate" with one another. How are flowers "sent" from one city or country to another?

## ON THE JOB
### FLORIST

Florists own and manage their own retail shops in which they sell fresh flowers, floral arrangements, and other related products. In addition to running a business and managing a staff, a florist needs to know about different kinds of flowers and plants, trends in floral design, and the traditions of using flowers for weddings and funerals. Useful high school courses for this fast-paced and creative career include art, marketing, business, and botany.

# UNDERSTANDING

1. Teruo wants to learn the business. What questions and remarks does he make that let us know he is sincere?

   List the types of work in which you are interested. Next to each job, write whether it is performed indoors or outdoors. What other elements of the work environment might come into play, given the types of work on your list? What work environment appeals to you the most?

2. Find evidence in the text of what "the game" is. How does Teruo accept his lesson about the game? What does Mr. Sasaki tell Teruo to do and why? Make a two-column chart for Teruo's dilemma. In the columns, list the pros and cons of each choice he has to make.

3. The other employees do not try to hide what Teruo is doing. Should they? To what extent should employees be loyal to one another? How might disclosures or cover-ups affect a person's job? Write a persuasive essay on how you think Tommy should have handled Teruo's situation. *Workshop 13*

## A LAST WORD

In "Say It with Flowers," the character Teruo struggles between lying and telling the truth to customers. What lesson can be learned from his way of resolving the conflict?

# CONNECTING

1. Selling perishables is tricky, since the materials are good for only a limited amount of time. What items other than flowers are perishable? How are they sold? Interview the produce manager at a grocery store, asking about spoilage and other issues related to perishable products. Write a display ad for the store that includes graphics. Emphasize the freshness of the produce as well as the availability of discounted items. *Workshop 26*

2.  When one worker tells on another, it is called "whistle-blowing." Search the Internet or your local libary for articles on this issue. Working with a group, role-play for the class a situation that you uncover in your research. Have the students in the class create a chart of options for the characters in your scene. Discuss the options and act them out. *Workshop 21*

3. A circumstance could arise that is ethically intolerable for you. Write a letter to explain a situation on a team, in a club, among friends, or at work in which you do not agree with or cannot comply with the wishes of the leader (coach, boss, or the like). Explain the issue and state that you can no longer participate in the group. *Workshop 17*

# The Bird
# Like No Other

## EXPLORING

Family matters can be difficult at times, and the unwritten rule seems to be, "Don't tell." Sometimes it would feel so much better to complain to others about our families, yet that might be disloyal. Have you ever had a story so wonderful or horrible that you could hardly wait to tell it to someone else? What if telling the story would be disloyal? Does that make it more difficult to keep as a secret?

## THEME CONNECTION...
## A LESSON IN SELF-CONTROL

To set standards of conduct and loyalty for oneself and maintain them requires self-control. In this simple story, a kindly neighbor shelters a boy who learns that after a while the anger goes away, and he is able to maintain loyalty to his family.

## TIME & PLACE

The story takes place where people spent summers in cottages near a body of water. Getting out of the city for at least several weeks in the summer was fairly common in the 1940s and 1950s, especially near the east coast of the U.S. Mothers would take their children "to the lake" or "to the cottage," and fathers would join their families on weekends. Warm and long-lasting relationships sometimes were formed between "summer neighbors."

## THE WRITER'S CRAFT
### VISUAL EFFECTS OF VERBS

When a writer chooses carefully the verbs in a story, the writing sizzles with action. Verbs carry content in the following phrases from the story: "the old glider *screeched* and *groaned*," and "he *flung* himself." The reader can visualize activity, motion, or energy with each verb.

# The Bird Like No Other

## Dorothy West

Colby ran through the woods. He ran hard, as if he were putting his house and family behind him forever. The woods were not a dark forest of towering trees. They were just scrub oak and stunted pine with plenty of room for the sun to dapple the road. The road, really a footpath worn by time, was so much a part of Colby's summers that at any point he knew how many trees to count before he reached the one with the hollow that caught the rain and gave the birds a drinking cup.

As the clearing came in sight with its cluster of cottages, Colby began to call Aunt Emily, the **stridency** in his voice commanding her to shut out the sweeter sounds of summer.

Whatever Aunt Emily was doing, Colby knew, she would stop what she was doing. Wherever she was, she would start for the porch, so that by the time Colby pounded up the stairs, she would be sitting on her old porch glider, waiting for him to fling himself down beside her and cool his hot anger in her calm.

Aunt Emily was a courtesy aunt, a family friend of many years. When Colby's mother was a little girl, she played with Aunt Emily's little boy when they came on holiday from their separate cities. Then Aunt Emily lost her little boy in a winter accident on an icy street. When vacation time came again, it took all her courage to reopen her cottage. But she knew she must do it this saddest summer of all if she was ever to learn to live in a world that could not bend its tempo to the slow cadence of grief.

Colby's sister made frequent visits with her dolls. She brought the dolls that didn't cry or didn't wet because they were always rewarded with a tea party for their good behavior. She eased the summer's sorrow for Aunt Emily, who felt an obligation to show this trusting child a cheerful face and to take an interest in her eager talk.

All the same, though Aunt Emily felt a bit ungrateful thinking it, a little girl dressing her dolls for a tea party is no substitute for a little boy playing cowboys and Indians at the top of his lungs.

Colby's family would have agreed with her. His mother adored him because he was her long-awaited son, five years younger than the youngest of his three sisters. His father was pleased and proud to have another male aboard.

But Colby couldn't see where he came first with anybody. As far as he was concerned he was always at the bottom of a heap of scrapping sisters. No matter how good he tried to be, his day most generally depended on how good his sisters decided to be. His rights were never mightier than their wrongs.

Aunt Emily had been Colby's sounding board ever since the summer he was

### About the Author

Dorothy West's writing career spans eight decades. Of her career, West once said, "I have no ability nor desire to be other than a writer, though the fact is, I whistle beautifully." The only child of an ex-slave and his wife, she was born in Boston in 1902. At the age of seven, she won a prize for her short story "Promise and Fulfillment." She published her first novel, *The Living Is Easy,* in 1948. Her second novel, *The Wedding,* was published in 1995.

stridency—
harsh insistence

four. One day that summer, his mother postponed a promised boat ride because his sisters had fought with each other all morning over whose turn it was to use the paint box that somebody had given them together. When they began to make each other cry, they were sent upstairs as punishment, and the outing was postponed.

Colby felt he was being punished for blows he hadn't struck and scars he hadn't caused. He had to tell somebody before he burst. Since he knew the way to Aunt Emily's, he went to tell her.

She took a look at his clouded-over face, plumped him down on her old porch glider, then went inside to telephone his mother that Colby wasn't lost, just **decamped.** His mother told her what had happened, and Aunt Emily listened with uncommitted little clucks. She wasn't any Solomon to decide if it was more important to punish the bad than to keep a promise to the good.

She could hear him banging back and forth on the glider, waiting in hot impatience to tell his tale of woe. The old glider screeched and groaned at his assault on its unoiled joints.

Standing inside her screen door, wincing in sympathy, Aunt Emily knew that neither she nor any nearby neighbor could take that tortured sound much longer. She tried to think of something to distract Colby's mind until he calmed down. A blue jay flew across her line of vision, a bird familiar to the landscape, but the unexciting sight bloomed into an idea.

Shutting the screen door soundlessly, approaching Colby on whispering feet, she put her finger to her lips and sat down beside him.

As he stared at her round-eyes, his swinging suspended, she said softly, "Colby, before you came the most beautiful bird I ever saw was sitting on my hydrangea bush. He almost took my breath. I never saw a bird of so many colors. When you came running, he flew away. But if we don't talk or make any noise, he may come back."

After a moment of reflection, Colby's curiosity pulled out the plug in his sea of troubles, and he settled back.

That was the way this gentle fiction began. When Aunt Emily decided that the beautiful bird was gone for the day, Colby was wearing an agreeable face of a normal color. Taking the initiative, a shameless triumph over a small boy, Aunt Emily plunged into a story before Colby could get his mouth open to begin his own.

For the rest of that summer, and in the summers that followed, when Colby came glad or when Colby came only a little bit mad, the right to speak first was his automatically. But when Colby came breathing fire, by uncanny coincidence, the bird like no other had just left the yard.

It was soon routine for Colby to seal his lips and settle down to wait.

Now he was eight, and on this angry morning when he flung himself up Aunt Emily's stairs, and flung himself down beside her on the poor old glider that

decamped—suddenly departed

> ● ● ● ● ● ● ● ●
> "It was soon routine for Colby to seal his lips and settle down to wait."
> ● ● ● ● ● ● ● ●

The Bird Like No Other

**339**

confluence—
flowing or
coming together

responded as expected to a sudden shock, it was plainly a morning to search the sky for the bird like no other.

Before Aunt Emily could comb a fresh story out of her memory, Colby got a speech in ahead of her. He said in an excited whisper, "I see it, I see it. I see the bird you said was so beautiful. I guess he's every color in the world."

Jerking upright in stunned surprise, making the glider wearily protest, Aunt Emily asked in a shaken voice, "Where?"

"On that tree over there, see, over there."

By a **confluence** of golden sunlight and blue sky and green leaves and shimmering summer air, a bird on a swinging bough took on an astonishing beauty.

For a moment Aunt Emily couldn't believe her eyes. But in another moment her eyes stopped playing tricks. And suddenly she wanted to stop playing tricks, too.

"Colby, look again. That's a jay. There never was a bird like the one I told you about. I made him up."

As if to give credence to her confession, the bird on the bough released itself from its brief enchantment and flew away in the dress of a blue jay.

Colby spoke slowly. "Why did you make up a bird to tell me about?"

Aunt Emily started to answer, but asked instead, "Don't you know why, Colby?"

"I think so," he said soberly.

"Will you tell me?"

"To make me sit still so I wouldn't say bad things about my family when I was mad. But you didn't want to make me sit still like a punishment. So you made me sit still like we were waiting to see something wonderful."

"I see the wonderful thing I've been waiting for. I see a little boy who's learned about family loyalty. It's as beautiful to look at as that bird."

Colby got up. He scuffed his sneakers. "Well, I guess I'll go home now. See you, Aunt Emily."

He bounded down the stairs and began to run home, running faster and faster. Aunt Emily's eyes filled with sentimental tears. He was trying to catch up with the kind of man he was going to be. He was rushing toward understanding. ❖

# ON THE JOB
## FAMILY COUNSELOR

Family counselors work with entire families or with individual family members. They help clients understand themselves and their relationships with others, and they try to guide their clients to use their new understanding to develop better relationships. Counselors work in mental health centers, hospitals, schools, for social service agencies and in private practices. Excellent listening and communication skills are essential. High school psychology courses offer a useful introduction to counseling work.

## FOCUS ON...
## LITERATURE

Dorothy West was a distinguished writer of the Harlem Renaissance, a period of great creativity in African-American art and literature during the 1920s. Other legendary writers of the Harlem Renaissance include Zora Neale Hurston, Langston Hughes, and Countee Cullen. Research this extraordinary era in African-American literature. Working in small groups, prepare a multimedia presentation of this movement, its artists, and its influences.

# UNDERSTANDING

1. Find lines in the text that describe Aunt Emily's relationship with Colby. What event strengthens her relationship with him? In a T-chart, list other characters in the story and the impact they have on Colby. Could a different character have had the same influence on his life at that moment?

   In a similar T-chart, list people who have had an important impact on you. Write their names on one side of the chart; write their effects on the other.

2. Authors select descriptive phrases carefully to add to the content of their stories. Find examples of details that tell about Colby and the theme of the story. In a paragraph, explain the story's theme. Then relate that theme to your own life in a journal entry. *Workshop 8*

3. Aunt Emily has a notion of what Colby needs. Find evidence in the text of what she thinks that is. Describe how she is able to help him see what he needs. Consider why family loyalty is a beautiful thing. Plan a family reunion. Include as many generations as are alive and available. Design activities that will enhance the closeness of your relationships.

4. Why was Aunt Emily surprised when Colby said, "I see it, I see it. I see the bird . . . "? Why does Aunt Emily confess that she made up the story about the bird? Does it strengthen or weaken her as a character? Write a letter to Aunt Emily from the boy when he is a man. What will he say in the letter about the events of this story? *Workshop 16*

## A LAST WORD

Colby learns a valuable lesson about patience and understanding from Aunt Emily. How might we all benefit from waiting for "the bird like no other"?

The Bird Like No Other

## CONNECTING

1. Businesses often require loyalty to maintain company secrets. In fact, the keeping of secrets—or confidentiality—is sometimes required and stated in employee manuals and handbooks. Strict adherence to security measures could make the difference between keeping and losing a job. Working with a group, research and review contracts and security measures for a company in your area. Write a confidentiality clause for the employee manual of a security-sensitive business of your creation. *Workshop 21*

2. Character references are frequently required when applying for a job. Write a letter of recommendation for yourself as if it were written by someone you know very well. What will the letter say about your demonstrated ability to be loyal? *Workshop 17*

# WRAP IT UP

UNIT 6

1. "Beauty Is Truth," "A Day's Wait," and "The Bird Like No Other" teach us about family bonds and loyalty. Think of a time in your life when you truly understood the ways in which family loyalty can bring family members together and tear them apart. Prepare a five-minute speech describing your experience, the lesson you learned, and how you changed because of the experience. Compare your experience with the experience of one of the characters in these three stories.

2. In "The Savings Book," "Translating Grandfather's House," and "Say It with Flowers," the characters face struggles and doubts. Write an essay in which you compare and contrast the struggles faced by each of these characters and what they learned from their experiences.

# WORKSHOPS

# WORKSHOP 1

## Elements of Fiction

### WHAT IS FICTION?

*Fiction* is writing about imagined, or made up, characters and events. Some events or characters described in a work of fiction may be based on real-life experiences, but the story itself comes from the imagination of the writer. A writer's main purpose in writing fiction is to entertain while exploring events, themes, and human behavior.

### POINTERS: FICTION WRITING

Two major types of fiction are novels and short stories. Although a novel is a long, complex work of fiction and a short story a brief work of fiction, they have in common certain elements.

1. **Character** A *character* is a person in a novel or short story. The character's actions, words, and thoughts reveal his or her qualities. The most important characters are the *protagonist* and the *antagonist*. The protagonist is the central figure, and the antagonist opposes the protagonist.

2. **Setting** The *setting* is the time and place the story happens. The setting consists of such things as the writer's descriptions of landscape, buildings, weather, and seasons.

3. **Mood** Mood refers to the emotion a story creates in the reader. A story's mood may convey, for instance, joy, sorrow, or anxiety. Writers use careful word choice to create mood.

4. **Conflict** Every story has a *conflict* around which events revolve. In a conflict, things struggle against each other. Usually, the main character is involved in the conflict, struggling against another character, nature, society, or himself or herself in order to reach a specific goal or desire.

5. **Plot** A *plot* is the series of events that occur in a story. Usually, a plot is made up of several parts. A story's *exposition* is the opening, which provides background information. The *inciting incident* introduces conflict. During the *rising action* of a story, a series of events happens in which the characters' actions and feelings intensify as problems become more complicated. The *climax* is the point of highest suspense or intensity. A story's *falling action* follows the climax and describes the results of the earlier events. The *resolution,* or ending of the story, occurs when the conflict is resolved. After the resolution, the writer may still need to tie up loose ends of the story. This final part of the plot is called the *dénouement.* The diagram below is often used to show the elements of plot.

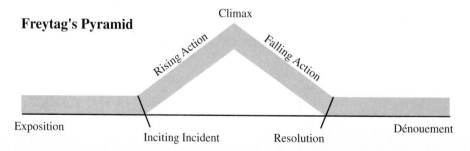

**Freytag's Pyramid**

Climax

Rising Action

Falling Action

Exposition

Inciting Incident

Resolution

Dénouement

6. **Theme** The *theme* is a story's main idea.

## Fiction Writing Sample

The following fiction excerpt is taken from the beginning of the short story "A Mother in Mannville," written by Marjorie Kinnan Rawlings.

| | |
|---|---|
| **The story's setting is established.** | The orphanage is high in the Carolina mountains. Sometimes in winter the snowdrifts are so deep that the institution is cut off from the village below, from all the world. Fog hides the mountain peaks, the snow swirls down the valleys, and a wind blows so bitterly that the orphanage boys who take the milk twice daily to the baby cottage reach the door with fingers stiff in an agony of numbness. |
| **The opening, or exposition, of the story provides important background information.** | "Or when we carry trays from the cookhouse for the ones that are sick," Jerry said, "we get our faces frostbit, because we can't put our hands over them. I have gloves," he added. "Some of the boys don't have any. . . ." |
| **The narrator, one of the main characters in this story, is introduced.** | I was there in the autumn. I wanted quiet, isolation, to do some troublesome writing. I wanted mountain air to blow out the malaria from too long a time in subtropics. I was homesick, too, for the flaming of maples in October, and for corn shocks and pumpkins and black-walnut trees and the lift of hills. I found them all, living in a cabin that belonged to the orphanage, half a mile beyond the orphanage farm. When I took the cabin, I asked for a boy or man to come and chop wood for the fireplace. The first few days were warm, I found what wood I needed about the cabin, no one came, and I forgot the order. |
| **The introduction of another main character intensifies the action of the story and makes the reader want to know what will happen next.** | I looked up from my typewriter one late afternoon, a little startled. A boy stood at the door, and my pointer dog, my companion, was at his side and had not barked to warn me. The boy was probably twelve years old, but undersized. He wore overalls and a torn shirt, and was barefooted. |

## PRACTICE

Use one of the following assignments to help you practice your fiction writing skills:

1. Write an exposition, the opening of a short story, that establishes the setting and provides background information about the main character.

2. Using Freytag's Pyramid, outline the plot of a short story you would like to write. For each of the plot elements in the pyramid, write a paragraph describing what will happen in your story.

3. Write a short story using the traditional elements of plot illustrated in Freytag's Pyramid.

# WORKSHOP 2
## Elements of Poetry

**WHAT IS POETRY?**
How would you describe or define poetry? What effect does poetry have on you when you read it? The poet Samuel Taylor Coleridge said, "prose = words in their best order; poetry = the best words in their best order." Poets use words with great control, arranging them to express emotions, experiences, and ideas. Poems capture the essence of an event or character.

**POINTERS:** **WRITING POETRY**
Poets use imagery, lines, stanzas, rhyme, rhythm, and sounds of letters to communicate images, emotions, ideas, sounds, and even stories. Read poetry aloud to hear its sounds.

1. **Imagery** An *image* is a word or phrase that describes how something looks, sounds, feels, tastes, or smells. A group of these sensory images is called *imagery.*

2. **Figurative language** refers to special combinations of words that poets use to make images. Similes, metaphors, personification, and hyperbole are examples of figurative language.

3. **Stanzas** Poems are often written in lines that are grouped together according to rules in stanzas. Poets don't always use stanzas, however. Sometimes they use *free verse,* when lines follow no stanza rules or patterns.

4. **Rhyme** The repetition of sounds at the ends of words, such as "moon" and "balloon," is called *rhyme.* Rhyming words that appear within lines of poetry are called *internal rhyme.*

5. **Rhythm** *Rhythm* is the beat of poetry created by combinations of stressed and unstressed syllables. The rhythmical pattern of a poem is called its *meter.* Poetry that is not written in a regular rhythmical pattern is known as *free verse.*

6. **Sound** The sound of a word is important in poetry. Sounds of words create feeling and music in a poem. *Alliteration* is the repetition of consonant sounds at the beginnings of words. *Assonance* is the repetition of vowel sounds within words. *Consonance* is the repetition of consonants at the ends of words. *Onomatopoeia* is the use of words that sound like the things to which they refer, such as "pop" and "creak."

7. **Speaker** The *speaker* of a poem is the character who speaks, but the speaker and the poet are not necessarily the same person. The speaker may be a person living in another time or place, an object, or an animal or insect. The speaker brings his or her viewpoint to the poem and the ideas expressed in it.

8. **Theme** The *theme* of a poem is its central, or main, idea. Through theme, the author presents a point of view or focuses on a particular idea.

**Poetry Sample**

Look at the use of rhyme and rhythm in this example from "If I can stop one Heart," written by Emily Dickinson.

| | |
|---|---|
| Repeats sounds in the words *breaking* and *Aching* and in *vain*, *Pain*, and *again* | If I can stop one Heart from breaking<br>I shall not live in vain<br>If I can ease one Life the Aching<br>Or cool one Pain |
| Uses a pattern of accented and unaccented syllables to create a steady, regular rhythm | Or help one fainting Robin<br>Unto his Nest again<br>I shall not live in Vain. |

**Poetry Sample**

In "Women," the poet Alice Walker uses rhythms of everyday speech and imagery to help you hear and see the women of her mother's generation.

Uses sounds and vivid verbs to create the sense of battle

Uses imagery to help readers see and hear the women

They were women then
My mama's generation
Husky of voice—Stout of
Step
With fists as well as
Hands
How they battered down
Doors
And ironed
Starched white
Shirts
How they led
Armies

Headragged Generals
Across mined
Fields
Booby-trapped
Kitchens
To discover books
Desks
A place for us
How they knew what we
*Must* know
Without knowing a page
Of it
Themselves.

**PRACTICE**

Here are some ways you can practice using different elements of poetry in your poetry writing:

1. Write a poem about someone you admire. In your poem, use the following elements: stanza form, free verse, imagery, and figurative language.

2. Write a poem describing an outdoor activity, such as raking leaves, playing basketball, or walking with a friend. In your poem use any three or more elements of poetry. Identify the elements used and explain in a brief paragraph why you chose them.

# WORKSHOP 3
## Elements of Nonfiction

**WHAT IS NONFICTION?**

*Nonfiction* is a type of writing that presents facts, ideas, or opinions about real people, actual places, and true events. Autobiographies, biographies, essays, and articles are four of the types of nonfiction.

**POINTERS:** NONFICTION WRITING

Keep the following pointers in mind when writing nonfiction:

1. **Know your purpose.** Decide whether you are writing to inform, to express an opinion, to persuade, or to entertain. You may have more than one purpose in mind.

2. **Know your audience.** What do your readers already know about the topic? What information do you need to explain? Will they be receptive to your topic? Tailor your writing to their experience.

3. **Begin with a clear thesis statement.** This statement identifies the topic, your main idea, and your viewpoint on the topic. Your choice of words will reveal your *tone,* or attitude, toward the subject.

4. **Choose a method of organization.** Your purpose(s) for writing will help you decide how to organize your work such as chronologically or around main ideas.

5. **Use transitional words and phrases to clarify the order and relationship of ideas, events, and details.** Examples of transitional words and phrases are *first, mainly, as a result,* and *for example.*

6. **Conclude your nonfiction work with a summary of the main points, events, or ideas.** Explain the connection between the summary of main points or ideas with your beginning thesis statement.

### Nonfiction Writing Sample

| | |
|---|---|
| Begins with thesis statement | Eleanor Roosevelt is a role model for many people. She is my role model, however, because of her courage. She once said, "You gain strength, courage and confidence by every experience in which you really stop to look fear in the face." Those words are written on a faded $3 \times 5$ notecard, which is tacked to my bulletin board. Six years ago when I was diagnosed with leukemia Eleanor Roosevelt and her words of courage came into my life. While I was in the hospital, a friend brought me a book about Eleanor Roosevelt. Mrs. Roosevelt's words of courage bolstered my tired and frightened spirits. Now my cancer has been in remission for a year, which is a big reason to celebrate. But, I keep that $3 \times 5$ notecard tacked to the bulletin board, just in case I need a courageous reminder. |
| Uses first-person point of view for an autobiographical account | |
| Uses transitions to help establish organization | |
| Summarizes the main idea in closing sentences | |

**PRACTICE**

Complete one of the following assignments to practice your nonfiction writing skills:

1. Write about an important event in your life, using the first-person point of view.

2. Write an essay on a subject about which you have strong feelings such as cutbacks in school sports or arts programs. In your essay, persuade your audience to take specific action.

# WORKSHOP 4

## Elements of Drama

### WHAT IS DRAMA?

A *drama* is a play, a story performed by actors in front of an audience. Drama can take many forms, including theater plays, radio plays, television programs, and movies.

### POINTERS: UNDERSTANDING DRAMA

All forms of drama have certain elements in common.

1. **Playwright** The *playwright* is the author of the play.

2. **Script** A *script* is the written form of the play, created from the imagination of the playwright.

3. **Stage directions** *Stage directions* are a set of instructions written by the playwright. They describe how something in the play should look, sound, or be performed. Stage directions may describe scenery, props, lighting, costumes, music, or sound effects. They may also describe elements related to the acting of the play, such as entrances and exits, tone of voice, or gestures and movements.

4. **Cast** The *cast* is the list of characters appearing in the play. Usually, the cast is listed in the order of appearance. This helps the audience to recognize each character as he or she appears on stage.

5. **Dialogue** *Dialogue* is the speech recited by the actors in a play. Dialogue reveals the character's personalities and moves the story or plot forward.

6. **Act and Scene** An *act* is a major section of a play. A *scene* is a short part of an act and happens in one place and time. When the setting of a play, changes, a new scene begins.

### Script Sample

The following excerpt appears in Shakespeare's *Romeo and Juliet*.

| | |
|---|---|
| Drama is divided into acts and scenes. | Act III, scene i<br>*(In a public place in Verona.)*<br>*Enter* MERCUTIO, BENVOLIO, *and* MEN. |
| Stage directions | BENVOLIO. I pray thee, good Mercutio, let's retire.<br>    The day is hot, the Capulets abroad,<br>    And, if we meet, we shall not 'scape a brawl,<br>    For now, these hot days, is the mad blood stirring. |
| Dialogue | MERCUTIO. Thou are like one of these fellows that, when he enters the confines of a tavern, claps me his sword upon the table and says 'God send me no need of thee!' and by the operation of the second cup draws him on the drawer, when indeed there is no need. |

### PRACTICE

Use one of the following assignments to help you practice your drama writing skills:

1. Write a dialogue between two characters who are having a disagreement.

2. Write one scene in a play set at a local shopping mall.

# WORKSHOP 5

## Strategies for Reading

## WHAT ARE STRATEGIES FOR READING?

When you read, you often do so for a reason: to learn information, to study, to take notes, to review, or to summarize. Learning to read more actively will help you get more out of the materials you read.

## POINTERS: READING STRATEGIES

Here are a few strategies to help you read more actively:

1. **Question** When you read a word, phrase, or statement that is unclear or confusing, question it. You may be able to make sense of the word by its context in a sentence or paragraph.

2. **Connect** Relate what you are reading to people, places, and things you already know.

3. **Predict** Try to figure out what will happen next.

4. **Clarify** Return to questions you had earlier, and try to answer them.

5. **Evaluate** Draw your own conclusions about the characters, actions, and events in the story.

### Applying Reading Strategies

The following excerpt is from Sandra Cisneros's story "Three Wise Guys: A Christmas Story."

**Question:** I'm not familiar with this holiday.

**Predict:** This story might be about the meaning of a Christmas gift.

**Connect:** The river must be the Rio Grande.

**Question:** What do these words mean?

**Clarify:** The Day of the Three Kings must be related to Christmas.

**Evaluate:** The parents are hardworking people.

The big box came marked DO NOT OPEN TILL XMAS, but the mama said not until the Day of the Three Kings. Because in Mexico where she was raised, it is the custom for boys and girls to receive their presents on January sixth and not Christmas, even though they were living on the Texas side of the river now. Not until the sixth of January.

Yesterday the mama had risen in the dark same as always to reheat the coffee in a tin saucepan and warm the breakfast tortillas. The papa had gotten up coughing and spitting up the night, complaining how the evening before the buzzing of the *chicharras* had kept him from sleeping. By the time the mama had the house smelling of oatmeal and cinnamon, the papa would be gone to the fields, the sun already tangled in the trees and the *urracas* screeching their rubber-screech cry.

## PRACTICE

Here are some ways you can practice using strategies for reading:

1. Select a short story from your textbook that you have not yet read. As you read the story, write notes for each of the strategies: question, connect, predict, clarify, and evaluate.

2. Apply the strategies for reading to a story that you have already read. Write a paragraph evaluating the story, explaining the conclusions you have drawn about the characters and events in it.

# WORKSHOP 6
## Active Listening

**WHAT IS ACTIVE LISTENING?**

You have the opportunity to use active listening skills every day, all day long. When you talk with a good friend, listen closely to a teacher, or watch a movie or television program, you should be engaged in active listening. *Active listening* means thinking critically and carefully about what you hear. As a listener, your job is to understand and evaluate a speaker's words.

**POINTERS:** **HOW TO LISTEN**

Effective communication depends on active listening. Sharpen your active listening skills by following these guidelines:

1. **Identify the main idea.** What is the speaker's main topic? What is his or her position on the topic?

2. **Concentrate on the topic.** As you listen to a speaker, think about what he or she is saying. To avoid distraction, mentally follow the speaker's train of thought. If possible, take notes of the main idea and supporting points.

3. **Ask questions.** Whenever you do not understand something, ask questions of the speaker. If you are unable to address the speaker, ask yourself the questions. Then predict what the speaker might say, as if you and the speaker were having a conversation.

4. **Notice verbal cues.** Transition words are verbal cues that help listeners follow what the speaker is saying. Transition words such as *next, then,* and *furthermore* indicate that the speaker is going to make another important point. Transitions such as *on the other hand* or *however* indicate that the speaker is about to make a contrast with a previous point. Other transitions include *but, like, similarly, therefore,* and *in conclusion.*

5. **Watch for nonverbal cues.** Nonverbal cues are facial expressions, hand gestures, and other kinds of body language that people use. These cues might help the speaker emphasize important points, brighten a speech with humor, or provide additional insight as to his or her attitude toward the topic.

6. **Keep an open mind.** Do not let your emotions get in the way of hearing what the speaker is saying. Keep an open mind, even if you do not agree with the speaker's opinions.

7. **Separate fact from opinion.** A fact is a piece of information that can be proven or verified. An opinion is a person's view of a fact or situation. When evaluating a conversation, speech, or presentation, consider the facts separately from the opinions expressed by the speaker.

**PRACTICE**

Here are some ways you can practice using your active listening skills:

1. Listen to a press conference or other oral presentation on television. If possible, record the presentation on audio- or videotape. Summarize the presentation for your classmates. Then review the tape to see if your summary covered the speaker's main points.

2. Listen to a classmate's speech. Afterwards, write a summary of the speech, including the speaker's main topic and supporting points. Include a description of the speaker's verbal and nonverbal cues and explain how they made the speech easier or more difficult to understand.

# WORKSHOP 7
## The Writing Process

**WHAT IS THE WRITING PROCESS?**

Think of a piece of writing you recently completed. What steps did you take? No two writers approach writing the same way, but there are several steps in the *writing process* that are common.

**POINTERS:** DEVELOPING YOUR WRITING PROCESS

Every writer has a different work style, but all writers work through the same five steps of the writing process. As you write, you may move back and forth among the following steps:

1.  **Prewriting** Prewriting is everything you do before you begin to write your memo, essay, article, or report. Prewriting occurs when you plan, ask questions, make notes, and narrow your topic. When you explore ideas about your topic, gather information, and organize your ideas, you are prewriting.

    During this stage you should identify your purpose and audience. Before you write, determine what your readers know, what they need to know, and why they need to know it. Knowing your audience will influence your purpose, tone, and presentation.

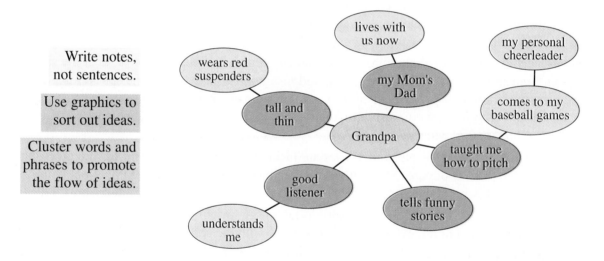

2.  **Drafting** Getting your ideas down in rough sentences and paragraphs with a beginning, middle, and an end is the drafting stage of the writing process. If your prewriting plan is detailed and well organized, your rough draft may be fairly complete. If your prewriting notes are loosely organized, your draft may be somewhat unstructured. The important thing to remember when writing a draft is to get your ideas down in an understandable form, with a beginning, a middle, and a conclusion.

### Rough Draft Sample

> Writer begins the paragraph with a solid topic sentence.
>
> Writer gets the ideas down without worrying about spelling, grammar, and mechanics.

My Grandpa is my personal cheerleader. Last year he moved into our apartment with my Mom and me. I tiptoe into his room sometimes, where I listen to his stories until midnight. His days playing basball make the funnyest stories. They traveled by bus to their out-of-town games. One time, the team drove off in the bus, leaving the driver behind while he was still in the stadiem. Wearing red suspenders, my Grandpa is easily visible to me from the pitcher's mound. After each game, Grandpa and I talked about my pitching. He listens and understands when I feel frustrated. I know that I'll always think of him as my cheerleader.

3. **Revising** The revising stage involves evaluating and improving your draft. In revising, focus on the organization of your ideas. Use clear sentences with strong supporting details and active verbs.

4. **Editing** In this stage, review your sentences and paragraphs for clear, correct construction and smooth transitions. Proofread your work word-by-word for errors in grammar, usage, and mechanics. Then set aside your writing for a day or two before carefully reading it again. You may evaluate your own draft, or you may choose to ask a peer reviewer to read it and make constructive comments. Then make any necessary changes.

### Revised and Edited Draft

> Writer has added detail and improved some phrasing.
>
> Errors in mechanics and spelling have been corrected.
>
> Errors in verb tense have been corrected.

My Grandpa doesn't wave paper pompoms or shout cheers from the bleachers, but he is my personal cheerleader. Last year he moved into our apartment and now sleeps in the room next to mine. Sometimes, late at night, I tiptoe into his room to listen to his funny stories about playing baseball for an Iowa minor league farm team. One time, to play a prank on the bus driver, the team drove off in the bus, leaving the driver behind while he was still in the stadium buying a hot dog. Wearing red suspenders, my Grandpa is easily visible to me from the pitcher's mound. Grandpa and I talk about each game. He listens and understands when I feel frustrated about how I'm pitching. Years from now, I know that I'll still think of my Grandpa as my cheerleader.

5. **Presenting/Publishing** How you present or publish your work depends on your audience and purpose for writing. For example, you may present or publish in the form of a class report, a news article, a letter to the editor, or a computer bulletin board memo.

## PRACTICE
Complete one of the following assignments using the five steps of the writing process:

1. In an essay, explain the influence a mentor has had on your decisions regarding education and work.

2. Write an article about an exciting or humorous event.

# WORKSHOP 8
## Writing a Paragraph

**WHAT IS A PARAGRAPH?**

A *paragraph* is usually made up of two or more sentences that are related to the topic sentence that presents the paragraph's main idea.

**POINTERS:** **WRITING A PARAGRAPH**

To write an effective paragraph, include the following elements:

1. **Topic sentence** The topic sentence states the paragraph's main idea. Usually, the topic sentence appears at the beginning of the paragraph.

2. **Supporting sentences** Supporting sentences develop and elaborate on the main idea presented in the topic sentence. Sensory details, facts and statistics, examples, and quotations are often used in supporting sentences. Transition words or phrases may be used to show how the supporting sentences relate to one another and to the topic sentence.

3. **Closing sentence** The closing sentence of a paragraph summarizes what has been said or restates the main idea of the paragraph.

### PARAGRAPH SAMPLE

Topic sentence presents the main idea.

Supporting sentences develop the main idea.

Closing sentence restates the main idea.

The aroma of apples laced with cinnamon greeted the children as they returned home. Still wrapped in layers of hats, mufflers, mittens, and boots, the children burst into the kitchen, stomping snow from the door to the table. Their cheeks were red, and their teeth chattered. Two hours ago, they had left behind the warm embrace of the house for an adventure in the fresh morning snow. At the sight of the steaming apple pie, the children clapped their mittened hands and squealed with hungry delight.

**PRACTICE**

Use one of the following assignments to practice writing a paragraph:

1. Write a paragraph that explains your opinion on the value of extracurricular school activities.

2. Write a paragraph describing the face of a relative or close friend.

3. Write a paragraph about your favorite holiday.

# WORKSHOP 9

## Narrative Writing

### WHAT IS NARRATIVE WRITING?

*Narrative writing* is writing that tells what happened. You may narrate a personal experience, an event at home, work, or school, or a historical episode. Knowing the elements of narrative writing will help you understand what you read and write.

### POINTERS: NARRATIVE WRITING

Narrative writing describes an event or a series of events (in real life or as depicted in fiction), and is usually presented with specific details about time, place, people, and feelings or impressions.

1. **Sketch out a timeline to identify the key events about which you want to write.** Make certain that your narrative has a beginning (introduction), a middle (body), and an end (conclusion).

2. **Choose a method of organizing the details and the events.** In narrative writing, events are often organized in the order in which they happened. However, spatial order or order of importance may also be appropriate. (See *Workshop 10* for more on methods of organization.)

3. **Start with a thesis statement.** Identify your subject, main idea, and viewpoint.

4. **Introduce the problem or conflict.** Describe and expand the problem with specific details and events in the middle of the narrative.

5. **Use transition words to show order.** Transition words such as *first, next,* and *afterwards* will clarify the order of events and details.

6. **End your narrative with a solution to the problem or a summary of events.**

### Narrative Writing Sample

| | |
|---|---|
| A thesis identifies the central idea. | My part-time job has turned out to be a great lesson on attitude. As a mystery shopper, my job is to make a purchase at a store and then write an observation report on employee knowledge and courtesy. Before this job, I hadn't thought about the effect employees' attitudes might have on customers. One day, I asked a clerk where I would find detergent. Without making eye contact, he said, "I don't know. Maybe try aisle 4 or 7." Most recently, a checkout clerk at a grocery store said to me, "Man, I can't wait until my shift ends!" That remark made me feel unwelcome. I doubt many business owners want their customers to feel unwelcome. I have learned a very important lesson on this job: how to say "please" and "thank you!" |
| The problem is introduced and developed. | |
| Transitions help establish organization. | |
| Concluding sentences summarize the solution. | |

### PRACTICE

Complete one of the following assignments to practice your narrative writing skills:

1. Write about an unusual or unexpected event that happened in your childhood.

2. Write an account of your "typical day," using chronological order to organize the events and details.

# WORKSHOP 10
## Descriptive Writing

## WHAT IS DESCRIPTIVE WRITING?

*Descriptive writing* uses precise, vivid details to create a picture of a character, scene, or event. Sensory details that appeal to readers' senses of sight, hearing, smell, taste, and touch are often used. In a description, elements are organized in an appropriate way to achieve unity and logic, and transition words and phrases help establish the relationship between details.

## POINTERS: DESCRIPTIVE WRITING

In all effective writing, ideas are connected to one another. In descriptive writing, the details must be arranged for the best effect. Methods of organization may be combined. For example, a writer may combine chronological order, spatial order, and order of impression to create a particular mood, such as suspense. When choosing a method of organization, refer to the following suggestions:

1. **Chronological order** Chronological order presents details and events in the order in which they happen. This method of organization is often used to describe a process or tell about a series of events. To show time relationships, use transitional words and phrases, such as *first, next, after, during, second, finally,* and *last.*

2. **Order of importance** Another way to organize your writing is to arrange details in order of importance, either from most important to least important, or from least to most.

3. **Spatial order** Spatial order arranges details by their physical location. When describing a place or object, spatial order may be particularly effective. To show the location of objects and their relationship to each other, use prepositional words and prepositional phrases, such as *above, below, behind, next to, on the left,* and *on the right.*

4. **Order of impression** In this method, details are placed in the order a character notices or perceives them. Sometimes, a writer arranges details simply in the order of the impression he or she is trying to convey to the reader.

### Sample Descriptive Writing

Spatial order helps to create a unified description of a place. Sensory details help readers see, hear, and smell the place. Prepositions show the relationship of one object to another.

Outside the frost-crackled window, a tangle of dead Black-eyed Susans provided cover for the purple finches. Tap-tapping their tiny beaks on the dried flower heads, the finches pecked for seeds. Along the garden path, leaves fluttered and skipped, as if heading for an autumn dance held in their honor. Overhead, billows of dark blue and gray clouds pressed down into the waiting arms of the ancient oak tree.

## PRACTICE

Here are some ways you can practice using different methods of organization in your descriptive writing:

1. Describe a process with which you are familiar, such as making spaghetti sauce or delivering the morning newspaper. Use chronological order in your description.

2. Describe a new clothing store you have visited, using order of impression.

3. Describe a book you would recommend to a friend, using order of importance.

## POINTERS: INCIDENT REPORT

An incident report describes an incident, or event, in detail. Usually, the details in an incident report are organized in chronological order. To write an incident report, use the following guidelines:

1. **State the vital statistics.** Begin your report by identifying all of the vital elements of the incident, such as the time, location, people involved, conditions related to the cause of the incident, specific positions of items and people, and so on.

2. **Describe what happened.** Describe the events in the order they happened.

3. **List results.** Conclude your report by describing the results of the incident and the present status of the case or investigation.

### Sample Incident Report

Vital statistics are identified in specific detail.

**Date:** November 12, 199–
**Time:** 7:16 A.M.
**Location:** Intersection of Hwy J and 34th Street
**Parties involved:** Terry Baxter, 338 34th Street, driver of car; Michael Ortiz, 882 65th Street, Apt. B, operator of bicycle.
**Scene description:** Dark blue 1975 Dodge Dart, license plate OU33WT, five feet beyond E. soft shoulder, skid marks measure 10 feet 3 1/4 inches. Weather conditions of fog and mist may be a contributing factor.
**Incident description:** Baxter drove north on 34th Street at 40 mph. The speed limit is 45 mph. Baxter observed a bicyclist moving on the east side of the shoulder. Ortiz stated that the shoulder was difficult to maneuver because of the wet conditions and crossed from the shoulder to the road. Baxter swerved to avoid hitting the bicyclist. He applied his brakes and skidded onto the shoulder, then off. Baxter acknowledged driving too fast for the road conditions.
**Status:** Baxter was cited for driving too fast for the road conditions.

Events are described in chronological order.

Report conludes with results or status of case.

## PRACTICE

Complete one of the following assignments to practice using descriptive writing in an incident report:

1. Use chronological order to write an incident report describing an attempted burglary.

2. You are a server at a restaurant. Write an incident report describing for your supervisor an incident in which one of your customers sent back her order.

# WORKSHOP 11
## Action Plan

### WHAT IS AN ACTION PLAN?

To solve a problem or meet a goal, you often need help from others. Before group members can work together, however, everyone must have a clear understanding of what needs to happen. An *action plan* explains the steps that should be taken to solve a problem or meet a goal.

### POINTERS: WRITING AN ACTION PLAN

To create an effective action plan, you must write your ideas in a clear and organized manner. Here are some guidelines to follow when making an action plan:

1. **State your goal clearly.** Get your reader's attention immediately by stating the purpose of your plan.

2. **Lay out the steps of the plan.** Describe a set of steps that are organized and easy to follow.

3. **Anticipate questions or doubts about the plan.** Include details that will make your readers feel comfortable carrying out the plan and give them confidence in the actions you recommend.

4. **Use active verbs.** Since your plan is a call to action, use active verbs to describe the necessary steps.

5. **End with confidence.** Restate your goal and sum up the key steps in your action plan.

### SAMPLE ACTION PLAN

A strong introduction includes a clear goal.

Clear details and active verbs support each step.

Strong concluding statement

If we are to save the historic Talman Building from being torn down, we need to accomplish three tasks. First, we need to make our neighbors aware of the problem. We should distribute flyers throughout the neighborhood, explaining why the Talman Building has historic importance and why we need to save it from demolition. Second, we must make the local media aware of our campaign. To do so, we should write letters to the editor of the newspaper and make phone calls to the news departments of local television and radio stations. Third, we need to make the mayor aware of our plan. We must ask all of our neighbors to send persuasive letters and e-mail to the mayor's office, urging her to stop the city's demolition plans. If we carry out these tasks, we can save the Talman Building from the wrecking ball and, in doing so, preserve the history and beauty of our neighborhood.

### PRACTICE

Complete one of the following assignments to create an action plan:

1. Write an action plan that details how to get more students involved in an after-school tutoring program.

2. Explain your plan for turning an empty lot in your neighborhood into a community garden.

# WORKSHOP 12
## Writing Instructions

**WHAT ARE INSTRUCTIONS?**

*Instructions* are written directions that explain how to carry out a process. Detailed and easy-to-understand instructions can be a great help to peers and co-workers.

**POINTERS:** WRITING INSTRUCTIONS

People need clear, easy-to-follow instructions to help them carry out a specific task. These guidelines will help you write instructions:

1. **Begin with an introduction.** Explain in a heading or in one or two sentences when the instructions should be followed and what they accomplish. Also, list any materials or equipment needed.

2. **Write and number each step in the order in which it should be done.** Begin each step with an action verb, such as *lift, place,* or *press.*

3. **Think about what your readers know and what they need to know.** Include all necessary steps, but leave out obvious ones, such as "Turn on the photocopier."

4. **Indent explanations.** Readers will feel comfortable with a new task if you include explanations of what should happen. Indent the explanation under the numbered step to which it refers.

5. **Include pictures and diagrams if they would be helpful.**

**Sample Instructions**

**How to Enlarge a Document on a Photocopier**

Begin with introduction

You will need a clean copy of the document that you want to enlarge.

1. Lift the cover and place the sheet of paper face down on the glass.

Number steps in order

2. Position the original between the appropriate size marks.

Indent explanations

    Use the guide placed to the left of the glass to position the original. For example, if your original measures 8 1/2 by 11 inches, place it between the marks that read "8 1/2 x 11."

3. Lower the cover.

4. Press the preset copy ratio key. Continue to press the key until the copy ratio for enlargements lights up.

    Each time the copy ratio key is pressed, a different ratio will light up. To enlarge a document, light up the ratio that reads "Max. 141%."

5. Press the Start key.

6. Once the copy has been made, lift the cover and remove the original.

**PRACTICE**

Practice writing instructions by completing one of the following assignments:

1. Tell readers how to send electronic mail.

2. Explain the process of switching gears on a bicycle, grooming a pet, or repotting a plant.

# WORKSHOP 13

## Persuasive Writing

### WHAT IS PERSUASIVE WRITING?

You probably have strong opinions on many subjects. But how can you convince others of your point of view? Mastering the art of *persuasive writing* is one way to get others to see things your way.

### POINTERS: WRITING A PERSUASIVE ESSAY

In a persuasive essay, you want to convince your reader to share your beliefs or take certain actions. Persuasive essays can focus on many different topics. Refer to the following guidelines:

1. **Select an appropriate topic.** Any topic you choose should have at least two distinct "sides." Also, it should grab your readers' attention.

2. **State your position.** Clearly state the main idea of your essay in a thesis statement.

3. **Support your opinion with evidence.** Use facts, statistics, examples, opinions from experts, or observations that back up your opinion and make your argument stronger.

4. **Know your audience.** Think about what your audience already believes or knows about the topic. Develop arguments that will persuade them to share your opinion.

5. **Address possible opposing arguments.** Think about how your audience might argue against your opinion. Then use clear and precise language to defend your position.

6. **Avoid errors in logic.** Do not use stereotypes or oversimplifications, such as either/or statements that only present an issue in two ways. Be careful not to generalize your view of the topic.

7. **Organize your information.** Arrange your paragraphs in a logical order. You might present your most important points first. Perhaps you will address opposing arguments at the beginning, or you may put these arguments at the end. In any case, include a strong introduction and conclusion.

### Sample Persuasive Essay

| | |
|---|---|
| Thesis statement | The proposed increase in bus and subway fares is unfair to our city's workers and students. The current fares, $1.50 for adults and $1.25 for |
| Supporting arguments | students, are already among the highest fares in the nation. Over the past five years, our city's public transportation fares have increased at a |
| Supporting opinion | faster rate than in any other metropolitan area. At the same time, services have been unfairly reduced. Fewer buses run at night and on the weekends. At the beginning of this year, the city eliminated weekend |
| Conclusion | service on the North subwayline altogether. The city should seek other revenue sources before raising fares and cutting services. |

### PRACTICE

Use one of the following assignments to help build your persuasive skills:

1. Write a persuasive essay asking your school principal to adopt a new school subject or activity.

2. Write an essay to convince a parent to let you participate in a student exchange program.

# WORKSHOP 14
## Cause and Effect

### WHAT IS CAUSE AND EFFECT?
A *cause* makes something else happen. An *effect* is the result of something happening. Sometimes several causes together cause one or more effects.

### POINTERS: CAUSE AND EFFECT ORGANIZATION
As you use cause-and-effect organization in your writing, keep the following guidelines in mind:

1. **Choose a topic and decide whether to describe cause, effect, or both.** You might explain the cause of a character's actions and the effects of those actions on other characters.

2. **State your topic as a question.** If you were writing about "Grandmother and the Workmen." You might ask, "What effect does the Grandmother have on the laborers' work ethic?"

3. **Brainstorm possible causes or effects that answer this question.** Put these causes or effects into a logical order—order of importance or chronological, the order the causes or effects happened.

4. **Add supporting details.** Support your topic with examples, definitions, facts, or an expert's opinion.

5. **Show connections between events with transitional words.** Transitional words such as *because, as a result,* and *therefore* help readers see relationships.

6. **Check your logic.** Do not assume that a cause has only one effect. Be careful not to assume that an earlier event is the cause of a later event just because it happened first.

7. **End with a summary of your main point.** Summarize your main point clearly and creatively.

### Sample Cause-and-Effect Essay

| | |
|---|---|
| The topic is introduced. | In "Grandmother and the Workmen," the grandmother's actions produce a noticeable change in the laborers' performance. At first, the laborers could hardly believe that a grandmother could swing a pick. |
| Effects are listed in chronological order. | They "laughed uproariously at her." Their laughter did not stop the grandmother, however. After a while, the men just went back to work. With the grandmother working alongside them, though, the men did |
| Supporting details | more work than usual. Finally, the superintendent convinced the grand-mother to exchange her pick for a job bringing the laborers water. As a |
| Transitional words | result, the laborers greatly improved their quality of work and their work ethic. In the words of the author, "I think they were a little sad |
| Main point is summarized. | when they finished the job and had to move to another neighborhood." |

### PRACTICE
Complete one of the following assignments to practice explaining cause and effect.

1. Write an essay explaining the effects dyslexia has had on the author of "On Being Seventeen . . ."

2. Research and write a report explaining what causes people to have heart attacks.

# WORKSHOP 15
## Comparison and Contrast

**WHAT IS COMPARISON AND CONTRAST?**

When you *compare and contrast* items, you explain how they are alike and different. School and work assignments will ask you to compare and contrast information, ideas, events, and people.

**POINTERS:** COMPARISON AND CONTRAST ORGANIZATION

Comparison and contrast is an effective method for organizing information in an essay, report, or article.

1. **Select the items to compare and contrast and gather information about their similarities and differences.** Explore similarities and differences in a Venn diagram. Draw two overlapping circles. List what the two items have in common in the center space, where the circles overlap. List the differences between the items in each of the outer parts of the circles.

2. **Write your topic sentence or thesis statement.** State your purpose and general subject.

3. **Decide how to organize the information.** The *whole-to-whole pattern* compares one whole topic to another by describing all features of one entire topic before going to the next. The *feature-to-feature pattern* compares the individual features common to both topics.

4. **Write your first draft and make revisions.** If one pattern isn't working well, try the other pattern of organization. Close by drawing a conclusion about the similarities and differences of your topic.

5. **Use transitions to make connections between features or ideas.** Use transitions such as *likewise, similarly, however,* and *on the other hand* to emphasize similarities and differences.

6. **Edit your comparison/contrast for grammar and spelling.**

### Sample Comparison/Contrast Essay

|  |  |
|---|---|
| Thesis statement | "Birdfoot's Grampa" and the excerpt from *Wouldn't Take Nothing for My Journey Now* both show the influence of grandparents. However, the lessons that each grandparent teaches about life differ. |
| Organized on the whole-to-whole pattern | Birdfoot's Grampa is a patient man who rescues toads from the road. He gently teaches his grandson to respect nature and to understand the balance between nature and humans. |
| Transitions | In contrast, Maya Angelou's grandmother firmly teaches that whining is graceless. Her no-nonsense dialogue states, "So you watch yourself about complaining, Sister. What you're supposed to do when you don't like a thing is change it." |
| Conclusion | One grandparent's way of teaching is patient. The other's is blunt. Yet, both grandparents deliver important messages about life. |

**PRACTICE**

Complete one of the following assignments to practice using a comparison and contrast:

1. In an essay, compare and contrast the sons in "All the Years of Her Life" and "A Rupee Earned."

2. Write a report comparing and contrasting the benefits packages offered by two different companies.

# WORKSHOP 16
## Personal Letters

### WHAT IS A PERSONAL LETTER?
By writing a *personal letter*, you could take the time to tell your reader every detail. Personal letters are an important way for friends and family members to keep in touch with one another. Informative and entertaining, personal letters foster a meaningful communication between people.

### POINTERS: WRITING A PERSONAL LETTER
As you write personal letters, keep the following guidelines in mind:

1. **Keep your reader in mind.** Write about topics that your reader will find interesting. Be thoughtful and ask about a particular event or situation in your reader's life.

2. **Avoid vague and boring language.** Be creative and original. Use specific details and vivid verbs.

3. **Follow the form for a personal letter.** Include your return address, a greeting, the body of the letter, an appropriate closing, your signature, and, if you wish, an additional comment, or postscript.

### Personal Letter Sample

Return address and date

> 477 Beach Road
> Tampa, FL 13312
> June 10, 199–

Greeting followed by a comma

Dear Aunt Marina,

Body of the letter

> I've just received the most wonderful news! The Tampa Town Council has formed a Youth Council for Community Affairs, and I've been named chairperson! Before next month's Town Council meeting, I need to write a mission statement, outlining my goals for the coming year. One of my goals is to establish a literacy program for senior citizens. This would be an excellent way for teens my age to help others in the community. As the mayor of your city, you probably have all sorts of wonderful ideas and advice to pass along. Do you have a Youth Council? What is its role in the community? I look forward to hearing from you. I'll write an update after our next meeting.

Closing followed by a comma

> Your niece,

Signature

> *Tina*

### PRACTICE
Complete one of the following assignments to practice your personal letter writing skills:

1. Write a letter to a friend or relative thanking him or her for helping you with a project.

2. Write a letter to a friend or relative describing a recent important event in your life.

# WORKSHOP 17
## Business Letters

### WHAT IS A BUSINESS LETTER?

A *business letter* is a piece of correspondence written to a workplace for a specific purpose.

### POINTERS: WRITING A BUSINESS LETTER

1. **Include the basic parts of a letter.** The heading gives the sender's address at the top left of the stationery. Add the date, and the name (if known), title, and address of the recipient. The salutation includes the recipient's title and last name. The body consists of the message and ends with a closing such as "Sincerely yours" on a separate line. Sign the letter above your typed name.

2. **Type business letters in block form or modified block form.** To use block style, place each part of the letter flush left (aligned at the left margin).

### Letter of Request

A letter of request asks for specific information in a polite and clear manner. Explain what you need, why, when, and where to send it. Thank the recipient for taking the time to respond.

| | |
|---|---|
| Heading, date, and address | 123 Holly Lane<br>Chester, WI 55500-3227<br><br>October 31, 199–<br><br>Volunteer Director<br>Canine Companions for Independence<br>4989 State Route 37 East<br>Delaware, OH 43015-9682 |
| Salutation | Dear Director: |
| Request for information | I am interested in volunteering as a puppy raiser for CCI. Please send me the guidelines for your program and an application form. |
| Thanks | I look forward to joining CCI. Thank you for the information. |
| Closing, your signature, and your typed name | Sincerely,<br><br>*Max Chan*<br>Max Chan |

### PRACTICE

Complete one of the following assignments to practice writing a business letter:

1. Write a letter of request to a local branch of a nonprofit organization, such as Habitat for Humanity or the Salvation Army, asking for information about areas where volunteer efforts are needed.

2. Write to an organization that offers a course locally that interests you, such as small engine repair, CPR, or swimming. Ask the organization for information about meeting times and fees.

# WORKSHOP 18

## E-mail/Memo

### WHAT IS AN E-MAIL/MEMO?

A *memo* is a brief message usually written from one company employee to another for a specific purpose. *E-mail,* or electronic mail, is a memo sent rapidly through a computer network.

### POINTERS: E-MAIL/ MEMO

To create an e-mail or memo, follow these guidelines:

1. **Begin with a heading.** Include who is receiving the memo, sender, date, and subject.

2. **State your main point.** State the main point or purpose of your memo as soon as possible.

3. **Be clear and concise.** Clearly explain what you want the recipient to know. Many memos announce a policy change or ask for action to be taken. Make clear what you want the recipient to do.

4. **Use an appropriate tone.** Remember that the recipient of your memo cannot see your face. He or she may be offended by a comment that you meant to be funny or sarcastic.

5. **Use upper- and lower-case letters.** Using all capitals in e-mail is difficult to read and is considered the equivalent of shouting—an undesirable mode of office communication.

6. **Find out your recipient's computer network address.** You can send e-mail messages only to others on the same network or a connecting network. You must use the person's exact address.

7. **Remember others may read e-mail.** Don't write anything that would be damaging if it were read by others. Fix errors, and always avoid offensive language.

### Sample E-mail Memo

| | |
|---|---|
| Network addresses | To: All Super Company Employees@SuperCo.com |
| | From: JanineFreeman@SuperCo.com |
| | Date: November 1, 199- |
| Memo headings | Subject: Personal and Sick Days |
| Main point | Effective immediately, all employees must use all accumulative personal and sick days by December 29. Please note that failure to do so will result in loss of days earned. |

### PRACTICE

Complete one of the following assignments. Make up network addresses, if necessary.

1. Write an e-mail memo informing a co-worker of the car pool schedule.

2. Write a memo announcing a change in the company dress policy for Fridays only.

# WORKSHOP 19

## News and Feature Writing

### WHAT ARE NEWS AND FEATURE WRITING?

Newspapers and magazines can include both *news writing* and *feature writing*. News writing, or reporting, gives readers up-to-date information. Feature writing provides readers with more human-interest information. News writers describe events and facts in an objective way; in other words, they do not show their personal opinions about the events or facts presented. Feature writers can focus on their readers' personal interests and emotions. A feature deals with facts but highlights the people and opinions surrounding the facts.

### POINTERS: NEWS WRITING

Think of a news article as an upside-down pyramid. The first sentence, or lead, gives the most important information. Each of the next sentences offers less important details and facts.

1. **Answer the basic questions first.** Write the words *who, what, why, when, where,* and *how* on a piece of paper. Answer these questions in as few words as possible. (Omit any questions that are not important to your article.) Combine your answers into one or two sentences.

2. **Decide which other details to include.** Think about other details readers might want to know, such as how a certain news event might affect them. You may want to use quotations from people you interviewed. Then choose as many details as you have space to include in your article.

3. **Arrange the details in decreasing order of importance.** If the editor must shorten the article, details from the end of the article will be cut first.

4. **Make your first draft brief and objective.** Stick to the facts and important details. Do not reveal your feelings about the facts. Avoid opinion words such as *good,* and *unfortunately.*

5. **Revise and edit your article.** Make sure you have used terms readers will understand. Consider whether you have answered questions the readers might have. Use transitional words and phrases to make smooth connections. Check your grammar, spelling, and punctuation for correctness.

6. **Check your facts.** Make sure times, locations, dates, titles, and names are correct.

### News Writing Sample

Lead sentence answers basic questions

Objective terms used

Least important fact is last

    Drama adviser Mr. Kurt Bays announced that auditions for the fall play will be held in the auditorium on Tuesday, October 8, from 2:00 P.M. to 6:00 P.M. Mr. Bays, who will direct the play, has chosen Thornton Wilder's "Our Town" for the late November production. Auditions are open to all students who sign up for an audition time before 4:00 P.M. on October 7. Sign-up sheets are posted in Mr. Bay's classroom, Room 208. Students may also sign up for technical roles, such as stage manager, costume director, and lighting assistant. Mr. Bays directed last spring's musical production, "Oklahoma!", which achieved record attendance.

## PRACTICE

Develop your news writing skills by completing one of the following assignments:

1. Write a news article about a positive change made by teenagers in your school or community. Be sure to stick to the facts and report the story in an objective way.

2. Write a news article about a recent tragic event in your school or community. Remember to keep your personal feelings and opinions out of the article.

## POINTERS: FEATURE WRITING

A feature article can include facts, but it is not written as an upside-down pyramid. Instead, its organization depends on the subject matter. Use the following pointers as you write your features:

1. **Select a topic that will interest your readers.** Look for the human-interest side of a news story. For example, you might write about how recent job layoffs have affected community members. You could conduct interviews with current and former students of this year's Teacher of the Year. You might write a historical feature explaining the history of a school or community event.

2. **Gather information.** This information may come from personal interviews, library research (especially if you are writing a historical feature), or computer databases and the Internet.

3. **Follow the rest of the writing process to complete your article.** Write your first draft, revise it, edit it, and perhaps arrange to have it published in the school or local newspaper. Begin your article with an engaging personal story or fact that will grab the readers' attention. Also make sure that any facts or other information you've included is correct.

### Feature Writing Sample

Begins with a sentence that grabs readers' attention

Focuses on the human aspect of the story

While her friends spent the summer hiking in the mountains or working at the corner yogurt shop, Trina Mendez spent most of her vacation covered in dirt. Trina was one of three local high school students to receive a summer archaeological internship. Trina traces her interest in archaeology back to her childhood. She would spend hours digging up rocks in her backyard and inventing stories about where they came from. Last summer, working at an excavation site in western Kentucky, Trina and her co-workers helped to uncover bits of bone, pottery, and other artifacts. Despite the intense heat, dust, and mosquitoes that swarmed the work site, Trina says the six-week internship was the greatest experience of her life.

## PRACTICE

Complete one of these assignments to practice writing a feature story:

1. Interview your classmates or family members about their response to a recent news event. Then write a feature story for your school or local paper.

2. Review recent news stories in your local or school newspaper. Then list possible human-interest topics based on the stories. Choose one topic and write a feature article. Gather any necessary information.

# WORKSHOP 20

## Brochure

### WHAT IS A BROCHURE?

A *brochure* advertises products or services with colorful pictures and graphics and an attention-grabbing format. Its folded form makes it easy to hold or carry.

### POINTERS: CREATING A BROCHURE

1. **Make an outline.** Decide what information you need to include and organize it in an outline. For example, if you are writing to advertise a baby-sitting service, you might include a list of your services, a description of your experience, and how customers can contact you.

2. **Write engaging copy.** Use vivid verbs and inviting adjectives to describe your product or service. Emphasize what you have to offer your customers.

3. **Arrange information to get your readers' attention.** Use small paragraphs, numbered or bulleted items, and short direct sentences to make your brochure easy to read.

4. **Add visuals.** Eye-catching photographs and simple charts emphasize the written information.

5. **Choose an attractive design.** Select the best quality paper available to you, add color where possible, and use lettering that stands out and is easy to read.

**Sample Brochure**

### PRACTICE

Complete one of the following assignments to create a brochure:

1. Create a brochure that describes a product or service that you are offering to members of your community. Explain what you are offering and why your neighbors should buy your product or service.

2. Create a brochure that advertises a vacation spot you would like to visit. Use appealing language and engaging graphics to get readers' attention.

3. Create a brochure that describes a club or organization at school. Explain what the club does and why people should become members.

# WORKSHOP 21

## Research Methods

**WHAT ARE RESEARCH METHODS?**
Use a variety of *research methods* to help you write an engaging, convincing, and factual research paper.

**POINTERS:** **SUCCESSFUL RESEARCH**
Keep the following methods in mind as you research information for a report:

1. **Get to know your library and its resources.** Find out where the card catalog or computer card catalog is located and how to use it. Searching a catalog will often be the first method you use to look for books on your topic. Also find out where the reference materials are located.

2. **Ask the reference librarian for help.** Remember that asking questions is as important as finding answers. The reference librarian is familiar with the many sources of information a library offers. He or she can suggest materials that you may not know about or that might not have occurred to you.

3. **Use a variety of reference materials.** Searching encyclopedias is a good first research method. But don't forget about other reference materials. Almanacs and yearbooks, which are published each year, provide up-to-date facts and statistics. Atlases contain maps and other geographical information. Biographical references provide information about the lives of noteworthy people. You can find some of the most current information about your topic in periodicals, such as newspapers and magazines. Computer databases and the Internet are other excellent sources of information.

4. **Consider primary sources.** A primary source is a firsthand account. For instance, rather than reading an encyclopedia's summary of Lewis and Clark's travels, you could read the journal that Lewis kept during the expedition. Using primary sources can lend a fresh outlook to your research paper.

5. **Gather your own information.** Conduct interviews or make firsthand observations of a topic that you are researching. For example, if you are researching how plant hybrids are created, you might interview the manager of a plant nursery about the special types of roses the nursery grows.

6. **Take careful and thorough notes.** Most reference materials cannot be checked out of the library. Therefore, it is important to take careful notes of the information you gather from printed sources. When conducting interviews or making live observations, you might use a tape recorder or video camera to document the information. Remember that you will need to document and credit any ideas that are not your original thoughts.

## PRACTICE
Choose one of the following research topics. Then, practice your research methods by listing at least three different ways you would gather information about the topic.
1. The national holidays of Mexico
2. How the electoral college works
3. The scientific workings of hot-air balloons

# WORKSHOP 22
## Reading Charts and Graphs

**WHAT ARE CHARTS AND GRAPHS?**

You've probably heard the saying, "A picture is worth a thousand words." Instead of using words, *charts and graphs* use pictures to show information. Newspapers, magazines, textbooks, and business reports often use charts and graphs to show statistics and other numerical facts. These pictures allow readers to analyze information quickly and easily. Knowing how to read pie charts and bar graphs, two common types of charts and graphs, will help you understand many types of information.

**POINTERS:** ▌READING A PIE CHART▐

A *pie chart* is a round chart that is divided into sections. The sections are the parts of a whole. Each part, or piece of the pie, represents a certain percentage of the whole subject.

1. **Read the title.** The title refers to the whole subject. The pieces of the pie are the parts of this whole.

2. **Compare the parts to each other.** Glance at the size of each part to get a general idea of how the parts compare to each other. Examine the information more closely to find out the exact number or percentage that each part represents.

3. **Compare the parts to the whole.** The total parts of a pie chart will always equal 100 percent. Usually, the parts are shown in percentages.

**Sample Pie Chart**
Favorite School Subject among Jefferson High School Students

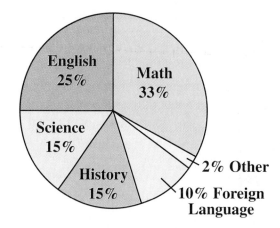

**PRACTICE**

Practice reading a pie chart by answering the following questions about the pie chart on this page:

1. What subject is the favorite of most Jefferson High School students?

2. Which subjects do equal numbers of students prefer?

3. What is the second most popular subject among students?

## POINTERS: READING A BAR GRAPH

A *bar graph* shows how things compare to each other or how they change over time. Information is organized on a horizontal axis and on a vertical axis. One axis displays numbers. The other axis shows bars that stand for the subjects being compared.

1. **Read the graph title and bar titles.** The titles tell what information is being compared.

2. **Look at the height or length of each bar.** To find out the amount that each bar represents, line up the end of a bar with a number on the opposite axis.

3. **Compare the bars.** Analyze the information by comparing the lengths or heights of bars and the amounts they stand for.

**Sample Bar Graph**
Earth Day Fundraising Totals

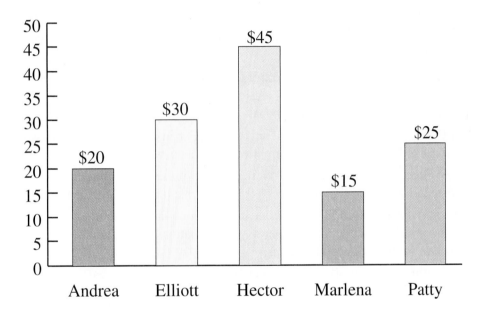

## PRACTICE

Practice reading a bar graph by answering the following questions about the bar graph on this page:

1. Who raised the most money? How much did he or she raise?

2. Who raised more money, Andrea or Marlena?

3. Who was the third most successful fundraiser?

# WORKSHOP 23

## Critical Thinking

### WHAT IS CRITICAL THINKING?

When you use *critical thinking,* you examine your own thinking and the thinking of others to see if it makes sense. You use critical thinking skills when you analyze a problem or situation, use cause-and-effect reasoning, compare and contrast things, and summarize.

### POINTERS: APPLYING CRITICAL THINKING

To apply critical thinking to an issue or problem, you should do the following:

1. **Describe the real issue or problem.** Before you can try to solve a problem, you must be able to describe it. For example, in the poem "Birdfoot's Grampa," the problem is not how to rescue toads from the highway. The problem is how humans can learn to live in harmony, or balance, with nature.

2. **Raise important issues that relate to the issue.** After reading "Raymond's Run," you might ask how being the younger sister of two brothers has shaped Squeaky and her feelings about being a girl.

3. **Recognize your own biases and those of others.** The critical thinker tries to put aside his or her own likes or dislikes and look at an issue objectively. As a critical thinker, you should also look for signs of bias when considering others' opinions.

4. **Avoid assumptions.** Use evidence to draw conclusions. For instance, rather than assume that a co-worker cannot handle a new task, you might evaluate a co-worker's skills and ability to learn.

5. **Be open to new ideas and other points of view.** Listen with an open mind to others' opinions. Try not to feel threatened or attacked simply because another person has a different point of view.

6. **Evaluate new information.** Carefully consider information—and its sources—before you accept it as true. Realize that sometimes you might get new information that will cause you to think differently than before or to draw new conclusions.

7. **Consider implications and possibilities.** In Act III, scene i, of Shakespeare's play *Romeo and Juliet,* Romeo slays Tybalt. A critical thinker might ask whether Romeo considered the consequences of such an action and whether he is prepared to face banishment from Verona.

8. **Support opinions with evidence.** Others are more likely to accept your opinions if you support them with evidence or examples. Be prepared to explain your conclusions with logical reasons.

### PRACTICE

Answer one of the following questions to practice using your critical thinking skills:

1. Why is the husband, Monsieur Loisel, in "The Necklace" a sympathetic character?

2. In "Say It with Flowers," Teruo insists on being honest to customers. Are Teruo's values inappropriate in the business world?

3. Your boss has asked you and a co-worker to create a new filing system. You think the files should be organized by subject matter. Your co-worker suggests that the files be arranged alphabetically. What critical thinking skills can you apply to this task?

# WORKSHOP 24
## Critical Viewing

**WHAT IS CRITICAL VIEWING?**

As a viewer, you need to develop *critical viewing* skills to distinguish between facts and opinions represented in the media. Looking for and recognizing bias in news programs and advertisements will help you become a critical viewer.

**POINTERS:** DEVELOPING CRITICAL VIEWING

To develop your critical viewing skills, keep the following points in mind:

1. **Analyze the images you see.** Make a habit of asking questions about what you see. In advertisements, products can be photographed or manipulated to be more attractive. Remember that advertisers want to create an image that will appeal to viewers and make them spend money on their products.

2. **Identify loaded language and connotations.** *Loaded language* includes words that have strong emotional, and often negative, associations. *Connotations* are the images or feelings associated with certain words. For example, while reporting about a demonstration, one reporter describes an "angry mob" and another describes a "group of concerned citizens." Although they both refer to the same event, the two reporters create vastly different images. "Angry mob" is an example of loaded language with negative connotations. "Concerned citizens" has a positive connotation. However, neither is necessarily closer to the truth of the event. As a critical viewer, you must consider the people involved in a news event and the biases they might bring to a story.

3. **Remember that advertisers want to sell their products.** Commercials exist to encourage viewers to spend their money. As a critical viewer, you should always think carefully about the claims made in commercials, especially claims that seem too good to be true.

4. **Carefully weigh information.** TV news programs must cover many stories in a short amount of time. Often, stories are summarized or simplified. Complex issues are presented as having two clear and opposing sides. As you watch news reports, ask whether you are getting the whole story.

5. **Look for evidence to support news reports and advertising claims.** News reports sometimes cite "unidentified sources." These words should make viewers question why the sources wish to remain anonymous. Viewers should be equally wary of television advertisements that link products to appealing pictures. For instance, a soft drink company might show attractive people having fun while drinking their product. A critical viewer should consider whether a person becomes more attractive or popular simply by buying the product.

**PRACTICE**

Complete one of the following activities to practice your critical viewing:

1. Choose a current news event that interests you. Watch three news programs about the event. Take notes on the reports. Then analyze what you have seen. Try to identify any bias in the programs you view.

2. Write a critical analysis of a television commercial that you like. Explain why you think the commercial is appealing, how the ad appeals to your emotions, and what facts support the claims.

# WORKSHOP 25

## Speaking Skills/Oral Presentations

### WHAT ARE SPEAKING SKILLS AND ORAL PRESENTATIONS?

Developing your *speaking skills* will help you in school and on the job. As a student, you might deliver an oral report in class or give an election speech to your fellow students. As an employee, you might give an *oral presentation,* in which you share information and visual aids with co-workers or customers.

### POINTERS: PRESENTATION TECHNIQUES

Public speaking makes many people nervous. You can feel more relaxed and confident if you follow these techniques for delivering an oral presentation:

1. **Know your topic.** Do any necessary research to familiarize yourself with the subject. If possible, choose a topic that you know about and that will interest your audience.

2. **Identify your purpose.** What do you want to accomplish with your oral presentation? Decide whether you want to provide information, persuade your audience, or motivate them.

3. **Analyze your audience.** How much does the audience already know about your topic? What information will you need to explain or provide? If your purpose is to convince your audience, think about how you will respond to any opposing attitudes or beliefs.

4. **Organize your presentation.** Plan the order in which you will cover your points. Prepare an outline that includes all your major points and some brief details about each. If you plan to use notecards during your talk, arrange them according to your outline.

5. **Prepare visuals.** A few visual aids will make your presentation more interesting and easier to understand. Graphs, drawings, photographs, models, videotapes, or actual equipment are types of visuals you may want to use. Display the visuals so that all audience members can see them.

6. **Practice your delivery.** Ask someone to listen to your presentation and offer suggestions on how to improve it, or record your presentation on video- or audiotape and review it yourself. Make sure you are speaking clearly and loudly enough and maintaining eye contact with your audience. Listen to how fast you speak. Be careful not to sound as if you are reading rather than speaking your ideas. Avoid using interrupters such as "um" or clearing your throat frequently.

7. **Deliver your presentation.** Remember what you rehearsed. Direct the audience's attention to your visual aids at the appropriate times. Refer to your notecards when necessary. Follow your outline and speak naturally.

### PRACTICE

Practice your speaking skills by preparing an oral presentation for one of these situations:

1. Your supervisor at a toy company has asked you to prepare a presentation about the marketing of a new toy. Prepare a presentation for your co-workers, explaining the new toy and how you and your co-workers will help to market the product. Create visuals to aid your presentation.

2. Your team coach has asked you to give an oral presentation to new members. Prepare a presentation in which you share your team's history and explain your goals for the coming year.

# WORKSHOP 26

## Information Interviewing

## WHAT IS INFORMATION INTERVIEWING?

Often, other people can be a rich and interesting source of information. *Information interviewing* is the process of asking people prepared questions about themselves or their activities and recording the information they give. You might use your information interviewing skills as you conduct research for a report or explore different careers and job opportunities.

## POINTERS: CONDUCTING INTERVIEWS

The following pointers will help you prepare for an information interview:

1. **Pick a subject for your interview.** Decide which person you want to interview and what information you want. You might interview a businessperson about his or her job responsibilities. Perhaps you need to ask a factory worker how an assembly line works.

2. **Make an appointment.** Call or write the person you wish to interview. Briefly explain the purpose of your interview and request a convenient time to meet. Remember to be courteous.

3. **Do background research.** To be fully prepared for your interview, you may need to do some background research about the person you are interviewing or the person's business or industry.

4. **Write your interview questions.** Write at least four or five questions. As you think of your questions, keep the question words *who, what, when, where, why,* and *how* in mind. Questions that begin with these words will lead you to more informative, detailed answers. Try to avoid questions that can be answered simply with "yes" or "no."

5. **Make a good impression.** When you meet for the interview, you should be dressed neatly. Be polite and courteous—shake hands, smile, and make eye contact with the person you will be interviewing.

6. **Take good notes.** Make careful and detailed notes of the answers you receive. If you choose to tape-record the interview, ask the person's permission before you begin recording.

7. **Listen carefully.** Pay attention to the answers the person gives. In some cases, you may want to ask a follow-up question to part of an answer.

8. **Send a thank-you note.** After the interview, send a personal note to the person, thanking him or her for taking the time for the interview.

## PRACTICE

Practice information interviewing by completing one of the following assignments:

1. Interview a human resources person and find out the qualities he or she looks for in employees.

2. Talk with a local store owner about employee problems, such as theft or absenteeism.

3. Interview an attorney about common courtroom procedures.

# WORKSHOP 27
## Peer Editing

### WHAT IS PEER EDITING?

*Peer editing* is reading and responding to a piece of writing done by a classmate, or peer. A peer editor might spot mistakes that you missed because you know how your writing *should* read. Often, a peer editor can suggest a new solution to a problem that you've been unable to solve in your writing.

### POINTERS: FOR THE WRITER

1. **Introduce your work.** Name the purpose and intended audience for your writing.

2. **Explain what feedback you need.** Point out specific problems you've been having with the writing. State whether you'd like written comments from the reader or whether you'd prefer to discuss the response.

3. **Listen carefully and politely to your peer editor's comments.** Let your reader explain his or her comments without interruption. Remember not to take constructive criticism personally.

4. **Ask follow-up questions.** If you are unclear about any of your reader's comments, ask him or her to explain them again and point out specific examples.

### POINTERS: FOR THE READER

1. **Focus on the type of feedback the writer wants.** Listen to what the writer wants and focus your attention on those issues. If the writer is concerned about flow of ideas, focus on organization, not on spelling or grammar.

2. **Take time to respond.** Remember that the writer has spent a good deal of time writing the paper. Take time to focus on your task and read the paper carefully and thoughtfully. It is a good idea to read the paper more than once before sharing your comments.

3. **Be positive.** Don't begin by focusing on problematic areas. Point out sections or passages that you like best. Then suggest some improvements that could make the paper stronger.

4. **Make specific suggestions.** Suggest concrete ways that the writer could improve a problem area. For example, if you think a certain sentence is confusing, suggest a clearer wording.

5. **Be considerate of the writer's feelings.** Your comments should be honest, but they should also be tactful. Remember to critique the writing, not the writer.

### PRACTICE

Practice peer editing by completing one of the following activities:

1. Choose a piece of your writing in progress, and prepare it for a peer editor. Make a list of the steps you will go through as you make your preparations.

2. Exchange a piece of writing with a classmate. Act as a peer editor and write comments on how the piece could be improved. Remember to note strong passages as well as areas that need improvement.

# GRAMMAR WORKSHOP

## Parts of Speech Overview

**THE PARTS OF SPEECH**

A working knowledge of the parts of speech helps you to communicate your thoughts and ideas to others. Review the following parts of speech:

1. **Noun** A *noun* is a word that names a person, place, thing, or idea.

   Examples:   ballerina, Springfield, stage, hope
   Sentence:   The young *ballerina* seemed to float across the *stage.*

2. **Pronoun** A *pronoun* is a word that may be used in place of a noun or another pronoun.

   Examples:   I, me, we, us, you, she, her, he, him, they, them, it
   Sentence:   Carmen enjoys studying geography, and *she* hopes to continue studying *it* in college.

3. **Verb** A *verb* is a word that expresses an action or a state of being.

   Examples:   sleep, fold, crash, is, feel
   Sentence:   After I *folded* the towels, sheets, underwear, and socks, I *felt* tired.

4. **Adjective** An *adjective* is a word that modifies a noun or a pronoun.

   Examples:   freckled, small, narrow, short
   Sentence:   A *small, freckled* face suddenly appeared in the *steamy* window.

5. **Adverb** An *adverb* is a word that modifies a verb, an adjective, or another adverb.

   Examples:   delightfully, quickly, quietly, very, really, hardly
   Sentence:   The flutist played the music *delightfully;* she must be a *very* dedicated young musician.

6. **Preposition** A *preposition* relates a noun or pronoun to another word in the sentence.

   Examples:   across, among, behind, in place of, outside, under, without
   Sentence:   The treasure map directed us *around* the moat, *behind* the castle, and *into* the forest.

7. **Conjunction** A *conjunction* is a word that connects two or more words or groups of words.

   Examples:   and, but, yet, or, nor, as soon as, in order that, therefore, unless
   Sentence:   Rosa *and* Raymond will help set the table, *as soon as* dinner is ready.

8. **Interjection** An *interjection* is a word, or group of words, that expresses feeling or emotion.

   Examples:   ouch, oh, hello, help, hey, yes, no
   Sentence:   *Hey!* That pot of chili is hot!

**PRACTICE**

Identify the part of speech for each italicized word in each sentence:
1. The *green parakeet paced* back and forth on its perch.
2. *Yikes!* You *really frightened* us with your monster costume!
3. Like *butterflies,* yellow *and* red leaves fluttered *around* the trunk of the *maple.*
4. Samantha *carefully* placed the *small* notebook *inside* the bottom bureau drawer.
5. *We* hope to visit you in *Hawaii soon.*

# GRAMMAR WORKSHOP

## Pronouns

**POINTERS**

**1. A pronoun should refer clearly to an easily identified noun (its antecedent).**

    Unclear:    Marie told her mother **she** couldn't go.

It's not clear at all whether Marie or her mother is unable to attend. Writers substitute pronouns for nouns to avoid repetition and to make sentences more readable—but not at the expense of clarity. Add enough information or reword the sentence so that readers can tell what the pronoun's antecedent is.

    Clear:    Marie told her mother that parents couldn't go.

**2. A pronoun must agree with its antecedent in number.**

    Incorrect:    Each **student** took **their** seat on the bus.

*Their* is a plural pronoun, but *student* is a singular noun. Here are three ways to correct the problem:

        Make both the pronoun and the antecedent singular.
    Correct:    Each **student** took **his** or **her** seat on the bus.

        Make both the pronoun and the antecedent plural.
    Correct:    **Students** took **their** seats on the bus.

        Reword the sentence so that a pronoun is not needed.
    Correct:    All **students** took seats on the bus.

**3. A subject pronoun should be in subject position; an object pronoun should be in object position.**

    Correct:    **He** and **I** agreed to meet at the street festival.

Pronouns can be subjective or objective. If the pronoun is the subject of the sentence or phrase, use a subject pronoun. If the pronoun is the object of the verb or of a preposition, use an object pronoun. Subject pronouns are: *I, you, we, he, she, it, they, who.* Object pronouns are: *me, you, us, him, her, it, them, whom.*

    Correct:    **She** had seen **him** and **me** at last year's festival.
        In this sentence, *him* and *me* are the objects of *had seen.*

    Correct:    **We** were glad Halley was going with **us** again.
        In this sentence, *we* is the subject pronoun and *us* is an object pronoun.

    Incorrect:    **Me** and **Sam** had always wanted to see the Bulls in person.
        In this sentence, me is an object pronoun being used as a subject.

**PRACTICE**

Find and correct the pronoun problem in each sentence:

**1.** She leaned her bike against a tree, but it wouldn't stand up.

**2.** Everyone has their own opinion about religion.

**3.** Me and Sarah always enjoy playing music together.

**4.** I wouldn't let anything come between he and I.

# GRAMMAR WORKSHOP

## Adjectives and Adverbs

### POINTERS

1. **Adjectives modify nouns and pronouns.** Adjectives describe who, which, what kind, or how many.

   Under the **warm** sun, we lay in the **long, green** grass of the **unmowed** yard.

   In this sentence, *warm* modifies the noun *sun, long* and *green* describe the noun *grass,* and *unmowed* modifies the noun *yard.*

2. **Adverbs modify only verbs, adjectives, and other adverbs.** Adverbs tell when, how, to what extent, or where, sometimes referred to as "time, manner, and place." Many adverbs end in *ly;* this makes them easy to recognize.

   We played **poorly** in the semifinals, but we won **easily** anyway. (The adverb *poorly* modifies the verb *played;* the adverb *easily* modifies the verb *won.*)

   It was an **impossibly** difficult assignment. (The adverb *impossibly* modifies the adjective *difficult.*)

   The bus went **especially slowly** today. (The adverb *especially* modifies the adverb *slowly;* the adverb *slowly* modifies the verb *went.*)

3. **Some important adverbs do not end in ly.** Put the tape **there.** You came out **ahead.** We have to leave **now.** It was a **very** hard rainfall. They are **always** late.

4. **Adjectives and adverbs have comparative and superlative forms.** A **comparative** form compares two things. Add *er* to a word or use *more* to make the comparative form.

   This is a **harder** test than I expected.
   This is a **more** difficult test than I expected.

   A **superlative** form considers three or more, or all. Add *est* to a word or use *most* to make the superlative form.

   I think it may be the **hardest** test I ever took.
   I think it may be the **most** difficult test I ever took.

   Some adverbs and adjectives have irregular comparative and superlative forms. Become familiar with them.

   good, better, best
   bad, worse, worst
   little, less, least

### PRACTICE

Identify each word in boldface type as an adjective or adverb and determine what each modifies.

1. We took a **quick** trip to the grocery store.
2. Sean answered **pleasantly.**
3. You got off to a **better** start this time.
4. It was the **worst** storm of the century.
5. The planes took off **quickly.**

# GRAMMAR WORKSHOP

## Prepositions

## POINTERS

**1. A preposition often identifies location.** A preposition along with a noun (called the *object of the preposition*) and any modifiers of the object make up a prepositional phrase.

Example:    Kyle chipped the ball **over the sprawling goalie.**

The preposition is *over; goalie* is the object of the preposition; and *the* and *sprawling* are modifiers describing the object, *goalie.*

**2. Learn to recognize prepositions.** A prepositional phrase is usually easy to identify. Familiarize yourself with this list of prepositions:

| | | | | | |
|---|---|---|---|---|---|
| aboard | as | but | in | out | toward |
| about | at | by | inside | outside | under |
| above | before | concerning | into | over | underneath |
| across | behind | despite | like | past | until |
| after | below | down | near | pending | unto |
| against | beneath | during | of | regarding | up |
| along | beside | except | off | since | upon |
| amid | besides | excepting | on | through | with |
| among | between | for | onto | throughout | within |
| around | beyond | from | opposite | to | without |

**3. Use prepositional phrases so that they are clear.** Because prepositional phrases serve as modifiers, where you put them may affect your readers' understanding.

Unclear:    We couldn't see the musicians clearly **in the back of the hall.**

Who is in the back of the hall? Choose a different preposition or rearrange the phrases for clarity.

Clear:    We couldn't see the musicians clearly **from** the back of the hall.
Clear:    We **in the back of the hall** couldn't see the musicians clearly.
Clear:    **From the back of the hall,** we couldn't see the musicians clearly.

In formal writing, avoid ending a sentence with a preposition.

Informal:    She got the necklace from an **aunt** she lives **with.**
Formal:    She got the necklace from an aunt **with whom** she lives.

## PRACTICE

**1.** Write a sentence for each of these prepositional phrases. Use the example as a guide.

Example:    below the surface
Sentence:    We saw species that live far below the surface of the ocean.

above the window          between two cities
in their minds          near the intersection

**2.** Find two prepositions from the list above that don't identify location. Write a sentence using each.

# GRAMMAR WORKSHOP

## Subject-Verb Agreement

### POINTERS

A verb must agree in number with its subject.

1. **Make sure the verb agrees with the subject and not the object of a preposition.**

   Incorrect: The students in this class is smart.

   Correct: The **students** in this class **are** smart.

2. **A sentence may contain a noun or pronoun that follows a linking verb and describes the subject. The verb still agrees with the subject.**

   Incorrect: Cluster diagrams is an effective tool to use in the prewriting stage.

   Correct: **Cluster diagrams are** an effective tool to use in the prewriting stage.

3. **Watch for sentences in which the subject comes after the verb. The verb still should agree with the subject.**

   Incorrect: Behind the stage was two anxious actors.

   Correct: Behind the stage **were** two anxious **actors.**

4. **When a compound subject is joined by *or* or *nor,* the verb agrees with the subject that is closer to it.**

   Incorrect: Either the president or the directors addresses the board first.

   Correct: Either the president or the **directors address** the board first.

5. **Watch for intervening phrases or expressions.** Phrases such as *in addition to, as well as,* or *together with* do not change the number of the subject.

   Incorrect: The forest ranger, as well as her staff, are keeping a close watch on the wilderness fires.

   Correct: The **forest ranger,** as well as her staff, **is keeping** a close watch on the wilderness fires.

6. **Indefinite pronouns may be singular or plural.** Some indefinite pronouns, such as *anyone, everything,* and *each,* are always singular. Others, such as *few, both,* and *many,* are always plural. A few (*some, all, most,* and *none*) can be singular or plural. Determine the number of the indefinite pronoun. Then make the verb agree with it.

   Incorrect: Most of the best seats in the theater is taken.

   Correct: **Most** of the best seats in the theater **are taken.**

### PRACTICE

Correct the agreement error in each sentence.

1. Either Mimi or Emanuel are going to review my paper.

2. Charts is the best visual to use in your presentation.

3. The employees in the financial department is working late tonight.

4. Everyone in the school are going to the pep rally.

5. Underneath the shrub was two shivering kittens.

6. Did you know that Walter Lawler, along with his brother, are going to France?

# GRAMMAR WORKSHOP

## Complete Sentences

### POINTERS

1. **A sentence needs two basic parts to express a complete thought: the subject and the predicate.** The subject includes the noun or pronoun and all the words that modify, or describe, it. The predicate includes the verb or verb phrase and all the words that complete its meaning.

```
     ┌────── subject ──────┐  ┌───── verb ─────┐
The LeBlanc Company in Wisconsin makes musical instruments.
```

2. **Some sentences do not follow usual subject-predicate order.** Some place the subject after the verb.

```
     ┌────────── verb ──────────┐  ┌───── subject ─────┐
Behind the cans of tomatoes and peas is hidden the bag of holiday treats.
```

In imperative sentences, the subject *you* is understood rather than expressed.

```
┌subject┐ ┌─────────── predicate ───────────┐
(You)    Remember to put new batteries in the smoke alarm.
```

3. **A sentence fragment lacks a subject, a verb, or both.** Every sentence must contain a verb. Unless the subject is understood, it also must be included in the sentence.

   Fragment:   Asked me to work on Saturday. (lacks a subject—who asked you?)
   Better:     Mr. Kibbles asked me to work on Saturday. (includes a subject—*Mr. Kibbles*)

   Fragment:   The incident report. (lacks a verb—what about the incident report?)
   Better:     The incident report described the bicycle accident. (includes a verb—*described*)

4. **A run-on sentence is two or more complete sentences written as if they were one sentence.** Incorrect punctuation causes run-on sentences. When only a comma separates two main clauses, for instance, a run-on occurs.

   Run-on:   Kevin has an exam tomorrow in algebra, he will study late tonight.
   Better:   Kevin has an exam tomorrow in algebra, so he will study late tonight.

Another type of run-on sentence is two main clauses with no punctuation between them.

   Run-on:   Evelyn has a strong voice perhaps she will pursue a career in public speaking.
   Better:   Evelyn has a strong voice; perhaps she will pursue a career in public speaking.

### PRACTICE

Indicate whether each item below is a fragment or a run-on sentence and correct each:

1. Rebecca applied for a part-time job at a florist's shop, the owner asked her to return for a second interview.

2. Called early that morning.

3. The small red box.

4. Amanda is eating lunch her baby brother is taking a nap.

# GRAMMAR WORKSHOP

## Capitalization

### POINTERS

Here are a few guidelines to follow when deciding what to capitalize.

1. **Capitalize the first word of every sentence.**

   **W**ho knocked on the door?
   **T**he yellow dog thumped its tail against the floor.

2. **Capitalize the first word of a quotation if the quotation is a complete sentence.** In a divided quotation, capitalize the first word of the second part, only when that word begins a new sentence.

   Bradley urged, "**W**henever you have a question, please ask."
   "**I**'d like to know," Hannah asked, "what classes will help me prepare for a job in law enforcement."
   "**M**r. Jacobs is on the phone," Mike said. "**H**e wants to talk about the car pool schedule."

3. **Capitalize proper nouns. A proper noun names a specific person, place, thing, or idea.**

   The **S**antiago family toured the **W**hite **H**ouse when they vacationed in **W**ashington, **D.C.**
   **S**hari plans to volunteer for **H**abitat for **H**umanity this summer.

4. **Capitalize titles that are used before a proper name or in direct address.** Titles that follow a proper name or are used alone are not capitalized.

   At the train station, **P**resident **R**oosevelt waved to the crowd.
   Tomorrow **A**unt Gina will take us on a picnic with our uncle and cousins.

5. **Capitalize proper adjectives.** A proper adjective is formed from a proper noun. Do not capitalize the noun it modifies unless the noun would be capitalized when used alone.

   Have you eaten at the new **C**hinese restaurant yet?
   The **E**gyptian tombs are an engineering marvel.

6. **Capitalize the main words in titles of works such as books, magazines, songs, and stories.** The article preceding a title is capitalized only when it is actually part of the title.

   Have you read *The Old Man and the Sea?*
   Do you like the song "**H**old **M**y **H**and" by the group Hootie & the Blowfish?

7. **Capitalize the days of the week, the months of the year, and names of holidays.**

   We hope to meet our fund-raising target by **F**riday, **D**ecember 19.
   The early autumn weather was perfect for the **L**abor **D**ay holiday.

### PRACTICE

Find and correct the capitalization errors in these sentences. State the rule that should be followed.

1. have you ever ridden on the riverboat *delta queen*?
2. We viewed so many beautiful victorian gardens in england.
3. Do you want to apply for the internship in the marketing department of johnson wax company?
4. Did you enjoy reading *romeo and juliet?*

# GRAMMAR WORKSHOP
## Commas

## POINTERS

1. **Use a comma and a coordinating conjunction (*and, but, nor, or, for, so, yet*) to separate two independent clauses.** In this example, either clause could stand as an independent sentence.

   > I was fascinated by the movie, **but** Antonia thought it was boring.

2. **Use a comma after an introductory participle or participial phrase. A participle is a verb that functions as an adjective.**

   > **Grinning,** Lu-yin handed me the backup disk with our report on it.
   > **Surfing through channels,** Gerald paid no attention to the doorbell.

3. **Use a comma after an introductory adverb clause.** Set off an internal adverb clause with commas if it interrupts the flow of the sentence.

   > **While applying for one job,** Greg discovered another one he wanted more.
   > Tomas, **ahead by 10 yards on the last turn,** broke into a smile.

4. **Use commas to separate items in a series.** Separate three or more words, phrases, or clauses with commas. Put a conjunction before the final item.

   > The Yankees had runners on first, second, and third.
   > You must plan cautiously, prepare carefully, and perform confidently.

5. **Use commas when writing dates, addresses, and numbers.**

   > Her date of birth was June 16, 1980, as it said on her new license.
   > We lived at 51 Ruckle Street, Indianapolis, Indiana, in those days.
   > The car's sticker price was twenty-one thousand, two hundred four dollars.

   When writing digits, insert a comma every three digits (counting from the right). If the number has only four digits, the comma is optional.

   > 23,217                    7,645,332,614                    6151 or 6,151

6. **Do not use commas to join two sentences.**

   > Incorrect:    Luis had pleased his mother immensely, his gift was just what she wanted.
   > Correct:      Luis had pleased his mother immensely, for his gift was just what she wanted.

## PRACTICE

Correct comma flaws in each of these sentences:

1. The Congress President and Supreme Court make up the legislative executive and judicial branches.
2. Impatiently waiting Sam checked his watch every 10 seconds.
3. Sue would not accept money for helping the old woman with her groceries, that didn't seem right.
4. The company's regional headquarters is 300 Barton Drive Chicago Illinois.
5. Speeding the car passed on the right as well.

# GRAMMAR WORKSHOP

## Apostrophes

### POINTERS

1. **Use an apostrophe to form the possessive of a noun.** For a singular noun, use an apostrophe followed by *s*, even if the word ends in *s*.

| | | |
|---|---|---|
| the **candle's** glow | the day's labor | the **girl's** book |
| **Keats's** poetry | **Jones's** house | **Carlos's** jeans |

Exception: Some words that have three close *s* sounds use only the apostrophe.

**Achilles'** heel          for **goodness'** sake

For a plural noun, put an apostrophe at the end of the word.

| | | |
|---|---|---|
| the **girls'** books | **alligators'** skins | **computers'** impact |

A plural noun that does not end in *s* forms its possessive the same way a singular noun does.

| | | |
|---|---|---|
| the **geese's** route | **children's** laughter | **reindeer's** antlers |

2. **Use an apostrophe to form contractions.** Contractions shorten two words into one. An apostrophe replaces the missing letter or letters.

| | | |
|---|---|---|
| do not = **don't** | can not = **can't** | are not = **aren't** |
| they are = **they're** | she will = **she'll** | he had = **he'd** |

Spelling tip: Remember that the apostrophe replaces a missing *letter*, not a missing space.

Incorrect:   Are'nt
Correct:     Aren't

3. **Apostrophes note the omission of one or more digits in a number.**

The summer of '**68**          The class of '**01**

4. **Apostrophes sometimes form past participles of verbs derived from nouns.**

Tyson K.O.'d him in the second round.
I think I'm *Star Trek*'d out.

### PRACTICE

1. Use an apostrophe to create the possessive form. Follow the example given.

| | | |
|---|---|---|
| Example: | the rattle of the baby | the baby's rattle |
| | the smile of Sarah | the hooves of a horse |
| | the habits of mice | the red glare of rockets |
| | the journey of Odysseus | the conclusion of a story |

2. Form contractions for the following words.

| | |
|---|---|
| she would | we are |
| you will | will not |

# GRAMMAR WORKSHOP

## Quotation Marks

**POINTERS**

**Use quotation marks in the following situations:**

1. **To set off direct speech in dialogue.** Direct speech is enclosed in quotation marks.

   "What's the matter with all the pooches?" he said. "Where's Spot?"
   "He's out with them," his mother said. "They've probably got a porcupine treed. Dogs go crazy in the spring."

   Note that the question marks, commas, and periods go inside the quotation marks.

2. **To set off quoted material in text.** Short quotations (less than five lines) should be placed within quotation marks.

   Dorothy West sets the scene by writing, "The woods were not a dark forest of towering trees."

3. **To distinguish certain titles.** The titles of essays, poems, articles, stories, and chapters should be enclosed in quotation marks.

   The essay by Gary Soto, "The Savings Book," was my favorite selection.
   Wallace Stegner's "The Colt," was first published in a collection of short stories.
   Read Chapter 9, "The Industrial Revolution," by Friday.

4. **To set off definitions.** Writers sometimes define words in text. The word itself is in italics, with the definition enclosed in quotation marks.

   The margin note explained that *bedlam* means "a scene of confusion."

5. **To provide special emphasis.** Quotation marks call special attention to the words they enclose.

   The term "Iron Curtain" became common once Winston Churchill used it.

**PRACTICE**

Correct each error in the use of quotation marks.

1. After we read A Mother in Mannville, we talked about the Depression.

2. "The interview went very well, he said, "until I tripped over a chair."

3. I agree with the poet's claim that When you let proud words go, it is not easy to call them back".

4. The essay claims that *responsibility* means "accepting the consequences of our actions.

# GRAMMAR WORKSHOP

## Spelling

## POINTERS

1. **The rule is 100% accuracy.** Whether you are writing schoolwork, a personal letter, or a workplace memo, your words must be spelled accurately. Your readers make judgments based on your writing. Your words convey meaning, which might not be clear if the words are spelled incorrectly.

2. **Look for your own spelling errors.** Don't rely on peer editors, teachers, or computer spell checkers. Peer editors and teachers have more important things to do. And spell checkers can make mistakes, too. Consider this sentence, which would never be questioned by a computer spell checker:

   The character inn the story did knot no weather two weight ore too go ahead.

   Here's an old proofreader's trick. Proofread your work from end to beginning. Start reading from the last word and move backwards to the first word. When your mind is not caught up in the meaning of the words, you will be less likely to overlook errors in spelling or punctuation.

3. **Learn certain spelling rules.** Know how to form plural nouns by adding *s* or *es*. Remember to form the past tense of regular verbs by adding *ed*. Learning rules such as these can take you a long way toward 100% accuracy.

4. **Keep your own personal spelling list.** Is there one word that always sends you to the dictionary because you're just not sure? Tackle that word by keeping it on your own spelling list. It will be easier to look up, and once you write it correctly a few more times, you will remember it and be able to cross it off your list.

5. **Watch out for frequently misspelled words.** Homonyms, or words that sound alike but are spelled differently, are often troublesome. Much of the confusion in the example sentence in Pointer #2 above is caused by homonyms. Here is the correct version of the sentence. Compare the sounds and the spellings of the words.

   The character in the story did not know whether to wait or to go ahead.

   The only way to conquer homonyms is to memorize the words and their meanings. Some writers create sentences to help them distinguish between homonyms. In this example, you can keep the words straight because they fall in alphabetical order in the sentence.

   He went **to** the store, **too,** for **two** loaves of bread.

## PRACTICE

Correct the spelling or word-choice errors in each sentence.

1. The boss beleives that his new policy coveres all employees.

2. Theyre advise was to keep my ankle stationery and too remain as quite as possible.

3. I wanted to chose recycling as my topic; its second nature to me.

4. I hopped to earn a spot on the committee.

# GLOSSARY OF LITERARY TERMS AND SKILLS

**act**   a major section of a work of drama

**alliteration**   the intentional repetition of the same beginning consonant sound in words that are close together

**analogy**   a comparison through simile or metaphor that explains something by illustrating its likeness to something else

**analysis**   a thorough examination of a problem, question, or issue in which the writer's opinion is clearly stated and other sources are presented to support that opinion

**anecdote**   a brief narrative about an incident or event that illustrates a specific point a writer or speaker wants to make; generally anecdotes are amusing and often biographical

**antagonist**   the character or force that works against the protagonist (central character) in a story

**argument**   the expressing and supporting of one's beliefs, in the attempt to convince others

**assonance**   the intentional repetition of vowel sounds within words

**atmosphere**   the general feeling that a piece of writing conveys

**autobiography**   the story of a person's life, told in the words of that person

**ballad**   a song-like poem that tells a story

**bias**   a personal belief, attitude, or judgment (either positive or negative) that prevents a person from being objective

**biography**   a form of nonfiction; the story of a person's life, written by someone else

**blank verse**   poetry that follows a regular rhythm but contains no rhyme

**brochure**   a folded document that advertises products or services (also known as a flyer or pamphlet) attracting readers with colorful pictures and graphics

**cast**   a list of characters appearing in a play, usually listed in order of appearance with a brief description

**cause-and-effect relationship**   a sequence in which one event (a cause) makes another event (an effect) happen

**characterization**   process through which an author reveals the qualities of a character, through the character's own words and actions, physical descriptions of the character, and the reactions of other characters

**characters**   the people portrayed in a novel, short story, or drama that take part in its events

**chorus**   a group of actors or a dancing company in a drama that speak together, commenting on the action of the play and often foreshadowing events to come

**chronological order**   the organization and presentation of details and events according to the order in which they occur

**climax**   the crisis, or most exciting point in a plot where emotion peaks and the conflict is at its worst point

**comedy**   drama that is intended to amuse through its light-hearted approach and happy ending

**compare**   to examine and explain how two or more things are similar

**conclusion**   a final observation or decision made after a reasonable number of facts are known

**conflict**   a clash of ideas, attitudes, or forces; a problem or struggle around which the story events revolve. Characters can have internal conflicts, in which they struggle with issues within themselves, and external conflicts, in which they have a problem with other characters or outside forces.

**connotation**   the images or feelings associated with certain words and phrases

**consonance**   the intentional repetition of consonant sounds at the ends of words

**contrast**   to examine and explain how two or more things differ

**crisis**   the climax, or most exciting point in a plot

**definition**   structured and objective words and phrases that explain or describe the characteristics or qualities of a subject

**dénouement**   the stage in plot development in which the conflict is resolved; all events that occur during the falling action

**description**   concrete and vivid words and phrases that appeal to the senses and enable the reader to re-create a scene, person, or image in the mind's eye

**dialect**   a special version of any language spoken in particular regions of a country; used to show a reader a specific culture or region

**dialogue**   a conversation between two or more characters in a work of fiction or drama

**diction**   word choice

**drafting**   the stage of the writing process in which a writer creates an unstructured draft of a work in rough sentences and paragraphs

**drama**   a story told only through action and dialogue, intended to be performed in front of an audience in a series of acts with several scenes each. Each scene typically depicts a secific place and time. Drama can take many forms including radio plays, television programs, and movies.

**dramatic irony**   when an audience knows more about what is happening in a play than do the characters involved in the events

**editing**   the stage of the writing process in which a writer reviews sentences and paragraphs for clear, correct construction and smooth transitions and proofreads word-by-word for errors in grammar, usage, and mechanics.

**epic poetry** long narrative poetry that tells a story of great adventure, usually of the glorious deeds of a nation's heroes, and often handed down orally. *Beowulf* and *The Odyssey* are examples.

**essay** a brief, structured nonfiction discussion of a single topic, in which the writer introduces a thesis, or main point, presents supporting evidence with examples and details in subsequent paragraphs, and draws a conclusion

**evaluation** an important reading strategy in which a reader makes judgments about the quality or value of something

**fable** a short tale told in poetry or prose to teach a moral lesson. When the main characters are animals that behave like humans to make a point about human behavior, these tales are called *beast fables*.

**fact** something that can be proven to be true beyond a reasonable doubt

**falling action** events in a plot that resolve the crisis

**fantasy** a form of fiction that involves fashioning an entirely original world of imaginary times and places tht are filled with magic and the supernatural. Familiar and realistic details are also included to help the reader willingly accept the world of fantasy.

**farce** a comedy that contains humorous characterizations and improbable plots

**feature writing** nonfiction writing presented in magazines and newspapers that focuses on information of general interest and attempts to involve readers emotionally through creative presentation of real people and events. It should include statements from witnesses and/or authorities and not introduce the writer's opinion.

**fiction** writing that is imagined, or made up, by a writer to communicate something about life to the reader. It may be based on real life experiences, but the story itself comes from the imagination of the writer.

**figurative language** imaginative words and phrases that often compare or describe two unlike things in a manner that is not meant to be taken literally; phrases that create a vivid image

**first-person** the perspective of a narrator who speaks from his or her own point of view

**flashback** an interruption in a natural time sequence used to describe earlier events. This technique allows an author to present the beginning of a story in a dramatic way.

**folk tale** a traditional story handed down through the generations, usually by word of mouth, that preserves a culture's ideas, customs, and wisdom gathered over time

**foreshadowing** a technique in which a writer gives clues or hints about a story's outcome

**frame story** a story within a larger story

**free verse** poetry that contains little or no regular rhyme or rhythm, freeing the poet from stanza patterns and measured lines

**genre** a category of literature characterized by a particular style, form, or content. Generally, literature is divided into three genres: *poetry, prose* (fiction and nonfiction) and *drama*

**haiku** a special form of poetry developed by the Japanese that captures a brief moment in nature. Consisting of three lines, it follows a strict syllable pattern; five syllables in the first line, seven in the next, and five in the last.

**humor** quality in writing that evokes laughter and relieves tension

**imagery** a mental picture created for the reader by the writer's skillful choice of words and details that appeal to the senses

**inciting incident** the stage in plot development where the story's main conflict is introduced

**internal conflict** a disturbance (often spiritual or moral) that occurs within an individual

**interpretation** the process of determining the meaning or importance of writing, speech, art, music, or actions

**interview** A source of information consisting of a conversation in which one person asks another prepared, open-ended questions that move the conversation toward revealing the knowledge desired

**irony** a tone in a piece of writing when there is a surprising difference between what is expected to happen and what actually occurs

**jargon** technical terminology that relates to only one area of interest (such as computers or medicine)

**journal** a personal diary or notebook in which a writer records his or her activities, experiences, thoughts, and feelings

**legend** a popular story that comes from past generations. Many legends offer explanations of how things came to be, but usually contain no historical information that can be verified.

**letter** a piece of correspondence directed to a particular audience and designed to achieve a specific purpose

**limited omniscient point of view** the third person point of view from which the narrator can enter one character's mind to let the reader know his or her motives, emotions, and thoughts

**loaded language** words that have strong emotional, and often negative, associations; used in media as a form of bias

**main idea** the most important point that a writer wants to communicate

**memo** a brief piece of business correspondence directed to a particular audience in the workplace; used to inform, request, instruct, or persuade

**metaphor** a direct comparison in which two things are described as if they were one and the same, that is, without the use of the words *like* or *as*

**meter** the number and pattern of syllables and stresses in a line of poetry

Glossary of Literary Terms and Skills

**monologue** an emotional, and revealing speech by one character with another character listening

**mood** the general feeling or atmosphere that a piece of writing conveys

**moral** an instructive lesson about right and wrong taught in a fable, parable, short story, or poem; sometimes a moral is clearly stated; sometimes it must be implied from the actions and words of the characters

**motivation** the reason or force that drives a character to behave in a certain way

**myth** a fictional tale that explains the actions of gods or heroes or the origins of elements of nature

**narrative** fiction, nonfiction, or poetry that details an event or series of events that have taken place

**narrator** the person or character who is telling a story. A skillful narrator moves the action along, helping readers untangle details of time and place.

**news writing** nonfiction writing presented in newspapers and magazines that presents readers with the most timely and accurate information about a current event using only objective and concise reporting of facts. It must answer the questions who, what, when, where, and why, in a brief manner.

**nonfiction** writing that informs, concerning real people, places, and events. Examples of nonfiction are biography, autobiography, essays, speeches, letters, manuals, and narratives.

**nonstandard English** words and phrases that do not meet the grammar and spelling conventions of written or spoken English; used by a writer to express a precise thought or create a special mood

**novel** a book-length work of fiction

**objectivity** the ability to present information without being influenced by emotion or personal opinions

**omniscient point of view** the third person point of view from which the narrator is all-knowing and can freely enter character's minds to let the reader know their motives, emotions, and thoughts

**onomatopoeia** the use of words whose sounds seem to express or reinforce their meanings. Examples are *splash* and *boom*

**opinion** a belief that cannot be proven absolutely but that can be supported

**oral tradition** the handing down of stories, folktales, parables, ballads, legends, and myths by word of mouth from generation to generation

**parable** a short story written to point out a moral truth, in which a main character is often required to take a journey or to complete a task with several opportunities to make mistakes and learn the intended lesson

**paraphrase** a summary of a work that presents the main ideas and helps clarify the difficult vocabluary and concepts in the original work

**personification** figure of speech in which something that is not alive or not human is given human characteristics

**persuasion** language a writer uses to convince a reader to think or act in a certain manner; a writer must state a clear position, support it with evidence, and address possible opposing arguments

**play** a work of drama

**playwright** the author of a work of drama

**plot** the sequence of events in a story, consisting of an *introduction* or *exposition*, in which background information is provided for the reader; *inciting incident*, in which the story's main conflict is introduced; *rising action*, in which events become complicated and rise to a crisis; *climax*, where the crisis is at its worst and the story is at its highest point of suspense, *falling action*, which describes the results of the major events, and *resolution* and *dénouement* where the conflict is resolved and all loose ends are tied up

**poem** concentrated, relatively brief work of literature, generally intense and emotional, that often uses figurative language to make an observation

**point of view** the perspective of the narrator, such as third-person (a narrator who is an outside observer), first-person (a narrator who speaks from his or her own point of view), or second-person ( a narrator who directly addresses the reader)

**prediction** a reading strategy in which a reader constantly guesses about what is going to happen next

**prewriting** the first stage of the writing process in which a writer plans, asks questions, makes notes, and narrows a topic before writing

**propaganda** ideas, facts, or allegations used intentionally and improperly for the purpose of swaying an audience

**proposal** a report that uses persuasion to convince a reader (usually an employer) to act on information provided

**prose** the literary genre that is the ordinary form of written language including fiction and nonfiction forms

**protagonist** the central character of a short story or novel

**publishing** the final stage of the writing process in which a writer formats and presents a final work

**quatrain** a four-line stanza where the final sounds of the first and third lines and the final sounds of the second and fourth lines are rhymed and each line stresses three syllables. Many of Emily Dickinson's poems are in quatrains.

**realism** fiction that is believable, but not actually true, taking place in today's world, involving characters who act like real people and deal with life's actual problems, and containing no miracles or supernatural figures

**repetition** the use of a word or phrase over and over again to emphasize specific meaning; used often in poetry and speeches

**resolution** the stage in plot development in which the conflict is resolved

**review** an evaluation in the form of a commentary about an artistic work

**revising** the stage of the writing process in which a writer evalutes and improves a draft by focusing on the organization of the ideas presented and the clarity of the language

**rhyme** repetition of sounds at the ends of words in the lines of a poem

**rhyme scheme** a pattern of rhyming words that gives structure to a poem

**rhythm** the pattern of sounds and beats, stressed and unstressed syllables, formed by words in the lines of a poem

**rising action** events in a plot leading up to the crisis

**romance** exaggerated, unbelievable stories about incidents remote from ordinary life. Among the earliest romances were medieval stories about knights, kings, ladies in distress, enchantments, and adventures

**satire** a story that ridicules personal behavior or political institutions, often through the use of humor, irony, clever language, and absurd situations

**scene** a smaller section of a work of drama; a section within an act that happens in one place and time

**science fiction** the term given to short stories and novels that draw upon real science and technology and actual social institutions and problems to protray an imaginary future

**script** the written form of a play

**sensory language** words and phrases that engage a reader by appealing to the reader's senses

**setting** the time and place where the action of a story, novel, or drama occurs

**short story** fiction writing with clear setting, characters, plot, and theme, that presents a specific event in a compact time frame, generally focusing on one major conflict and how it is resolved

**simile** a figure of speech in which two things are compared through the use of the words *like* or *as*

**soliloquy** a long, emotional, and revealing speech by one character alone on stage

**stage directions** set of instructions or notes written by the playwright. These directions may describe scenery, props, lighting, costumes, music, or sound effects. They may also describe elements related to the acting of the play, such as entrances and exits, tone of voice, or gestures and movements.

**stanza** two or more lines of poetry that are grouped together to divide a poem into its form

**subjective** based on personal judgments, reactions, and emotions rather than on objective facts

**summary** a shortened version of an original work in which only the most important facts (main ideas) are presented in the order in which they originally appeared

**supporting detail/evidence** fact that provides more information about a main idea

**surprise ending** an interesting twist to the ending of a story that cleverly untangles the plot; used to trick or amuse the reader and show the strange behaviors of human beings

**suspense** the element in fiction or nonfiction that keeps a reader in a state of uncertainty and forces the reader to keep reading to find out what will happen next

**symbol** something that exists in and of itself and at the same time is used to represent something else

**symbolism** figurative language in which an object, person, or event represents something else; used to give deeper meaning to a poem or piece of fiction and to help readers understand events, characters, and themes.

**theme** the broad, general statement or belief about life or human nature presented in a piece of writing; a story's main idea.

**third-person** the perspective of a narrator who speaks as an outside observer

**tone** the attitude or feeling that a piece of writing conveys

**topic sentence** the sentence that states a paragraph's main idea, usualy at the beginning of the paragraph

**tragedy** a drama that ends in great misfortune or ruin for a major character, especially when a moral issue is involved

**verbal irony** when a speaker means the opposite of, or far more than, he or she actually says

**visuals** charts, graphs, diagrams, tables, and maps that can convey data with greater impact than words alone. Newspapers, journals, manuals, and business publications, and presentations use visuals extensively.

**word choice** a writer's choice of words, phrases, and techniques used to express thoughts and feelings and create clear characters, images, and events

# GLOSSARY OF VOCABULARY TERMS

## A

**abate**　(v.) die down

**abstracted**　(adj.) absentminded

**accosted**　(v.) approached and spoke in a challenging way

**acute**　(adj.) sharp

**afford**　(v.) allow

**affront**　(n.) insult

**alcove**　(n.) nook, a small part of a room set back from the rest of the room

**amass**　(v.) collect; store up

**amerce**　(v.) penalize

**amoral**　(adj.) without moral sense or principles

**angular**　(adj.) bony and lean, gaunt

**anomalous**　(adj.) different from the usual arrangement, irregular

**anthology**　(n.) a book made up of literary works by a variety of authors

**anthropologist**　(n.) one who studies human origins, culture, races, and social relations

**antidote**　(n.) a remedy to counteract the effects of poison

**armory**　(n.) supply

**aspiration**　(n.) strong desire

**aspired**　(v.) risen to

**atrocious**　(adj.) exceptionally bad

## B

**barrage**　(n.) a rapid, heavy series of blows

**beau**　(n.) boyfriend

**bedlam**　(n.) a scene of confusion

**benevolent**　(adj.) kindly

**bestir**　(v.) motivate; bother

**bivouac**　(n.) temporary camp

**blazoned**　(v.) displayed boldly

**bout**　(n.) an athletic match; a fight (in boxing)

**buckskin**　(n.) soft leather made from a deer's hide

## C

**cadences**　(n.) the rising and falling pitches of a voice

**caprice**　(n.) whim

**chic**　(adj.) fashionable

**chloroform**　(n.) toxic chemical formerly used as an anesthetic

**chock-full**　(adj.) full to the brim

**compact**　(n.) a small container of cosmetics or makeup; an agreement

**complacent**　(adj.) unconcerned, unwilling to act

**composure**　(n.) calmness

**concludes**　(v.) brings to an end

**concoction**　(n.) odd mixture

**conduct**　(v.) guide

**confiscate**　(v.) to seize with authority, often in exchange for unpaid money

**confluence**　(n.) flowing or coming together

**consciousness**　(n.) awareness

**consecrated**　(adj.) declared sacred

**conservative**　(adj.) tending to preserve established traditions

**conspiratorially**　(adv.) schemingly, secretly

**constricted**　(adj.) squeezed tightly together

**contrition**　(n.) sincere remorse; regret for wrongdoing

**convalescence**　(n.) recovery

**conventional**　(adj.) usual

**coquettishly**　(adv.) shyly, flirtatiously

**coveted**　(v.) desired what belonged to someone else

**covey**　(n.) small flock of birds

**curvaceous**　(adj.) rolling, hilly

## D

**decamped**　(v.) suddenly departed

**defaulted**　(v.) failed to meet an obligation

**degenerate**　(v.) sink

**derisively**　(adv.) laughingly, cruelly

**detained**　(v.) held against one's will

**devotees**　(n.) people devoted to something

**dignitaries**　(n.) persons of high rank or office

**disarmed**　(v.) won over

**discords**　(n.) contradictions; in music, tones that are out of harmony

**discounted**　(v.) ignored

**disdain**　(n.) dislike, scorn

**disheveled**　(adj.) in disorder

**dispelled**　(v.) driven away

**disposition**　(n.) temperament, personality

**dissever**　(v.) to separate

**divulge**　(v.) make known

**doggedly**　(adv.) stubbornly, determinedly

**dowdy**　(adj.) shabby

**downtrodden**　(adj.) burdened with difficulties

**dowry**　(n.) the property that a woman brings to her husband at marriage

**draught**　(n.) drink; inhaling

**draw**　(n.) a tie

**drunk**　(adj.) dominated or overwhelmed by a feeling

**dyslexia**　(n.) a condition that causes a disturbance in the ability to read

## E

**ecstatically**　(adv.) excitedly and extremely happily

**eliciting**　(v.) bringing out

**emaciation**   (n.) thinness; wasting away

**encroachment**   (n.) going beyond proper limits

**enjoined**   (v.) directed, commanded

**enraptured**   (adj.) filled with delight

**ensuing**   (adj.) following

**equilibrium**   (n.) balance

**ermine**   (n.) a weasel whose brown or white fur is often used to line capes or hoods

**exorbitant**   (adj.) exceeding the customary or appropriate limits

**exuberant**   (adj.) joyously enthusiastic

## F

**feature**   (v.) prefer

**feinted**   (v.) faked

**fitted out**   (adj.) equipped

**fivescore**   (n.) 100 years; a score is twenty years

**foliage**   (n.) leaves

**forlorn**   (adj.) sad and lonely

**formidable**   (adj.) causing fear or awe

**formula**   (n.) a milk-like drink containing nutrients required by infants

**fortitude**   (n.) strength

## G

**gallantries**   (n.) polite gestures or remarks

**garish**   (adj.) boldly, unattractively bright

**glockenspiel**   (n.) an instrument similar to a xylophone

**gluttonous**   (adj.) given to excessive eating

**gnarled**   (adj.) twisted

**groveling**   (v.) crawling humbly; living without freedom

**guile**   (n.) cleverness

**guttering**   (adj.) flickering

## H

**hallowed**   (adj.) sacred

**hankering**   (v.) longing for

**harmonize**   (v.) to bring into line with

**homage**   (n.) publicly expressed honor or respect

**humility**   (n.) the state of being humble; not arrogant or assertive

## I

**ills**   (v.) troubles

**immolate**   (v.) to kill or destroy as a sacrifice

**impelled**   (v.) driven to do something

**implications**   (n.) consequences, involved meanings

**implicit**   (adj.) unquestioning

**inextricably**   (adv.) incapable of being separated

**innate**   (adj.) inborn; possessed at birth

**insolent**   (adj.) disrespectful, rude

**interdict**   (n.) command

**interminably**   (adv.) seemingly without end

**intimidate**   (v.) to frighten with threats

**irresolute**   (adj.) undecided

## J

**jeers**   (n.) comments meant to be rude or to ridicule

## K

**kids**   (n.) young goats

## L

**lamentation**   (n.) an expression of sorrow or mourning

**lathered**   (adj.) sweaty

**legitimate**   (adj.) rightful

**level**   (n.) an instrument that indicates when something is perfectly horizontal

**limbo**   (n.) a neutral, temporary waiting place

**lithe**   (adj.) flexible, graceful

**longevity**   (n.) length of life

## M

**maidenhair**   (n.) type of fern used as greenery in floral arrangements

**manacles**   (n.) a type of handcuff once used on African slaves

**mantle**   (n.) cloak

**mass**   (n.) a religious ceremony observed by Catholics

**mercantilism**   (n.) an economic system, also called commercialism

**mess hall**   (n.) a place where meals are served to a group of people

**mewl**   (v.) whimper

## N

**necrotic**   (adj.) dead

**noisome**   (adj.) unhealthy; offensive to the senses

**nostrum**   (n.) a medicine of unknown makeup, recommended by its maker but with no scientific proof of its effectiveness

**novelty**   (n.) something new or unusual

## O

**omen**   (n.) sign

**oscillate**   (v.) swing back and forth

## P

**pallor**   (n.) paleness

**parching**   (adj.) hotly drying

**parturition**   (n.) the process of giving birth

**pensively**   (adv.) thoughtfully

**phosphates**   (n.) carbonated beverages

**picketed**   (adj.) tied to a stake in the ground

**pinions**   (n.) wings

**plaintive**   (adj.) sad

**poignancy**   (n.) painfully emotional quality

**prate**   (v.) chatter

**predicated**   (adj.) previous, or practiced

**primatologist** (n.) one who studies primates, an order of mammals including humans, apes, and monkeys

**privy** (n.) outhouse

**prodigious** (adj.) numerous and lofty

**prodigy** (n.) a highly talented child

**promissory note** (n.) a written promise to pay a sum of money in the future

**propelled** (v.) moved

**providence** (n.) divine guidance

**province** (n.) area of specialty

**pub** (n.) short for "public house"; a restaurant or gathering place

**put up** (v.) save

## Q

**qualms** (n.) uneasiness

## R

**rank** (n.) row

**rappelling line** (n.) rope used by mountain climbers

**rapt** (adj.) wholly absorbed; engrossed

**rash** (adj.) sudden, unreasonable

**redemptive** (adj.) bringing about restoration, or freeing from distress

**redolent** (adj.) full of fragrance

**reeds** (n.) dry grasses

**remonstrances** (n.) protests, usually ineffective

**reproach** (n.) scolding, blame

**repugnance** (n.) strong dislike

**rescinded** (v.) voided; taken back

**retire** (v.) go back inside

**revelation** (n.) something that is revealed

**reverberation** (n.) vibration, as an echo

**rueful** (adj.) regretful

## S

**salve** (v.) soothe

**sashaying** (v.) walking slowly so as to call attention to oneself

**savory** (adj.) delicious

**sepulchre** (n.) a place of burial, a tomb

**seraphs** (n.) angels

**shambling** (v.) moving slowly and awkwardly

**signify** (v.) send a signal

**simple** (adj.) stupid

**sloughing** (adj.) dead and separating

**sloughlike** (adj.) swampy

**snake** (v.) wind or curl

**solicitude** (n.) concern

**spectacle** (n.) sight; scene

**sphinx-like** (adj.) mysterious

**spray** (n.) a decorative, flat arrangement of flowers and foliage

**stoically** (adv.) showing no response or emotion

**stooge** (n.) someone who plays a subordinate, or inferior, role to someone else

**stoop** (n.) a small porch or stepped platform by the door of an apartment building

**straitly** (adv.) narrowly

**stridency** (n.) harsh insistence

**struts** (n.) the stiff, supporting part of a wing

**subject** (adj.) likely

**subterfuge** (n.) a purposely deceptive action

**suffused** (v.) spread over

**sullen** (adj.) gloomily silent

**superimposed** (v.) placed over or above

**susurrus** (n.) whispering or rustling sound

**sweltering** (adj.) extremely hot

## T

**tax** (n.) cost

**temperament** (n.) the distinguishing emotional traits of a person

**tenement** (n.) low-rent, often run-down apartment building

**testimony** (n.) evidence of a fact

**tranquilizing** (adj.) excessively calming; numbing

**tremulous** (adj.) trembling, shaky

**trussed** (v.) bound or secured tightly

**tumult** (n.) noisy confusion

**tureen** (n.) large serving bowl

**tweed** (n.) woolen fabric with flecks of color in it

## U

**unaccountable** (adj.) unexplainable

**unbridled** (adj.) set loose, unrestrained

**unyoking** (v.) unhitching from the plow

**uproariously** (adv.) heartily

**upswept** (adj.) lined

**usurers** (n.) ones who lend money at a very high rate of interest

## V

**vengeance** (n.) punishment in return for an insult

**veritable** (adj.) actual, not imaginary

**vermilion** (adj.) bright reddish orange

**vernacular** (n.) common, everyday speech

**virulent** (adj.) extremely poisonous

## W

**wallow** (v.) remain helpless

**wharves** (n.) piers along the shore

# UTHOR/TITLE INDEX

# GENERAL INDEX

# ACKNOWLEDGMENTS

*Continued from copyright page*

"Advice to the Young" by Miriam Waddington. From *Collected Poems* by Miriam Waddington. Copyright © Miriam Waddington, 1986. Reprinted by permission of Oxford University Press Canada.

"All The Years of Her Life" by Morley Callaghan. Reprinted by permission of the Estate of Morley Callaghan.

"Amigo Brothers" by Piri Thomas. From *El Barrio* by Piri Thomas. New York: Alfred A. Knopf, Inc., 1978.

Excerpts from "Basketball for Women" by Nancy Lieberman-Cline and Robin Roberts. Reprinted by permission, from Nancy Lieberman-Cline and Robin Roberts, 1996. *Basketball for Women* (Champaign, IL: Human Kinetics Publishers), 41, 110-111.

"Be Daedalus" by Nanina Alba.

"Beauty is Truth" by Anna Guest.

"The Bird Like No Other" by Dorothy West. From *The Richer, The Poorer* by Dorothy West. Copyright © 1995 by Dorothy West. Used by permission of Doubleday, a division of Bantam Doubleday Dell Publishing Group, Inc.

"Birdfoot's Grampa" by Joseph Bruchac. From *Entering Onandaga* by Joseph Bruchac. Copyright © 1975. Reprinted by permission of Barbara S. Kouts.

"The Colt" by Wallace Stegner. From *Women On The Wall* by Wallace Stegner. Copyright © 1943 by Wallace Stegner. Reprinted by permission of Brandt & Brandt Literary Agents, Inc.

"Daedalus" by Bernard Evslin. From *Heroes, Gods & Monsters of the Greek Myths*. Reprinted by permission of Writer's House, Inc. acting for the estate of Bernard Evslin.

"A Day's Wait" by Ernest Hemingway. Excerpted with permission of Scribner, a Division of Simon & Schuster, from *Winner Take Nothing* by Ernest Hemingway. Copyright 1933 Charles Scribner's Sons. Copyright renewed © 1961 by Mary Hemingway.

"Dreams" by Langston Hughes. From *The Dream Keeper And Other Poems* by Langston Hughes. Copyright © 1932 by Alfred A. Knopf, Inc. and renewed 1960 by Langston Hughes. Reprinted by permission of the publisher.

"Ex-Basketball Player" by John Updike. From *The Carpenetered Hen and Other Tame Creatures* by John Updike. Copyright © 1957, 1982 by John Updike. Reprinted by permission of Alfred A. Knopf, Inc.

Abridged excerpt from *Farewell To Manzanar* by James D. Houston and Jeanne Wakatsuki Houston. Copyright © 1973 by James D. Houston. Reprinted by permission of Houghton Mifflin Company. All rights reserved.

"First Lesson" by Phyllis McGinley. From *Times Three* by Phyllis McGinley.

"The Fly" by Mai Vo-Dinh. From *The Toad is the Emperor's Uncle* by Mai Vo-Dinh. Copyright © 1970 by Mai Vo-Dinh. Reprinted by permission of the author.

"Good Hot Dogs" by Sandra Cisneros. From *My Wicked Wicked Ways* in English; from *Cool Salsa* in Spanish. Copyright 1987 © by Sandra Cisneros, published in English by Third Woman Press and in hardcover by Alfred A. Knopf, Inc.; in Spanish by Henry Holt. Copyright © 1994 by Sandra Cisneros. Reprinted by permission of Susan Bergholz Literary Services, New York. All rights reserved.

"Grandmother and the Workmen" by Anthony Quinn. Reprinted by permission of the author.

Excerpts from *Hey, I'm Alive!* by Helen Klaben with Beth Day. Reprinted by permission of Curtis Brown, Ltd. Copyright © 1964 by Helen Klaben.

"Hobbyist" by Fredric Brown. Reprinted by permission of the Author's estate and its agent, The Scott Meredith Literary Agency, LP.

"I, Icarus" by Alden Nowlan. From *Bread, Wine & Salt*. Reprinted with permission of Stoddant Publishing Co. Limited, North York, Ontario Canada.

Excerpt from "I Have a Dream" by Martin Luther King, Jr. Reprinted by arrangement with The Heirs to the Estate of Martin Luther King, Jr., c/o Writer's House, Inc., as agent for the proprietor. Copyright © 1963 by Martin Luther King, Jr. Copyright renewed 1991 by Coretta Scott King.

"In Just-" by E. E. Cummings. Copyright 1923, 1951, © 1991 by the Trustees for the E. E. Cummings Trust. Copyright © 1976 by George James Firmage, from *Complete Poems*, 1904-1962 by E. E. Cummings, Edited by George J. Firmage. Reprinted by permission of Liveright Publishing Corporation.

"In Response to Executive Order 9066" by Dwight Okita. © 1996 by Dwight Okita from *Crossing with the Light* by Dwight Okita (Tia Chucha Press). Reprinted by permission of the author.

"Interview With The Chimp Lady" by Jane Goodall with Vicki Gabereau from *This Won't Hurt a Bit!* by Vicki Gabereau.

# HOTO & ILLUSTRATION CREDITS

Illustrations on pages 9, 13, 21, 28, 33, 41, 48, 87, 112, 125, 153, 165, 169, 230, 242, 247, 264, 269, 307, 312, 316, 320, 344, 352, 368 were created by South-Western Educational Publishing; **80** National Geographic Society. From *Greece and Rome: Builders of Our World,* 1977. Reprinted by permission of National Geographic Society; **92** Visgaitis, Gary. From "Wildfires in the West" by Gary Visgaitis, *USA Today,* August 15, 1994. Copyright © 1994, USA TODAY. Reprinted with permission; **203 top and bottom** Derks, Scott. From *The Value of A Dollar, 1860–1989.* Edited by Scott Derks. Copyright © 1994 Gale Research, Inc. Reproduced by permission. All other illustrations are in the public domain.

**iv–xiii** © 1995, PhotoDisc, Inc.; **6** Courtesy of National Archives Trust; **11** © 1995. PhotoDisc, Inc.; **17, 19** © Corbis-Bettman; **27, 31, 35** © 1995, PhotoDisc, Inc.; **39** © David Austen/Tony Stone Images, Inc.; **42, 43, 51, 53, 62, 63, 68** © 1995, PhotoDisc, Inc.; **70** © Corbis-Bettman; **72, 73** © 1995, PhotoDisc, Inc.; **75** © Corbis-Bettman; **83** Courtesy of the Jordan Information Bureau; **84** © Corbis-Bettman; **85** © 1995, PhotoDisc, Inc.; **89, 90** Courtesy of the U.S. Forest Service; **91** © 1995, PhotoDisc, Inc.; **97, 99** © Corbis-Bettman; **103** © Jeff Greenberg; **105** © Corbis-Bettman; **114, 118, 128, 136** © 1995, PhotoDisc, Inc.; **138, 140** © Corbis-Bettman; **146 top** © 1995, PhotoDisc, Inc.; **146 bottom** © Jeff Greenberg; **150** © 1995, PhotoDisc, Inc.; **151** © Christopher Burki/Tony Stone Images, Inc.; **155** © Jeff Greenberg; **163, 172, 175** © 1995, PhotoDisc, Inc.; **179** © Corbis-Bettman; **186** Courtesy of Bill Roughen; **190** © Tony Stone Images, Inc.; **196** © Corbis-Bettman; **202** © 1995, PhotoDisc, Inc.; **207** © Jeff Greenberg; **208, 209** © 1995, PhotoDisc, Inc.; **210, 216** © Corbis-Bettman; **219** © Corel Images; **227** © 1995, PhotoDisc, Inc.; **233** © Tony Stone Images, Inc.; **235** Photo by Alan Brown/Photonics Graphics; **239, 244** © 1995, PhotoDisc, Inc.; **249, 250** © Corbis-Bettman; **255** © 1995, PhotoDisc, Inc.; **257** © Don Smetzer/Tony Stone Images, Inc.; **270, 280** © Corbis-Bettman; **288** © 1995, PhotoDisc, Inc.; **296** The Metropolitan Museum of Art, Fletcher Fund, 1956; **298** © 1995, PhotoDisc, Inc.; **301** © William Thompson/Photonica; **302** © 1995, PhotoDisc, Inc.; **304** © Corbis-Bettman; **305** © 1995, PhotoDisc, Inc.; **309** Library of Congress; **311** Photo by Alan Brown/Photonics Graphics; **317** © Christopher Burki/Tony Stone Images, Inc.; **318, 322, 326, 328** © 1995, PhotoDisc, Inc.; **335** Courtesy of IBM; **340** © 1995, PhotoDisc, Inc.; **341** © Corbis-Bettman.